Issues and Methods in Comparative Politics

Building on the strengths of the second edition, this highly regarded textbook continues to provide the best introduction to the strategies of comparative research in political science.

Divided in three parts, the book begins by examining different methods, applying these methods to dominant issues in comparative politics using a wealth of topical examples from around the world, and then discusses the new challenges in the area. The book is thoroughly revised throughout with extensive new material on quantitative and qualitative analytical techniques, principles for selecting and comparing a small number of countries, and the value of single-country studies for the development of empirical theories of politics. New to this edition:

- Features explanation of regression analysis with accompanied briefing boxes.
- New discussion of the assumptions, research design, and the use of statistics characteristic of many-country comparisons.
- Single and multi-country studies – how to compare countries and address problems of comparison, especially the principles for selecting countries.
- New chapter on the intersection between international relations and comparative politics.
- Greater attention to the role of theory in comparative politics.
- All chapters have been updated with new publications and research output relevant to the discussion.

Balancing reader-friendly features with high quality analysis makes this popular academic text essential reading for everyone interested in comparative politics and research methods.

Dr Todd Landman is Reader in the Department of Government at the University of Essex. He is author of *Studying Human Rights* (Routledge 2006), *Protecting Human Rights* (2005), and co-author of *Governing Latin America* (2003) and *Citizenship Rights and Social Movements* (1997).

Issues and Methods in Comparative Politics: An Introduction

■ Third Edition

Todd Landman

Routledge
Taylor & Francis Group

LONDON AND NEW YORK

First published 2000
Second edition, 2003
Reprinted 2004 (twice), 2005, 2006, 2007
by Routledge
2 Park Square, Milton Park, Abingdon, Oxon, OX14 4RN

Simultaneously published in the USA and Canada
by Routledge
270 Madison Avenue, New York, NY 10016

Routledge is an imprint of the Taylor & Francis Group, *an informa business*

Reprinted 2008, 2009

Typeset in Sabon by
Keystroke, 28 High Street, Tettenhall, Wolverhampton
Printed and bound in Great Britain by
TJ International, Padstow, Cornwall

British Library Cataloguing in Publication Data
A catalogue record for this book is available from the British Library

Library of Congress Cataloging in Publication Data
Landman, Todd.
    Issues and methods in comparative politics: an introduction/Todd Landman. — 3rd ed.
        p. cm.
    Includes bibliographical references and index.
    1. Comparative government. I. Title.
    JF51.L346 2008
    320.3—dc22   2007037620

ISBN 10: 0–415–41236–6 (hbk)
ISBN 10: 0–415–41237–4 (pbk)
ISBN 10: 0–203–92978–0 (ebk)

ISBN 13: 978–0–415–41236–0 (hbk)
ISBN 13: 978–0–415–41237–7 (pbk)
ISBN 13: 978–0–203–92978–0 (ebk)

Contents

Figures

Tables

Briefing boxes

Acknowledgements

It has been both a challenge and a pleasure writing and revising this book. I am grateful to Patrick Proctor, who approached me while at a book launch in London ten years ago and asked me whether I would like to write a book on methods in comparative politics. Mark Kavanagh and Craig Fowlie encouraged me to write the second edition. Tom Mackie at Strathclyde University kindly reviewed the first edition, and I am indebted to Claudio Cioffi-Revilla at George Mason University, Kenneth Newton at the University of Southampton, Richard Dunphy at the University of Dundee, and Paul Pennings at Vrije Universiteit Amsterdam for their very helpful comments on the proposed second edition. This is now the third edition (thanks again to Craig Fowlie's encouragement). This new edition clarifies and expands the methodological discussions in Part I by providing a separate treatment of each of the main comparative methods, adding a discussion of regression analysis, and expanding the critical examination of the comparison of few countries, as well as how single-country studies have a significant role to play in comparative politics. Part II includes additional examples in each of the chapters and a new chapter on the connections between comparative politics and international relations, both in looking at the influence of domestic factors on international state behaviour, and how comparative analysis, now more than ever, needs to include important international factors to explain domestic political developments. Part III expands its concluding discussions on new issues facing comparative politics.

From my experiences of teaching comparative politics and research methods in the United States, the United Kingdom, Italy, Germany, Norway, China, and Brazil, it became apparent that few students understand the logic and purpose of systematic comparative analysis. My own intellectual formation comprised sound training in research methods. After studying political science at the University of Pennsylvania and Latin American Studies at Georgetown University, my formal study of comparative methods began at the University of Colorado, where I had the pleasure of working with Claudio Cioffi-Revilla, J.Samuel Fitch, Sven Steinmo,

ACKNOWLEDGEMENTS

Jeffrey Kopstein, T.J. Pempel, and Mark Lichbach. At the University of Essex I have been fortunate to benefit from a stimulating intellectual community and an outstanding research environment. While the facilities and surroundings provided the necessary support and infrastructure to complete the various editions of the book, it has been the people in the Department of Government over my many years at Essex that have mattered the most. I wish to thank Hugh Ward, David Sanders, David Howarth, Albert Weale, Christian Anglade, John Bartle, Thomas Plümper, Kai Arzheimer, Vera Troeger, and Roman Krznaric for their comments, discussion, suggestions, and assistance. Paul Carter, my research assistant in the summer of 1998, read many drafts of the first edition to provide an undergraduate perspective. Thanks to Joe Foweraker from Oxford University, Attracta Ingram from the National University of Ireland, Dublin, Bert Lockwood from the University of Cincinnati, Neil Robinson from University of Limerick, and Darren Hawkins from Brigham Young University. Thanks to Alice Cooper for working with me on the democratic peace literature, which forms part of the discussion of Chapter 12. I would also like to thank my many students on whom I have inflicted the logic of inference and to whom I have evangelized the virtues of systematic comparative analysis. In particular, I would like to thank Marcelo Gameiro, Anna Mackin, Marco Larizza, Jaime Baeza Freer, Edzia Carvalho, and Ricardo Luna Corral.

A number of personal friends and family have made my time in the United Kingdom an absolute pleasure, and the social network that has built up over the years makes my daily life a joy. Dave Smith, Leigh Amos, Malcolm, Sibel, and Max Latchman, Pavlenka and Stephen Small, have all been dear friends throughout the process of writing. Across the 'pond', thanks to Drew and Kate Landman, Hank Landman, and my mother Laura Landman. Finally, I want to extend my huge and heartfelt thanks to Melissa, Oliver and Sophia for making every day so much fun and filled with so much laughter. It is to them that I dedicate this third edition.

Todd Landman
Colchester, Essex

Introduction

This book is intended to be an accessible text on the strategies of comparative research in political science. It is aimed at upper-level undergraduate and first-year postgraduate students taking courses or doing degrees in political science, comparative politics, area studies (European politics, Russian and post-communist politics, Latin American politics, Third World politics, African politics, or Asian politics), public policy, human rights, and political explanation. The book self-consciously puts method first, and then interrogates a variety of 'big issues' in comparative politics through the lenses of the methodologist in an effort to teach students to think about the logic behind comparison as well as the need for systematic research in political science. In this way, the book sees comparison as an important means to an end: namely, explanation of observed political phenomena.

The book is necessarily grounded in a certain way of 'doing' political science. Without becoming mired in the ongoing debate about different approaches to political science and social science in general, suffice it to say that this book assumes there are observable political events, actors, interests, structures, and outcomes about which political scientists can make reasoned, informed, and intelligent analytical statements.[1] Variously called 'positivism', 'behaviouralism', or 'post-behaviouralism' (Fay 1975; Von Wright 1971; Sanders 1995; Lane 1996; Flyvberg 2001; Brady and Collier, 2004; Caterino and Schram 2006), this style of political science concentrates on *observable* political behaviour and events at the individual, group, or national level, and assumes that explanations of that behaviour are 'susceptible to empirical testing' (Sanders 1995:58). It is thus grounded in the position that the ultimate objects of comparative politics exist for the most part independent of and prior to their investigation (see Lane 1996; Lawson 1997). Moreover, it argues that the world of politics consists of important empirical puzzles to which political scientists apply a set of theories and methods in order to provide meaningful explanation and understanding (see Gordon 1991:629–30). This book is meant to aid those with a similar outlook on studying the political and social world in making statements about politics based on the best empirical evidence available, given the natural constraints on resources. In this way, it accepts that these statements are imperfect and uncertain, but by advocating systematic and well-grounded 'procedures of inquiry' (King et al. 1994:6) it aims to help students of politics make such statements the best that they can be.

To achieve these main objectives, the book is organized into three parts, which can be read separately or in the order in which they are presented here. Part I establishes the scientific justification for doing comparative politics, including why political scientists compare countries (Chapter 1), how they compare countries and the problems that may encounter in so doing (Chapter 2), strategies and methods for comparing many countries (Chapter 3), few countries (Chapter 4), and how single-country studies serve important comparative functions (Chapter 5). Part I shows how comparative methods can help students explain and understand observed political phenomena in the world. It shows what analytical leverage can be added to a research problem by comparing one country to another, a few countries together, or many countries at once. It shows how comparative methods help generate, clarify, and support important theories and propositions of political science. It shows the key problems to avoid in order to maximize the impact of comparative research. Finally, it seeks to unify these comparative methods into one logic of inference (King *et al*. 1994), where no one method is favoured over another. Rather, it outlines the strengths and weaknesses of the methods as to their ability to achieve valid inferences.

Part II uses the comparative 'architecture' established in Part I to address some dominant issues in comparative politics. These issues were chosen using the following criteria: (a) they receive wide attention in the extant comparative literature, (b) they have a certain resonance with and attraction for students of comparative politics, and (c) they are particularly suited to examining the different ways in which comparative methods can be applied. The comparative issues include economic development and democracy (Chapter 6), violent political dissent and social revolution (Chapter 7), non-violent political dissent and social movements (Chapter 8), transitions to democracy (Chapter 9), institutional design and democratic performance (Chapter 10), human rights (Chapter 11), and the overlap between international relations and comparative politics (Chapter 12).

Each chapter in Part II identifies the main research problem or question, specifies the ideal ways in which to investigate the problem with different comparative methods, and reviews the main findings of comparative research on the topic. In this way, the chapters in Part II seek to 'compare comparisons' in an effort to demonstrate how scholars choose research questions, formulate theories, specify hypotheses, and use comparative methods to test their hypotheses. Students who are new to comparative politics can begin by reading the chapters in Part II to get a flavour of the types of issues that have received significant attention in the comparative literature. They can then return to the chapters in Part I to see how the different methods of comparison have developed and how each offers different strengths and weaknesses for the study of politics. For students who have been studying comparative politics, or other related disciplines, it is suggested that the book be read in the order in which it has been presented. For all readers, it is suggested that they read Part III last.

Part III summarizes the main conclusions from Part II and looks forward to the challenges that the field will face in the foreseeable future. Chapter 13 highlights the common themes, methodological trade-offs, and sources of difference that arise from the comparison of comparisons in Part II. Chapter 14 concludes with an examination of the substantive and methodological challenges that the field will confront in the future. The chapter reviews briefly the evolution of the field since its early 'public law phase' (Valenzuela 1988), examines new methods that are being developed for cross-national comparison, argues for ways in which to transcend traditional dichotomies in the field, and discusses new issues that will capture the attention of comparativists. The text also includes tables and figures drawn from the findings of comparative research; 'briefing' boxes in each chapter clarifying concepts, terms, and relationships; suggestions for further reading at the end of each chapter; a glossary of terms; and a bibliography. Taken together, the book progresses from a discussion of different comparative methods, through a treatment of issues popular in comparative politics, to reflections on the field in the past and the future. As primarily a text on method, it should be read as a companion volume to more theoretically oriented comparative textbooks, such as Dogan and Pelassy (1990) *How to Compare Nations*; Chilcote (1994) *Theories of Comparative Politics*; Lichbach and Zuckerman (1997) *Comparative Politics: Rationality, Culture, and Structure*; Peters (1998) *Comparative Politics: Theory and Methods*; Lichbach and Kopstein (2000) *Comparative Politics: Interests, Identities, and Institutions in a Changing Global Order*; Hay (2002) *Political Analysis*; Brady and Collier (2004) *Rethinking Social Inquiry*; George and Bennett (2005) *Case Studies and Theory Development*, and Gerring (2006) *Case Study Research: Principles and Practice*.

Note

1   The divisions in political science are discussed in Almond (1990), Goodin and Klingemann (1996b), Caterino and Schram (2006); the post-modern criticisms of social science are well outlined in Rosenau (1992) and Howarth and Glynos (2007); general criticisms about science can be found in Kuhn (1970) and Feyerabend (1993); and responses to these criticisms can be found in Gordon (1991), Gross and Levitt (1994), and Couvalis (1997).

Part I

WHY, HOW, AND PROBLEMS OF COMPARISON

The chapters in this part of the book establish the rationale for the systematic comparison of countries, demonstrate the different ways in which countries can be compared, and examine the various problems that scholars have confronted or will confront when comparing countries. Too often, both the choice of countries and the way in which they are compared are decided for reasons not related to the research question. In contrast, these chapters argue that the comparative research strategy matters. From the initial specification of the research problem, through the choice of countries and method of analysis, to the final conclusions, scholars must be attentive to the research question that is being addressed and the ways in which the comparison of countries will help provide answers.

To this end, Chapter 1 shows that the comparison of countries is useful for pure description, making classifications, hypothesis-testing, and prediction. It then shows how methods of comparison can add scientific rigour to the study of politics in helping students and scholars alike make stronger inferences about the political world they observe. This is followed by a discussion of key terms needed for a science of politics including theory and method; ontology, epistemology, and methodology; cases, units of analysis, variables, and observations; levels of analysis; and quantitative and qualitative methods. Chapter 2 delves deeper into the different ways in which countries can be compared and why these different methods matter for making inferences. It argues that scholars face a key trade-off between the level of conceptual abstraction and the scope of countries under study. It shows how comparing many countries, few countries, or single-country studies all fit under the broad umbrella of 'comparative politics', and that all have different strengths and weaknesses for the ways in which political scientists study the world. It continues by outlining the main problems that confront comparativists and suggests ways in which to overcome them. These problems include 'too many variables and too few countries', establishing equivalence between and among comparative concepts, selection bias, spuriousness, ecological and individualist fallacies, and value bias.

The next three chapters are devoted to a fuller discussion of the strengths and weaknesses of the comparison of many countries (Chapter 3), few countries (Chapter 4), and single-country studies (Chapter 5). The discussion centres on the underlying assumptions of the methods, the types of research questions they address, and the advantages and disadvantages they have for drawing inferences. Chapter 3 contains a basic introduction to regression analysis. Chapter 4 lays out the two main forms of comparative analysis of few countries (most similar systems design and most different systems design) and then discusses the different ways in which they have been expanded and enhanced. Chapter 5 concludes this part of the book with a full discussion on the value of single-country studies for comparative analysis, including description, plausibility probes and generating hypotheses, confirming and infirming theory, and process tracing and exploring casual mechanisms. Together, these chapters offer a synthesis of comparative methods and provide a 'toolchest' for students and scholars that can be used to approach both existing and new research questions in political science.

Why compare countries?

Making comparisons is a natural human activity. From antiquity to the present, generations of humans have sought to understand and explain the similarities and differences they perceive between themselves and others. Though historically, the discovery of new peoples was often the product of a desire to conquer them, the need to understand the similarities and differences between the conquerors and the conquered was none the less strong. Since the new millennium, citizens in all countries continue to compare their position in society to those of others in terms of their regional, ethnic, linguistic, religious, familial, and cultural allegiances and identities; material possessions; economic, social and political positions; and relative location in systems of power and authority. Students grow up worried about their types of fashion, circle of friends, collections of music, appearance and behaviour of their partners, money earned by their parents, universities they attend, and careers they may achieve.

In short, to compare is to be human. But beyond these everyday comparisons, how is the process of comparison scientific? And how does the comparison of countries help us understand the larger political world? In order to answer these important questions, this chapter is divided into four sections. The first section establishes the four main reasons for comparison, including *contextual description*, *classification* and 'typologizing', *hypothesis-testing* and theory-building, and *prediction* (Hague *et al.* 1992:24–27; Mackie and Marsh 1995:173–176). The second section specifies how political science and the sub-field of comparative politics can be scientific, outlining briefly the similarities and differences between political science and natural science. The third section clarifies the terms and concepts used in the preceding discussion and specifies further those terms and concepts needed for a science of politics. The fourth section summarizes these reasons, justifications, and terms for a science of comparative politics.

Reasons for comparison

Today, the activity of comparing countries centres on four main objectives, all of which are mutually reinforcing in any systematic comparative study, but some of which receive more emphasis than others, depending on the aspirations of the scholar. *Contextual description* allows political scientists to know what other countries are like. *Classification* makes the world of politics less complex, effectively providing the researcher with 'data containers' into which empirical evidence is organized (Sartori 1970:1039). The *hypothesis-testing* function of comparison allows the elimination of rival explanations about particular events, actors, structures, etc. in an effort to help build more general theories. Finally, comparison of countries and the generalizations that result from comparison allow *prediction* about the likely outcomes in other countries not included in the original comparison, or outcomes in the future given the presence of certain antecedent factors and conditions

Contextual description

This first objective of comparative politics is the process of describing the political phenomena and events of a particular country, or group of countries. Traditionally, in political science, this objective of comparative politics was realized in those countries that were different to those of the researcher. Indeed, as the field developed in American political science, a comparativist was considered anyone who carried out research on a country other than the United States. Through often highly detailed description, scholars sought to escape their own ethnocentrism by studying those countries and cultures foreign to them (Dogan and Pelassy 1990:5–13). The comparison to the researcher's own country is either implicit or explicit, and the goal of contextual description is either more knowledge about the nation studied, more knowledge about one's own political system, or both. The comparative literature is replete with examples of this kind of research, and it is often cited to represent 'old' comparative politics as opposed to the 'new' comparative politics, which has aspirations beyond mere description (Mayer 1989; Apter 1996). But the debate about what constitutes old and new comparison often misses the important point that all *systematic research begins with good description*. Thus description serves as an important component to the research process and ought to precede the other three objectives of comparison. Purely descriptive studies serve as the raw data for those comparative studies that aspire to higher levels of explanation, and provide initial hunches about which topics of research may be of interest and which factors may be important to explain observed phenomena that are related to those topics.

In the field of Latin American politics, Macauley's (1967) *Sandino Affair* is a fine example of contextual description. The book is an exhaustive account of Agusto Sandino's guerrilla campaign to oust US marines from Nicaragua after a presidential succession crisis. It details the specific events surrounding the succession crisis, the role of US intervention, the way in which Sandino upheld his principles of non-intervention through guerrilla attacks on US marines, and the eventual death of Sandino at the hands of Anastasio Somoza. The study serves as an example of what Almond (1996:52) calls 'evidence without inference', where the author tells the story of this remarkable political leader, but the story is not meant to make any larger statements about the struggle against imperialism. Rather, the focus is on the specific events that unfolded in Nicaragua, and the important roles played by the various characters in the historical events. None the less, the account could provide a wealth of evidence for comparative and single-case studies examining the role of indigenous resistance to outside intervention, the history of the rise of military authoritarianism in Central America, the roots of revolutionary movements (the contemporary Sandinistas from whom President Daniel Ortega comes), among many other relevant topics found in comparative politics both inside and outside Latin America.

Classification

In the search for cognitive simplification, comparativists often establish different conceptual classifications in order to group vast numbers of countries, political systems, events, etc. into distinct categories with identifiable and shared characteristics. Classification can be a simple dichotomy such as that between 'authoritarianism' and 'democracy', which draws on a set of theoretically-derived criteria that help determine where particular countries would fall. Or classification can be a more complex array of regimes and governmental systems that provides greater differentiation. Like contextual description, classification is a necessary component of systematic comparison, but in many ways represents a higher level of comparison since it seeks to group many separate descriptive entities into simpler categories. It reduces the complexity of the world by seeking out those qualities that countries share and those that they do not share. Moreover, classification schemes can be the first step towards capturing cross-national variation in political phenomena, such as democratic and authoritarian countries, developed and under-developed countries, core and peripheral countries, military and civilian regimes, among many other distinctions.

The process of classification is not new. The most famous effort at classification is found in Aristotle's *Politics* (Book 3, Chapters 6–7), in which he establishes six types of rule. Based on the combination of their form of rule (good or corrupt) and the number of those who rule (one, few, or many), Aristotle derived the following six forms: monarchy, aristocracy, polity, tyranny, oligarchy, and democracy (see Hague *et al.* 1992:26). A more recent attempt at classification is found in Finer's (1997) *The History of Government*, which claims that since antiquity (*ca.* 3200 BC) all forms of government have belonged to one of the following four basic types: the palace polity, the church polity, the nobility polity, and the forum polity. Each type is 'differentiated by the nature of the ruling personnel' (ibid.: 37). In the palace polity, 'decision-making rests with one individual' (ibid.: 38). In the church polity, the church has a significant if not exclusive say in decision making (ibid.: 50). In the nobility polity, a certain pre-eminent sector of society has substantial influence on decision-making (ibid.: 47). In the forum polity, the authority is 'conferred on the rulers from below' by a 'plural headed' forum (ibid.: 51). Aristotle's classification was derived deductively and then 'matched' to actual city states, while Finer's classification scheme is based on empirical observation and inductive reasoning (see below for the distinction between these two types of reasoning). Both scholars, however, seek to describe and simplify a more complex reality by identifying key features common to each type (see Briefing box 1.1).

Hypothesis-testing

Despite the differences between contextual description and classification, both forms of activity contribute to the next objective of comparison, hypothesis-testing. In other words, once things have been described and classified, the comparativist can then move on to search for those factors that may help explain what has been described and classified. Since the 1950s, political scientists have increasingly sought to use comparative methods to help build more complete theories of politics. Comparison of countries allows rival explanations to be ruled out and hypotheses derived from certain theoretical perspectives to be tested through examining cross-national similarities and differences. Scholars using this mode of analysis, which is often seen as the *raison d'être* of the 'new' comparative politics (Mayer 1989), identify

Briefing box 1.1 Making classifications: Aristotle and Finer

Description and classification are the building blocks of comparative politics. Classification simplifies descriptions of the important objects of comparative inquiry. Good classification should have well-defined categories into which empirical evidence can be organized. Categories that make up a classification scheme can be derived inductively from careful consideration of available evidence or through a process of deduction in which 'ideal' types are generated. This briefing box contains the oldest example of regime classification and one of the most recent. Both Aristotle and Samuel Finer seek to establish simple classificatory schemes into which real societies can be placed. While Aristotle's scheme is founded on normative grounds, Finer's scheme is derived empirically.

Constitutions and their classifications

In Book 3 of *Politics*, Aristotle derives regime types which are divided on the one hand between those that are 'good' and those that are 'corrupt', and on the other, between the different number of rulers that make up the decision-making authority, namely, the one, the few, and the many. Good government rules in the common interest while corrupt government rules in the interests of those who comprise the dominant authority. The intersection between these two divisions yields six regime types, all of which appear in Figure 1.1. The figure shows that the good types include monarchy, aristocracy, and polity. The corrupt types include tyranny, oligarchy, and democracy. Each type is based on a different idea of justice (McClelland 1997: 57). Thus, monarchy is rule by the one for the common interest, while tyranny is rule by the one for the one. Aristocracy is rule by the few for the common interest, while oligarchy is rule by the few for the few. Polity is rule by the many for the common good, while democracy is rule by the many for the many, or what Aristotle called 'mob rule'.

		Those Who Rule		
		One	Few	Many
Form of Rule	Good	Monarchy (kingship)	Aristocracy	Polity
	Corrupt	Tyranny	Oligarchy	Democracy (mob rule)

Figure 1.1 Aristotle's classification scheme
Sources: Adapted from Aristotle (1958: 110–115); Hague *et al.* (1992: 26); McClelland (1997: 57)

Types of regime

Finer (1997: 37) adopts an Aristotelian approach to regime classification by identifying four 'pure' types of regime and their logical 'hybrids'. Each regime type is based on the nature of its ruling personnel. The pure types include the palace, the forum, the nobility, and the church. The hybrid types are the six possible combinations of the pure types, palace–forum, palace–nobility, palace–church, forum–nobility, forum–church, and nobility–church. These pure and hybrid types are meant to describe all the regime types that have existed in world history from 3200 BC to the modern nation state. Finer concedes that there are few instances of pure forms in history and that most polities fit one of his hybrid types. These pure forms, their hybrids, and examples from world history appear in Figure 1.2. The diagonal that results from the intersection of the first row and column in the figure represents the pure forms, while the remaining cells contain the hybrid forms. Many regime types that were originally pure became hybrid at different points in history. Of all the types, the pure palace and its variants have remained the most common through history, and despite its popularity today, the forum polity that represents modern secular democracies is a relatively rare and recent regime type (Finer 1997: 46).

	Palace	Forum	Nobility	Church
Palace	*Pure Palace* Persian, Roman, Byzantine, Chinese, and Islamic Empires; 18th-century absolutisms	*Palace–Forum* Greek tyrants, Roman dictators, Napoleonic France, modern dictatorships and totalitarian regimes	*Palace–Nobility* Court of Louis XIV, Britain 1740–60, Poland, Mamluk Regime in Egypt, and pre-1600 Japan	*Palace–Church* Traditional Thailand: the *sangha*; European Middle Ages
Forum		*Pure Forum* Greek *poleis*, Roman republics, and medieval European city-states; modern secular democracies	*Forum–Nobility* Roman republic, Republic of Venice	*Forum–Church* Ephrata Mennonites 1725, Amish 1700–present,[†] both near Lancaster, Pennsylvania
Nobility			*Pure Nobility* 17th- and 18th-century Poland	*Nobility–Church* Teutonic Order 1198–1225
Church				*Pure Church* Vatican; Tibet 1642–1949

Figure 1.2 Pure and hybrid regime types with examples from history
Source: Adapted from Finer (1997: 34–58)
Note: [†] Author's addition

important variables, posit relationships to exist between them, and illustrate these relationships comparatively in an effort to generate and build comprehensive theories.

Arend Lijphart (1975) claims that comparison allows 'testing hypothesized empirical relationships among variables'. Similarly, Peter Katzenstein argues that 'comparative research is a focus on analytical relationships among variables validated by social science, a focus that is modified by differences in the context in which we observe and measure those variables' (in Kohli *et al.* 1995:11). Finally, Mayer (1989:46) argues somewhat more forcefully that 'the unique potential of comparative analysis lies in the cumulative and incremental addition of system-level attributes to existing explanatory theory, thereby making such theory progressively more complete'. In other words, comparison of countries and testing hypotheses contributes to the progressive accumulation of knowledge about the political world. Multiple symposia on comparative politics in *World Politics* (Kohli *et al.* 1995), *American Political Science Review* (vol. 89, no. 2, pp. 454–481), and *Political Analysis* (Brady *et al.* 2006), as well as new monographs containing critical reflections on the state of comparative methodology suggest that questions of theory, explanation, and the role of comparison continue to be at the forefront of scholars minds (see, e.g., Flyvbjerg 2001; Brady and Collier 2004; George and Bennett 2005).

Furthermore, the publication of truly comparative books in the field continues to demonstrate the fruitfulness of this mode of analysis. For example, Luebbert (1991) compares Britain, France, Switzerland, Belgium, The Netherlands, Denmark, Norway, Sweden, Czechoslovakia, Germany, Italy, and Spain to uncover the class origins of regime type in inter-war Europe. Rueschemeyer *et al.* (1992) compare the historical experiences of the advanced industrial countries with those of the developing world to uncover the relationship between capitalist development and democracy. Wickham-Crowley (1993) compares instances of revolutionary activity in Latin America to discover the causal configuration of successful and unsuccessful social revolution in the region. Foweraker and Landman (1997) compare the authoritarian cases of Brazil, Chile, Mexico, and Spain to illustrate the relationship between citizenship rights and social movements. Dryzek and Holmes (2002) examines the ways in which citizens think and view democracy across eleven post-communist countries. Hawkins (2002) uses the single case of Chile to examine how international mobilization condemning human rights abuses led 'rule-oriented' factions of the Pinochet regime to push for a democratic transition, the inferences from which are applied to the cases of Cuba and South Africa (see Chapter 11). Finally, Inglehart and Welzel (2005) compare cross-national survey and other data to assess the complex relationship between and among processes of modernization (or postmodernization), changing value systems, and democracy. In all these works, key explanatory and outcome variables are carefully defined and the relationships between them are demonstrated through comparison of empirical evidence (see Briefing box 1.2).

Briefing box 1.2 Hypothesis-testing

Voting participation

In *Contemporary Democracies*, Powell (1982) examines a number of key hypotheses concerning voter participation in twenty-nine democratic countries. Participation is measured using voter turnout, or the percentage of the eligible voters who actually voted in national elections. He argues that voting participation ought to be higher in countries with higher levels of economic development (per capita GNP), a representational constitution, electoral laws that facilitate voting, and a party system with strong alignments to groups in society (Powell 1982: 120–121). His statistical analysis of the data from these countries reveals positive effects for all these variables on voter participation, which are depicted graphically in Figure 1.3.

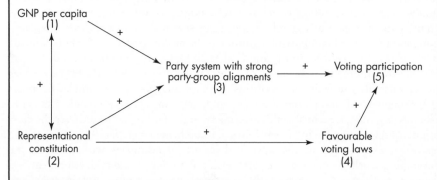

Figure 1.3 Four hypotheses on voting participation
Source: Adapted from Powell (1982: 121)

Moreover, his analysis shows that the level of economic development and constitutional structure are not directly related to voter participation, but that they 'lead to or help sustain the development of party systems and the choice of voting laws, which do get the voters to the polls' (ibid.: 120). This causal ordering is depicted in the figure with the arrows and the numbering of each variable.

Prediction

The final and most difficult objective of comparative politics is a logical extension of hypothesis-testing, namely, to make predictions about outcomes in other countries based on the generalizations from the initial comparison, or to make claims about future political outcomes. Prediction in comparative politics tends to be made in probabilistic terms, such as 'countries with systems of proportional representation are more likely to have multiple political parties'. In this example, a political scientist would know the likely effect of a nation switching its electoral system from a plurality or 'first-past-the-post' rule to a proportional one (Hague *et al.* 1992). Another predictive example involves the benefits accrued to political incumbents in contesting future elections. Based on the empirical observations of past electoral contests, political scientists could be reasonably secure in predicting that the incumbent in any given election has a higher probability of winning the election than the non-incumbent (see King *et al.* 1994).

Although prediction is less an aspiration of comparativists today than in the past, there are those who continue to couch their arguments in predictive language. For example, weak predictive arguments are found in Huntington's (1996) *The Clash of Civilizations and the Remaking of the New World Order*, and strong predictive arguments are found in Vanhanen's (1997) *The Prospects of Democracy*. Huntington (1996) identifies nine key cultural groupings which he believes currently characterize the world's population, and predicts that future conflicts will be more likely to appear in the areas where two or more of these cultures meet or 'clash'. Not only does he seek to predict future conflicts in the world, but claims that his 'civilization' approach accounts for more post-Cold War events than rival approaches. His predictions became all the more relevant after the terrorist attacks on the World Trade Center and the Pentagon on September 11, 2001, which many saw as proof of a clash between the 'Western' and 'Islamic' civilizations outlined in his book. Subsequent analysis on pairs of states (or 'dyads') between 1969 and 2003 has shown that Huntington's 'West' civilization has been significantly more targeted than other civilizational groups and that the Islam–West dyad encounters more terrorism, but in contrast to Huntington's prediction, the Islamic group is not more violent *per se*, while overall levels of terrorism did not increase significantly after the Cold War (Neumayer and Plümper 2006).

Similarly, based on observations of the presence of economic resources and the occurrence of democracy in the world from the middle of the nineteenth century until today, Vanhanen (1997:99–154) predicts the degree to which individual countries and regions in the world are likely to become democratic, where his various results invite further research on the dynamics of democratization that moves beyond consideration of his socio-economic variables (see Briefing box 1.3). Finally, in the field of human rights, Poe and Tate (1994) find from their analysis of the cross-national variation in the protection of human rights that economic development and democracy have a positive effect on the protection of human rights while involvement in international and civil war have a negative effect. Using these findings, Poe and Tate (1994: 861–866) predict the likely over-time increases in repression (i.e. violations of human rights) due to the loss of democracy, involvement in international war, and experience of civil war, as well as predict the decrease in repression due to the increase in economic standing.

The science in political science

The preceding section specified the four main objectives of comparison in political science and hinted, through reference to questions of explanation, theory building, and prediction, how the comparison of countries might be considered a science. The

Briefing box 1.3 Making predictions

Democracy in East and Southeast Asia

Using similar methods as Burkhart and Lewis-Beck (1999), Vanhanen (1997) seeks to predict the expected level of democracy in specific countries and regions of the world based on their distribution of 'power resources'. Democracy is measured by a combination of the smallest parties' share of the vote and the percentage turnout (ibid.: 35). The distribution of power resources is measured by an index that combines the urban population, the non-agricultural population, proportion of students, the size of the literate population, the number of family farms, and the degree of decentralization of non-agricultural economic resources (Vanhanen 1997: 59–60). By examining the relationship between the level of democracy and the distribution of power resources from 1850–1993, Vanhanen compares the actual 1993 values of democracy to those that were predicted using regression analysis. Figure 1.4 shows the actual and predicted values of democracy for sixteen

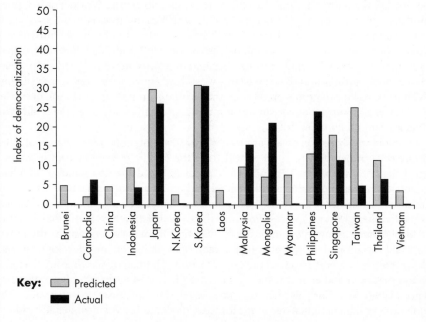

Key: ▢ Predicted
■ Actual

Figure 1.4 Predicting democracy in East and Southeast Asia
Source: Adapted from Vanhanen (1997: 88–89)

countries from East and Southeast Asia. The sixteen countries are listed along the horizontal axis and the values of the index of democratization are listed on the vertical axis. The predicted scores of democracy represent the level of democracy that each country ought to have obtained by 1993, given its corresponding distribution of power resources. The actual level is the score for 1993. The difference between the two values is known as the residual. Japan and South Korea appear to have obtained the levels of democracy that were predicted, while Malaysia, Mongolia, and the Philippines have higher levels of democracy than expected and Brunei, China, and Taiwan have lower scores than were expected. These varied results have several implications. First, the discrepancy between the actual and the predicted values may mean that something other than the distribution of power resources accounts for the level of democracy (see Chapter 3). Second, the deviant cases whose level of democracy is unexpected for 1993 may be temporary exceptions to the overall pattern. Third, the indicators that were used may not accurately reflect the concepts Vanhanen seeks to measure (see Chapter 3). Overall, however, the process of making predictions can raise new research questions and identify the need to focus on those cases that do not 'fit' the pattern (see Chapter 2).

key term used throughout the discussion was *inference*. Simply put, making an inference is 'using facts we know to learn something about facts we do not know' (King *et al.* 1994:119 after Mill; see also Couvalis 1997). Gabriel Almond (1996) observes that 'the object of political science . . . is the creation of knowledge, defined as inferences or generalizations about politics drawn from evidence'; and Mayer (1989:56) claims that 'comparative analysis . . . [is] a method that plays a central role in the explanatory mission of political science itself'. Thus, comparative politics seeks to achieve the goal of inference about politics through comparing countries. This section of the chapter clarifies how the process of making inferences is the underlying principle of comparative politics, and how the methodological assumptions of natural science are important to a science of politics.

For the purposes of this volume, science is defined as the gradual accumulation of knowledge about the empirical world through systematic practices of inquiry, including the collection of evidence, the generation and testing of hypotheses, and the drawing of substantive inferences.[1] But beyond this basic definition, what are the parallels between political science and natural science? What are the main differences between the two? And how does comparison help resolve these differences? The strong case for a science of politics suggests that both (comparative) political science and natural science share the same basic goals, namely, description, classification, hypothesis-testing, and prediction. Both activities require the systematic collection of evidence; an ordering of the evidence and the search for discernible patterns; the formulation and testing of contending explanations for the occurrence of the patterns; and the building of more general theories. Thus, a science of politics always contains this 'evidence-inference methodological core' (Almond 1996:52), or the 'customary pair' of theory and observation (Feyerabend 1993:23; see also Gordon 1991: 589–634).

Two examples from the natural sciences may help make these points clearer. Both the theory of evolution and the theory of gravity are based on the systematic collection of evidence. Charles Darwin sought to document the entirety of the Earth's flora and fauna. Originally in an effort to demonstrate the glory of God's creation,

Darwin soon discovered a pattern in what he was observing for which an alternative explanation was possible. The theory of evolution, buttressed later by the theory of natural selection, emerged as the new explanation for the variety of species found in the natural world. Similarly, Isaac Newton formulated the theory of gravity based on the collection of evidence (the falling apple!). Neither scientist had actually seen evolution or gravity but merely observed its effects. In this way, evolution and gravity are mental constructs, whose repeated empirical verification has given them a law-like status.

Political scientists also collect evidence systematically (e.g. archival records, interviews, official statistics, histories, or surveys), search for discernible patterns in the evidence, and formulate theories to account for those patterns. In comparative politics, the political scientist compares countries in an effort to verify the theories that have been formulated. Thus, both the natural and political sciences seek to make inferences based on the empirical world they observe, and both seek to maximize the certainty of these inferences. Despite these general similarities between natural science and political science, there remain two important (albeit not absolute) differences: experimentation and the generation of scientific 'laws'. These differences are discussed in turn.

The first difference between natural science and political science is the role of experimentation. While for some areas of natural scientific research, such as astronomy and seismology, experimentation is not possible, the advances in natural science are generally supported by evidence gathered through experimentation, which involves the controlled manipulation of the subject under study in an effort to isolate causal factors. Evidence in political science, on the other hand, tends not to be gathered through experimentation, even though some political scientists use experiments in their research (e.g. those who work on game theory, focus groups, and 'citizen-juries'). Comparative politics, in particular, cannot use experimentation for both practical and ethical reasons. For example, it would be impossible to re-run the same election in the same country with a different electoral system to observe the differences in the outcome of the two systems. Ethically, it would be impossible to redistribute income intentionally in a developing country to see if civil strife erupts. Both these examples demonstrate the need for using *counterfactuals*, or situations in which the researcher imagines a state of affairs where the antecedent factors to a given event are absent and where an alternative course of events or outcomes is considered (Ferguson 1997b).

Whether it is different electoral systems, different distributions of income, different levels of economic development, or the absence of particular revolutionary groups, political scientists implicitly suggest a counterfactual situation when making claims about important explanatory factors. The claim that 'single-member district electoral systems tend to produce two-party systems' is in effect also claiming that countries *without* such electoral systems will necessarily have different political party systems. While some historians may construct alternative historical scenarios based on 'calculations about the relative probability of plausible outcomes' (ibid.: 85), political scientists compare countries that differ in ways that supply the requisite counterfactual situation. For example, by comparing the political party systems across countries with different electoral systems, the comparativist seeks to demonstrate that the type of electoral system has some bearing on the type of party system. In this way, comparative research 'simulates' experimentation (Lieberson 1987:45; Ferguson 1997b; see also Tetlock and Lebow 2001).

The second difference between natural science and political science involves the law-like status that is given to certain scientific theories. Experimentation and repeated empirical verification give theories in the natural sciences the status of laws (e.g. the law of conservation of energy, Newton's laws of motion, or Boyle's Law of Gases); however, the nature of evidence marshalled in support of theories of political science is such that law-like generalizations are rare. Three famous 'laws' of political science are well known. Michels' 'Iron Law of Oligarchy' suggests that the natural processes observable in the dynamics of organizations and small groups are such that over time, all groups and organizations develop a hierarchical structure of authority with a small elite at their head. In an example from the comparative literature, this law has been tested in the examination of social movement organizations, where evidence suggests that the most successful and long-standing social movement organizations tend to have formal bureaucratic structures and authoritative bodies composed of elites from the movement (see Tarrow 1994). The second law, called 'Duverger's Law', states that electoral systems based on single-member districts tend to produce two parties while systems with proportional representation tend to produce multiple parties. This law has been repeatedly tested in comparative studies on electoral systems and on balance, is supported by the evidence (see Rae 1971; Lijphart 1994a).

The third law on 'the democratic peace' states that democracies do not go to war with other democracies (Babst 1964; see also Chapter 12 in this volume), while a corollary law claims that democracies are less likely to be involved in militarized disputes than non-democracies (see Russett and O'Neal 2001). Repeated comparative studies in international relations of war 'dyads' (i.e. pairs of countries that engage in war with each other), demonstrate that '[t]he number of wars between the democracies during the past two centuries ranges from zero to less than a handful depending on precisely how democracy is defined' (Levy 1989:87–88). Scholars argue that this 'absence of war between democracies comes as close to anything we have to an empirical law in international relations' (ibid.: 88). Moreover, combined with the process of democratization, which has become more pronounced since 1974 (see Chapter 7), the law of democratic peace offers optimism about future conflict in the world, since a larger proportion of democracies in the world means fewer inter-state wars (see Ward and Gleditsch 1998; Przeworski *et al.* 2000; Gelpi and Griesdorf 2001; Russett and O'Neil 2001).

Aside from these three 'laws' of political science, the bulk of comparative research eschews making such strong claims. What then are the main conclusions about comparative politics that can be drawn from this cursory comparison with natural science? First, for practical and ethical reasons, comparative politics relaxes some of the rigours of natural science, but still employs the same logic of inference. Second, comparative politics is a non-experimental (or quasi-experimental) social science that seeks to make generalizations based on the best available evidence (Campbell and Stanley 1963; Lijphart 1975:162; Lieberson 1987). Third, as a substitute for experimentation, comparison allows for *control* (Sartori 1994:16), holding certain things constant while examining and accounting for observed differences (see Chapter 2). Fourth, while not seeking ironclad laws, comparative politics seeks clarity, understanding, and explanation of political phenomena about which it can be reasonably certain. The goal of this book therefore, is to provide the necessary tools for students of politics to achieve this clarity, understanding, and explanation while avoiding the pitfalls and obstacles that limit such an enterprise.

Scientific terms and concepts

Before concluding this chapter, it is necessary to define and clarify terms that have been used thus far, as well as terms that will be encountered throughout the book. These are general terms used throughout the social sciences that all students of politics ought to know if they aspire to a more scientific approach to understanding the political world. These terms include theory and method; ontology, epistemology, and methodology; cases (or countries), units of analysis, variables, and observations; levels of analysis; and quantitative and qualitative methods. Throughout the discussion every effort is made to show how the book uses these terms and concepts of social science.

Theory and method

There are two basic types of theory in political science, normative and empirical. Normative theory specifies how things in society *ought to be*, given a desired set of outcomes and philosophical position. From the Greeks and Romans to contemporary scholars such as John Rawls, normative political theorists establish frameworks for realizing the common good and address key problems of society through theoretical argumentation. For example, Rawls (1971) carries on the tradition of liberal contract theory found in Locke, Rousseau and Kant, by deriving principles of justice from an idealized thought experiment that involves the key concept of the 'veil of ignorance', behind which individuals are unaware of their age, class, gender, wealth, ethnic identity, etc. In contrast, empirical theory seeks to establish relationships between two or more concepts in an effort to explain the occurrence of observed political phenomena. For example, an empirical theory of social revolution may posit a series of socio-economic factors that account for revolutionary behaviour in certain types of people, which would then be tested using evidence (see Chapter 7). In addition, theories in political science can be deductive or inductive. Deductive theories arrive at their conclusions by applying reason to a given set of premises (Stoker 1995:17; Lawson 1997:16–19; Couvalis 1997). For example, the rational choice perspective in political science assumes that all political actors maximize their own personal utility, or self-interest, when choosing between alternatives. From that basic assumption, the scholar logically deduces the range of possible outcomes (Ward 1995:79; Levi 1997). Inductive theories, on the other hand, arrive at their conclusions through observation of known facts (Couvalis 1997). For example, a scholar observing higher instances of peasant rebellion in geographical areas with higher levels of land and income inequality will arrive inductively at the conclusion that inequality is related to rebellion. Comparison of evidence from other countries or geographical regions would seek to confirm this generalization.

Method, on the other hand, is the means by which a theory is derived and tested, including the collection of evidence, formulation and testing of hypotheses, and the arrival at substantive conclusions. Evidence can be collected, for example, through the examination of historical records, the collation and analysis of open-ended interviews of political activists, the systematic reporting of the participant observation of social movement activities, or the construction and analysis of mass surveys of a sample of the population. In formulating and testing hypotheses, method makes the decision rules and the rejection of rival hypotheses explicit. Finally, substantive conclusions are drawn from the theories and the evidence. As the preceding discussion in this chapter suggests, this book, although not primarily concerned with different theories of comparative politics, seeks to demonstrate the different ways in which comparative methods can be used to test deductive and inductive empirical theories of politics.

Ontology, epistemology, and methodology

Ontology, epistemology, and methodology are terms that occur in the discussion of the philosophy of science and the distinctions between them often become blurred in the comparative literature. Ontology is, quite literally, the study of being, or the metaphysical concern with the essence of things, including the 'nature, constitution, and structure of the objects' of comparative inquiry (Lawson 1997:15). It concerns what can be studied, what can be compared, and what constitutes the political. In other words, for comparative politics, ontology concerns the countries, events, actors, institutions, and processes among other things that are observable and in need of explanation. Epistemology is the study of the nature of knowledge, or how scholars come to know the world, both through a priori means and through a posteriori means of observation, sense impression, and experience. In contrast to ontology, it concerns what knowledge of the political world is possible and what rules of inquiry scholars follow in knowing the political world. In the history and philosophy of science, epistemology has moved from the strong claim made by positivists that a unity of the natural and social sciences is possible to one that recognizes a certain plurality of approaches grounded in the link between evidence and inference of the kind that this book advocates (see Gordon 1991:589–668). In contrast to ontology and epistemology, methodology concerns the ways in which knowledge of the political world is acquired. As its name suggests, methodology is the study of different methods or systems of methods in a given field of inquiry. There are thus rules of inquiry specific to qualitative and quantitative methods, even though both strive to provide explanation and understanding of observed political phenomena. These three concepts also have ordered and 'directional dependence' such that ontology establishes what is knowable, epistemology how it is knowable, and methodology how it is acquired systematically (Hay 2002:61–66).

Having defined these terms, it is helpful for the reader to know how the discussions throughout the rest of this book are grounded in certain ontological, epistemological, and methodological assumptions. Without entering a philosophical debate, this book is grounded in the ontological belief that animate and inanimate objects in the world exist in and of themselves, and by extension observable events exist in and of themselves. The object of political science is to account for and understand these events in terms of why they happened, how they happened, and the likelihood of them happening again in the future, as well as in different parts of the world. While adhering to the notion that history is 'open ended' (Popper 1997), this book accepts that there are certain 'event regularities' (Lawson 1997) in the world that political science seeks to describe, explain, and understand.

Epistemologically, comparative politics inhabits a broad spectrum. One end of the spectrum contends that all things political and social are knowable through the process of deduction based on indisputable assumptions about human nature. Typically labelled 'nomothetic-deductive', such an epistemological position adheres to the positivist quest for law-like generalizations about political behaviour. The other end of the spectrum claims that all knowledge is culturally bound and relative, suggesting that it is impossible to know anything beyond the strict confines of the local cultural context (Kohli *et al.* 1995). Such a position suggests that a science of comparative politics is not possible, since political concepts would not 'travel' across different cultural contexts and there would be fundamental differences in their meaning (see Macintyre 1971).

In an effort to be inclusive of different methods of comparison, this book is located somewhere in between these two extremes. On the one hand, it accepts that certain deductive theories of politics can be tested in the real world and that generalizations about the world of politics are possible given the proper adherence to rules of inquiry. On the other hand, it recognizes that knowledge of the political world cannot be 'value-free' and that the processes of theory generation and observation may not be mutually exclusive (Feyerabend 1993:27; Sanders 1995:67–68; Couvalis 1997). It therefore accepts that certain kinds of cross-cultural comparisons and cross-national comparisons can be made if certain procedures are adopted (see Chapter 2 in this volume). Methodologically, the book is concerned with the application of comparative methods to real research problems in comparative politics in an effort to help students make more valid generalizations about the political world they observe. These different methods of comparison, as well as their advantages and disadvantages are outlined in Chapter 2.

Cases, units of analysis, variables, and observations

These four terms are vital aspects of systematic research in comparative politics. Cases are those countries that feature in the comparative analysis. For example, in *States and Social Revolutions* (1979), Theda Skocpol examines the cases of France, Russia, and China. Units of analysis are the objects on which the scholar collects data, such as individual people, countries, electoral systems, social movements, etc. Variables are those concepts whose values change over a given set of units, such as income, political party identification, propensity to join a protest movement, etc. Observations are the values of the variables for each unit, which can be numeric, verbal, or even visual. For example, a hypothetical study of social movements in Britain, France, The Netherlands, and Germany may have a variable entitled 'strategy', which has categories denoted 'political lobbying', 'peaceful demon-stration', 'violent direct action', 'grass-roots organizing', and 'consciousness-raising'.

In this hypothetical study, the cases are the countries, the units of analysis are the movements, the variable is 'strategy', and the observation is the value of the strategy variable for a given movement in a given country.

In addition to the different values that variables assume, they can either be *dependent* or *independent*. Dependent variables (alternatively referred to as outcome variables, endogenous variables, or the explanandum) are those political outcomes that the research is trying to explain. An independent variable, on the other hand, is that which explains the dependent variable (and is alternatively labelled a causal variable, an explanatory variable, an exogenous variable, or the explicandum). The distinction between dependent and independent variables is derived from the specific research question of a comparative project and the particular theoretical perspective that has been adopted. Since most political events have multiple explanations, it is possible to have more than one independent variable for a given dependent variable. In formal models of politics and in standard notation used for regression equations the dependent variable is often depicted by a y, and the independent variable is often depicted by an x (see Chapter 3).

For example, a dependent variable may include votes for a leftist party, military coups, revolutions, or transitions to democracy. These are all examples of outcomes of interest to political scientists. Independent variables to account for each of these dependent variables may include, respectively, social class, economic crisis, the commercialization of agriculture, or elite bargaining. In his study of guerrillas and revolution in Latin America, Wickham-Crowley (1993) seeks to explain the occurrence of successful social revolutions. In this example, successful social revolution is the dependent variable. The independent variables include the presence of a guerrilla group, the support of workers and peasants, sufficient guerrilla military strength, the presence of a traditional patrimonial regime, and the withdrawal of US military and economic support for the incumbent regime (Wickham-Crowley 1993:312; see Chapter 7 in this volume).

Levels of analysis

Levels of analysis in political science are divided between the micro, or individual level, and the macro, or system level. Micro-political analysis examines the political activity of individuals, such as respondents in a mass survey, elite members of a political party or government, or activists in a protest movement. Macro-political analysis focuses on groups of individuals, structures of power, social classes, economic processes, and the interaction of nation states. As in other divisions in political science, there are those who believe all of politics can be explained by focusing on micro-level processes, and there are those who believe that all of politics can be explained by a focus on macro-level processes. This is sometimes called the 'structure-agency' problem of politics (see Hay 1995, 2002). Micro-analysts believe that the world of politics is shaped by the actions of 'structureless agents', while macro-analysts believe that that world is shaped by the unstoppable processes of 'agentless-structures'.

The comparative politics literature is rich with examples of these different levels of analysis. In *The Rational Peasant*, Samuel Popkin (1979) argues that revolutionary movements are best understood by focusing on the preferences and actions of individual peasants (a micro-level analysis). Support for this assertion comes from his intense study of peasant activity in Vietnam. In contrast to Popkin, Jeffrey Paige (1975) in *Agrarian Revolution*, demonstrates that revolutions are most likely in countries with a particular structural combination of owners and cultivators. This macro-level analysis is carried out through comparing many countries at once, and then verifying the findings in the three countries of Vietnam, Angola, and Peru (see Chapter 2). In *Liberalism, Fascism, or Social Democracy*, Gregory Luebbert (1991) claims that the types of regime that emerged in inter-war Europe had nothing to do with 'leadership and meaningful choice' (ibid.: 306), but were determined structurally by mass material interests, social classes, and political parties (a macro-level analysis). Finally, in *The Breakdown of Democratic Regimes*, Stepan (1978) finds the middle ground in accounting for the 1964 breakdown of democracy in Brazil, where he suggests that macro-political conditions at the time of breakdown certainly limited but did not determine the actions of individual leaders. This present book does not privilege one level of analysis over another. Rather, it demonstrates the ways in which different levels of analysis fit into different comparative methods and how different comparative studies have addressed the key tenets of dominant empirical theories in political science (see Chapter 13 this volume).

Quantitative and qualitative methods

Simply put, quantitative methods seek to show differences in number between certain objects of analysis and qualitative methods seek to show differences in kind. Quantitative analysis answers the simple question, 'How many of them are there?' (Miller 1995:154), where the 'them' represents any object of comparison that can either be counted or assigned a numerical value. There are many such objects in political science, such as protest events, social movement strategies (see above, p. 19), an individual's identification with political parties, democratic transitions (see Chapter 9) and the degree to which human rights are protected (see Chapter 11). Quantitative data can be official aggregate data published by governments on growth rates, revenues and expenditures, levels of agricultural and industrial production, crime rates and prison populations, or the number of hectares of land devoted to agrarian reform. Quantitative data can also be individual, such as that found in the numerous market research surveys and public opinion polls. Quantitative methods are based on the distributions these data exhibit and the relationships that can be established between numeric variables using simple and advanced statistical methods.

Qualitative methods seek to identify and understand the attributes, characteristics, and traits of the objects of inquiry, and the nature of the method necessarily requires a focus on a small number of countries. In comparative politics, there are three broad types of qualitative methods: macro-historical comparison (and its three subtypes) (Skocpol and Somers 1980; Ragin *et al.* 1996); in-depth interviews and participant observation (Devine 1995); and what is variously called interpretivism, hermeneutics, and 'thick description' (Geertz 1973; Fay 1975). In none of these types of method is there an attempt to give numerical expression to the objects of inquiry, and in all of them, the goal is to provide well-rounded and complete discursive accounts. These more complete accounts are often referred to as 'ideographic' or 'configurative', since they seek to identify all the elements important in accounting for the outcome. Through focus on a small number of countries, comparative macro-history allows for the 'parallel demonstration of theory', the 'contrast of contexts', or 'macrocausal' explanation (Skocpol and Somers 1980). Parallel demonstration of theory tests the fruitfulness of theory across a range of countries. The contrast of contexts helps to identify unique features of countries in an effort to show their effect on social processes, while bringing out the richness of the individual countries and aspiring to 'descriptive holism'. Macro-causal analysis seeks to explain observed political phenomena through the identification and analysis of 'master' variables (Luebbert 1991:5). In-depth interviews and participant observation strive to uncover a deeper level of information in order to capture meaning, process, and context, where explanation 'involves describing and understanding people as conscious and social human beings' (Devine 1995:140). Similarly, interpretivism, hermeneutics, and 'thick description' are concerned with interpretation, understanding, and the deeper structures of meanings associated with the objects of inquiry.

Over the years a division in political science has developed between those who use quantitative methods and those who use qualitative methods; however, it seems that this division is a false one if both methods adhere to the goal of making inferences from available evidence (Foweraker and Landman 1997:48–49). In other words, this book is grounded in the belief that the same logic of inference ought to apply equally to quantitative and qualitative methods (see King *et al.* 1994; see also Brady and Collier 2004). Perhaps more importantly, the qualitative distinction made among categories in comparative classification schemes necessarily precedes the process of quantification (Sartori 1970, 1994). And, as the ensuing chapters will demonstrate, it is clear that the field of comparative politics is richly populated with studies that use quantitative and qualitative methods (or both) at all levels of analysis, as well as across all methods of comparison.

Summary

This chapter has outlined the four main objectives of comparative politics and argued further that these should be seen not as mutually exclusive but as progressively cumulative and necessary for systematic research. Predictions cannot be made without well-founded theories; theories cannot be made without proper classification; and classification cannot be made without good description. The chapter has shown how comparative politics is scientific if it aspires to making inferences about the political world based on the best available evidence and coherent rules of inquiry. Finally, it defined the key terms that will be used throughout the book. The next chapter examines the different methods of comparison that are available to students, all of which can be used to make larger inferences about the political world that we observe.

Note

1   A slightly more cumbersome definition is offered by Goodin and Klingemann (1996a: 9): 'science . . . [is] systematic enquiry, building toward an ever more highly differentiated set of ordered propositions about the empirical world.'

Further reading

Brady, H. and Collier, D. (eds) (2004) *Rethinking Social Inquiry: Diverse Tools, Shared Standards*, Lanham, MD: Rowman and Littlefield.
   A considered and robust reflection on King *et al.*'s (1994) *Designing Social Inquiry*.

Chilcote, R.H. (1994) *Theories of Comparative Politics: The Search for a Paradigm Reconsidered*, 2nd edn, Boulder, CO: Westview.
   An overview of the main theories of comparative politics, including systems theory, state theory, political culture theory, modernization theory, dependency theory, and class theory.

Dogan, M. and Pelassy, D. (1990) *How to Compare Nations: Strategies in Comparative Politics*, 2nd edn, Chatham, NJ: Chatham House.
   A review of why and how to compare countries as well as a brief overview of popular concepts in comparative politics.

Hague, R., Harrop, M., and Breslin, S. (1992) *Political Science: A Comparative Introduction*, New York: St Martin's Press.
   A textbook on political science written from a comparative perspective.

Hay, C. (2002) *Political Analysis*, London: Palgrave.
   Excellent summary and exposition on the purpose and meaning of conducting political analysis.

King, G., Keohane, R.O., and Verba, S. (1994) *Designing Social Inquiry: Scientific Inference in Qualitative Research*, Princeton, NJ: Princeton University Press.
   Demanding but worthwhile effort to unify qualitative and quantitative research methods under one logic of inference.

Lichbach, M. and Zuckerman, A. (eds) (1997) *Comparative Politics: Rationality, Culture, and Structure*, Cambridge: Cambridge University Press.
   Advanced text on rational, cultural, and structural theories and how they are used in comparative politics.

Marsh, D. and Stoker, G. (eds) (1995) *Theories and Methods in Political Science*, London: Macmillan.
   Excellent reader on the main theories and methods of political science.

How to compare countries

Introduction

As the last chapter made clear, there are different strategies of comparative research in political science, including comparing many countries, comparing few countries, and single-country studies. In contrast to the claim of some comparativists (e.g. Lijphart 1971; Peters 1998), this book argues that all three of these strategies of research are subsumed under the broader umbrella of comparative politics (see Mackie and Marsh 1995:177), which can be unified under one logic of inference (King *et al.* 1994). The comparative literature is replete with examples of all these methods, but why have they come about and what are the advantages associated with each? Why do some comparativists use a global sample of countries, while others analyse smaller samples, or single countries? What are the perennial problems of doing comparative research? What are the rules of thumb to follow when selecting cases for comparison? How are some of the main problems of comparison overcome in ways that allow for drawing meaningful inferences and more robust empirical generalizations?

This chapter demonstrates that comparative methods *and* the solutions for many of the problems associated with comparing countries should be seen as a function of the explanatory aspirations of the researcher and the level of conceptual abstraction contained within a given study. The chapter first outlines briefly the different types of comparative methods and discusses how each is useful for drawing inferences, where no one method is privileged over another and the discussion shows that each method has its own set of advantages and disadvantages. It then outlines the main problems that confront comparative research, including *too many variables and too few countries*, *establishing equivalence*, *selection bias*, *spuriousness*, *ecological and individualistic fallacies*, and *value bias*. The discussion of the methods available, problems with comparison, and solutions to these problems paves the way for a more in-depth discussion of each main comparative method that follows in the ensuing chapters. Chapter 3 is on comparing many countries, Chapter 4 on comparing few countries, and Chapter 5 on single-country studies as comparison.

Methods of comparison

The distinction between different comparative methods should be seen as a function of the particular research question, the time and resources of the researcher, the method with which the researcher is comfortable, as well as the epistemological position he or she adopts. Different research questions require different methods. For example, someone wanting to know why Tony Blair and New Labour have continued to be successful in the 1997, 2001, and 2005 General Elections will necessarily focus on the United Kingdom. But someone interested in the electoral support for reformed left-of-centre political parties may choose all the countries in the European Union, or given recent developments, all the countries in Latin America. Second, time and other resources of researchers are often constrained, which limits the number of countries that can be feasibly researched in any one project. Third, some are comfortable using quantitative methods while others are not. Some enjoy large comparisons while others enjoy researching the fine details of particular countries. Finally, researchers who adhere to deductive theory may use different methods to those adhering to inductive theory. Those seeking more universal generalizations may use different methods from those who seek more contextually specific levels of explanation.

Despite these more practical and idiosyncratic considerations, however, the central distinction between different comparative methods depends on the key trade-off between the *level of abstraction* and the *scope of countries* being studied (Mair 1996). In general, the higher the level of conceptual abstraction, the more potential there is for the inclusion of a large number of countries in a study, where political science concepts 'travel' across different contexts (Sartori 1970, 1994). Alternatively, focus on one country or a few countries means that the researcher can use less abstract concepts that are more grounded in the specific contexts under scrutiny. For example, in the study of democratic institutions, a comparison of many countries may use a simple dichotomy between 'presidential' or 'parliamentary' political systems (Stepan and Skach 1993). A comparison of Latin American political systems, however, would have to adopt more refined categories of presidentialism since all the countries in the region are presidential (Shugart and Carey 1992; Sartori 1994; Jones 1995; Foweraker 1998). Finally, further refinements of the concept of presidentialism could be made in order to fit the nuances of a particular country, such as the United States.

Figure 2.1 summarizes these methods of comparison by showing this trade-off between the level of abstraction and the scope of countries. The cells identifying each method are determined by the intersection between the level of abstraction (high, middle, and low) and the scope of countries (one, few, and many). The figure is a heuristic device to illustrate this trade-off in stark terms. In reality, the lines of distinction between the various methods are more blurred, and there are studies that use several different methods at once. For example, Paige's (1975) *Agrarian Revolution* compares many countries at once to uncover the structural determinants of revolution in the world, and then compares the specific countries of Angola, Vietnam, and Peru to see if the cross-national findings hold at the local level. Rueschemeyer *et al.* (1992) interrogate the global statistical findings about the relationship between economic development and democracy by comparing a reasonably large number of countries (N = 53) qualitatively. Finally, Hawkins (2002) analyses the single case of Chile to examine the ways in which international mobilization around human rights violations affected the Pinochet regime and then extends his comparison to the cases of Cuba and South Africa (see Chapter 11 in this volume).

This representation of comparative methods differs slightly from that outlined in previous work on comparative politics (Lijphart 1971; Collier 1991:9–12). First, it includes all three methods under the comparative umbrella. In the past, Lijphart (1971) called comparing many countries using quantitative analysis the 'statistical' method and comparing few countries using qualitative analysis the 'comparative' method. For many, single-country studies are by their nature not comparative but may have comparative merit. Many such studies either use concepts that are applicable in other countries, develop new concepts that may become applicable in other countries, and/or embed their studies in a comparative context (Sartori

1994:15). This book argues that if the research strives to make larger inferences about politics through some form of comparison and uses concepts applicable to more than the country under study, then it is comparative (Lichbach and Zuckerman 1997:4; see also George and Bennett 2005; Lees 2006). Thus, all three methods are deemed comparative.

Second, comparing many countries is commonly referred to as 'large-n' comparison, and comparing few countries 'small-n' comparison, where n is the number of countries. It is important not to confuse the usage of n when carrying out a comparative study, since it can also refer to the overall number of observations. Many global quantitative studies use time-series cross-national data sets, where the total number of observations represents the product of the number of countries (N) times the number of years (T).

Moreover, it is possible to have single-country studies that have many observations, such the number of general elections, the number of respondents as in a national survey, the number of human rights violations over a givem time period, the number of violent political events, and so on (see Eckstein 1975:85; Ragin 2000:67–69). For example, Robert Putnam's (1993a) *Making Democracy Work* compares many regions within Italy, which, in this case, is a single-country study drawing inferences from a large-n. In similar fashion, Beer and Mitchell (2006) compare democracy and human rights across the states of India. To prevent confusion in this book, n is always used to denote the number of observations (King *et al.* 1994:51–52). For example, Burkhart and Lewis-Beck (1994) compare 131 countries from 1972–1989 ($n=2,358$), and Foweraker and Landman (1997) compare Brazil (1964–1990), Chile (1973–1990), Mexico (1963–1990), and Spain (1958–1983), producing $n=99$ (four countries times the total number of years compared). While the former study compared many countries and the latter a few countries, both could be considered 'large-n' comparative studies. Thus, in remaining consistent with this nomenclature, this book divides the three methods into *comparing many countries*, *comparing few countries*, and *single-country studies*.

Figure 2.1 Methods of comparison
Sources: Based on Sartori (1970) and Mair (1996)

Comparing many countries

Comparing many countries most closely approximates the experimental method found in natural science. The large number of countries makes this method of comparison particularly suited to quantitative analysis of aggregate data collected on different measures that vary across many countries (Lijphart 1971). Although there are examples of qualitative comparisons of many countries, such as Huntington's (1996) *The Clash of Civilizations* and Finer's (1997) *History of Government*, the majority of studies that compare many countries simultaneously use quantitative methods. Since this method compares many countries at once, it generally requires a higher level of abstraction in its specification of concepts. This method originated more generally through the emergence of the behaviourist revolution in the social sciences where political scientists and political sociologists working on large questions of political development and political stability sought to uncover empirical generalizations that held across large samples of countries. Since the early work in the 1950s and 1960s, data sets have become increasingly complex where larger and larger numbers of countries have been included and the dimension of time has also been taken into account. It is not uncommon for such data sets today to include between 150 and 194 countries that are compared over time periods ranging from twenty to fifty years. For example, the analysis in *Democracy and Development* (Przeworski *et al.* 2000) includes 150 countries from 1950 to 1990 (see Chapter 6).

The main advantages of this method of comparison include its ability to use statistical controls to rule out rival explanations and control for confounding factors, its extensive coverage of countries over time and space, its ability to make strong inferences that hold for more cases than not, and its ability to identify so-called 'deviant' countries or 'outliers' that do not have the outcomes expected from the theory that is being tested. The main disadvantages of this method of comparison include the limited availability of data for many countries and many times periods, the validity of measures that are often crude approximations of social scientific concepts, and the mathematical and computing skills needed to analyse increasingly complicated data sets whose structure and properties violate many of the assumptions of standard statistical methods of analysis. In addition, many see this method of comparison as inappropriate for analysing many topics involving complex causal mechanisms, historical processes, and deeper meanings and understandings that are highly dependent on the contextual specificities of discrete country cases. These and other features of this method of comparison are discussed at length in Chapter 3.

Comparing few countries

Comparing few countries involves the intentional selection of a few countries for comparison. This selection may involve anywhere between 2 to more than 20 countries, where the distinction between the comparison of few countries and many countries remains blurred to some degree. The defining feature of this method of comparison is the intentional selection of countries from the universe of possible cases. As we shall see, such a selection of cases in the absence of any rules of inquiry can lead to insecure inferences, limited findings, and in some cases, simply incorrect conclusions about a particular topic. One famous example comes from the analysis of the East Asian 'tiger' economies in which analysts sought to understand why these economies had been so successful when they did. Rather than comparing a sample of successful and unsuccessful countries from this region over a time period that covered the entire history of their emergence from agricultural dependence to export capitalism, this analysis focused on a very limited sample of successful economies over a shorter period of time, leading to incorrect inferences about the particular strategy of development that these countries followed (i.e. export-oriented industrialization, or EOI) and the particular role for strong government that repressed its labour force (see Geddes 1990; Brohman 1996; Stiglitz 2002). Large and highly consequential economic policies adopted by international financial institutions (IFIs) such as the World Bank (IBRD) and the International Monetary Fund (IMF) were based on these types of studies.

But this story suggests that it is possible to have good comparative analysis of a few countries. This method has been variously called the comparative method, the 'comparable cases strategy' (Lijphart 1975), or 'focused comparison' (Hague *et al.* 1992), and it achieves control through the careful selection of countries that are analysed using a middle level of conceptual abstraction. Studies using this method are more intensive and less extensive since they encompass more of the nuances specific to each country. The political outcomes that feature in this type of comparison are often seen to be 'configurative', i.e. the product of multiple causal factors acting together. This type of comparison has thus also been referred to as 'case-oriented' (Ragin 1994), since the country is often the unit of analysis, and the focus tends to be on the similarities and differences among countries rather than the analytical relationships between variables. There are two main types of research design that are included under this method of comparison. Some studies compare different outcomes across similar countries, which is known as the Most Similar Systems Design (MSSD); while others compare similar outcomes across different countries, which is known as the Most Different Systems Design (MDSD). In either research design, comparison of the similarities and differences is meant to uncover what is common to each country that accounts for the observed political outcome. These different strategies and their strengths and weaknesses are discussed at length in Chapter 4.

Single-country studies as comparison

As outlined above, a single-country study is considered comparative if it uses concepts that are applicable to other countries, develops concepts that are applicable to other countries, and/or seeks to make larger inferences that stretch beyond the original country used in the study. What should be recognized is that inferences made from single-country studies are necessarily less secure than those made from the comparison of several or many countries. Nevertheless, such studies are useful for examining a whole range of comparative issues. For Eckstein (1975), single-country studies are the equivalent of clinical studies from medicine, where the effects of certain treatments are examined intensively. Beyond this, however, single-country studies provide contextual description, develop new classifications, generate hypotheses, confirm and infirm theories, and explain the presence of deviant countries identified through cross-national comparison (see also Van Evera 1997; Gerring 2004; George and Bennett 2005; Lees 2006).

Despite the many limitations to single-country studies and their recent decline and marginality in the world of academic book publishing and dominant journals in political science (Lees 2006: 1088–1095), the field of comparative politics has benefited greatly from single country studies. Among the many examples are Tocqueville's (1888) *Democracy in America*, Dahl's (1961) *Who Governs?*, Lijphart's (1968) *The Politics of Accommodation* (the Netherlands), O'Donnell's (1973) *Modernization and Bureaucratic Authoritarianism* (Argentina), Scott's (1976) *Moral Economy of the Peasant* (Vietnam), Popkin's (1979) *Rational Peasant* (Vietnam), Tilly's (1986) *The Contentious French*, Tarrow's (1989) *Democracy and Disorder* (Italy), Putnam's (1993) *Making Democracy Work* (Italy), Varshney's (2002) *Ethnic Conflict and Civic Life* (India), and Wood's (2003) *Insurgent Collective Action and Civil War in El Salvador*. These examples are all studies of single countries that have formulated new concepts and generalizations that have been applied and or tested in subsequent single-country and comparative studies. The functions, contributions and limitations of single-country studies are discussed at length in Chapter 5.

This section of the chapter has shown that all three methods – comparing many countries, comparing few countries, and single-country studies – should be grouped under the umbrella of comparative politics if they seek to make generalizations through explicit comparison, or if they use and develop concepts applicable to other countries through implicit comparison. Comparing many countries is the best method for drawing inferences that have more global applicability. Through use of the method of difference and method of agreement, comparing few countries can lead to inferences that are better informed by the contextual specificities of the countries under scrutiny. Single-country studies can provide contextual description, generate hypotheses, confirm and infirm theories, and enrich our understanding of deviant countries identified through other comparisons. It has also been made clear that different strategies of comparison should be seen as the product of the trade-off between the level of conceptual abstraction and the scope of countries, as well as the arbitrary and practical factors surrounding any comparative research project. The next section examines the process of choosing countries, the main problems associated with comparison, and the possible solutions to many of these problems.

Choosing countries and problems of comparison

It should now be somewhat clearer as to why and how scholars compare countries. They compare to provide context, make classifications, test hypotheses, and make predictions. They do this by comparing many countries, few countries, or they provide in-depth studies of single countries. As there are many trade-offs associated with these different goals and methods of comparison, there are also important fundamental problems, which if not addressed explicitly can limit the types of generalizations that can be drawn from any study. While not representing insurmountable obstacles to comparison, it is important to address these problems and outline the strategies for overcoming them in ways that strengthen research design and bolster the resulting inferences.

Too many variables and too few countries

The first is the problem of too many variables and not enough countries (Collier 1991; Dogan and Pelassy 1990; Hague *et al.* 1992), also known more generally as 'too many inferences and not enough observations' (King *et al.* 1994:119). This problem arises when more factors of explanation for the observed outcome have been identified than there are countries (or observations) in the study, leading to what is called an *indeterminate research design*. Clearly this problem tends to be associated more often with single-country studies and those that compare few countries than with those studies that compare many countries. It can be illustrated initially with two simple examples, one from simple algebra and one from introductory economics. It is then illustrated using a hypothetical example from political science.

Algebra courses often present simple equations that take the following form:

$$x + 5 = 10 \tag{1}$$

In this equation, x is some unknown, whose value is solved by subtracting 5 from 10. A slightly more complicated problem would include two unknowns and takes the following form:

$$y = x + 10 \tag{2}$$
$$2x = y + 35 \tag{3}$$

In equations [2] and [3], the values of x and y are not immediately known; however, by combining the two equations through substitution, it is possible to solve for both x and y. Once the value of x has been determined, the value of y can be determined. The steps for substitutions and for moving terms from one side of the combined equation to the other are as follows:

$$2x = (x + 10) + 35 \tag{4}$$
$$2x = x + 45 \tag{5}$$
$$x = 45; y = 55$$

In economics, the price and quantity of any good in a market at equilibrium is a function of its supply and demand. Goods in short supply fetch a higher price than goods in abundance, and goods in high demand are more expensive than goods in low demand. If there is an upward shift in demand for a product, then a firm raises the price until it can produce more. Similarly, if a firm produces too much of a good, it is forced to lower its price until the excess supply is sold. Knowing only the supply or demand function for a particular good could not allow the market price or quantity to be determined. As in the algebra example above, the supply and demand curves can be approximated using equations for straight lines. The market price and quantity of a good are determined by setting the two equations equal to one another, which is the same thing as saying that they intersect. Thus, given specific demand and supply equations, the market price and quantity can be derived.

In both the algebra and economic examples, the idea of a system of two equations is similar to the problem of two many variables (or inferences) and not enough countries (or observations). On its own, equation [2] above is meaningless, and x and y can have any number of values that would satisfy it. Similarly, a demand equation without its complementary supply equation is equally meaningless if one wants to know both the quantity and price at market equilibrium. In comparative politics, if a study has too many unknowns (i.e. inferences or possible explanations) and not enough equations (i.e. countries or observations), then solving for the unknowns is problematic. Consider the following hypothetical example from political science. A scholar wants to know which factors are crucial for explaining high public expenditure. After reviewing the relevant literature, it is posited that public expenditure is high in wealthy countries controlled by left-of-centre governments. In this example, there is one dependent variable, public expenditure, and two independent variables, partisan control of government and wealth of the country. Logically, there are four possible combinations of the two independent variables (Figure 2.2). It would be impossible for a scholar to know the effects of these variables on the level of public expenditure if the comparison only looked at two countries or less. For example, if a left-poor country is compared to a left-rich country, partisanship is not allowed to vary. Similarly, if a left-rich country is compared to a right-rich country, then wealth is not allowed to vary. Adding a third case to either comparison (e.g. a right-poor country), allows both variables to vary, and the hypothesis can be tested with a determinate research design.

In extending this logic to an example already discussed, Wickham-Crowley (1993) could not know the explanatory relevance of the type of peasant if he only looked at peasants in one country. Similarly, Luebbert (1991) could not know the likely outcome of class alliances if he limited his study to Britain. In general, a study that has too many variables and not enough countries makes explanation of the outcome problematic. Although this problem is more frequent in single-country studies and those studies that compare few countries, it can also arise in those that compare many countries since there is a relatively small and finite number of them in the world (Hague *et al.* 1992:27) and it is possible to imagine a study that includes numerous multi-value variables.

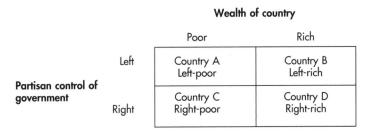

Figure 2.2 Logical combination of two variables in four countries

There are three solutions to the problem of too many variables and not enough countries, all of which are based on the principle that the number of variables (or inferences) must be less than the number of countries (or observations) (King *et al.* 1994:119–122). The first solution is to raise the number of observations to allow the key factors of the study greater overall variation, sometimes referred to as 'degrees of freedom'. This can be achieved by comparing instances of the political phenomenon and its hypothesized explanatory factors over time, by adding more countries to the study, or by comparing sub-units of the nation under scrutiny. Recent work in comparative politics has sought to compare many countries over many years using techniques in so-called 'pooled cross-section time series analysis' (see Stimson 1985; Beck and Katz 1995). Such analysis 'pools' repeated observations of countries by collecting country data for long periods of time (see Chapter 3 in this volume). As the discussion in Chapter 6 shows, Burkhart and Lewis-Beck (1994) compare 131 countries from 1972 to 1989, yielding a total of 2,358 observations, while Landman (1999) compares seventeen Latin American countries from 1972 to 1995 for total sample size of 408 observations. In each example, pooling the comparison of countries over time raises the number of observations. In studies that compare few countries, more instances of the phenomenon are drawn from history to increase the number of observations, and in single-case studies, sub-units or regions within the nation are compared, such as Putnam's (1993a) study of democratic performance across the regions of Italy, Hagopian's (1996) study of patrimonial politics in Brazil, or Beer and Mitchell's (2006) study of democracy and human rights in India.

The second solution to the problem is to use the most similar systems design (MSSD) to achieve focused comparison of few countries. As was outlined briefly above, the MSSD framework seeks to control for those factors that are similar across the countries in the study, while focusing on only those factors that are different that account for the outcome. Again, this strategy of comparison underlies the justification for area studies, but some argue that the MSSD framework simply provides 'overdetermined' outcomes (Przeworski and Teune 1970; Collier 1991:17), where many rival explanations are never truly eliminated. Another criticism of the MSSD framework involves one of perspective, in that similarities for one researcher may be differences for another, effectively lending little value to the approach (Collier 1991; King *et al.* 1994). Despite these criticisms, area studies continue to be carried out with implicit or explicit reference to the MSSD framework. Chapter 4 discusses the various strengths and weaknesses of both the MDSD and MSSD strategies in greater detail.

The third solution is to reduce the number of variables by focusing on the key explanatory factors that are hypothesized as important for explaining the outcome. This can be achieved either by using the most different systems design (MDSD) or by having stronger theoretical specifications. The MDSD framework intentionally compares a diverse set of countries, while concentrating on their key similarities. For example, Opp *et al.* (1995) compare the relationship between left–right ideological positions and support for social protest in Germany, Peru, and Israel. For them, the comparison of such different countries allows for a rigorous test of their main theoretical propositions (ibid.: 71–72). In applying a variation on MDSD, Parsa (2000) compares the social revolutions in Iran, Nicaragua, and the Philippines. All three countries shared 'similar experiences and structural features' (economic development, authoritarian rule, strong states, and US support), yet 'unlikely challengers were able to seize power' and the immediate outcomes of each revolution were different (ibid.: 3–4). In addition to comparing most different countries as in these two examples, a strong theory can highlight a parsimonious set of explanatory factors that can travel across space and over time. For example, the 'rational choice' perspective examines the role that 'selective incentives' play in the motivations of individuals to become involved in collective action. Such attention to selective incentives has been used to account for the actions of revolutionary peasants across the globe and over the centuries (see Lichbach 1994, 1995).

Establishing equivalence

The second problem is one of establishing equivalence both in the theoretical concepts that are used and the operational indicators of those concepts as they are applied in multiple contexts (Sartori 1970; Macintyre 1971; Mayer 1989). For example, the concept of political participation may mean very different things across different contexts, such as voting in one country, or mobilizing activists against nuclear power in another. Different understanding of a concept can, in turn, lead to different measures being developed for that concept (see Adcock and Collier 2001). Mayer (1989:57) argues that 'the contextual relativity of the meaning or the measures of indicators constitutes the most serious impediment to the cross-contextual validity of empirically testable explanatory theory'. In other words, is it possible to specify concepts and indicators that have shared meanings to allow valid comparisons? For example, does the concept of class apply equally in all societies? Does the idea of 'civic culture' (Almond and Verba 1963) mean the same thing in Brazil as it does in France? Is it possible to have 'new' social movements in Latin America (Fuentes and Frank 1989; Escobar and Alvarez 1992)? Does it mean the same thing when a British MP votes against his or her party as when a US Senator votes against his or her party (Hague *et al.* 1992:29)? The crux of the problem is not specifying identical, or even similar concepts, but *equivalent* ones so that their comparison is meaningful (Dogan and Pelassy 1990; Sartori 1994).

There are three intellectual positions that offer insight into this problem: (1) the universalist position, (2) the relativist position, and (3) the middle position. The universalist position argues that if theoretical concepts and their indicators are to have any explanatory power, they must be able to travel to all parts of the globe. For example, rationalist, functionalist, and structuralist approaches take such a position. Rationalists argue that all individuals maximize their own personal utility given a set of preferences and confronting a range of choices (Ward 1995). Functionalists argue that 'certain vital functions', such as interest articulation and interest aggregation, are 'fulfilled everywhere' (Dogan and Pelassy 1990:42). Structuralists argue that macro-structures such as the state, economic development, and social classes are omnipresent, but exist in varying degrees and are responsible for determining political outcomes.

The relativist position argues that all meaning is locally determined, and that a general 'science' of comparative politics is necessarily limited if not impossible (Macintyre 1971; see also Freeman 2001; Landman 2005a; 2006a). Ethnographic, interpretivist, and anthropological approaches tend to take this position (see Geertz 1973; Scott in Kohli *et al.* 1995). In a critique of Almond and Verba's (1963) study of political culture in Italy, Germany, Britain, the United States, and Mexico, Macintyre (1971:173) argues that indicators of commitment to government were never sufficiently examined to account for their cross-cultural differences in meaning. Thus, substantive comparison of these countries and the generalizations about civic culture must be treated with suspicion. Although not an extreme relativist, Sartori (1970, 1994) argues that 'stretching' a concept too far dilutes its meaning and precision, suggesting that once defined and operationalized, certain concepts can only travel so far. This relativist position has also featured in the debate over the universality of human rights, which in turn affects the degree to which they can be measured and compared (see Landman 2002, 2004).

The middle position argues that comparativists must not abandon all their concepts, but should modify them to be more sensitive to the cultural specificities of the contexts they are studying. In *Theorizing Social Movements*, Foweraker (1995) seeks to modify the North American rationalist and European culturalist perspectives on social movements to explain the patterns of social mobilization in Latin America. Key factors of explanation from the rationalist perspective (interests, strategies, micro-mobilization, and political opportunity structure) are combined with culturalist concerns of identity and expression in discussing the various origins, trajectories, and outcomes of Latin American social movements. Some comparativists consider themselves 'opportunists' as they modify, combine, and reconstitute concepts to fit the cases under study (Przeworski in Kohli *et al.* 1995:16), and argue that wilful sacrifice of insights from different perspectives may obscure important explanatory factors (Katzenstein in Kohli *et al.* 1995:15).

Since the relativist position obviates the reason for comparative politics, this chapter provides common solutions for those seeking to make larger inferences through comparison (i.e. those adhering to the universal and middle positions). These solutions include raising the level of abstraction (Sartori 1970), focusing on smaller numbers of countries for which the comparativist has thorough substantive knowledge (Sanders 1994), using 'specialist teams' in compiling cross-national data sets (ibid.), and specifying the functional equivalence between concepts or indicators (Dogan and Pelassy 1990). As in the solutions to the problem of 'too many variables not enough countries', there are important trade-offs associated with each of these solutions. The key to all is careful specification of concepts, thoughtful construction of indicators that operationalize them, careful application of them to multiple contexts, and honest recognition of their limitations.

In returning to the distinctions made in Chapter 1, raising the level of abstraction allows a study to be more inclusive, while lowering the level of abstraction makes it more exclusive. For example, in the comparative study of public administration, Sartori (1970:1042) argues that the term 'staff' is abstract enough to travel universally, 'administration' to all societies that have the presence of some form of bureaucracy, and 'civil service' to all societies with a fully developed modern state. In this way, as the level of abstraction decreases from 'staff' to 'civil service', the number of countries eligible for comparison necessarily decreases as well. Finer (1997:78) adopts terms that will travel through space and over time. His 'master variables' for classifying the world's regimes include territory (city, country, or empire), type of regime (palace, forum, nobility, church, and hybrids), the presence or absence of a standing military or civil bureaucracy, and the substantive and procedural limitations on the activities of rulers. Inglehart (1997) seeks to apply two-value continua to forty-three countries, which range on the one hand from citizens' concerns with 'survival' vs. 'well-being' to, on the other, their concerns with 'traditional' vs. 'legal-rational' forms of authority (see also Inglehart and Welzel 2005). In the latter two examples, important concepts are specified in such a way as to incorporate large samples of countries.

The second solution – focusing on a small set of countries for which the comparativist has thorough substantive knowledge – suggests that the analyst be 'extremely cautious about engaging in cross-national comparative research' (Sanders 1994:43). The explanatory power of concepts can be enhanced if they are applied in contexts with which the comparativist is most familiar. Thus, those who engage in area studies spend many years studying the history, economics, politics, and culture of a regional sub-set of countries in an effort to make more meaningful explanations of political phenomena. This 'local' knowledge can identify gaps between theoretical concepts and their application, and result in more meaningful comparison. Sanders (ibid.: 48) summarizes this point:

> It is only with detailed substantive knowledge that analysts can make informed judgements either about the relevance of the characterizations that they make of particular systems or about the identity of meaning attached to the questions that they pose to people living in different countries.

The third solution necessarily follows from the second. If truly informed comparison of many countries is limited, then those seeking to compare many countries 'should venture out of the security of the familiar if they are prepared to collaborate with other scholars' who possess specialist knowledge of the countries under scrutiny (Sanders 1994). This solution was used by Fitzgibbon (1967), who sought to measure democratic change in Latin America by using a questionnaire to measure general social and political factors he believed were both preconditions and manifestations of democracy. The questionnaire was sent to leading academics working in specific countries and regions in Latin America and was repeated at five-year intervals between 1945 and 1985. The resulting 'image index' is highly correlated with similar such measures (Foweraker and Landman 1997:61 fn. 14; Chapter 4). Another example that follows Sanders' prescription is Inglehart's (1997) *World Values Survey*, which uses local specialist teams to implement a similar survey in forty-three countries. It is also common practice in the human rights community to produce world reports on human rights protection such as the Amnesty International *Annual Reports*, the US State Department *Country Reports*, or Human Rights Watch *World Report*. These reports can then be used for secondary analysis, such as Poe and Tate's (1994) global analysis of the repression of human rights (see Chapter 9 in this volume). The final solution is the identification of 'functional equivalence' of concepts and indicators. This solution does not envisage concepts as identical or even similar, but functionally equivalent. If two entities share exactly the same qualities, properties, and characteristics, they are considered identical (apples are apples). If they share some qualities, properties, or characteristics, then they are said to be similar (apples and pears are fruit). If they share the same function, however, they are said to be functionally equivalent. For example, leaders of countries can serve three functions: symbolic representation of the nation, chief executive of state authority, and party leader. The French president embodies all three while the British monarch embodies the symbolic role and the British prime minister embodies the executive and party leader roles (see Dogan and Pelassy 1990:37). Depending on the functional focus and political systems of the comparison, the study may include an examination of one, two, or three individuals. Thus, functional equivalence allows entities with seemingly dissimilar characteristics to be grouped into useful and exclusive categories. In general, the analyst must specify clearly in which respect the concept is comparable.

Selection bias

The third problem of selection bias arises from the intentional choice of countries (Lieberson 1987; Geddes 1990; Collier 1995; King *et al.* 1994), as well as the use of historical accounts and sources that favour the particular theoretical position of the comparativist (Lustick 1996), which often violates the crucial scientific principle of using random samples. Comparison seeks to achieve experimental simulation, but experiments and mass attitudinal surveys in political science use *random selection* of individual respondents, while the essence of much of comparative politics is the *intentional selection* of countries. The basic experimental form has an experimental group and a control group. The experimental group receives the 'treatment' (stimulus, drug, or exposure to some independent factor), and the control group does not. The outcome of both groups after treatment is then compared. If the experimental group exhibits a different outcome than the control group, it is attributed to the treatment, given that all else is equal (known as the *ceteris paribus* condition). In mass attitudinal surveys, a completely random sample of individuals is selected and the subsequent data analysis of responses yields substantive inferences about the whole population from which the sample is drawn (see de Vaus 1991). In studies of electoral behaviour, a frequent finding is that those from a lower social class tend to vote for left-of-centre political parties while those of higher social class tend to vote for right-of-centre parties. The analysis of the survey data *compares* groups of individuals from each social class and determines the effects of that difference on their preference for particular political parties.

In both these examples, *the selection of individuals or units of analysis is not related to the outcome to be explained*. Selection bias in comparative politics occurs through the non-random choice of countries for comparison, or the deliberate selection by the comparativist (Collier 1995:462). Though selection of countries lies at the heart of comparison, selection without reflection may lead to serious problems of inference. The most blatant form of selection occurs when a study includes only those cases that support the theory. More subtle forms of selection bias, however, occur when the choice of countries relies on values of the dependent variable (Geddes 1990; King *et al.* 1994) and for qualitative studies, both the use of certain historical sources (Lustick 1996) as well as exclusive focus on contemporary political systems.

The problem of selection does not affect studies that compare many countries as much as those that compare few countries, and it is a major problem for single-country studies. Studies that compare many countries usually have a sufficient number of observations to avoid the problem of selection, and quantitative studies of many countries can use a number of statistical techniques to eliminate the problem (see Gujarati 1988; Fox 1997). For studies that compare few countries and single-country studies, however, selection can seriously affect the type of inferences that are drawn. Frequently in these types of studies countries are chosen because they exhibit only the outcome the comparativist seeks to explain, such as a social revolution, a military coup, a transition to democracy, the failure of deterrence, or high economic growth rates (Geddes 1990; Collier 1995). Selecting on the dependent variable in this way can lead either to an overestimation of effects that do not exist, or to an underestimation of effects that do exist (Geddes 1990:132–133). In other words, a study may claim that a set of explanatory variables is either more important in accounting for an outcome, or may neglect the importance of other explanatory variables. Both problems mean that the analysis is drawing false inferences.

For example, O'Donnell's (1973) study explains the advent of the bureaucratic-authoritarian state based on the case of Argentina in 1966. He argued that the presence of key independent factors – a collapse of a certain mode of dependent capitalist industrialization, economic stagnation, and an increase in popular demands – led the military to overthrow the democratic government, implement economic plans for recovery, and repress popular mobilization against the Argentine state. Subsequent research tested this theory both in Latin American countries that had similar experiences of authoritarianism and in countries that did not (Collier 1979). These studies showed that countries with similar authoritarian experiences did not share the same antecedent factors, while countries that sustained democracy did share these factors. Moreover, when the Latin American economy took another downturn in the early 1980s, no new instances of the bureaucratic-authoritarian state arose. Thus, the comparison across cases and time revealed that the strong connection between these independent factors and authoritarianism could not be upheld (Cohen 1987). O'Donnell's single-country study overestimated the effect of the antecedent factors on the political outcome he observed (see Briefing box 2.1). His results led him to issue a robust refutation of the thesis that economic development naturally leads to democracy.

In a less obvious but equally problematic example of selection bias, Skocpol (1979) compares countries that experienced social revolutions (Russia, China, and France) to contrasting countries where revolution did not occur (Japan, Prussia, and Britain) in an effort to demonstrate the explanatory relevance of certain structural factors to these revolutions. These structural factors include external military threats, regime reform, dominant class opposition, and state collapse (see Chapters 4 and 7 in this volume). The contrasting cases did not share these factors and did not experience social revolutions. Geddes (1990) argues that the comparison to these contrasting cases is good but still limited, since these countries represent the other extreme of her dependent variable. The comparison confirms Skocpol's theory, but Geddes (1990:143) asks, 'would a differently selected set of cases do so?' Comparison to the cases of Mexico, Guatemala, El Salvador, Honduras, Nicaragua, Ecuador, Peru, Bolivia, and Paraguay, which have similar structural factors and varying experiences with social revolution, would reveal the limits to the inferences about structures that Skocpol draws (ibid.: 144–145).

Briefing box 2.1 The problem of selection bias

The rise of the bureaucratic-authoritarian state

In explaining the rise of the bureaucratic-authoritarian state in Argentina, O'Donnell (1973) focused on two key explanatory factors: (1) the stagnation of the economy as measured by balance of payments deficits, low growth rates, rising inflation, and (2) the inability of the country to make the necessary transition from the 'easy phase' to the 'hard phase' of import-substitution-industrialization (ISI).

Under the easy phase of ISI, the state provided protection of the local economy with high tariffs and import quotas to allow new industries to develop the capacity to produce domestically what used to be imported from abroad. The policy included credit at concessionary rates, high wages for labour, and artificially high prices for traditional exports through manipulation of exchange rates. The hard phase of ISI, on the other hand, saw a shift to the domestic production of all intermediate goods necessary for finished capital goods, which was known as 'deepening' or 'vertical integration'. This phase required the attraction of foreign investment from multi-national corporations, the loosening of tariff and quota restrictions, a reduction in wages, and a readjustment of exchange rates.

In the Argentine case, economic stagnation preceded the military overthrow in 1966 and 'deepening' of the economy occurred after the coup. From this chain of events, O'Donnell theorized a connection between the antecedent factors, the advent of the bureaucratic state, and the subsequent economic policy of deepening. This reasoning is depicted in column three of Table 2.1. Subsequent comparison to the cases of Brazil, Colombia, and Venezuela revealed that while all three experienced economic stagnation, two (Colombia and Venezuela) *did not* experience military coups, and one (Brazil) had *already* started a process of deepening *before* the military overthrew the democratic government in 1964. These contrasting cases are listed in columns four, five, and six of Table 2.1. Thus, by relying on only the case of Argentina, O'Donnell's theoretical conceptualization and explanation suffered from selection bias.

Table 2.1 Explaining the bureaucratic–authoritarian state in Latin America

		Argentina	Brazil	Venezuela	Colombia
Explanatory factor 1	Economic stagnation	Yes	Yes	Yes	Yes
Explanatory factor 2	Failure to make transition to hard phase of ISI	Yes	No	Yes	Yes
Outcome 1	Military coup and implementation of BA state	Yes	Yes	No	No
Outcome 2	Deepening of domestic economy	Yes	Yes (pre-coup)	Yes	Yes

Source: Adapted from O'Donnell (1973); Serra (1979)

Ruth Collier (1999) compares seventeen historical cases and ten contemporary cases of democratization to examine the importance of working-class mobilization on the process of democratic reform. In all twenty-seven cases, the period of democratic reform pushed the countries 'across a threshold consistent with conceptualizing the political regime as democratic' (ibid.: 23), marked by an election and the installation of a new government. Collier is not concerned with the overall durability of the new regime, as many of the cases experience democratic breakdown later on, but she is interested in determining the role of labour mobilization in the reform process. The study is a curious example of selection bias since the dependent variable does not vary (all cases in the sample experienced democratic reform), the choice of countries depends on the outcome that is to be explained (historical and recent cases of democratic reform), and labour mobilization was present in some cases and absent in others. Collier (1999:167) argues that based on these comparisons labour mobilization is not a 'decisive or even necessary, no less sufficient, factor in democratization'. But her study is an example of how an attempt to raise the number of observations by comparing many instances of democratic reform still yields an indeterminate research design. Like the problem outlined in Figure 2.1, Collier's problem can be depicted by a 2×2 matrix that is the product of the intersection between her two main variables: (1) labour mobilization (yes or no), and (2) democratization (yes or no). Her observations only cover half of all the possible combinations in the matrix (i.e. cases of democratic reform with or without labour mobilization). For a definitive rejection of the hypothesis that labour mobilization matters for democratization, she would ideally have to add cases to her sample that either (1) did not experience democratic reform and had labour mobilization, or (2) did not experience democratic reform and did not have labour mobilization. It could be that labour mobilization has a *negative* impact on democratic reform. Without adding examples of either of these two combinations of variables, her analysis suffers from indeterminacy stemming from a selection of cases on the dependent variable (see above discussion on too many variables and too few countries).

In both the O'Donnell and Skocpol examples, selection on the dependent variable led to an overestimation of the importance of certain explanatory factors, while in the Collier example, selection bias may have led to the underestimation of effects that do exist. In general, there are three solutions to the problem of choosing on the dependent variable. The first solution is to have a dependent variable that varies: i.e. countries in which the outcome has occurred and those in which it has not. Only by comparing across the presence and absence of outcomes can the importance of explanatory factors be determined. Second, when comparing few countries, the choice of countries ought to reflect substantive knowledge of parallel cases (Laitin 1995:456). Third, stronger theory may specify more accurately a range of countries in which certain outcomes and their explanations would obtain (ibid.). Fourth, and related to the third solution, strong theory will also identify which countries represent 'least likely' instances of the phenomenon under investigation (Caporaso 1995:458). All four solutions demand close attention to the types of inferences that are being drawn when intentionally choosing countries for comparison.

A second form of selection bias arises in qualitative studies that rely on historical sources, where the analyst chooses historical accounts either intentionally or unintentionally whose description of events fits the particular theory being tested. As Lustick has pointed out, 'the work of historians cannot be legitimately treated as an unproblematic background narrative from which theoretically neutral data can be elicited for the framing of problems and the testing of theories' (Lustick 1996:605). Historiography varies in its description of how the past actually unfolded, which events receive emphasis, as well as the different theoretical dispositions of the historians themselves. Thus, inferences drawn from studies using descriptive historical accounts that 'are organized and presented according to the categories and propositions of theories they are testing' will necessarily be biased (ibid.: 610). Solutions to this form of selection bias include using multiple sources to arrive at a 'mean' account of the events and identifying the tendencies within each source to acknowledge possible sources of bias.

A third form of selection bias can occur from the time periods that are used in the comparison, especially for those studies seeking to analyse social behaviour that has a very long history, such as warfare, trade, and the emergence of states and regimes. Selecting contemporary time periods (even those throughout the twentieth century) and drawing inferences about longer-term processes is a form of historical selection bias. In this sense, the selection is taking place at a particular time or at an arbitrary end to a time-line of events, and inferences drawn from such a comparison will necessarily be less secure (Geddes 1990). There are examples of studies in comparative politics and international relations that avoid such a problem of selection. As noted above, Finer (1997) compares ancient, medieval, and modern forms of government. Arrighi (1994) examines the relationship between capital accumulation and state formation over a 700-year period. Cioffi-Revilla and Landman (1999) analyse the rise or fall of Mayan city-states in ancient Mesoamerica from 2000 BC to AD 1521. Midlarsky (1999) examines the effects of inequality on state formation and warfare in ancient and modern societies. Finally, the work on the 'democratic peace' compares warfare 'dyads' from the middle of the nineteenth century to the late twentieth century (see Russett and O'Neal 2001). In each of these examples, there is an attempt to provide generalizations about an important aspect of politics by comparing whole systems over long periods of time.

Spuriousness

The fourth problem is spuriousness, or the omission of key variables that may account for both the outcome and other explanatory factors already identified. A spurious explanation is one in which some unidentified factor is responsible for the outcome, while the identified factor is mistakenly attributed to having an effect on the outcome. Also known as omitted variable bias (King *et al.* 1994:168), this problem frequently arises in comparative politics and is related to selection bias since the choice of cases may overlook an important underlying factor that accounts for the outcome. Consider the following ridiculous example. An industrious graduate student spends the summer holidays working in resorts around the United States. Over the years, the student recognizes that wherever he works, there appears to be both a high number of flamingos and retired people. He decides to spend his leisure time collecting data on the geographical distribution of flamingos and retired people.

Cognizant of the problem of selection bias, the student extends the collection of data to include all the states in the US. After the data are collected, the student finds a positive correlation between the number of flamingos and the number of retired people. From these robust statistical results, he concludes that flamingos cause retired people. It is clear that the unidentified factor in this example is climate. On balance, both flamingos and retired people in the United States 'flock' to those areas with warmer climates. Thus, the mistaken connection between the two is due to the unidentified factor (see Briefing Box 2.2). By omitting the variable of climate, the student mistakenly concluded that flamingos *cause* retired people. If the student had only collected data in Florida, he may have reached the same conclusion, but one that was additionally influenced by selection bias.

In comparative politics, it has been frequently asserted that authoritarian regimes are better at promoting economic development than democratic regimes, since their 'relative autonomy' from society allows them to control more easily instances of political dissent. Global analysis of the relationship compares indicators of authoritarianism and economic performance and finds a strong positive association between the two. What these studies fail to identify, however, is that authoritarian governments tend to fall during periods of economic downturn, since much of their legitimacy rests on their ability to deliver economic benefits (Przeworski *et al.* 2000). Once discredited in economic terms, authoritarian regimes tend to lose their grip. Democracies, on the other hand, endure through periods of thick and thin. In terms of the overall relationship, this fact means that authoritarian regimes are only in power during times of good economic performance. Thus, by ignoring the important factor of regime 'attrition', the original finding in support of the connection between authoritarian regimes and economic performance is spurious (Przeworski and Limongi 1993, 1997).

As seen above, the solutions to the problem of spuriousness are related to the number of countries in a comparative study; moreover the trade-offs associated with these solutions can often be a source of frustration. The easiest solution for spuriousness is to specify all the relevant variables that may account for the observed outcome. This solution is fine if the comparison is across many countries or many observations, but if the study is one of few countries or one country, specifying additional variables can overlap with the first problem identified in this chapter (too many variables, not enough countries). It is important not to specify irrelevant variables as they may simply cloud the analysis. The second solution is to select countries that fit the criteria of the theory that has been specified, but this solution overlaps with the problem of selection bias. Thus, the comparativist is forced to recognize these various trade-offs while maximizing the types of inferences that can be made given the countries and the evidence in the study.

Ecological and individualist fallacies

The fifth problem – ecological and individualist fallacies – arises when a study seeks to make inferences about one level of analysis using evidence from another (Robinson 1950; Scheuch 1966, 1969; Miller 1995). For example, a theory of revolution may concentrate on individual psychological factors that account for rebellious behaviour,

Briefing box 2.2 Spuriousness

Simple explanations of events often take the form 'if event *x* then event *y*' (Sanders 1994, 1995; Lawson 1997), which can be depicted graphically as follows:

In this example, *x* and *y* are the only variables that have been identified. Suppose data collected on the occurrence of *x* and *y* shows that whenever (or wherever) *x* occurs, *y* also occurs. The regular and concomitant occurrence of both would lead to either the weak conclusion that *x* and *y* are *associated* with each other, or the strong conclusion that *x* actually causes *y*. But what if some other factor *z* also occurs regularly with *x* and *y*? The analyst risks specifying a relationship between *x* and *y* that may actually be the result of *z* acting on *x* and *y* independently. This situation is depicted as follows:

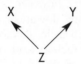

In this case, there is no direct relationship between *x* and *y*, but a common underlying factor to both, which explains their occurrence. Failure to specify this third variable and its effects on *x* and *y* constitutes the problem of spuriousness. The assertion that authoritarian regimes (*x*) are better at promoting economic development (*y*), failed to identify that authoritarian regimes tend to collapse in times of economic hardship (*z*).

In another example, Lieberson and Hansen (1974) found a negative relationship between language diversity (*x*) and development (*y*), when they compared a sample of countries at one point in time. Had they stopped there, they would have concluded that language diversity inhibits development. Further analysis showed, however, that for a given nation *over time*, there was no relationship between language diversity and development. What they did find, however, was that the *age of a nation* (the previously unspecified *z*) was negatively related to language diversity and positively related to development. Thus, the original relationship between language diversity and development was spurious (see Firebaugh 1980). This example of spuriousness is summarized as follows:

In both these examples, failure to identify the common underlying factor can lead to a false inference regarding the relationship between the two variables specified originally.

but the comparison to test the theory may use aggregate statistics across countries on levels of inequality and instances of political violence. There are two types of data in the social sciences: *individual* data and *ecological* data. Individual data, as the name suggests, comprise information on individual people. Ecological data comprise information that has been aggregated for territorial units, such as voting districts, municipalities, counties, states, and countries (Scheuch 1969:136). Individual data are collected through the use of periodic censuses carried out on the whole of a particular population, through other 'official' means, or through surveys carried out on a representative sample of the population. The twin problems of ecological and individualist fallacies occur when inferences are drawn about one level of analysis using evidence from another. An ecological fallacy occurs when results obtained through the analysis of aggregate-level data are used to make inferences about individual-level behaviour. Alternatively, an individualist fallacy occurs when results obtained through analysis of individual-level data are used to make inferences about aggregate-level phenomena. For example, claiming that women support the right to abortion by correlating the percentage of women in electoral districts with votes in support of an abortion measure is an ecological fallacy. Claiming that Germany is a more 'authoritarian' society than Britain by comparing responses to standardized survey questions is an individualist fallacy.

Both fallacies are a problem since analysis carried at one level may overestimate relationships at another level (Robinson 1950:353), and both fallacies originate from the same sources, namely, the ontological predispositions of the researcher and data availability. In the first case, some scholars may assume that data at one level represent a higher degree of reality than data at another level. As Scheuch (1969:134) argues, 'individual behaviour may be treated as being the only real phenomenon, while system properties are abstractions, or individual behaviour may be viewed as mere reflection of the only reality, namely structural properties'. In either case, the source of the fallacy is due to a certain ontological predisposition that serves as the starting point of the inquiry. As outlined in the previous chapter, rationalist explanations see collective behaviour as having no particular status other than the individuals who comprise it (Lichbach 1997:245). Structuralist explanations, on the other hand, focus on the political, social, and economic connections among people, such as '[h]istorically rooted and materially based processes of distribution, conflict, power, and domination, thought to drive social order and social change' (ibid.: 247–248). Thus, a rationalist may collect information on individuals to make larger claims about groups, while a structuralist may collect information on groups of people to make larger statements about individuals.

Data availability is the second source of ecological and individualist fallacies, since scholars may be forced to substitute data from one level to examine a research question specified at another level. The first example of such a problem appears in a study of voting behaviour of newly enfranchised women in the US State of Oregon. In trying to count women voters, Ogburn and Goltra (1919) correlated the percentage of women in electoral districts with the percentage of people who voted 'no' on selected referenda in the same districts. They assumed that women would have been more likely to vote 'no' on this select set of referenda and this could therefore indirectly estimate the number of women voting in each district. Ogburn and Goltra were aware that there may be a problem drawing inferences about women voters by combining aggregate data on the female population with individual data on referenda votes (see King 1997:3–4). Similar problems have been encountered in studies that try to estimate the socio-economic characteristics of people who voted for the Nazi Party during the Weimar Republic.

Examples of ecological and individualist fallacies are not only isolated to single-country studies. Gurr (1968) posited that a sense of relative deprivation was the prime motivating force behind rebellious activity. Relative deprivation is a psychological condition that obtains when individuals perceive that those 'goods and conditions of life to which they are rightfully entitled' fall short of those they are actually capable of achieving, given the social means available to them (Gurr 1970:13). He posited that high levels of relative deprivation ought to be related to high levels of political violence. Since individual-level data on relative deprivation were unavailable, Gurr tested this hypothesis using aggregate data on 114 countries, which showed a positive association between his measures of relative deprivation and political violence. In this case, aggregate data were used to falsify a hypothesis at the individual level (Sanders 1981:30–31).

In *Modernization and Postmodernization*, Inglehart (1997) commits an individualist fallacy in his study of values in forty-three societies. Using a standard battery of questions ranging from the importance of God to protection of the environment, Inglehart constructs 'clusters' of values that cohere into distinct geographical patterns. These patterns, Inglehart argues, are meaningfully distributed around the globe according to general cultural groups, including Latin America, Northern Europe, Eastern Europe, Catholic Europe, South Asia, Africa, and North America. In this study, Inglehart is aggregating individual-level responses to questions to establish simplified classifications of countries based on culture. Grouping percentages of individuals who responded similarly to a battery of survey questions and ascribing cultural 'types' to them is a clear illustration of the individualist fallacy, which confuses systemic properties with individual characteristics (see also Inglehart and Welzel 2005). Whiteley's (2000) examination of the relationship between social capital and economic growth also commits an individualist fallacy. He compares thirty-four countries using individual-level measures of social capital and aggregate measures of economic growth. His analysis includes a scatterplot of the percentage of respondents in the *World Values Survey* who claimed they trust people against GDP per capita (Whiteley 2000:455). His multivariate regression analysis includes individual-level data on social capital alongside aggregate measures of investment, education, population growth, among other control variables in order to account for changes in the average growth rate of the countries in his sample. While he does find a statistically significant relationship between high levels of trust and economic growth, the inference that social capital matters for growth is insecure owing to the problem of individualist fallacy.

In both the Inglehart (1997) and Whiteley (2000) examples, individual-level data drawn from national surveys are aggregated into country scores and then included in analytical models alongside aggregate data. Each study assumes that countries can be grouped into different cultural clusters, or classified into groups that have strong and weak social capital on the basis of individual level data. Scheuch (1966:158–159) shows that making these types of inferences is not possible. For example, a democratic system may comprise many individuals who respond positively to a series of questions probing their authoritarian tendencies, none the less the system is still democratic. Similarly, an authoritarian system may comprise individuals who respond positively to a series of questions probing their democratic tendencies or 'civic culture' (Almond and Verba 1963), but nevertheless remains authoritarian. In short, to ascribe a certain cultural or systemic trait to a country based on a sample of the population is to draw an incorrect inference about that system based on an incorrect level of analysis.

The solution for avoiding both fallacies is straightforward. The data used in any research ought to minimize the chain of inference between the theoretical concepts that are specified and the measures of those concepts that are ultimately adopted in the analysis. Known as the 'principle of direct measurement' (Scheuch 1969:137), the solution means that research that specifies questions at the individual level ought to use individual data, and vice versa for research questions that specify systemic relationships. For quantitative analysis, Miller (1995:155–156) argues that 'analysis of individuals can only lead to precise quantitative conclusions about individuals; an analysis of places to precise conclusions about places; and analysis of times only to conclusions about times'.[1] The pragmatic aspects of research may not allow the direct measurement of the phenomena, but the overall point remains that this measurement must be as close to the level of the phenomena being examined as possible.

Value bias

The final problem for all comparativists to consider is that of value bias, where the particular cultural, political, and philosophical predisposition of the researcher necessarily biases the conduct and conclusions of the enquiry. Over the course of the last century, social science has come to recognize that knowledge is not 'value-free'. Classification, analysis, and substantive interpretation are all subject to the particular perspective of the researcher. Modern empirical analysis accepts that to some degree 'what is observed is in part a consequence of the theoretical position that the analyst adopts in the first place' (Sanders 1995:67), but the quest to 'separate fact and value' is still considered worthwhile (Hague et al. 1992:30). The key to making valid comparisons is to be as public as possible (King et al. 1994:8) in terms of the judgements that have been made in the overall construction of the comparative study. These judgements include the theoretical perspective upon which the study is based, the identification of its key variables, the specification of its research design, and the limits to the type of inferences that can be drawn from it.

Summary

This chapter has given a brief overview of the different comparative methods that are available and the many standard problems that are associated with these different methods. The overview of methods has included the comparison of many countries, the comparison of few countries, and single-case studies and argued that these methods are grounded in one logic of inference. The strategy adopted may well depend on the specific research question, the time and resources of the researcher, and the general approach to studying politics that the researcher adopts. It also involves the trade-off between the level of abstraction and the number of countries that feature in the analysis. These different methods are discussed further in the next three chapters.

In addition to outlining the possible methods for comparison, the chapter also identified a series of associated problems and argued that if they are not addressed, may well lead to making insecure inferences. Specifying too many inferences without having enough observations constitutes an indeterminate research design that often affects single-country studies and those that compare few countries. Establishing cross-cultural equivalence in terms of theoretical concepts and their operational indicators is a constant worry for studies that compare many countries, since the global travel of concepts may undermine the precision of their meaning. The intentional selection of countries that support the theory being tested or are related to values on the dependent variables can lead to an overestimation of a relationship that does not exist or the underestimation of a relationship that does. Failing to specify important 'control' or other relevant variables can lead to the overestimation of relationships. Transcending different levels of analysis can also affect the type of inferences. Finally, ignorance of the cultural and theoretical perspective that underlies a study can colour its substantive conclusions.

These problems were outlined not to paralyse comparative researchers, but to highlight possible sources of bias in drawing valid inferences. Careful attention to these problems at the outset of any comparative inquiry will maximize the types of inferences that can be drawn. Acceptance of the natural limits of comparative inquiry is a healthy step along the winding road to the production of knowledge. Taken together, the discussion thus far has identified why political scientists compare countries, how they compare countries, and the types of problems they frequently encounter along the way. Table 2.2 summarizes the methods of comparison and assesses their strengths and weaknesses both in terms of their ability to arrive at valid inferences and the trade-offs for the researcher that are associated with each.

Comparing many countries is susceptible to statistical analysis, which helps eliminate possible sources of selection bias and spuriousness. The large number of observations means that these types of studies are good at making strong inferences, which in turn contribute to theory-building. The comparison of many countries is good for identifying deviant cases that invite closer scrutiny both of the cases as well as of the theory that is being tested. On the other hand, comparison of many countries can rely on measures that are invalid owing to the limitations of available data. The connections established between variables may be considered too abstract and simplistic. The collection and analysis of the data may be time-consuming and may require mathematical and computing training which many comparativists are not willing to undertake.

Comparing few countries achieves control through the careful selection of countries that fit within either the most similar systems design (MSSD) or the most different systems design (MDSD). These types of studies are intensive and are good for theory generation. They avoid conceptual stretching since they rely on specialist knowledge of a few cases. These studies tend to see their objects of analysis as a configuration of multiple explanatory factors that depend on the careful comparison of history of the chosen countries. Alongside these benefits, studies that compare

Table 2.2 Comparative methods: an assessment

Method	Strengths	Weaknesses/challenges
Comparing many countries	Statistical control Limited selection bias Extensive scope Strong inferences and good for theory-building Identify deviant countries	Invalid measures Data availability Too abstract/high level of generality Time-consuming Mathematical and computer training
Comparing few countries	Control by selecting 1 Most similar systems design (MSSD) 2 Most different systems design (MDSD) Good for theory-building Intensive, less variable-oriented Avoid 'conceptual stretching' Thick description Areas studies Configurative analysis Macro-history	Less secure inferences Selection bias: 1 Choice of countries 2 Choice of historical account Language training Field research
Case study	Intensive, ideographic, path-dependent, and configurative analysis Six types: 1 Atheoretical 2 Interpretive 3 Hypothesis-generating 4 Theory-confirming 5 Theory-infirming 6 Deviant countries	Insecure inferences Selection bias: 1 Choice of countries 2 Choice of historical account Language training Field research

few countries are not able to draw strong inferences owing to problems of selection bias both in terms of the choice of countries and the choice of the historical accounts used for evidence. Finally, many comparativists who consider themselves 'generalists' do not want to spend their time and energy learning the languages and conducting the field research in the countries that comprise these types of studies.

Studies of single countries constitute the most intensive of the comparative methods and still make up a large proportion of research in the field of comparative politics. Single-country studies useful for comparison are those that generate hypotheses, confirm and infirm theories, and elucidate deviant cases identified through other modes of comparison. Since they are the least extensive, single-country studies are most susceptible to problems of selection bias, too many variables and not enough observations, and indeterminate research designs that yield less secure inferences than the other modes of comparison. As with area specialists, 'country specialists' invest a tremendous amount of their time learning the local language and culture of their particular country, a commitment that other comparativists may find too demanding.

Note

1   Recent work in this area claims to have resolved the problem of ecological fallacy using advanced statistical techniques and the creation of specific software (King 1997), which is available for those wanting to pursue this line of research. Thus far, the new technique has been applied to voting rights cases in the United States in which aggregate data is used to make inferences about individual voting behaviour based on categories of race and social class. The extension of the method to aggregate data on nation states will certainly follow, but will involve more complicated techniques. For those not willing to pursue this line of work, however, theories that posit relationships to exist at the individual levels ought to be tested with data at the individual level, and the same rule of thumb should apply for theories that posit relationships at the aggregate level.

Further reading

Collier, D. (1991) 'New Perspectives on the Comparative Method', in D.A. Rustow and K.P. Erickson (eds) *Comparative Political Dynamics: Global Research Perspectives*, New York: Harper Collins, 7–31.
    An excellent review of comparative methods.

Dogan, M. and Pelassy, D. (1990) *How to Compare Nations: Strategies in Comparative Politics*, 2nd edn, Chatham, NJ: Chatham House.
    This book provides a good discussion of establishing functional equivalence in comparative politics.

Eckstein, H. (1975) 'Case-study and Theory in Political Science', in F.I. Greenstein and N.S. Polsby (eds) *Handbook of Political Science*, Vol. 7: Strategies of Inquiry, Reading, MA: Addison-Wesley, 79–137.
    The most comprehensive review of the scientific value of single-country studies.

Faure, A.M. (1994) 'Some Methodological Problems in Comparative Politics', *Journal of Theoretical Politics*, 6(3):307–322.
    This essay outlines the most similar and most different systems design as well as their 'mirror images'.

Geddes, B. (1990) 'How the Cases You Choose Affect the Answers You Get: Selection Bias in Comparative Politics', *Political Analysis*, 2:131–150.
    An excellent article on selection bias using real examples from the comparative literature.

Hague, R., Harrop, M., and Breslin, S. (1992) *Political Science: A Comparative Introduction*, New York: St Martin's Press.
    Chapter 2 makes brief statements about value bias, too many variables not enough countries, and equivalence.

Lieberson, S. (1987) *Making It Count: The Improvement of Social Research and Theory*, Berkeley, CA: University of California Press.

   Chapter 2 provides an exhaustive review of problems with selection bias.

Lijphart, A. (1971) 'Comparative Politics and Comparative Method', *The American Political Science Review*, 65(3):682–693.

   The original statement about comparative method, locating it as a non-experimental and non-statistical social science.

—— (1975) 'The Comparable Cases Strategy in Comparative Research', *Comparative Political Studies*, 8(2):158–177.

   This essay presents further reflections on comparative method.

Lustick, I. (1996) 'History, Historiography, and Political Science: Multiple Historical Records and the Problem of Selection Bias', *American Political Science Review*, 90 (3):605–618.

   A good review of historical sources of selection bias.

Mackie, T. and Marsh, D. (1995) 'The Comparative Method', in D. Marsh and G. Stoker (eds) *Theory and Methods in Political Science*, London: Macmillan, 173–188.

   A brief overview of comparative methods.

Ragin, C.C. (1994) 'Introduction to Qualitative Comparative Analysis,' in T. Janoski and A. Hicks (eds) *The Comparative Political Economy of the Welfare State*, Cambridge: Cambridge University Press, 299–320.

   This essay distinguishes between 'variable-oriented' and 'case-oriented' approaches and proposes a way to unify them.

Sanders, D. (1994) 'Methodological Considerations in Comparative Cross-national Research', *International Social Science Journal*, 46.

   This article presents a strong argument in favour of using only those countries with which the comparativist has good substantive knowledge.

Sartori, G. (1970) 'Concept Misinformation in Comparative Politics', *American Political Science Review*, 64:1033–1053.

   The classic statement on 'conceptual stretching' and the 'ladder of abstraction'.

—— (1994) 'Compare Why and How: Comparing, Miscomparing and the Comparative Method', in M. Dogan and A. Kazancigil (eds) *Comparing Nations: Concepts, Strategies, Substance*, London: Basil Blackwell, 14–34.

   A restatement of the main claims in 1970 and that 'to compare is to control'.

Skocpol, T. and Somers, M. (1980) 'The Uses of Comparative History in Macrosocial Inquiry', *Comparative Studies in Society and History*, 22:174–197.

   This essay outlines the uses of comparative history as well as Mill's methods of agreement and difference.

Comparing many countries

The previous chapters have introduced the many reasons for comparison and outlined briefly the different methods for comparing countries, as well as examining the many associated problems of comparison and solutions to those problems that are available for comparativists. This chapter addresses one form of comparison in which a large sample of countries is compared simultaneously in an effort to arrive at a set of empirical generalizations about a particular topic in comparative politics. As we shall see, the substantive topics in Part II of this book have been examined using this method of comparison and each discusses the various strengths and weaknesses of this method with reference to the other main methods of comparison. In order to provide a better sense and understanding of this method of comparison, this chapter outlines the main assumptions that lie behind it, discusses the advantages with adopting it, outlines the problem of measurement, introduces the main features of regression analysis, and concludes with a discussion of the limitations of this method as a way to anticipate the content of the next two chapters on comparing few countries (Chapter 4) and single-country studies (Chapter 5).

Starting assumptions

The comparison of countries is based on the idea that all countries can be seen as 'units' on which certain pieces of information can be collected and compared. For the comparison of many countries, however, the number of units is quite large, since the world now comprises 194 independent nation states. Countries have different features that vary between one another (known as 'between-unit' variation) as well as varying over time or across sub-national units (known as 'within-unit' variation). For example, comparing the level of democracy or the level of per capita GDP across a global sample of countries at one point in time is an example of between-unit variation. Comparing those variables over time in one country, or across sub-national units such as states in federal systems are examples of within-unit variation. In addition, some variables tend to exhibit quite a lot of change over time, while others do not. For example, a country's level of inflation, social protest, or civil conflict may vary quite a lot over a short period of time, while its basic institutional design may not vary at all. Indeed, European countries have parliamentary forms of government and it is unlikely that they will suddenly switch to presidential forms, while Latin American countries have presidential forms of government and are unlikely to switch suddenly to parliamentary forms.

This chapter demonstrates that although it is entirely possible to compare a large number of countries qualitatively, such a practice is relatively rare, where it is clear that a large sample of countries lends itself more readily to quantitative analysis. Thus the comparison of variation in features across a large sample of countries assumes that these features can be measured (see below), that the features being measured are similar across the countries (the idea of conceptual travel and functional equivalence outlined in the previous chapter), and that the variation in these features in one country is largely independent of the variation of the same features in other countries (also known as unit independence). These assumptions are often the subject of much debate and criticism from those who doubt the ability to make such broad comparisons across so many units (see Ross and Homer 1976). Others doubt the equivalence of units themselves, since the world is made up of very large countries, such as India, China, Russia, and the United States; very small countries such as Caribbean islands, the Seychelles, the Solomon Islands, and Samoa; and large countries that are sparsely populated, such as Mongolia, which is three times the size of France and has only 2.5 million people. In addition to the vast differences in size and population, the main criticism of this method of comparison focuses on the fact that there may well be more 'within-unit' variation than 'between-unit' variation, which precludes making any sort of meaningful inferences that apply to each of the units under comparison (see Peters 1998).

The main underlying assumption of statistical analysis in general is that events and facts in the world exhibit certain distributions, which can be described, compared, and analysed. But the comparison and analysis of these distributions of data in comparative politics is done from a collected sample of *countries* during specific periods of time. The comparison of the distributions is carried out in an effort to see if a relationship exists between them for the sample, and whether this relationship would hold for all countries in all periods of time. This basic practice of making inferences from a sample (some countries during one period of time) to a population (all countries in all time), lies at the heart of statistical analysis in comparative politics. This basic principle of statistical analysis can be demonstrated using a deck of playing cards (see Knapp 1996). A deck of playing cards has a known population of fifty-two cards. Each card has known characteristics, including the four suits (clubs, hearts, spades, and diamonds), the two colours (red and black), and the different values (Ace through King). There is thus a distribution of suits (thirteen cards in each), colours (twenty-six red cards and twenty-six black cards), and values (four cards of each value). Assuming that the entire deck of cards represents all countries for all time, it is possible to see how the examination of a sample of cards from the deck could tell us much about the whole population. Using a sample of twenty cards from a well-shuffled deck, a student could get a first approximation of any of the distributions of a deck's attributes (suits, colours, and values). Replacing the sample, drawing repeated samples, and noting the distributions of the various characteristics would allow the student to get a more accurate picture of the whole deck. This process of sampling and inference is precisely what comparativists are trying to do when they collect and compare aggregate statistics from many countries.

But as the previous chapters have made clear comparing many countries moves one step beyond the descriptive level to test hypotheses about possible relationships between variables. If a relationship exists, there ought to be some association between the distribution of values for one variable and the distribution of values for another variable. For this reason, the comparison of many countries using statistical analysis is referred to as 'variable-oriented', since its primary focus is on 'general dimensions of macro-social variation' (Ragin 1994:300) and the relationship between variables at a global level of analysis. The extensive coverage of countries allows for stronger inferences and theory-building, since a given relationship can be demonstrated to exist with a greater degree of certainty. For example, Gurr (1968:1015) demonstrates that levels of civil strife across 114 countries are positively related to the presence of economic, political, short-term, and long-term deprivation. His analysis also explains that this relationship holds for roughly 65 per cent of the countries (see Chapter 5 and Sanders 1995:69–73). More recently, Helliwell (1994) has shown that for 125 countries from 1960–1985 there is a positive relationship between per capita levels of income and democracy. After controlling for the differences between OECD countries, Middle Eastern oil-producing countries, Africa, and Latin America, this relationship is demonstrated to hold for about 60 per cent of the countries.

A second advantage of comparing many countries lies in the ability to identify so-called 'deviant' countries or 'outliers'. These are countries whose values on the dependent variable are different than expected, given the values on the independent variables. In testing for the positive relationship between income inequality and political violence in sixty countries, Muller and Seligson (1987:436) use a simple scatterplot to identify which countries fit their theory and which do not. For example, Brazil, Panama, and Gabon were found to have a lower level of political violence than was expected for the relatively high level of income inequality. On the other hand, the UK was found to have a particularly high level of political violence given its relatively low level of income inequality. By identifying these 'outliers', scholars can look for other explanations that account for their deviance, and they can remove them from their analysis to make more accurate predictions for the remaining countries. Thus, in this case the unexpected level of political violence observed for the UK was due to the Northern Ireland conflict. Such deeper analysis of outliers is also known as conducting a 'crucial' case study (see Chapter 5).

As mentioned above, qualitative comparison of many countries is rare and is made difficult for two reasons. First, qualitative analysis generally requires a richer level of information, such as deep history of all the countries, which is often difficult to collect and synthesize. Indeed, Finer's (1997) attempt to compare regime types over 5,000 years and across the globe represents a monumental task that occupied all the years of his retirement and produced a three-volume study with 1,700 pages. Second, it is more difficult to draw strong inferences from these data since they cannot be subjected to the kind of systematic comparison that statistical analysis offers. Thus, Finer is able to describe and analyse different regime types as they have appeared in history to show how those in existence today are products of innovations from the past, but he is unable (or unwilling) to make any larger causal inferences. Even though he 'privilege[s] those governmental innovations that are still relevant today', he is adamant in stating that these regime types are not the product of a process of 'linear evolution' (ibid.: 88–89). There is one example of a study that combines the logic of statistical analysis with the depth and advantages associated with qualitative techniques. In *Capitalist Development and Democracy*, Rueschemeyer *et al.* (1992) compare over fifty countries qualitatively to determine the degree to which significant socio-economic transformations are related to the installation of democracy in Europe, Latin America, and the Caribbean (see Chapter 6).

Measuring concepts

Given the difficulties associated with the qualitative comparison of many countries, most studies that compare many countries adopt the quantitative method, which is predicated on the development of numerical measures for concepts. As Chapter 1 outlined, a measure is a quantified representation of a concept and includes the enumeration of anything that can be counted (e.g. choices, elections, democracies, protest events, civil wars, military coups, human rights violations) or assigned a numerical value (e.g. ethnic fractionalization, religious fragmentation, attitudes, perceptions, understandings, and intentions). In other words, measurement involves moving from a broad notion of a 'background concept' to the provision of 'scores on units' (Adcock and Collier 2001). Background concepts include such things as democracy, human rights, development, conflict, etc. Through careful theorizing, scholars provide a set of *systematized* concepts, which give further definition to the concept and may outline its different dimensions and components. This move is then followed by the operationalization of the systematized concept into a set of meaningful, valid, and reliable *indicators*. Finally, using these indicators, scores are assigned to the units of observation, which can be in individuals, groups, sub-national units, countries, and regions. Typically for the comparison of many countries, the various scores on units are aggregated to the country level and then analysed using statistical techniques.

The concept of democracy provides a useful example to illustrate these different levels in the process of measuring concepts. Democracy is a classic 'essentially contested' (Gallie 1956) concept since there is not now, nor is there likely to be, a final consensus on its definition or full content. The numerous attempts to define democracy can be grouped into three broad categories: *procedural democracy, liberal democracy*, and *social democracy* (see Landman 2005d). For the purposes of this example, let's assume a scholar wants to measure the level of procedural democracy for all the countries in the world. Procedural definitions of democracy, made most notably in Robert Dahl's (1971) seminal work *Polyarchy*, include the two dimensions of *contestation* and *participation*. Contestation captures the uncertain peaceful competition necessary for democratic rule, a principle that presumes the legitimacy of some opposition, the right to challenge incumbents, protection of the twin freedoms of expression and association, the existence of free and fair elections, and a consolidated political party system. Participation, on the other hand, captures the idea of popular sovereignty, which presumes the protection of the right to vote as well as the existence of universal suffrage.

This definition of procedural democracy represents an example of an attempt to provide a systematized concept and immediately suggests a number of indicators that could be collected on all the countries in the world. For example, the definition makes reference to elections, voting, and the protection of certain rights about which there is substantial information available that can be used to develop different types of measures of democracy. The collection of various indicators on these democratic features then allows for a variety of measurement and coding strategies. Some scholars provide simple *dichotomous measures* (democracy or non-democracy) of procedural democracy in which a set of essential criteria have to met in order for a country to be classified as a democracy (see Przeworski *et al.* 2000; Boix 2003). Some have provided polychotomous measures of procedural democracy that rank countries in categories of stable and unstable democracies on the one hand and stable and unstable dictatorships on the other (Lipset 1959). Some have created interval scales of democracy, in which checklists on different attributes and dimensions of democracy are used to rank order countries (e.g. Jaggers and Gurr 1995). And yet some others have constructed more 'objective' measures of democracy that combine indicators of competition (share of votes for the smallest political party) and participation (voter turnout) (Vanhanen 1984, 1990, 1997, 2003).

In each of these examples, the concept of procedural democracy has found quantitative expression through converting a set of attributes of the concept into numerical values that vary across different countries and over different periods of time. Beyond democracy, comparative politics has used existing measures of concepts from sociology and economics, such as per capita gross domestic product and income inequality as a measure of wealth, or imports and exports as a percentage of gross domestic product as a measure of 'trade openness'. The discipline has produced a vast array of measures for different concepts, such as unitary and federal systems, parliamentary and presidential systems (e.g. Stepan and Skach 1994), executive–legislative relations (Jones 1995); plurality and majoritarian electoral systems (Lijphart 1994a), the effective number of political parties (Laakso and Taagepera 1979), protection of civil and political rights (Poe and Tate 1994), levels of political violence (Hibbs 1973; Sanders 1981; Muller and Seligson 1987), civil war (Gleditsch 2002), post-material values (Inglehart 1977, 1990, 1997; Inglehart and Welzel 2005); and the number of terrorist attacks (Enders and Sandler 2006).

Basic regression analysis

The veritable workhorse of the social sciences for conducting quantitative analysis on a large number of comparable units is *linear regression*. It is vital for a book such as this to provide a rudimentary understanding of this analytical technique. In order to demonstrate its basic features and discuss how it can reveal underlying relationships, we shall use an example from the literature on human rights (see also Chapter 11). For this example, we will use three variables for a sample of countries in the year 2000: (1) the violation of 'personal integrity rights', which is measured using a scale that ranges from 1 (low violations of rights) to 5 (high violations of rights) (see Poe and Tate 1994); (2) income inequality, which is measured using a scale ranging from 0 (perfect equality) to 100 (perfect inequality) (see Todaro 1997); and (3) the level of democracy, which is measured using a scale ranging from −10 (perfect autocracy) to +10 (perfect democracy) (see Jaggers and Gurr 1995). Table 3.1 shows the summary statistics for these three variables, including the number of observations (i.e. the number of countries), the average value for each variable (i.e. the sum of the values for each country divided by the total number of countries), the standard deviation (a measure of the relative spread of values in each variable), and the minimum and maximum values for each variable.

Figure 3.1 is a simple scatterplot between the violation of human rights and income inequality. It contains a straight line fitted to the scatter of points, which helps in defining a relationship between the two variables. Notice from the graph that many points lie on the line or very close to the line, while some are quite far off the line. For example, a typical country with high levels of income inequality and problems with human rights violations is Cameroon. Its location on the graph is within theoretical expectations. China, on the other hand, it a country where income distribution is much more equal than in other countries of the world, yet its human rights record is not particularly good. Qatar, a tiny country with fewer than 1 million

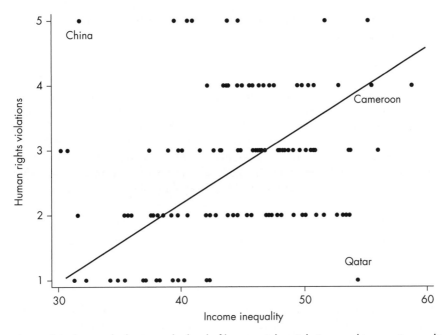

Figure 3.1 Scatterplot between the level of human rights violations and income inequality

Table 3.1 Summary statistics for three variables

Variable	Observations (countries)	Mean	Standard deviation	Minimum value	Maximum value
Human rights violation	138	2.73	1.10	1	5
Income inequality	137	44.19	6.34	30.23	58.79
Democracy	156	2.96	6.64	–10	10

inhabitants formed from Bedouin tribes in the Arab marshes, has a higher concentration of income, but far fewer human rights violations. Thus, Cameroon serves as a typical case, while China and Qatar represent outliers.

The point of linear regression is to explore whether there is a significant statistical relationship between levels of income inequality and levels of human rights violations, thereby capturing a general tendency while leaving open the possibility for exceptions to the rule, such as China and Qatar. Linear regression fits a straight line to the scatter of points that represent the intersection of the two variables. Before seeing how this works, we need to review basic linear algebra using the data example in Figure 3.1. If we label the horizontal axis in the figure x and the vertical axis y , we can then use the following equation for a straight line to depict the linear relationship between x and y :

$$y = mx + b \qquad [1]$$

where y = the observed values of the y variable (i.e. the level of human rights violations), x = the observed values of x variable (i.e. inequality), b = the point where the line crosses the y-axis (i.e. the level of human rights violations under conditions of perfect income equality), and m = the slope or 'rise over run' between x and y. For perfect linear relationships, using the values of x and y for two different points in the scatterplot, it is possible to calculate m and b, and then express the whole relationship as an equation. The following two formulas are used to calculate m and b:

$$m = \frac{(Y_2 - Y_1)}{(X_2 - X_1)} \qquad [2]$$

$$b = Y_1 - mX_1 \qquad [3]$$

In this case, one would identify two points, each with Y and X coordinates on the scatter (i.e. X_1, Y_1 and X_2, Y_2). The value for m is calculated by dividing the difference between Y_2 and Y_1 by the difference between X_2 and X_1. Once the value for m is known, it can be used in equation [2] to calculate the value for b. These values can then be used in equation [1] to illustrate the linear relationship between X and Y.

But in the social sciences, there are no perfect linear relationships, so regression analysis estimates the degree to which a straight line fits the scatter of points. The standard equation for a line used in regression analysis takes the following form:

$$\hat{Y} = \alpha + \beta X + \varepsilon \qquad [4]$$

where $\hat{Y}$ = the 'predicted' values of the dependent variable (i.e. the level of human rights violations), X = the observed values of inequality, α = the point where the line crosses the y -axis (i.e. the level of human rights protection under conditions of perfect income equality), β = the slope or 'rise over run' between X and Y, and ε = error since the scatter of points in the figure does not fall precisely on the line. The fact that the scatter of points does not fall precisely on the line means that we need to use modified formulas to calculate α and β. The line is fitted to minimize the distance between the observed values and the predicted values. The mathematical solution is called the 'least sum of squares' or 'ordinary least squares' (OLS) regression technique, which relies on the following two formulas:

$$b = \frac{\Sigma(X_1 - \bar{X})(Y_1 - \bar{Y})}{\Sigma(X_1 - \bar{X})^2} \qquad [5]$$

$$a = \bar{Y} - b\bar{X} \qquad [6]$$

Here, the formulas calculate the difference between actual values of X (i.e. those values of income inequality that have been collected on each country) and Y (i.e. those values for the level of human rights violations collected on each country) on the one hand, and the means of those values on the other. The product of these differences is summed and then divided by the sum of the squared differences between actual X values and the mean of X. Using the data from Table 3.1 produces the following regression equation depicting the relationship between income inequality and the level of human rights violations:

human rights violations = 0.04 + 0.06*(income inequality)   [7]

These statistical results can be interpreted literally. For the relationship in equation 7, the level of human rights violations starts at a political terror level of 0.04 (i.e. low violations), but increases by 0.06 for every increase in income inequality. In less literal terms, the analysis shows that higher levels of income inequality are related to higher levels of human rights violations.

But how confident in statistical terms are we with these results? In addition to calculating α and β, regression analysis also calculates their relative significance and the degree of fit achieved by the straight line. The relative significance calculation shows how confident we are in the fact that the mean values of α and β are significantly different from zero. In other words, if there were no relationship between x and y, β would not be significantly different from zero. The calculation of this significance is a function of the mean of the value itself and its standard error (see Lewis-Beck 1980:30–37). As a general rule of thumb, if the mean of β divided by its standard error is less than 2, β is unlikely to be significant at the standard level of statistical confidence, 95 per cent (ibid.). Including the standard error values for our results in equation 7 produces the following:

human rights protection = 0.04 (0.72) + 0.06 (0.02)*   [8]
    (income inequality)

In applying the general rule of thumb, dividing the β value above by its standard error yields a figure that is larger than 2 for our measure of income inequality (the actual value is 3.81), so our results are statistically significant at the 95 per cent level of confidence for income inequality. This means that if we used the same variables for a similar selection of countries at a different point in time, we would have very similar results. The statistics for α, on the other hand, are not significant, since dividing 0.04 by 0.72 yields 0.06, which is far below our critical value of 2 at the 95 per cent confidence level. We would conclude that we are unsure of the level of human rights violations under conditions of perfect equality, but we do know that as inequality increases, so too does the violation of human rights.

Finally, the degree of fit calculation examines how much of the variation in y is explained by the variation in x. The statistical value for the degree of fit is called R^2, which represents a ratio of explained variance to unexplained variance and ranges from 0 to 1. For example, an R^2 value of 0.43 means that 43 per cent of the variation in y is explained by the variation in x. In our example above, the R^2 value for income inequality and human rights is 0.10, which suggests that the variation in income inequality alone explains 10 per cent of the cross-national variation in human rights violations. Some would say that such an account of variation is not particularly high, but imagine how many other variables might account for the variation in human rights violations and it is possible to be fairly optimistic about the results for income inequality alone.

This separate illustration of a simple relationship is an example of *bi-variate statistical analysis*, since it examines the co-variation of two variables only and does not control for any other factors. But linear regression techniques can be applied to any number of factors, providing that there are enough observations in the sample of data that is being analysed (see also Chapter 2). The same basic linear equation is used in this *multivariate statistical analysis* but across all the variables included in the analysis. Thus, using the data from Table 3.1, we can estimate the following general equation, which depicts the level of human rights violations as a function of income inequality *and* the level of democracy:

$$\text{human rights violations} = \alpha + \beta_1 * (\text{income inequality}) \qquad [9]$$
$$+ \beta_2 * (\text{democracy}) + \varepsilon$$

Here, the regression analysis holds one variable constant while estimating the relationship for the other variable and then vice versa, thereby producing estimates for α, β_1, and β_2, their standard errors, and an overall R^2 value for the whole equation. The output, with standard errors in parentheses is as follows:

$$\text{human rights violations} = 1.0\ (0.78) + 0.04\ (0.02)* \qquad [13]$$
$$(\text{income inequality}) - 0.05\ (0.02)*(\text{democracy})$$
$$R^2 = .16$$

For this sample of countries in the year 2000, we have a total coverage for all three of our variables for 114 countries. Our analysis tells us that the level of human rights violations increases by 0.04 for every 1-point increase in income inequality and decreases by 0.05 for every 1-point increase in the level of democracy. We can thus conclude that more equitable distribution of income and higher levels of democracy are related to better human rights protection, while both variables taken together account for 16 per cent of the variation in human rights protection with 84 per cent of variation in human rights protection remaining *unexplained*. It is also interesting to note that since the scale of income inequality ranges from 0 to 100 and the democracy scale from −10 to +10, the relative impact of income redistribution may actually be greater than the impact of an improvement in democracy.

Extending the basic regression model

This kind of analysis and interpretation of the statistical results is a dominant feature of the extant global comparisons on human rights (see Chapter 11). While the simple linear regression model has featured in numerous comparative studies, there are many ways in which the basic analysis has been extended. For the purposes of this book and its themes in subsequent chapters, the discussion will focus on the inclusion of 'dummy' variables and the use of time. To control for major differences around the globe between particular sets of countries, the quantitative comparison of many countries often includes variables that assign numerical values to countries for being part of a particular set or for being outside that particular set. The variable for such groups is called a dummy variable and is effectively like a little 'switch' that is either turned 'on' or 'off'. For example, dummy variables have been used for regions (EU, Africa, Latin America), type of democracy (old, third wave, or fourth wave), position in the world economy (core, semi-periphery, periphery), or Huntington's (1996) type of 'civilization'.

We can illustrate the use of dummy variables through our human rights data example from above and test whether the relationship between income inequality and human rights is different if we take into account countries in the world that are involved in civil war. We create a variable called 'CWAR', which is coded 1 for all countries that are engaged in a civil war in the year 2000 and 0 for those that are not. The basic regression equation in [4] above is modified to include this new variable, which we denote with a D and whose coefficient we denote with an γ:

$$\hat{Y} = \alpha + \beta X + \gamma D + \varepsilon \qquad [10]$$

Since D is 1 for all countries engaged in civil war, and 0 for all others, it effectively divides the sample into two distinct groups and we can hypothesize that these groups matter for the relationship between income inequality and human rights. We can split equation [10] into two separate equations, one for the countries not involved in civil war (shown in [11]), where D = 0 and the equation is the same as [4] and one for the countries involved in civil war (shown in [12]), where D =1 and the equation adds $\alpha + \gamma$ while estimating the independent effect of X (or income inequality).

$$\hat{Y} = \alpha + \beta X + \gamma(0) + \varepsilon = \alpha + \beta X + \varepsilon \qquad [11]$$
$$\hat{Y} = \alpha + \beta X + \gamma(1) + \varepsilon = (\alpha + \gamma) + \beta X + \varepsilon \qquad [12]$$

In other words, the inclusion of the dummy variable provides a way of knowing whether there is a significant shift in the intercept of a relationship (i.e. the place where the line crosses the y-axis) for a particular group of countries. The results for the regression equation with the dummy variable are as follows:

human rights violations = 0.45 (0.64) + 0.05 (0.01)*   [13]
(income inequality) + 1.73 (0.30)* (civil war)
R^2 = .29

The results show that the general positive relationship between high levels of income inequality and a high level of human rights violations is upheld, but that the level of human rights violations in civil war countries in the first place (i.e. without taking income inequality into account) is much higher than the level of human rights violations in other countries. Civil war countries, unsurprisingly, start out with a worse record for human rights and high concentration of income adds additional problems for the protection of human rights. The inclusion of the dummy variable has added additional information on the explanation of the cross-national variation in the level of human rights violations. Indeed, the R^2 value is much higher, and suggests that a total of 29 per cent of the variation in the level of human rights violations is explained by the inclusion of income inequality and the civil war dummy variable.

Time

Thus far, the discussion about comparing many countries has focused on carrying out the comparison at one point in time. This is known as a synchronic comparison since the movement of time is not taken into account. The early studies that compared many countries engaged in this kind of analysis. For example, Lipset's (1959) seminal study of economic development and democracy compared many countries at one point in time, yet his inferences implied a dynamic process of development that would provide the social requisites for long-term democratic stability. The studies on political violence (e.g. Gurr 1968; Hibbs 1973) also compared many countries at one point in time but through their inferences, these studies implied a set of dynamic processes that were highly time dependent. Countless other topics in comparative politics have adopted the synchronic research design and yet the real substantive arguments have continued to focus on political processes over time.

In response to the theoretical demand for methods that could analyse political processes over time, scholars began to adopt comparative frameworks that analysed variables across space and time. The result has been a spate of comparative studies that use the so-called 'pooled cross-section time-series' analysis, or PCTS. As Chapter 6 shows, both Burkhart and Lewis-Beck (1994) and Helliwell (1994) adopt this research design. Poe and Tate (1994), Camp Keith (1999), Neumayer (2005), Landman (2005b) among others adopt the same basic research design for human rights. As Chapter 12 shows, international relations research has adopted a similar strategy but many studies construct time-series data sets comprised of 'dyads' or pairs of states. For example, Russett and O'Neal (2001) compare such dyads from the late 19th century to the late 20th century, where the total number of observations (i.e. dyad-years) exceeds 40,000.

Clearly, the immediate benefit of including time is that a study would naturally raise the number of observations and thus provide additional degrees of freedom to strengthen the inferences that are drawn from the analysis. In many cases, such comparative studies contain more than 4,000 country-year observations. The cost of including time, however, has been that many of the assumptions that make regression possible are violated, and many variables show little variation over time. PCTS data sets vary tremendously in their construction, where some are 'flat' and 'shallow' (more countries than time) and others are 'thin' and 'deep' (i.e. more time than countries). Thus, the PCTS research design has presented a series of challenges to political methodologists who have sought to find ways of overcoming the problems of comparing large number of countries over time in ways that can yield the strongest inferences and avoid the kinds of biases that may lead to drawing false inferences (see Stimson 1985; Beck and Katz 1995; Plümper and Troeger 2007). Failure to address the challenges presented by these data sets has meant that scholars run the risk of declaring that a significant relationship exists that actually does not, or declaring that a significant relationship does not exist when in fact one actually does.

Limitations to global comparative analysis

Despite the advantages of comparing many countries, there are some distinct disadvantages, including the availability of data, the validity of measures, and the mathematical and computing skills needed to analyse data. First, collecting relevant data on the independent nation states of the world can be difficult and time-consuming. Aggregate data are often published only for selected years or selected countries, making comprehensive comparison difficult. Scholars, research institutions, and international organizations have sought to improve the quality and quantity of data that have been made available in the public domain for academic research and analysis. Websites such as the Penn World Tables (http://pwt.econ. upenn.edu/) and the World Bank (www.worldbank.org) have large databases of hundreds of indicators that are useful for the quantitative comparison of many countries. In addition, there are good resources for data on democracy (http://www. cidcm.umd.edu/polity/) human rights (www.humanrightsdata.com), and warfare (http://www.correlatesofwar.org/) among other popular political concepts that have been the subject of much quantitative analysis.

Second, there are problems of validity and reliability in many measures that have featured in the comparison of many countries. Valid measures closely approximate the true meaning of a concept, or what the researcher thinks he or she is measuring (King *et al.* 1994:25). For example, per capita GDP is often seen as only an approximate measure of the level of economic development since it does not take into account the distribution of income. Our examples above used the latest available data on income inequality, which is often used in combination with per capita GDP to provide a multi-faceted measure of development. Vanhanen's 'objective' measure of democracy outlined above has been criticized for not taking into account the electoral system and the electoral threshold (see Chapter 11), which have an impact on the number of parties that have a chance of gaining seats in the legislative chamber. Scales of human rights measures and/or political freedom have been criticized for not being transparent about the coding procedures that have been used to convert raw information on human rights abuse into numerical values (see Landman 2004b; 2006).

Many students eschew quantitative comparison of many countries since it requires mathematical and computing skills. Statistical analysis of data requires an understanding of basic four-figure mathematics, algebra, probability theory, and calculus. It also requires knowledge of computers, spreadsheets, and statistical software packages. In response to these worries of students, there are several important things to consider. First, many undergraduate and most graduate programmes in political science require their students to take courses in statistics and political explanation, and some universities offer intensive data analysis training.

Second, the development of computer technology combined with the availability of data makes this type of analysis much easier than in the past, and it is not unreasonable to assume that it will continue to do so. Third, a large portion of published literature in comparative politics uses quantitative analysis. Students who avoid learning even the basics can shut themselves off from important sources in the field. Thus, all students of comparative politics ought to achieve a basic under-standing of the principles of quantitative analysis in order to evaluate studies that use it and employ it when appropriate (Collier 1991:25).

Finally, there are countless topics in political science for which the quantitative comparison of many countries is simply inappropriate. This method of analysis cannot 'unpack' important historical, political, and sociological relationships at a lower level of analysis. It cannot be used to analyse discrete moments of political negotiation, consensus building, or the establishment of particular political 'pacts' between elite groups or between elites and masses. It cannot be used to examine different political strategies adopted by social movements, trade unions, revolu-tionary movements, or other forms of collective action. It is not appropriate for 'process tracing' in an effort to establish the links at the domestic level made between actors and their propensity to reform political institutions. It cannot map the inter-subjective meanings and different cultural understandings of political concepts and practices, among other deeper processes of meaning investigated through different methods of comparative analysis. In short, the quantitative comparison of many countries is not particularly appropriate for analysing a number of topics in political science that involve complex causal mechanisms, historical processes, and deeper meanings and understandings that are highly dependent on the contextual specificities of discrete country cases.

Summary

This chapter has provided a discussion of how scholars compare a large number of countries. While not ruling out the qualitative comparison of many countries altogether, the chapter emphasized the natural affinity between this method of comparison and statistical analysis. It outlined the assumptions and main advantages to this method of comparison and then discussed the question of quantitative measurement and regression analysis using real world examples to illustrate the basics of interpreting regression outputs, as well as examining briefly the different ways in which the basic regression model has been expanded for comparative politics. The chapter has concluded with a discussion of the main limitations of the method of comparison in which it has been made clear that there are numerous significant questions in political science for which the quantitative analysis of a large number of countries is simply inappropriate. Despite these limitations, however, it should be stressed that the quantitative comparison of many countries can deliver useful and parsimonious empirical generalizations about the political world that help shape our understanding of significant phenomena and yield tremendous insights into how to carry forward particular research agendas using the same form of analysis or by adopting other methods of comparative analysis, to which the next two chapters now turn.

Further reading

Beck, N. and Katz, J.N. (1995) 'What to Do (and Not to Do) with Time-Series Cross-Section Data', *American Political Science Review*, 89(3):634–647.
   A thorough treatment of the problems and solutions for comparing many countries over time and space.

Dogan, M. (1994). 'The Use and Misuse of Statistics in Comparative Research' in M. Dogan and A. Kazancigil (eds) *Comparing Nations*, Oxford: Blackwell.

Classic argument about the limits of cross-national research that compares many countries.

Ersson, S. and Lane, J.E. (1996) 'Democracy and Development: A Statistical Exploration', in A.Leftwich (ed.) *Democracy and Development*, Cambridge: Polity, 45–73.
   A good example of the quantitative analysis of many countries over time on the relationship between democracy and development.

Jackson, R.W. (1985) 'Cross-national Statistical Research and the Study of Comparative Politics', *American Journal of Political Science*, 29(1):161–182.
   A good overview of using quantitative analysis to compare a large number of countries.

Pennings, P., Keman, H., and Kleinnijenhuis, J. (1999) *Doing Research in Political Science: An Introduction to Comparative Methods and Statistics*, London: Sage.
   Provides a good overview of political science methods and an in-depth presentation of regression analysis.

Poe, S.C. and Tate, C.N. (1994) 'Repression of Human Rights to Personal Integrity in the 1980s: A Global Analysis', *American Political Science Review*, 88(4): 853–872.
   A good example of the quantitative analysis of many countries over time in the field of human rights.

Plümper, T. and Troeger, V. (2007) Efficient Estimation of Time Invariant and Rarely Changing Variables in Panel Data Analysis with Unit Effects, *Political Analysis*, Spring 2007(15): 124–139.
   Discussion of regression in time and space and how to control for variables that rarely change.

Ross, M. and Homer, E. (1976) 'Galton's Problem in Cross-National Research', *World Politics*, 29(1): 1–28.

An overview of many of the pitfalls associated with qualitative approaches in comparative politics.

Stimson, J. (1985) 'Regression in Space and Time: A Statistical Essay', *American Political Science Review*, 29: 914–947.
   Good overview of the problems and solutions to analysing a large number of countries over time and space.

Comparing few countries

The previous chapter provided a discussion of how the comparison of a large number of countries can yield important inferences and empirical generalizations about the political world. It showed that there is a natural affinity between the comparison of many countries and statistical analysis, the techniques of which are grounded in a number of assumptions about units, time, the capacity for measurement, the availability of data, and the distributions in those data. While there are many advantages associated with the comparison of many countries, the chapter made clear that such analysis suffers from several weaknesses and may well be inappropriate for a large number of research topics in political science. It is from these various limitations that this chapter takes its point of departure. As in the last chapter, the discussion in this chapter includes the advantages and weakness of this method of analysis, which are illustrated with extant studies from the comparative politics literature. To this end, the chapter begins with outlining the assumptions behind the comparison of few countries, and then follows with how this method enhances validity, addresses the problem of case selection, outlines the parameters of the 'most similar' and 'most different' research designs, discusses the importance of non-variant and negative cases, how this method uses both qualitative and quantitative analysis, and finishes with a consideration of its main limitations.

Assumptions

In contrast to both the method and the kinds of studies that appeared in the last chapter, the methods for the comparison of countries presented here concern research designs in which the universe of countries has been *intentionally* selected and is *significantly smaller than a global selection*. The number of countries in such a comparison may vary at the upper limit, but by definition is always greater than or equal to two. Otherwise, we would be considering single-country studies, which are the topic of the next chapter. The precise maximum number of countries selected depends on the research question that is posed; the regional, historical, linguistic, and cultural expertise of the researcher; the methodological benefits of raising the number of observations; and the resource constraints imposed on any given research project. This chapter assumes that there are no resource constraints and focuses on the logic of inference and how that relates to the selection and comparison of countries using qualitative and quantitative analysis.

The comparison of few countries shares many of the same assumptions as the comparison of many countries, such as the idea that countries represent units on which comparable data and information can be collected; that in the case of the quantitative comparison of few countries, features of countries that are similar can be measured; and that the events and outcomes in each country are largely independent of events and outcomes in other countries. Despite these similar starting assumptions, the comparison of few countries has a number of differences, including its attention to the deeper context of each case, the intensive focus on variation within countries rather than on variation between countries, the lower level of conceptual abstraction and the enhancement of validity, and the ability to engage in qualitative analysis using different kinds of social and political information. These differences and various qualifications relating to them are considered in turn.

First, the comparison of few countries has been described as 'case-oriented' (Ragin 1987) rather than 'variable-oriented', since the focus of the analysis is much more on the specific unfolding of events and variation in political developments within each country than variation in macro-variables between countries. While there are numerous examples of comparative research in which there is much greater focus on the individual countries that comprise the sample, there are many other examples that maintain their focus on macro- and micro-variables of interest and seek to make larger (in some cases, causal) inferences that apply to countries outside the original sample. While this distinction helped in identifying a significant difference between global comparisons using quantitative analysis and the comparison of smaller samples of countries, it is too easy to draw a false dichotomy between the two methods. And it is Ragin (1987) who developed an important methodological tool for combining the systematic rigour of the quantitative approach with the more context sensitive nature of the methods described in this chapter (see below), where significant attention is still paid to examining the relationship between macro-variables of interest.

Second, the comparison of few countries has been described as being more *intensive* than *extensive* since those factors considered do not vary across a wide range of countries, but vary over time and across sub-national units within a smaller sample of countries, which allow the researcher to probe more deeply into each individual case comprising the sample. By intentionally limiting the number of countries under comparison, the method sacrifices in some degree the broad generalizations made possible through the comparison of many countries, but gains a deeper understanding of the countries that feature in the analysis, as well as their similarities and differences. In addition, as Chapter 2 pointed out, the comparison of few countries can benefit from comparisons over time, which are seen as one way to increase the number of observations and avoid in some degree the problem of too many variables, not enough countries (Collier 1991; King *et al.* 1994).

Third, while the comparison of few countries sacrifices the ability to make broad empirical generalizations, it means that they may well be located at a lower level of abstraction in which concepts and ideas are operationalized in ways that fit more closely with the contextual specificities of the countries used in the comparison. Operating at a lower level of abstraction means that the concepts do not need to 'travel' as much and that establishing equivalence may be easier in some research designs where the countries under comparison share a number of similar features (see below). This also suggests that the comparison of few countries enhances the validity of the concepts since they are operationalized in ways that capture more particular and nuanced understandings relative to the context of the countries being compared. For example, a comparison of patrimonial politics in Latin America could operationalize the notion of neo-patrimonialism in ways that are sensitive to deeper historical understandings of patron–client networks, large kinship structures, and land tenure patterns, while the operationalization of neo-patrimonialism in Africa would necessarily take into account tribal identification among other factors that are particular to that region. In both instances, the overarching concept may be the same, but the ways in which it is understood and practised, as well as its impact on politics will vary considerably between the two regions. Thus, a comparison of few countries within each of these regions would achieve greater validity for a particular under-standing of neo-patrimonialism.

Taken together, there are a number of distinct advantages to the comparison of few countries that in many ways address the limitations of the comparison of many countries outlined in the previous chapter. But how do scholars wishing to adopt this method of analysis know which countries to choose? What are the criteria by which to choose countries? Does it matter how many countries have been chosen? Does it matter why they have been chosen? Does the selection of countries affect the kinds of answers that are obtained? How secure are the inferences that are made from the comparison of few countries? These and other questions are addressed in the balance of this chapter. The discussion begins by examining principles of case selection and research design, which outlines the main differences and problems associated with 'most similar' and 'most different' systems design. This is followed by a discussion of qualitative, quantitative and mixed techniques for comparative analysis, and then the final section outlines the remaining limitations surrounding the comparison of few countries.

Case selection and research design

The method of comparing few countries is divided primarily into two types of system design: 'most similar systems design' and 'most different systems design' (Przeworski and Teune 1970; Faure 1994). Most similar systems design (MSSD) seeks to compare political systems that share a host of common features in an effort to neutralize some differences while highlighting others. Based on J.S. Mill's (1843) method of difference, MSSD seeks to identify the key features that are different among similar countries and which account for the observed political outcome. Most different systems design (MDSD), on the other hand, compares countries that do not share any common features apart from the political outcome to be explained and one or two of the explanatory factors seen to be important for that outcome. This system is based on Mill's method of agreement, which seeks to identify those features that are the same among different countries in an effort to account for a particular outcome. In this way, MDSD allows the researcher to distil out the common elements from a diverse set of countries that have greater explanatory power (Collier 1993:112). Table 4.1 clarifies the distinction between these two systems and shows to which of Mill's methods they adhere. For MSSD on the left-hand side of the table, the countries share the same basic characteristics (a, b, and c), and some share the same key explanatory factor (x), but those without this key factor also lack the outcome which is to be explained (y). Thus, the presence or absence of the key explanatory factor is seen to account for this outcome, a state of affairs that complies with Mill's method of difference. For MDSD on the right-hand side of the table, the countries have inherently different features (a through i), but share the same key explanatory factor (x) as well as the presence of the outcome to be explained (y). In this system, the outcome to be explained is due to the presence of the key explanatory factor in all the countries (x), and thus adheres to Mill's method of agreement. In both systems, the presence of x is associated with the presence of y, and some would

Table 4.1 Most similar systems design (MSSD) and most different systems design (MDSD)

	MSSD Difference[†]			MDSD Agreement[†]		
	Country 1	Country 2	Country Φ	Country 1	Country 2	Country Φ
Features	a	a	a	a	d	g
	b	b	b	b	e	h
	c	c	c	c	f	i
Key explanatory factor(s)	x	x	not x	x	x	x
Outcome to be explained	y	y	not y	y	y	y

Source: Adapted from Skocpol and Somers (1980:184)
Note: [†] Based on J.S. Mill's (1843) method

argue that x actually causes y. The difference between the two systems resides in the choice of countries.

Most similar systems design is particularly well suited for those engaged in area studies (Przeworski and Teune 1970:33). The intellectual and theoretical justification for area studies is that there is something inherently similar about countries that make up a particular geographical region of the world, such as Europe, Asia, Africa, and Latin America. Whether it is common history, language, religion, politics, or culture, researchers working in area studies are essentially employing most similar systems design, and the focus on countries from these regions effectively controls for those features that are common to them while looking for those features that are not. For example, Jones (1995) compares the institutional arrangements of Latin American countries, which not only share the same cultural and historical Iberian legacies, but also share the same basic form of presidentialism. Similarly, Collier and Collier (1991) compare the experiences of eight Latin American countries to uncover the 'critical junctures' during which labour movements were incorporated into the political system. Bratton and van der Walle (1997) and Lindberg (2006) compare countries from sub-Saharan Africa to explain the emergence and maintenance of democracy in that region.

Where quantitative analysis requires mathematical and computer skills, area studies require language training and extensive field research, which have been seen as distinct disadvantages to comparing countries from a given region. It can take years to learn the languages needed to compare countries in Asia or Africa. Even within Latin America, students must learn Spanish and Portuguese, let alone the various dialects of each that are spoken in different parts of the region. Extensive field research can mean long periods living under adverse conditions to which the researcher is unaccustomed. Moreover, funding organizations may be less inclined to support projects that envisage long periods of field research. These problems represent the practical considerations that all researchers confront, and they highlight the different ways in which comparative methods can be seen to be a function of the training and disposition of the researcher. Nevertheless, comparative studies from particular regions have provided tremendous insight into general and enduring questions of political science, including guerrillas and revolution (Wickham-Crowley 1993), collective action and repression (Brockett 2005), survival of presidential democracies (Jones 1995), transitions from authoritarian rule (O'Donnell, Schmitter and Whitehead 1986; Linz and Stepan 1996), and models for successful economic development (Porter 1990; Wade 1992) to name a few.

In contrast to most similar systems design, where a particular outcome varies across similar countries, most different systems design comprises a selection of countries in which the outcome does not vary across very different countries. This kind of research design is typical of comparative studies that identify a particular outcome that is to be explained, such as revolutions, military coups, transitions to democracy, or 'economic miracles' in newly industrialized countries (Geddes 1990:134–141). The countries that are selected are all instances in which the outcome of interest has occurred and one or more independent variables common to all the cases are identified as explaining the particular outcome. For example, Wolf (1969) compares instances of revolutionary movements that had significant peasant participation in Mexico, Russia, China, North Vietnam, Algeria, and Cuba. Though these countries share few common features, Wolf argues that the penetration of capitalist agriculture is the key explanatory factor common to each that accounts for the appearance of the revolutionary movements and their broad base of peasant support. This kind of intentional choice of countries based on the presence of the same outcome constitutes one form of 'selection bias' (Geddes 1990; King *et al.* 1994), which necessarily limits the types of inferences that can be drawn from comparison. For example, with respect to the superior economic performance of East Asian newly industrialized countries, Geddes (1990) argues that had the analysis included successful, less successful, and unsuccessful cases of economic performance, then its findings would have been completely different, from which she concludes along with King *et al.* (1994) that selecting on the dependent variable in this way leads to false inferences.

Dion (1998), however, has argued that in certain instances, selecting on the dependent variable is acceptable, if, and only if, the research is seeking to test for necessary (as opposed to sufficient) conditions for a particular outcome of interest. For example, Porter (1990) compares ten successful countries from East Asia and argues that their success is to due to the presence of the following four necessary conditions: (1) factor conditions, (2) demand conditions, (3) related and supporting industries, and (4) firm strategy, structure, and rivalry (Dion 1998:129). He claims that these four conditions are only *necessary* and not sufficient, and in Dion's (1998) view it is thus appropriate to choose on values of the dependent variable. The main problem with such an approach is that it is often not the case that researchers are clear or explicit about the kind of explanatory claim that they are making about a particular outcome for which they are providing an account. Often, the language elides the concepts of *necessary* and *sufficient* or lapses into stronger causal language that implies that the independent variables are necessary and sufficient for the

Briefing box 4.1 Most similar and most different systems design

Both system designs are used in comparative politics, particularly by those who compare few countries. Both these examples show how Mill's methods of agreement and difference can be applied to research questions. The first example shows how the most similar systems design is applied to six Latin American countries in an effort to uncover the sources of peasant support for revolutionary activity. The second example shows how the most different systems design is used to account for different regime types in fourteen European countries during the inter-war period.

Most similar systems design (MSSD): sources of peasant support for guerrillas

As part of a more comprehensive effort to account for revolutionary activity in Latin America between 1956 and 1970, Wickham-Crowley (1993: 92–117) uses the most similar systems design to examine the type of peasants that are most likely to support guerrillas in the region. Drawing on the work of Jeffery Paige (1975), he argues that guerrilla strongholds and support for revolutionary behaviour ought to be higher in rural areas in which there are peasants whose livelihood is the most vulnerable to negative influences from the structure of the agricultural system of production. His hypothesis is stated as follows:

> If the guerrillas gain support in an area with a relatively high prevalence of sharecroppers, squatters, or perhaps tenants, my working assumption is that there is an 'elective affinity' between the two, and that guerrillas would not have received such support in more ordinary agricultural regions.
>
> (Wickham-Crowley 1993:95)

To test the hypothesis, he compares the regional breakdown of Cuba, Venezuela, Guatemala, Colombia, Peru, and Bolivia to determine whether such a relationship

Table 4.2 Most similar systems design

Case	Cuba	Venezuela	Guatemala	Colombia	Peru	Bolivia
Key peasant groups	Squatters	Share-croppers	Tenants	Share-croppers	Serfs	Small-holders
Outcome to be explained	Guerrilla support	Guerrilla support	Guerrilla support	Guerrilla support	Guerrilla support	No guerrilla support

Source: Adapted from Wickham-Crowley (1993:92–117)
Note: Cases cover the period 1956–1970

Table 4.3 Most different systems design

Group 1

Cases	Britain	France	Switzerland	Belgium	The Netherlands
Class alliance	Middle class vs. working class	Middle class vs. working class	Middle class vs. working class	Middle class vs. working class	Middle class vs. working class
Outcome	Liberalism	Liberalism	Liberalism	Liberalism	Liberalism

Group 2

Cases	Denmark	Norway	Sweden	Czechoslovakia
Class alliance	Working class + middle peasantry	Working class + middle peasantry	Working class + middle peasantry	Working class + middle peasantry
Outcome	Social democracy	Social democracy	Social democracy	Social democracy

Group 3

Cases	Germany	Italy	Spain
Class alliance	Middle class + middle peasantry	Middle class + middle peasantry	Middle class + middle peasantry
Outcome	Fascism	Fascism	Fascism

Source: Adapted from Luebbert (1991)

exists. Table 4.2 summarizes the comparison and shows that in all the cases except Bolivia, there are present both the specified types of peasants and the outcome to be explained. Bolivia has a prevalence of smallholders, who according to the theory are not likely to support guerrilla activity, and in this case, do not. Thus, across similar cases, the presence of the key explanatory factor is associated with the presence of the outcome to be explained.

Most different systems design: the origins of regimes in inter-war Europe

In seeking to account for the different regime types that emerged in twelve countries in Europe during the inter-war period, Luebbert (1991) claims that the key explanatory variable is the particular class alliance that formed within these countries. The three regime types include liberalism, social democracy, and fascism. The twelve countries are grouped according to these three outcomes and within each group, the countries share few features in common apart from the same class alliance and the same outcome. Thus, Luebbert matches the presence of a particular class alliance to a particular regime type. Table 4.3 summarizes this analysis, and shows that liberalism is the product of a strong middle class versus a weak working class. Social democracy is seen to be a product of an alliance between the working class and the middle peasantry. And fascism is seen to be a product of an alliance between the middle class and the middle peasantry. In this example, the most different systems design is applied to each group of countries.

outcome that is being explained. In such cases where strong causal language is adopted in ways that imply the presence of necessary and sufficient independent variables, then selecting on the dependent variable is not acceptable. It is in these instances that the warnings issued by Geddes (1990) and King *et al.* (1994), as well as those outlined here apply to a comparative study.

While is it typical for scholars to use either MSSD or MDSD, some comparativists use both system designs. In *Problems of Democratic Transition and Consolidation*, Linz and Stepan (1996) use MSSD to compare the experiences of democratic consolidation within the separate regions of South America, Southern Europe, and Eastern Europe; and then use MDSD to compare across these three regions. Similarly, Rueschemeyer *et al.* (1992) use MSSD to examine the relationship between capitalist development and democracy within Latin America, and MDSD to compare Latin America to the advanced industrial world. De Meur and Berg-Schlosser (1994) employ both designs to analyse the conditions of survival or breakdown of democratic systems in inter-war Europe. Lindberg (2006) effectively employs MSSD to compare the longevity of democracy in Africa across 232 elections in 44 countries between 1989 and 2003. What remains important to all these methods of comparing few countries (and here the Lindberg example pushes the upper limit) is the proper specification of the outcome that is to be explained, the reasons for adopting either system design, as well as the choice of the particular countries under scrutiny.

Extending MDSD and MSSD

The discussion above shows the simple distinction between the two methods, where the main difference lies in which set of variables vary and which do not. For MSSD, there are a number of variables common to all the countries that are held constant (i.e. they do not vary), while the key independent variables and the dependent variable vary across countries. For MDSD, the key independent variable and the dependent variable do not vary, while the remaining variables that make the countries under comparison *most different* do vary. Apart from the inherent problems of too many variables and not enough countries for both methods, as well as the problem of selection bias in MDSD (i.e. the countries are chosen according to values on the dependent variable), there is a further complication that is related to the number of countries that are compared.

As Chapter 2 outlined, comparative studies can include one, few or many countries. Increasing the number of countries will affect the ability of a scholar to meet the conditions required by doing either MSSD or MDSD. For MSSD, as the number of countries is increased, there are fewer and fewer variables that can be held constant since increasingly different countries are added to the sample. For example, a Latin American study that added Caribbean countries, an African study that added countries from North Africa and the Middle East, and an Asian study that compared countries from Southeast Asia, South Asia, and Central Asia would all sacrifice a large number of similarities as increasingly different countries are added to the sample. In Table 4.1, it could be that as more and more countries are added to an MSSD research design, variables *a*, *b*, and *c* would cease to be held constant. In similar fashion, MDSD comparisons of few countries can only increase the number of countries to the point at which the supply of countries with the outcome to be explained is exhausted. In other words there is a limited supply of countries that have experienced particular outcomes of interest, whether they be periods of successful economic growth, social revolutions, democratic transitions, among others.

There is an important conclusion that follows from this consideration of the limits to expanding the number of countries in either research design. At some point the inclusion of more and more countries forces both research designs to move into the realm of a many-country comparative design since MSSD loses its ability to hold shared characteristics constant and MDSD runs out of countries from which to choose. For MSSD the increasing variation in those variables that were formerly held constant means that the comparison moves to comparing different outcomes across different countries, while for MDSD the increase in the number of countries to include those without the outcome of interest moves in similar fashion to comparing different outcomes across different countries. Thus, there is a limit to the number of countries that can be compared in either research design if the scholar wants to take advantage of their logic. When either research design adds so many countries that the analysis compares different outcomes across different countries, it has become a many-country study, which ought to take full advantage of the statistical techniques outlined in the previous chapter.

Negative cases

In addition to the differences between MSSD and MDSD, as well as the variations on these basic research designs (see Faure 1994 for a full coverage of these variants), there is a remaining challenge for the comparison of few countries. If a study wants to include instances in which the outcome of interest does not occur (known as a negative case), it is not entirely clear which negative cases ought to be chosen. For example, Wolf's (1969) study on peasant wars compares positive cases of countries that have had revolutions with significant peasant participation, while Skocpol's (1979) study of social revolutions comprises positive and negative cases. She compares the successful social revolutions in France (1787–1800), Russia (1917–1921), and China (1911–1949) to the negative cases of England (1640–1689), Prussia (1807–1814), Germany (1848–1850), Japan (1868–1873), and Russia (1905–1907) (see Chapter 7 in this volume and Mahoney and Goertz 2004:659–660). While the inclusion of the five negative cases addresses a significant methodological concern over selection bias, it is not clear why these five negative cases were chosen and why other negative cases were not chosen. After all there is a large universe of cases from which to choose if one uses all countries from throughout world history; however, such a universe of cases includes the positive cases, the negative cases, *as well as a significant number of irrelevant cases*. What makes a case irrelevant and why is it a problem for comparative analysis?

Again, Skocpol's (1979) study is instructive in this regard. As Chapter 7 will outline in greater detail, her two main explanatory variables are the presence of a peasant revolt and the breakdown of the state. In the cases of France, Russia, and China both of these conditions were present and all three cases experienced social revolution. There are two types of negative cases that help confirm her theory. First there are cases in which peasant revolt is present, state breakdown does not take place, and social revolution does not occur. Second there are cases in which peasant revolt is absent, state breakdown does take place, and social revolution does not occur. In both types of cases, social revolution does not occur, an outcome that supports her theory since both peasant revolt and state breakdown must be present in order for a social revolution to take place. Beyond these cases, however, there are other types of cases with different combinations of peasant revolt, state breakdown and social revolution. Figure 4.1 summarizes the logical combination of these three variables, each of which has two possible values (i.e. the presence or absence of peasant revolt, state breakdown, and social revolution). For any set of three such dichotomous variables, there are eight possible combinations (i.e. $2^3=8$).

Cell I in the figure contains the positive cases in which there has been a peasant revolt, state breakdown, and social revolution (i.e. France, Russia, and China). Many studies of macro outcomes, such as Wolf's (1969) *Peasant Wars* use only this kind of selection of positive cases to provide support for a general set of propositions. But the figure shows seven other possible cases that could be examined. Cases in Cells IV and VI are classic negative cases, which if found in history would confirm Skocpol's (1979) theory of social revolution. She thus includes England (1640–1689), Prussia (1807–1814), Germany (1848–1850), Japan (1868–1873), and Russia (1905–1907) as examples of negative cases. Cases with combinations of variables in Cells II, III, and V, however, would disconfirm her theory since either social

		$\underline{X_1}$ (state breakdown)			
		Yes		No	
		Yes	No	Yes	No
$Y>$ (social revolution					
	Yes	I Positive (1, 1, 1)	II Disconfirming (1, 1, 0)	III Disconfirming (0, 1, 1)	IV Negative (0, 1, 0)
$\underline{X_2}$ (peasant revolt)	No	V Disconfirming (1, 0, 1)	VI Negative (1, 0, 0)	VII Impossible, but happens (0, 0, 1)	VIII Irrelevant (0, 0, 0)

Figure 4.1 Matrix of possibilities for social revolution using two dichotomized independent variables ($2^3 = 8$)

Source: Adapted from Mahoney and Goetz (2004:663)

revolution has taken place in countries with different combinations of peasant revolt and state breakdown, or it has not taken place in countries with different combinations of those two factors. Cell VII contains cases in which a social revolution has taken place in a country that has not had peasant revolt or state breakdown (impossible according to her theory), while Cell VIII contains cases that are irrelevant for testing her theory altogether since none of the factors are present.

This consideration of the logical combinations of variables for a typical comparison of few countries is instructive for two reasons. First, it identifies cases beyond the original comparison that ought to be examined to provide more definitive support for a theory. Second, it identifies those cases that do not need to be examined to test the theory. Eliminating the possible cases for inclusion is vital for scholars seeking to compare a small number of countries in greater depth while nevertheless providing an evidence base from which more secure inferences can be drawn and support for a general theory can be made. Mahoney and Goertz (2004) argue that cases need to be selected in which there is a *possibility* of the outcome of interest occurring, and thus their rule of thumb, known as 'the possibility principle' suggests that a full test of Skocpol's (1979) structural theory of social revolution would need to examine cases from Cells I–VI in Figure 4.1.

Combining quantitative and qualitative comparison

Most of the examples in the preceding section involved the qualitative comparison of few countries in which historical processes, macro outcomes, and the presence or absence of antecedent factors are examined in ways that test general theories in comparative politics that seek to explain significant social and political phenomena. But the comparison of a small number of countries need not preclude the use of quantitative techniques alongside attention to the historical, cultural, and political context of the countries under comparison. Indeed, time-series data analysis and 'pooled' time-series analysis across a limited number of countries provides ways in which the number of observations can be raised while remaining sensitive to the cultural specificities of the countries under comparison. Analysis of time-series data can be done in parallel across any number of countries. For example, Foweraker and Landman (1997) compare the fluctuation in the protection of citizenship rights and patterns of social mobilization over different periods of time in the cases of Brazil (1964–1990), Chile (1973–1990), Mexico (1963–1990) and Spain (1958–1983). In similar fashion, Brockett (2005) compares time-series patterns of repression and collective action in Guatemala and El Salvador. In both studies, these trends in quantitative data are examined in parallel and alongside a fuller consideration of the particular histories of the countries under comparison. The quantitative analysis provides a core of evidence that is linked with history in ways that support the overall argument developed in both studies.

Other studies have 'pooled' their data, where time-series trends are not considered in parallel across a set of countries, but countries and time are combined in ways that create a large matrix of data that is then examined using the same statistical techniques employed for the quantitative comparison of many countries outlined in the previous chapter. For example, Lijphart (1994b) compares data on democratic performance across eighteen established democracies (see Chapter 10 this volume), while Wilensky (2002) compares a multitude of socio-economic and political indicators across nineteen 'rich democracies' to examine exactly what is modern about these countries and how different types of political economy have an impact on system performance. Lindberg (2006) compares data on 232 elections in 44 countries between 1989 and 2003. For him, elections serve as the unit of analysis, which are repeated across the 44 countries in the sample, although the repetition is uneven since the electoral process has been interrupted in some countries of his sample. In all these examples, the 'small-N' problem has been overcome through comparing the sample of countries over time using quantitative data and various statistical techniques to establish the presence or absence of statistically significant similarities, differences, and relationships between variables of interest, while the analyses have been conducted on regions or sets of countries about which the scholar is knowledgeable.

Finally, other scholars have sought to harness the leverage of quantitative analysis and apply it to the qualitative comparison of few countries. Rueschemeyer *et al.* (1992) seek to capture this additional leverage by comparing groups of countries in Europe, the Caribbean and Latin America to test the general theory of a relationship between economic development and democracy with greater in-depth analysis of pathways and periods of democratization (see Chapter 6 in this volume). Wickham-Crowley (1993) is more explicit in applying the logic of 'boolean' algebra to set of 28 instances of attempts to foment social revolution in Latin America (see Chapter 7 in this volume). His analysis draws on a general framework developed by Charles Ragin (1987) in which logical combinations and configurations of 'causal' factors are compared to outcomes in ways that provide a form of analysis that moves beyond considering the independent effect of variables on one another to one that emphasizes the *combination* of these factors in accounting for a particular outcome (Ragin 1987, 1994; Ragin *et al.* 1996).

Rather than rely on time-series, pooled time-series data, or straight historical and narrative information regarding a particular comparative research topic, qualitative comparative analysis in the first instance requires outcomes and the possible causal factors for these outcome to be specified in dichotomous terms. Making judgements about the different categories into which these factors across different countries are classified requires deep qualitative and historical knowledge, while the resulting Boolean 'truth table' (Ragin 1987) lists all the countries in the comparison and the configuration of both the casual conditions and the outcomes of interest. Table 4.4 is a hypothetical truth table that could be constructed for a macro outcome of interest in comparative politics of the kind examined in this chapter. The hypothetical outcome is listed in column F on the far right of the table, while the five hypothetical causal conditions are listed in columns A through E.

The table shows that across the ten cases (let us assume they are countries) for which information has been collected and judged using the scholar's own criteria there is a complex set of combinations for the presence or absence of the causal conditions and the presence or absence of the outcome. The purpose of the truth table and subsequent analysis is to determine whether there are any discernible patterns across the causal conditions and the different outcomes. In this example, the shaded regions in the table shows that across cases 4, 5, 6, 9 and 10 there is the same combination of factors and outcome. Formally, Boolean analysis would list this set

Table 4.4 Hypothetical truth table

| Cases | Causal Conditions | | | | | Outcome |
	A	B	C	D	E	F
1	A	b	c	d	e	f
2	A	b	c	d	e	f
3	A	b	c	d	E	f
4	A	B	C	D	e	F
5	A	B	C	D	E	F
6	A	B	C	D	e	F
7	A	b	c	d	E	f
8	A	b	c	d	e	f
9	A	B	C	D	e	F
10	A	B	C	D	E	F

Key to table:
A = first causal factor
B = second causal factor
C = third causal factor
D = fourth causal
E = fifth causal factor
F = outcome to be explained

Capital letter = presence of condition or outcome
Lower case letter = absence of condition or outcome

of matches as a preliminary causal combination (A + B + C + D = F), where the combination of the presence of the four causal conditions matches the presence of the outcome to be explained (F).

Closer examination of the table reveals more insights. First, causal condition A is always present, which means its contribution to the outcome could be eliminated from this preliminary combination and the focus could be on the remaining combination of causal conditions B + C + D. Second, the obverse of the successful combination is also true, i.e., the absence of a combination of these causal conditions (b + c + d = f) matches the absence of the outcome to be explained. Third, causal condition E does not appear to be a necessary or sufficient condition for explaining the outcome of interest. There are cases with the presence this condition and presence of the outcome (i.e. 5 and 10); cases with the presence of the condition and the absence of the outcome (3 and 7); cases with the absence of the condition and the presence of the outcome (4, 6, and 9); and cases with absence of the condition and the absence of the outcome (1, 2, and 8). Thus across the cases, once could conclude that causal conditions A, B, C, and D are necessary and sufficient for the outcome to have occurred.

This example of a Boolean truth table demonstrates that qualitative comparative analysis offers a powerful tool for the comparison of few countries for four reasons. First, it allows for the inclusion of information that has not been measured precisely, but that is represented through reasonable judgements and the application of criteria that are defensible. Second, it uses the combinatory logics of binary variables found in Boolean algebra to simplify the complexity of the world in order to tease out the set of necessary and sufficient conditions that account for an outcome of interest. Third, it allows for an assessment to demonstrate how certain causal conditions *contribute* to an outcome, and how such a contribution needs to take place alongside the presence of other important factors in order for the outcome to take place. Fourth, beyond identifying this set of necessary and sufficient conditions, the technique also allows the assessment to determine the reasons for the outcome *did not* occur in certain cases, and thus draws on the insights provided in the discussion of negative cases above.

Limitations of few-country comparisons

There are a number of limitations to the methods for comparing few countries that once again reinforce the general position advanced in this book that comparative scholars will always face a trade-off between the scope of countries included in any one study and the level of abstraction and strength of the inferences that result from the number of countries that are compared. Unlike the global comparison of many countries in which sample sizes are maximized for increasing variation in the variables of interest, comparing few countries involves significant and intentional choices, any one of which may limit the inferences made possible. The problem of selection bias looms large, the choice of most similar and most different cases can appear at times arbitrary (depending on the selection criteria), and the inclusion of negative cases, while laudable, may nonetheless not have exhausted all cases that ought to be considered when analysing particular outcomes of interest.

It appears that the most different systems design (MDSD) remains somewhat weaker than the most similar systems design (MSSD), since its inferences relate only to the confirmation of the importance of the presence of certain explanatory factors and in some cases the identification of necessary conditions for a particular outcome. But by definition MDSD does not provide a framework in which negative cases can be included, since it necessarily must compare different countries that share the same outcome. For both methods, however, it has been shown that there is an upper limit to the number of countries that can be added to a comparison. On the one hand, MSSD can lose the control offered by using countries with 'most similar' variables through the inclusion of more countries that share fewer features. On the other hand, the analytical leverage offered by MDSD becomes sacrificed as the number of countries with a particular outcome becomes exhausted.

Summary

This chapter has examined the different ways in which scholars can and do compare a sample of countries that has been *intentionally* selected. The assumptions that lie behind the methods for comparing few countries include its ability to give greater attention to the deeper context of each country, the intensive focus on variation within countries rather than on variation between countries, its lower level of conceptual abstraction and the consequent enhancement of validity, and the ability to engage in qualitative analysis using different kinds of social and political information. As the chapters in Part II of this volume will demonstrate, there have been many great contributions to the pool of knowledge about the political world from the comparison of few countries. There is a wealth of well designed studies with sensible criteria for selecting countries that have given us a richer understanding of particular contexts and processes, while at the same time providing a rich evidence base with which to test propositions, establish empirical relationships, and chart the course for future comparative research that uses a small sample of countries.

Further reading

Collier, D. (1991) 'New Perspectives on the Comparative Method', in D.A. Rustow and K.P. Erickson (eds) *Comparative Political Dynamics: Global Research Perspectives*, New York: Harper Collins, 7–31.
An excellent review of comparative methods.

Faure, A.M. (1994) 'Some Methodological Problems in Comparative Politics', *Journal of Theoretical Politics*, 6(3):307–322.
This essay outlines the most similar and most different systems design as well as their 'mirror images'.

Geddes, B. (1990) 'How the Cases You Choose Affect the Answers You Get: Selection Bias in Comparative Politics', *Political Analysis*, 2:131–150.
An excellent article on selection bias using real examples from the comparative literature.

George, A.L. and Bennett, A. (2005) *Case Studies and Theory Development in the Social Sciences*, Cambridge: Cambridge University Press.

Excellent book length treatment of how case studies provide a useful means for the development of theory in the social sciences.

Gerring, J. (2006) *Case Study Research: Principles and Practice*, Cambridge: Cambridge University Press.

In-depth and comprehensive analysis of using case study research that adheres to general social scientific principles.

Lijphart, A. (1971) 'Comparative Politics and Comparative Method', *The American Political Science Review*, 65(3):682–693.

The original statement about comparative method, locating it as a non-experimental and non-statistical social science.

—— (1975) 'The Comparable Cases Strategy in Comparative Research', *Comparative Political Studies*, 8(2):158–177.

This essay presents further reflections on comparative method.

Mahoney, J. and Goertz (2004) 'The Possibility Principle: Choosing Negative Cases in Comparative Research', *American Political Science Review*, 98 (4): 653–669.

Innovative framework and criteria for selecting negative cases based on the possibility that an outcome of interest could occur.

Mahoney, J and Rueschemeyer, D. (eds) (2003) *Comparative Historical Analysis in the Social Sciences*, Cambridge: Cambridge University Press.

Comprehensive edited volume on the uses of comparative historical analysis in the social sciences.

Ragin, C. (1987) *The Comparative Method: Moving beyond Qualitative and Quantitative Strategies*, Berkeley: University of California Press.

A thorough account of the differences between quantitative and qualitative analysis, and how to combine them into Boolean truth tables.

Ragin, C.C. (1994) 'Introduction to Qualitative Comparative Analysis', in T.Janoski and A. Hicks (eds) *The Comparative Political Economy of the Welfare State*, Cambridge: Cambridge University Press, 299–320.

This essay distinguishes between 'variable-oriented' and 'case-oriented' approaches and proposes a way to unify them.

Skocpol, T. and Somers, M. (1980) 'The Uses of Comparative History in Macrosocial Inquiry', *Comparative Studies in Society and History*, 22:174–197.

This essay outlines the uses of comparative history as well as Mill's methods of agreement and difference.

Single-country studies as comparison

The previous two chapters have demonstrated the advantages, disadvantages, and challenges associated with the comparison of many (Chapter 3) and few (Chapter 4) countries. This chapter turns its attention to the use of single-country studies in comparative politics. By a single-country study, I refer primarily to any study in which a single country forms the basic unit of analysis, but which may also be broken down into smaller units across time and space, by examining sub-national variation across states in federal countries, other administrative units in unitary systems, as well as other appropriate units of analysis, such as individuals. As argued in the other chapters, it is entirely possible to raise the number of observations and bolster the inferences that one wishes to make even in single-country studies by including analysis across such units. You will recall from Chapter 2 that the methodological trade-offs between the scope of countries under comparison and the level of abstraction includes the single-country study (see the lower left corner of Figure 2.1). Within the framework adopted here, single-country studies are necessarily more *intensive* (i.e. have a lower level of abstraction) and less *extensive* (i.e. only examine one country) where it is possible to focus on the particular features of a country while at the same time relating those features to broader sets of research questions in the field of comparative politics.

Single-country studies are thus another method for carrying out comparative research, and like our other methods, have their own associated strengths, weaknesses, and basic rules of thumb that guide their selection and analysis. In contrast to the literature that is critical of the value that single-country studies add to our comparative understanding of politics, this chapter shows the conditions under which single-country studies can be used to draw inferences about significant research questions in the field and help advance our knowledge in ways that the other comparative methods cannot. The chapter outlines the main functions of single-country studies and discusses the procedures for case selection to show how selection relates to the strength of the inferences that can be made. It then provides strategies for raising the number of observations within single-country studies, and concludes by examining the main limitations of single-country studies in making inferences for comparative politics research.

Functions of single-country studies

As outlined in Chapter 1, one of the goals of comparison is *contextual description*, a function that has been clearly best served by single-country studies. Studies that merely describe or interpret political phenomena have been variously referred to as 'atheoretical' and 'interpretative' (Lijphart 1971:691), or 'configurative-idiographic' (Eckstein 1975:96) in which the main purpose of the study is to provide purely descriptive information. Many have observed that such studies are, strictly speaking, not comparative but nevertheless are useful for comparison purely for the information they provide, which may feed into a study that seeks to provide explanation and understanding that has merit beyond the original country. The second goal of comparison is *classification* and there are numerous single-country studies that provide new classifications and 'types' that have become essential for further comparative research across a range of topics. For example, in describing the

Franco regime in Spain, Juan Linz (1964) identified a new form of authoritarianism that was different from personalistic dictatorships and totalitarian states. The regime institutionalized representation of the military, the Catholic Church, and the Falange, as well as the Franco loyalists, monarchists, and technocrats. Unlike totalitarian states, the regime relied on passive mass acceptance rather than popular support (Linz 1964; Carr and Fusi 1979:31–35; Foweraker and Landman 1997: xxiii). Similarly, Guillermo O'Donnell (1973) established the concept of the 'bureaucratic-authoritarian state' in his examination of Argentine politics, a concept which would later be applied not only to other authoritarian regimes in Latin America but also to those in Southeast Asia.

Beyond contextual description and classification, single-country studies have numerous other functions, including hypothesis generation and 'plausibility probes', theory-informing and theory-confirming, the analysis of so-called 'deviant' and 'outlier' cases, and process tracing and the elaboration of causal mechanisms (see Eckstein 1975; George 1979; Brady and Collier 2004; George and Bennett 2005; Gerring 2006; Hawkins, forthcoming). Using single-country studies in these different ways rests very much on a set of procedures for selecting countries that are related to the analysis of those countries using other methods of comparison. Thus, in the mind of a comparativist there are very few instances of the perfectly *sui generis* case, but one that is selected for its importance in relation to other cases, other findings, and other comparisons that have already been conducted. Single-country studies are thus not plucked from thin air, but are specifically chosen for the merit in contributing to larger sets of questions in the field.

The generation of hypotheses often comes from the analysis of political events, outcomes, and behaviour in single countries that are well known to the scholar, that present new research puzzles for wider debates in the field, and that either explicitly or implicitly suggest that the generated hypothesis be tested in a larger selection of countries (Lijphart 1971:692; Eckstein 1975:108). For example, as Chapter 2 has shown, O'Donnell's (1973) work on authoritarianism developed the hypothesis that the 1966 military coup and subsequent authoritarian regime in Argentina was related to failings of a particular phase of dependent capitalist development (see Briefing box 2.1). This hypothesis was subsequently tested in other Latin American countries and found wanting on many grounds (see Collier 1979). In similar fashion, James Scott (1976) developed the idea of the 'moral economy' and how its violation through capitalist development led to peasant revolutionary activity in Vietnam; a hypothesis that was later tested against other accounts of revolutionary behaviour in the same country as well as in additional countries from around the world (see Popkin 1979; Wickham-Crowley 1993; Anderson 1994; Lichbach 1994). For both these examples it is important to stress that the hypotheses generated from the Argentine and Vietnamese cases were stated in such ways that other scholars could test them for other countries, and their rejection in certain instances led to the search for rival explanations (on authoritarianism see Collier 1979; Cohen 1987, 1994; on peasant politics, see Popkin 1979; Wickham-Crowley 1993; Anderson 1994; Lichbach 1994).

When someone gives a lecture using comparative evidence from many countries, a member of the audience may exclaim, 'But in my country, things are different!' This is undoubtedly true, but more importantly the comment illustrates how single-country studies can be used to confirm and infirm existing theories, or illuminate known deviant countries. Theory-confirming and theory-infirming studies draw on known findings from existing studies that have been conducted a larger sample of countries (usually global quantitative studies of the kinds detailed in Chapter 3). They are thus grounded within the confines of known generalizations (Lijphart 1971:692) and in general terms, are often referred to as deviant cases or 'outliers'. As outlined above, comparison of many countries often reveals a host of deviant countries that do not conform to the theoretical expectations of the researcher. This deviance invites further research of the countries to establish which rival explanations had not been considered, and it forces the re-evaluation of how the key variables of the study were originally operationalized. Deviant country studies can weaken existing theories as well as further refine the concepts and measures used in the original comparative analysis (Lijphart 1971:692).

For example, as is shown in greater detail in Chapter 6, there has been considerable research on the empirical relationship between economic development and democracy. Over the years, the analysis of this relationship has expanded the number of countries that have been compared as well as the time periods over which they have been compared. These studies have shown that there is a positive and significant relationship between the level of the economic development on the one hand and the emergence and maintenance of democracy on the other hand. Despite this relatively robust set of findings, there are a number of countries in the world that could be identified as deviant cases. Consider the simple graphic in Figure 5.1, which depicts a stylized relationship between economic development and democracy. The x-axis has a measure of economic development that ranges from low to high, while the y-axis has a measure of democracy that also ranges from low to high. The upward sloping diagonal line depicts the positive and significant relationship between these two variables (see also Briefing Box 6.1).

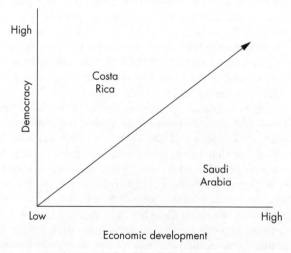

Figure 5.1 'Deviant' or 'outlier' cases for the relationship between economic development and democracy

It is typical in such analyses of this relationship that most of the countries are located somewhere along this line. Recall the explanation of regression analysis in Chapter 3, where the data points are scattered on and around the regression line. In this figure, there are two countries that fall significantly off the line, namely Costa Rica and Saudi Arabia. Both of these countries are considered 'outliers' or 'deviant cases'. Why? Costa Rica is an example of a relatively poor country that has had stable democratic institutions since 1948, while Saudi Arabia is a relatively rich country that has not established open, competitive democratic institutions. They are deviant cases since the outcome (i.e. democracy) is unexpected given the value of the explanatory variable (i.e. economic development). The goal of single studies of either of these two countries in this research area would be to find out why they do not conform to the expectations raised by an otherwise statistically significant relationship. These studies would then raise a series of new comparative research questions. Are there other so-called 'poor democracies' that have been established and survived in similar fashion to Costa Rica? Are there other rich non-democratic countries that appear not to be on the brink of democratic transition?

This 'Costa Rica–Saudi Arabia problem' (i.e. the presence of significant outliers) is typical across many other countries and many other research areas. The identification of outliers and the intentional selection of countries on that basis comprise what is often called the 'least likely' or 'most likely' method of comparison (Eckstein 1975:118). Most likely studies are carried out on countries where a theory suggests a particular outcome is definitely meant to occur (i.e. democratic transition, social revolution, civil war). If the outcome is observed as expected, then the theory is confirmed. If the outcome is not observed, then the theory is infirmed. Least likely studies are analogous but reverse the logic of comparison. These studies are carried out on a country where a particular theory suggests the outcome is not likely to occur (hence the term least likely). If the outcome is not observed, then the theory is confirmed, but if the outcome is observed, then the theory is infirmed. These crucial country studies do not definitively prove or disprove a theory (although a strict application of the Popperian principle of falsification would suggest otherwise), but merely confirm or infirm its applicability to other countries.

There are two examples in the literature on comparative democratization that illustrate the different application of most likely and least likely studies: Hawkins (2001) study of non-transition in Cuba and Howarth's (1998b) analysis of the successful democratic transition in South Africa. Hawkins' (2001) casts his analysis of Cuba's failure to undergo a democratic transition as a most likely study. Given the patterns in democratization in Latin America, the collapse of Communism in Eastern Europe and the reduction in Russian support to the country, as well as broader sets of socio-economic changes, Cuba appears to be an example of a most likely case of democratic transition, since many factors prominent in the democratization literature are present in the Cuban case. The fact that it is yet to undergo such a transformation makes Cuba an interesting case to examine. Hawkins' (2001) analysis reveals that classic structural explanations that link democratization to underlying socio-economic change cannot account for the absence of the transition in Cuba. Rather, the stability of the Cuban authoritarian system is based on the absence of key democratizing political actors, namely independent social groups and softline regime factions (Hawkins 2001:441). While not providing definitive empirical support for any causal relationship between the absence of the actors and democratization, his analysis provides a new set of hypotheses about Cuba's leadership and bases of legitimacy and lends significant support to 'agent-based' theories of politics. Moreover, his research design offers an excellent example of how a single-country study can contribute to larger debates in the field of comparative politics (see Chapter 13 in this volume).

In our second example, Howarth (1998b) provides an analysis of what he calls the 'best example of a least likely case' of democratic transition in South Africa. Given the hold that Apartheid had on the whole of South African society and the country's relative imperviousness to external sanctions, it was seen as highly unlikely that South Africa would experience a democratic transition. And yet, quickly after the release of Nelson Mandela, events proceeded very rapidly towards a democratic transition, new elections, and the formation of the new government controlled by the African National Congress. For Howarth (1998b:182–199), these events need much closer examination and the empirical analysis he conducts on the case leads him to question many of the dominant paradigms found in the literature on comparative democratization, including constitutionalism, institutional rational choice, elite pacts and 'transitology', Marxism, and discursive approaches. In this way, the single-country study serves as a basis for evaluating rival explanations as well as prescribing a research agenda that includes problematizing structures, agents, democracy, democratic institutions, and democratization itself (Howarth 1998b: 199–206).

Beyond these two examples of most likely and least likely cases, there are numerous other country examples that illustrate the utility of this method of analysis, such as the United States, China, and Brazil. For the United States, one area of focus has been on the absence of a large socialist party given that the US had a similar path of capitalist development over the course of the 19th and 20th centuries as in other advanced industrial economies (Lipset and Marks 2000). This and other 'unique' features of the United States has led to a sub-field of studies on 'American exceptionalism'; a concept originally introduced by Alexis de Tocqueville. The case of China, like Cuba, presents a paradox for studies in democratization given the survival of the communist regime after the 1989 'velvet revolutions' in Central and Eastern Europe (Hague *et al.* 1992:37–38), as well as its more recent period of successful economic development. For Brazil, the absence of a social revolution is puzzling given its history of land inequality, income inequality, and the persistence of poverty and social exclusion. Like the cases of Cuba and South Africa, these three countries represent a state of affairs that defies predominant theories in comparative politics, while the task of any one study of these countries is to provide an explanation for why they have experienced such an unexpected outcome.

Finally, single-country studies can be used to trace significant political processes and examine possible causal mechanisms that lie between two or more variables of interest. In both instances, the intensiveness of the single-country study allows for a more detailed look at underlying processes and mechanisms that simply cannot be investigated in studies that compare more countries. In this method of analysis, the scholar examines a variety of qualitative materials (histories, archival documents, interview transcripts, etc.) in order to see whether the causal process hypothesized by a particular theory is actually evident or not (George and Bennett 2005:6–7). In this way, the single country provides a rich source of material for presenting causal 'stories' that link causal chains together in ways that are relevant and verifiable (George and Bennett 2005:205; see also Tilly 1997).

Again, the work of Hawkins (2002) furnishes a good example of how process tracing provides deeper insight into causal mechanisms within a single county. In his study of authoritarianism in Chile and the response of the Pinochet regime to international human rights pressure, Hawkins (2004) examines thousands of internal communiqués within the Chilean military to show that there was a 'rule-oriented' faction within the regime that grew increasingly wary of the possible delegitimizing power of international human rights pressure. This faction increasingly gained ground within the regime, which ultimately held a national plebiscite for the new Constitution in 1980 and for President Pinochet himself in 1988. The defeat of Pinochet ushered in a relatively rapid transition to democracy. But the Hawkins (2004) analysis demonstrates several things that go far beyond the explanation of democratic transition in a particular country. First, he retains considerable leverage for the rationalist account of regime change that has been too easily dismissed by normative and constructive accounts. Second, he shows the discrete causal chains that lie between broader patterns of international human rights pressure and regime change by getting inside the factional tension within the regime itself. Third, he shows how the 'two-level' game (Putnam 1988, 1993b) originally devised to explain the behaviour of democratic regimes also applies to non-democratic regimes (see also Landman 2005b). Finally, he extends his findings from the Chilean case to South Africa and Cuba to test the applicability of his explanation to contexts outside the focus of the study.

While these different functions of single-country studies are methods of inquiry in and of themselves, they should also be seen as a set of criteria for selecting countries that make sense from a scientific perspective. While it is undoubtedly true that all countries are inherently interesting and worthy of study, pure random selection of countries, or selection on the basis of criteria unrelated to important research questions and puzzles in comparative political science are difficult to justify. Often undergraduate and graduate students choose a country simply because they have been there, they come from there, or some leading figure in international politics has declared the country to be meaningful in some way, but not because their country represents a puzzle for the larger research community in comparative politics. Such an arbitrary selection of a country necessarily raises the question, 'and this is a case of what, exactly?' Grounding one's case selection in one of the functions outlined here justifies the case in ways that make it relate to dominant debates in the field and offers a contribution to the accumulation of knowledge about politics.

Raising observations in single-country studies

In addition to the different functions of single-country studies and the related criteria for their selection, the explanatory leverage of a single-country study can be increased through strategies that raise the number of observations. These strategies are based on the general assumption that increasing the variation of any observable phenomena enhances the ability to make inferences and provide more systematic explanation (see

King *et al.* 1994; Brady and Collier 2004; George and Bennett 2005; Gerring 2006). Comparing any phenomenon across more and more units allows for a more systematic test of an empirical proposition about the relationship between two or more variables. Such a commitment does not unnecessarily wed one to a statistical approach. Rather it concedes the statistical point that more units means more 'degrees of freedom' or space over which units can vary. Such a move appears particularly suited to single-country studies, which have long been criticized for having the problem of *n* =1 (King *et al.* 1994: 208). But the strategies for raising the number of observations outlined here do not necessarily compromise the other benefits associated with the intensive nature of single-country studies.

It is clear that any strategy to increase the number of observations rests on three different but related parameters: time, space, and level of analysis. First, it is possible and desirable to raise the number of observations by comparing across different historical periods in the country or across continuous units of time, such as years, months, or days. Comparative historical analysis can compare one period of political transformation to another (e.g. early periods of populism to more recent periods of populism; periods of initial democratization to later democratic transitions; earlier experiences with economic crises to more recent experiences, etc.) in ways that can identify similarities and differences that help explain such phenomena. Events-based and other time-series methods compare incidences of social and political phenomena such as elections, protests, demonstrations, political-business cycles, inflation and other fluctuations. These types of data are often modelled statistically and take can advantage of long time-series to include a variety of explanatory variables.

Second, all countries have sub-national political units over which significant variables can be compared, such as states in federal systems (i.e. the US, India, Mexico, and Brazil), counties, regions, and cities. For example, the 28 Indian states and the 30 Mexican states have provided significant sub-national variation to analyse the relationship between democracy and human rights (Beer and Mitchell 2006; Mitchell and Beer 2004; see also Chapter 11 in this volume), while sub-national units in Nepal provided the context for an analysis of political violence (Mitchell *et al.* 2006). In *Making Democracy Work*, Putnam (1993a) compares measures of 'civicness' and institutional performance across different regions of Italy; an analysis which is complemented by a longer historical view on the divergent paths in the emergence of 'civcness' in the North and the South of the country (see Chapter 6 this volume). Clarke and Gaile (1998) compare the use of resources and entrepreneurial capacity of dozens of cities across the United States to examine the degree to which cities have changed in response to the forces of globalization. Varshney (2002) compares data on violent ethnic conflict between Hindus and Muslims across the Indian states and across 28 major cities.

Third, beyond the use of time and space, a single-country study can examine groups of people at a lower level of aggregation than states or administrative units, as well as analyse mass publics themselves with individual data. Research on 'contentious politics' compares the emergence, cycles of protest, and impact of different social movements within the same country, as well as communal and minority groups (see Gamson 1975; Tarrow 1989, 1994; Gurr 1993, 2000 and Chapter 8 this volume). Voting behaviour, electoral studies, and public opinion research relies on large random samples of the population at one point in time or over time to build complex models of human behaviour in single countries. Large samples of up to 15,000 respondents allow for significant degrees of freedom to test a large number of competing hypotheses, while at the same time holding the features of the particular country constant. So-called 'panel' studies carry out such surveys on the same sample over time to examine and explain changing attitudes of mass publics. In the field of human rights research, new data projects are emerging that code events down to the individual violations suffered by individual victims, which are then aggregated across time and space to reconstruct the main contours of violence during periods of conflict, such as the conflict in Peru from 1980 to 2000 (see, e.g., Ball *et al.* 2003, and Landman 2006: 107–125).

Limitations of single-country studies

Generalizations from single-country studies will always be limited, since the country unit itself is bound by particular characteristics, while the potential for comparing variation in political phenomena across units is bound by time and space. However many sub-national units are compared over however many days, months, and years, the inferences one draws from them will have to made with care. For example, Maxwell's (1995) study of the democratic transition in Portugal stretches all the way back to the colonial period to establish the context in which members of the military exiting Angola in the early 1970s became disillusioned with the Salazar regime and fomented the Movement of the Armed Forces (MFA). While his analysis of this disillusionment and subsequent mobilization to replace the dictatorship with a social democratic regime is well done, the limits of the study are certainly reached when he attempts to link these developments in 1974 to the collapse of the Soviet Union and then end of the Cold War. Even studies as robust as Putnam's (1993a) on Italy reach their inferential limits and necessarily require complementary analysis that compares that particular case to other cases, or extends the analysis for replication in other cases. As this chapter has sought to make clear, single-country studies by definition trade their ability to provide in-depth knowledge and understanding of particular contexts against the ability to draw generalizations that have wider applicability. The inherent limitations in single-country studies, however, can be overcome through the strategies outlined in this chapter.

Summary

This chapter has shown that single-country studies can play a critical role in comparative politics if they are used in particular ways and selected carefully. They can be used for pure contextual description that may feed into other comparative studies; provide new classifications for observed political phenomena; generate and probe hypotheses that can be tested in different countries; provide a solid strategy to confirm or infirm existing theories of politics; and reveal discrete processes of causal mechanisms that are often left underspecified in studies that compare a larger number of countries. There are natural limits to the use of single-country studies and it is paramount for scholars of such studies, as for other methods of comparison in this volume, not to claim too much for a particular study or for the events in a particular country. Rather, scholars should be open and transparent about the parameters of the country study, its purpose, the criteria for its selection, and the types of inferences that can be made securely from the evidence that has been collected and analysed. As with the other comparative methods covered in this section of the volume, the chapters in Part II will demonstrate the ways in which comparing many, few, and single countries have provided a rich base of evidence and accumulation of knowledge about a range of significant political problems confronting the world.

Further reading

Eckstein, H. (1975) 'Case-study and Theory in Political Science', in F.I. Greenstein and N.S. Polsby (eds) *Handbook of Political Science, Vol. 7: Strategies of Inquiry*, Reading, MA: Addison-Wesley, 79–137.
    Seminal and definitive treatment of the value of case studies, including single-country studies.

George, A.L. and Bennett, A. (2005) *Case Studies and Theory Development in the Social Sciences*, Cambridge: Cambridge University Press.
    Excellent exposition on the value of case studies, and in particular, a full chapter on 'process-tracing'.

Gerring, J. (2004) 'What is a case study and what is it good for?' *American Political Science Review*, 98: 341–354.
    Incisive examination of the value of case studies.

Gerring, J. (2006) *Case Study Research: Principles and Practice*, Cambridge: Cambridge University Press.
    Full treatment of the relationship between cases and observations, and a full outline of the different uses of case studies in social science research.

Part II

COMPARING
COMPARISONS

Part I established why countries are compared and how comparison helps generate, test, and refine theories of politics. It established a general 'architecture' of comparative methods that includes the comparison of many countries, few countries, and single-country studies. It demonstrated how these three types of comparison use quantitative and qualitative techniques at different levels of analysis. Finally, it highlighted the key problems associated with comparison and suggested how best to overcome them. Throughout the chapters, concrete examples from the comparative literature were used to demonstrate these points. The chapters that make up Part II of this text use these different methods to interrogate popular research topics in comparative politics. The topics chosen have received wide attention in the comparative literature, are attractive to students of comparative politics, and are well suited to examine the different ways in which comparative methods can be applied to real-world problems. In essence, the chapters in this part of the text compare comparisons in an effort to demonstrate the utility of different methods of comparison.

The post-war period brought a whole range of new research questions and political problems to the field of comparative politics. The initial years of the period witnessed: the rise of Communism; an end to colonial rule and birth of new nation states; the appearance of new forms of political conflict from peasants, workers, and other subordinate groups; military coups and the rise of authoritarianism; new experiences with democracy and the development of the international human rights system. The latter part of the period saw the collapse of Communism, the end of the Cold War, renewed attention to international terrorism, and transitions to democracy in Latin America, Southern Europe, Africa, Asia, and Central and Eastern Europe. These events raised intriguing questions for comparativists as they focused on global, regional, and local aspects of political change, and many of these studies were motivated by the concern for achieving political stability in the short term and promoting democratic rule in the long term (Valenzuela and Valenzuela 1978:535). In this sense, comparative political inquiry has responded to contemporary issues (Lichbach 1997:4), and has been motivated by a concern for the well-being of the people who comprise the modern world (Przeworski *et al.* 2000).

The chapters that comprise this section of the book reflect in part these challenges and concerns of comparativists. Chapter 6 examines the efforts to uncover the social and economic 'preconditions' (Karl 1990) for healthy democracy. Chapter 7 looks at attempts to explain violent political dissent and the surge of revolutionary movements. Chapter 8 compares efforts to explain the origins, characteristics, and impact of non-violent political dissent and social movement activity. Chapter 9 traces the comparative work that seeks to explain the 'third wave' (Huntington 1991) of democratic transitions that began in Portugal 1974. Chapter 10 examines the comparative work on democratic institutions and democratic performance. Chapter 11 examines the ways in which comparative politics examines the promotion and protection of human rights. Finally, Chapter 12 shows how comparative methods have been used to analyse problems that transcend national boundaries in ways that examine the domestic impact of international variables and the international impact of domestic variables. The discussion in each chapter is concerned primarily with the hypothesis-testing and theory-building functions of comparison (see Chapter 1), while the focus is on method and not on the theories themselves.

Each chapter begins with a statement of the basic research question and what motivated its emergence in the comparative literature, followed by a comparison of the attempts to investigate the problem using the methods outlined in the first part of the book. This comparison seeks to answer several important questions. First, do the different comparisons (i.e. many countries, few countries, single-country studies) arrive at the same conclusion about the research question? If not, why not? Second, for those studies that compare few countries, is the most different systems design or most similar systems design used? And, by extension, does the choice of research design make a difference to the substantive results? Third, are the various studies cognizant of the problems of comparison outlined in the first part of the book? For example, are there enough countries in the analysis? Do the comparisons establish equivalence? Is there a problem of selection bias? Are the relationships established spurious or not? Are there value biases that taint the analysis? Are there problems with ecological or individualist fallacies? Each chapter ends with a methodological discussion and summary table that includes the method of comparison, the exemplars used in the chapter, and their main findings with regard to the research question.

Economic development and democracy

The scholarly attention devoted to the relationship between economic development and democracy was initially motivated by the search for the 'preconditions' (Karl 1990:2–3) or 'requirements' (Landman 2001) of democracy. Focusing on both the 'old' democracies in the northwest triangle of Europe and North America and the 'new' democracies in the rest of the world, this research seeks to identify the key factors that help explain both the emergence and maintenance of democracy. Among the many factors that have been identified to account for democracy, the level of economic development continues to intrigue comparativists and policy makers in the international development community. This chapter compares the key efforts that examine the link between economic development and democracy to demonstrate whether or not different methods lead to the same result. It examines studies that compare many countries, those that compare few countries, and single-country studies. The discussion of each method of comparison focuses on how different theories specify the dependent and independent variables and nature of the relationship, how the analyses measure the concepts, the different problems that the analyses encounter, and the different results they obtain.

The research problem

Are wealthy countries more democratic? If they are, why are they? Does economic development create favourable conditions for the emergence of democracy? Once democracy is established, does continued economic performance help maintain democratic institutions? The model depicted in Figure 6.1 is a simple graphical representation of this research problem. It shows that democracy is the dependent variable and economic development is the independent variable. The arrow in the figure has both a plus and minus sign above it to indicate that economic development may have either a positive or negative effect on democracy. Over the years, this model has changed very little in terms of its basic concepts and the relationship between them.

What has changed, however, are the ways in which democracy and economic development are measured, the different forms the relationship takes, the selection of countries used as evidence (Landman 1999),[1] and the methods of comparison employed to support different theories about the relationship (Rueschemeyer et al. 1992). In terms of the concepts, some scholars argue that democracy is an all or nothing affair. Either a country is democratic or it is not. Others argue that it is possible to have degrees of democracy (Przeworski and Limongi 1997; Przeworski et al. 2000). Similarly, there have been different views on what constitutes economic development. Some authors argue that economic development is best understood as economic growth, while others claim it has more to do with the distribution of income and other economic resources (Todaro 1994:14–20), or overall levels of human

Figure 6.1 Economic development and democracy

development (Ersson and Lane 1996:59; Brohman 1996). The relationship has been specified in different ways, such as linear, curvilinear, and as a 'step' function (see Briefing box 6.1). Finally, different methods of comparison focus on different aspects of the relationship. Studies that compare many countries tend to use quantitative techniques to uncover uniform patterns of variation in a small number of variables. Studies that compare few countries and single-country studies use both quantitative and qualitative techniques to uncover the more historically contingent factors that intervene between processes of economic development and democracy, and tend to couch their arguments in more 'path-dependent' language (see Briefing box 6.2).

Briefing box 6.1 Possible relationships between economic development and democracy

The relationship between economic development and democracy can assume different *functional forms*, the most common of which include linear, curvilinear, and a 'step' function.

Linear relationship

A positive linear relationship between economic development and democracy suggests that as the level of economic development increases, the likelihood that a country will be democratic also increases. Thus, if a scholar measures both concepts and plots them on a graph, the scatter of points would be around a line that rises from the lower left-hand corner to the upper right-hand corner of the graph, as depicted in Figure 6.2. Moving along the line in the figure shows that a rise in one variable is associated with a rise in the other.

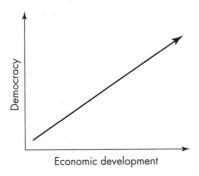

Figure 6.2 A linear relationship between economic development and democracy

Curvilinear relationship

A curvilinear relationship between economic development and democracy suggests that a positive change in economic development is accompanied by a positive

---

change in democracy, but unlike a linear relationship, the degree to which democracy increases tapers off with higher levels of economic development. In this case, there is a distinct range of economic development after which the likelihood a country becomes democratic does not change. This relationship is depicted in Figure 6.3, where this range, or 'threshold of democracy', is evident. A scatter of data points on this graph would group around the line, but it is clear from the figure that after a certain level of economic development, the level of democracy does not increase.

Figure 6.3 A curvilinear relationship between economic development and democracy

A 'step' relationship

A step-function is most different from the first two relationships. In this case, there is a distinct level of economic development after which the likelihood of a country being democratic does not change. Figure 6.4 shows that the democratic threshold is not a range of economic development, but a distinct 'take-off' point for democracy (Rostow 1961; Landman 1999)

Figure 6.4 A step relationship between economic development and democracy

Briefing box 6.2 Path-dependent arguments

A path-dependent argument focuses on the sequence of events in any given historical account. Its basic assumption is that once a particular event transpires, be it a war, election, revolution, or important decision, the course of events that succeeds it is altered forever. Consider the following two examples: an abstract example called the 'urn problem' (Jackson 1996:723) and one from political science concerning democratic consolidation (Burton et al. 1992).

First, consider an urn containing one red ball and one white ball. In the first instance, a ball is selected from the urn, then it and a ball of the same colour are placed back into the urn. If this operation is repeated a second and third time (or infinitely), the urn will develop a distribution of red and white balls that is highly dependent on the first few choices that are made. This situation is illustrated in Figure 6.5. The various possible distributions of red and white balls multiply rapidly with each successive round, but it is clear from the figure that each succeeding distribution is highly dependent on the previous round. For example, the left side of the figure shows that if a red ball is chosen on the first round, then two reds and one white are in the urn. If a red is chosen again, the urn will have three reds and a white, and so on. The bottom of the figure shows how many different types of distributions are possible, but what is clear is that the first two choices have a dramatic effect on the subsequent distributions.

Begin			R	W		
1		RRW			WWR	
2	RRRW	RRRW	WWRR	WWWR	WWWR	WWRR
3	RRRRW	WWWRR	RRRWW	WWWWWR	WWWRR	RRRWW
	(×6)	(×2)	(×2)	(×6)	(×2)	(×2)

Figure 6.5 The urn problem and path-dependence
Source: Adapted from Jackson (1996:723)

In the second example, Burton et al. (1992:23) develop a path-dependent argument to account for different types of democratic consolidation in Latin America and Southern Europe, which is illustrated in Figure 6.6.

For countries that experienced democratic transitions accompanied by popular mobilization, the figure shows initially two paths: elite settlement and mass mobilization, or no elite settlement and mass mobilization. The first path leads to stabilization, institutionalization, and consolidated democracy. The second path leads to a state of polarization between elites and masses, which in turn can lead to unconsolidated democracy, pseudo-democracy, or a reversion to authoritarianism. Crucial to their argument is that once a country reaches one of the nodes in the path,

Figure 6.6 A path-dependent argument about democratic consolidation
Source: Adapted from Burton *et al.* (1992:23)

certain outcomes are no longer available, suggesting that without an elite settlement and mass democratization, democratic consolidation is not likely. Macro-historical studies on economic development and democracy use path-dependent arguments (Moore 1966; Rueschemeyer *et al.* 1992), and such arguments can be found throughout political science, such as Collier and Collier's (1991) study of labour incorporation and regime formation in Latin America, or the historical analysis of war between countries (e.g. de Mesquita *et al.* 1997:17–19).

Comparing many countries

The initial efforts to identify a simple set of democratic preconditions compared many countries at one point in time. Seymour Martin Lipset (1959, 1960) carried out the seminal study on these preconditions by comparing 28 European and English-speaking countries with 20 Latin American countries (Lipset 1959:74). His definition of democracy is as follows:

> a political system which supplies regular constitutional opportunities for changing the governing officials. It is a social mechanism for the resolution of the problem of societal decision-making among conflicting interest groups, which permits the largest possible part of the population to influence these decisions through their ability to choose among alternative contenders for political office.
>
> (ibid.: 71)

Using this definition, Lipset then divides his sample of countries into four different groups. He divides the European and English-speaking countries into stable democracies on the one hand and unstable democracies and dictatorships on the other. He divides the Latin American countries into democracies and unstable dictatorships on the one hand and stable dictatorships on the other. For the first group, those countries that had an 'uninterrupted continuation of political democracy since World War I, and the absence over the past twenty-five years of a major political movement opposed to the democratic "rules of the game"' were considered to be democracies (ibid.: 72, emphasis in original). The Latin American countries were classified as democratic if they 'had a history of more or less free elections for most of the post-World War I period' (ibid.: 72–73).

The comparison provides a range of quantitative indicators of economic development for this sample of countries, including those for wealth, industrialization, education, and urbanization. Wealth is measured by per capita income, thousands of persons per doctor, persons per motor vehicle, telephones per 1,000 people, radios per 1,000 people, and newspaper copies per 1,000 people. Industrialization is measured by the percentage of males employed in agriculture and the per capita consumption of energy. Education is measured by the percentage of the population that is literate and enrolment in primary school, post-primary school, and higher education. Urbanization is measured by the percentage of cities with populations over 20,000, the percentage of cities with populations over 100,000, and the percentage of metropolitan areas (ibid.: 76–77). These various measures are seen as objective indicators of socio-economic development, where higher values indicate higher levels of economic development.

To demonstrate the relationship between the level of economic development and democracy, the study compares the averages of these indicators across both groups of countries. Across all these indicators, the European and English-speaking stable democracies and the Latin American democracies and unstable dictatorships score higher (or better) than their non-democratic counterparts, which means, on average, that democracies tend to have higher levels of socio-economic development than non-democracies. This pattern of results leads Lipset (ibid.: 80) to claim that all the factors 'subsumed under economic development carry with [them] the political correlate of democracy'. He also claims that the 'more well to do a nation, the more likely it will sustain democracy' (ibid.: 75). While not saying that economic development actually *causes* democracy, his study is the first to establish a correlation, or probable association, between the two, and thus paves the way for a succession of studies that seek to build on this original comparison.

Following Lipset, Cutright (1963) compares 77 countries in North America, South America, Asia, and Europe using scales of communications development, economic development, and political development. Unlike Lipset, however, he considers political development (or democracy) to exist on a continuum based on the prolonged presence of viable legislative and freely elected executive branches for the period 1940–1961. The correlation between communications development and political development is higher than that between economic development, yet both are high enough for Cutright (ibid.: 571) to conclude that there is an interdependence between political institutions and the level of social and economic development (see also Rueschemeyer *et al.* 1992:15). The overall confidence in his results leads him to predict the level of political development for the individual countries that comprise his sample based on the individual values of the various independent variables.

In responding to criticism that initial comparative efforts to examine the relationship were 'snapshot analyses', Cutright and Wiley (1969) compare 40 'self-governing' countries using data from before and after the Second World War to examine whether it can be sustained over time. Their dependent variable is political representation, which is defined as 'the extent to which the executive and legislative branches of government are subject to the demands of the non-elite population' (ibid.: 23–24). Annual scores on an index of political representation were compiled for each of four decades: 1927–1936, 1937–1946, 1947–1956, and 1957–1966. They also measure the difference between the scores for the successive decades to capture the change in political representation. Economic development is measured using the amount of energy consumed in any given year. The comparison of the 40 countries over the four decades reveals a significant and stable relationship between the level of economic development and political representation. Moreover, since the analysis uses four different time periods, Cutright and Wiley (ibid.: 29) conclude that the level of political representation is causally dependent on the level of economic development.

In *Polyarchy*, Robert Dahl (1971) seeks to formulate a classification of political forms of which democracy is one type, and then use the typology to examine the conditions that foster democracy. He conceives of democracy as having two critical dimensions: contestation and participation (ibid.: 4–9). Countries that have high levels of contestation (i.e. the degree to which members of a political system are free to contest the conduct of government) and participation (i.e. the proportion of the population entitled to participate in controlling the conduct of government) are considered 'polyarchies', or democracies. Using per capita GNP as a measure of economic development, his comparison of 118 countries and 33 polyarchies and near-polyarchies reveals a weak threshold effect (see Briefing box 6.1). In other words, countries that achieve a certain level of economic development (between 700 and 800 1957 US dollars per capita GDP) tend to be polyarchies. Dahl (ibid.: 68–69, 74) is cautious about this finding, since there are many deviant cases that have low levels of development and are polyarchies (e.g. India), or that have high levels of development and are not polyarchies (e.g. the Soviet Union and East Germany).[2] Moreover, history shows that the United States, Australia, New Zealand, Canada, Britain, Norway, and Sweden, among others, were polyarchies long before they achieved high levels of economic development (Dahl 1971:69–70; see also Rueschemeyer *et al.* 1992).

Jackman (1973:611) concentrates his comparison of 60 non-communist countries on the relationship between economic development and democracy, as well as the 'definition of democratic political development itself'. Drawing on the earlier studies conducted by Lipset (1959) and Cutright (1963), Jackman (1973) argues that democracy is best understood as a continuous rather than a dichotomous concept, and that both the linear and curvilinear forms of the relationship ought to be tested. His measure of democracy combines four indicators, including voter turnout, the competitiveness of the party voting system, the degree of electoral irregularity, and relative freedom of the press. Like Cutright and Wiley (1969), his measure of economic development is the level of energy consumption. His statistical analysis reveals that the curvilinear relationship is more significant than the linear relationship, effectively adding comparative evidence to the idea of a democratic threshold in line with Dahl (1971).

Bollen (1979) represents the last study in this earlier sample of comparative efforts that examine the relationship between economic development and democracy. In addition to focusing on the level of economic development, Bollen is also interested in the timing of development. It is possible that the countries that have developed long after those in Europe and North America may have had more difficulty in establishing democratic forms of governance (see below). For example, Britain's model of rapid economic development had profound effects on those countries that developed after it, such as France, Belgium, or the United States (ibid.: 573). When the so-called 'late developers' seek to 'catch up' to other countries in the world economy (Gerschenkron 1962), their efforts to do so may put undue pressure on their burgeoning political systems and thus lead to democratic breakdown. This type of argument suggests that countries that developed early are more likely to be democratic than those countries that developed later.

Thus, Bollen's comparison of 99 countries seeks to examine whether the level of democracy is higher in countries that developed early, whether it is higher in countries that have simply achieved better levels of economic development, or both. His index of democracy includes three indicators of popular sovereignty and three indicators of political liberties (Bollen 1979:580). Like Jackman (1973) and Cutright and Wiley (1969), the level of development is measured using energy consumption. The timing of development is measured by subtracting the starting year of development from 1966 (Bollen 1979:577). His statistical analysis reveals that the timing of development is not significant, but that the level of development has a significant and positive effect on democracy. In other words, for this sample of countries, a country's level of development, regardless of when it actually started developing, has an effect on the degree to which it is democratic.

Since this first phase of comparative work, new studies have been published that use increasingly sophisticated statistical techniques that allow scholars to compare many countries over time, thereby increasing the number of observations (see Chapters 1 and 3 in this volume). There are three notable studies that use this method of comparison. Helliwell (1994) compares 125 countries over the period 1960–1985 ($n=1,250$); Burkhart and Lewis-Beck (1994) compare 131 countries from 1972–1989 ($n= 2,358$); and Przeworski and Limongi (1997) and Przeworski et al. (2000) compare 135 countries between 1950 and 1990 ($n=4,126$). The first two studies find significant statistical evidence in support of a relationship between economic development and democracy. The third study casts serious doubt on these findings, and a comparison of all three reveals that their different results depend largely on their conceptualization of democracy and their specification of the relationship.

Helliwell (1994:226) selects a sample of countries for which 'it is possible to obtain comparable measures of per capita income and regular assessments of the extent of political and civil rights'. His index of democracy (or 'probability of political freedom') combines two separate measures of the protection of political and civil liberties[3] and ranges from low (no democracy) to high (full democracy). In addition to his measure of economic development, Helliwell (ibid.: 228–229) controls for different regional effects, including the OECD countries, the oil-producing countries of the Middle East, African countries, and Latin American countries. His statistical analysis reveals a strong positive effect of per capita income on the level of democracy.

In addition, his analysis shows positive effects for the OECD countries and Latin America, and negative effects for Africa and the Middle East. Overall, the statistical results confirm the relationship between economic development and democracy established by the comparative studies in the earlier phase.

Burkhart and Lewis-Beck (1994) use a slightly more robust collection of data than Helliwell (1994) and a similar measure of democracy ranging from low (no democracy) to high (full democracy). They use energy consumption to operationalize economic development and control for the effects of 'other social forces' and the 'world position' of the countries in the study. Other social forces are represented by past values of democracy, and the identification of a country's world position (core, semi-periphery, or periphery) is made on the basis of nine other studies (Burkhart and Lewis-Beck 1994:904–995). The results of the statistical analysis show that economic development and other social forces are positively associated with democracy, while both peripheral and semi-peripheral world positions detract from these positive effects. In other words, the effect of economic development on democracy is lower in newly developed and developing countries. By using more advanced statistical techniques than those employed by Helliwell (1994), they are able to claim with confidence that economic development causes democracy (Burkhart and Lewis-Beck 1994:907; see also Foweraker and Landman 2004).

The final studies in this section are those of Przeworski and Limongi (1997) and Przeworski *et al.* (2000), who are sceptical of the findings of earlier comparative work. They do not dispute the fact that the relationship between economic development and democracy has been demonstrated empirically, but they do object to the way in which the results have been interpreted. They classify countries according to strict rules of assessment, which include the election of the executive, the legislature, a competitive party system, and the alternation of power over time (Przeworski and Limongi 1997:178). Simple analysis reveals that the relationship between levels of economic development and democracy is strong. Rather than immediately proclaiming that economic development fosters democracy, however, they argue that 'either democracies may be more likely to emerge as countries develop economically, or they may be established independently of economic development but more likely to survive in developed countries' (ibid.: 156). Further analysis of the data that tests the likelihood of democratic transition, given levels of development, shows that 'democracies are almost certain to survive once they are established in rich countries' (ibid.: 166; Przeworski *et al.* 2000:137). Thus, a slightly different analysis/ interpretation of the empirical data avoids the strong causal language of the other two studies.

This review of studies that compare many countries reveals that there is a 'stable positive relationship between socio-economic development and democracy' (Rueschemeyer *et al.* 1992:26). The repeated empirical verification of the relationship, however, leads to two conclusions in the comparative literature. For the majority of studies, robust evidence in support of the relationship has led many to conclude that economic development causes democracy, a finding that has helped develop the 'modernization' perspective in comparative politics (see Briefing box 6.3 and Briefing Box 11.3). In this perspective, it is argued that the development of social institutions enhances the level of education of the population, improves its social and spatial mobility, and promotes the political culture that supports liberal democratic institutions (Lipset 1959; Valenzuela and Valenzuela 1978:538; Karl 1990:3; Inglehart 1997:5). The theory assumes that the process of socio-economic development is 'a progressive accumulation of social changes that ready a society to its culmination, democratization' (Przeworski and Limongi 1997:158). On the other hand, an emerging group of scholars points to the fact that while the relationship appears to hold over time and space, it may be spurious, since rich democracies tend not to collapse. This latter work has opened up a debate between those who support the idea of *endogenous democratization* versus those who support the idea of *exogenous democratization* (see Briefing box 6.3).

Briefing box 6.3 Endogenous and exogenous democratization

Within the empirical literature on democracy a significant debate has arisen as to the true causal nature of the relationship between economic development and democracy. The debate takes as its starting point the somewhat ambiguous statement made by Seymour Martin Lipset (1959:75) that the 'more well to do a nation, the more likely it will sustain democracy'. The statement is ambiguous since it does not specify whether economic development causes democracy or is a supporting condition for its long-term survival. In a subsequent article published in 1994, Lipset clarified that the correlations he found in the 1959 article and 1960 book, *Political Man* do not necessarily mean that development causes democracy. Nonetheless, scholars have sought to use increasingly sophisticated statistical analysis to uncover the true nature of the relationship.

The studies by Boix (2003) and Boix and Stokes (2003) use a pooled-cross section time-series data set that stretches back into the 19th century to capture the emergence of the so-called first and second wave democracies (see Huntington 1991), as well as the third and fourth wave democracies (see Doorenspleet 2005). The data analysis looks at the probability of a country 'switching' at different levels of economic development and they contend that their data show that economic development is a key causal condition for the emergence of democracy. They argue that these results support the general idea of *endogenous democratization*, which means economic development unleashes a set of social and economic changes that necessarily lead to democratization; a theoretical perspective that is largely in line with modernization theory (see Valenzuela and Valenzuela 1978; and Briefing box 11.3).

In contrast, studies by Przeworski and Limongi (1997) and Przeworski *et al.* (2000) use a similar data set that only includes data for the period from 1950 to 1990. They contend that one using a large data set such as theirs will always find a statistically significant relationship between the level of economic and democracy. However, they do not find any evidence of a statistically significant relationship between economic development and the *emergence* of democracy, and argue further that the probability of democratic collapse drops to near zero at high levels of economic development. In other words, for them, once democracy is established within a wealthy country, it tends not to collapse and it is this stability of democracy in rich countries that drives the overall statistical relationship. They label their theoretical perspective *exogenous democratization* since they posit that it is the presence of factors other than economic development that explains the emergence of democracy.

Both perspectives have little say over the political prospects for poor countries. There is an increasing number of 'outlier' countries in which democracy has become established and has become stable despite these countries having relatively low levels of economic development. Like the case of Costa Rica outlined in Chapter 5 of this volume, there are other cases in which democracy is flourishing under conditions of economic scarcity. For example, Mongolia has been democratic since the early 1990s when it threw off the Communist regime that had been in power since 1922. Throughout the 1990s, Mongolia privatized its economy while engaging in democratic reforms. It held competitive elections throughout the period in which the former Communists won, were displaced by an alliance of opposition parties, and then formed a grand coalition. This and other cases fit the category of 'least likely' countries since their ability to democratize without substantial progress in economic terms challenges the main tenets of the theories of endogenous and exogenous democratization.

Comparing few countries

As outlined in Chapters 2 and 4, studies that compare few countries use both quantitative and qualitative techniques. However, common to both is the intentional selection of countries for comparison based on criteria including theory, regional focus, data availability, and resources. As the review of the comparisons in this section will demonstrate, the choice of countries can affect the inferences that are drawn concerning the relationship between economic development and democracy (see also Chapter 3). This section first examines three studies that use quantitative techniques to compare few countries, namely Lerner's (1958) study of modernization in the Middle East, Neubauer's (1967) comparison of democratic development in 23 countries, and work on economic development and democracy in Latin America (Landman 1999, 2006a; Mainwaring and Perez-Liñan 2003). It then examines three qualitative studies that compare several countries, including de Schweinitz's (1964) study of industrialization and democracy in Britain, the US, Germany, and Russia. Moore's (1966) study of the 'three routes to modernity', and Rueschemeyer *et al.*'s (1992) comparison of developmental paths in advanced capitalist countries, Latin America, and the Caribbean.

Comparing few countries quantitatively

One year before Lipset (1959) provided the first cross-national study of economic development and democracy, Daniel Lerner (1958) published an ambitious study that examined patterns of modernization in the Middle East. His study starts with a comparison of 73 countries which shows a high level of association across a range of indicators of modernity, including urbanization, literacy, media participation, and political participation. This initial evidence leads him to establish such associations across a much smaller sample of countries, including Turkey, Lebanon, Jordan, Egypt, Syria, and Iran using surveys of individuals carried out by a team of country specialists. An initial combined comparison of these six countries is then followed by individual case studies of each country to identify particularities associated with each while remaining sensitive to the overall regularities that exist among them.

For Lerner (1958:89), modernization is a 'secular trend unilateral in direction-from traditional to participant lifeways'. This secular trend is characterized by physical, social, and psychic mobility whose culmination is a modern participant society with high levels of urbanism, literacy, media consumption, and an empathic capacity. While not directly assessing the connection between economic development and democracy, the study implies that democracy is the end-state for modernization and that for two of his most 'modern' societies-Turkey and Lebanon-the control of political power is decided by elections (ibid.: 84–85). History has shown, however, that both countries have had difficulty maintaining democracy as Turkey experienced military intervention in 1971 and 1980 while Lebanon suffered from civil war between 1975 and 1990. Initial comparisons of the six countries using aggregate data lead to the following ranking from low to high levels of modernization: Iran, Jordan, Syria, Egypt, Lebanon, and Turkey. This comparison is then followed by an analysis of the individual-level data from the six national surveys. Among the strongest regularities associated with modernity, Lerner (ibid.: 398–412) finds consistent patterns of happiness among urban dwellers, a decline in traditional forms of rule, increasing opportunities for both genders, and high levels of empathy, or willingness to tolerate the views of others. In the end, Turkey and Lebanon are viewed as having achieved balanced modernization, Egypt and Syria are considered to be 'out of phase', and Jordan and Iran as exhibiting no process of modernization.

The importance of Lerner's study for the comparative method is that he uses aggregate-level data and global comparisons to establish basic associations between important variables. He then uses individual-level data that measure what he believes are the key characteristics of modernity to allow intensive examination of six countries. This use of data at two levels of analysis seeks to minimize the problem of ecological fallacy (see Chapter 2 in this volume). His analysis has not 'proved' the theory of modernization, but has 'only explained and exemplified the regularities it posits', which for him are 'only more plausible hypotheses than they were before' (ibid.: 398). As the comparisons of many countries outlined above have demon-strated, considerable scholarly effort has been devoted to examining more fully the implications of these hypotheses. And as the comparisons of few countries reviewed below will demonstrate, the verification of these hypotheses is by no means a settled matter.

Drawing on the insights of the comparison of many and few countries, Neubauer (1967) compares 23 countries using an index of democratic development and indicators of economic development. The index of democratic development combines four indicators 'which measure the relative amount of *electoral equality* and *competition* present in a given political system' (ibid.: 1004–1005). He uses the same indicators of economic development as those employed by Cutright. The main difference between his study and those that compare many countries is the size of his sample. Neubauer (ibid.: 1006) argues that the 'data necessary for the democratic performance indicator come only from democratic countries', and that the findings of the comparison of many countries ought to hold for his smaller sample. His comparison of the 23 democracies reveals that there is 'simply no relationship between [the] level of democratic performance and measures of socio-economic development' (ibid.: 1007). His only significant correlation is between the level of communication and democratic performance. Overall, he concludes that there may be some threshold effect between economic development and democracy, but that for democratic countries, higher levels of economic development do not lead to improved democratic performance (ibid.: 1007).

Similar work in this area examines the relationship using a smaller sample of countries confined geographically to Latin America (Landman 1999; 2006a; Mainwaring and Perez-Liñan 2003). Seventeen Latin American countries are compared over the period 1972–1995 (Landman 1999), 1976–2000 (Landman 2006a) and for a much longer time series dating back to the 1940s (Mainwaring and Perez-Liñan 2003). Like Neubauer (1967), these three studies argue that the findings of the global comparisons ought to hold for smaller groups of countries, particularly those with great variation in both economic development and democracy. Unlike Neubauer's study, the countries in the sample are geographically proximate and culturally similar, therefore fitting squarely in the most similar systems design (see Chapter 2 and Chapter 4). The comparison controls for the cultural commonality of the region (similar Iberian heritage and patterns of economic development), and some of the models specify further controls for sub-regional differences between the Southern Cone and Central America, both of which had somewhat different patterns of development and democracy during the period. The statistical analysis tests for both the linear and non-linear forms of relationship, and finds no significant effects between economic development and democracy.[4] Thus, this smaller sample of most similar countries acts a 'most likely' test that infirms the theoretical propositions that have received strong empirical support at the global level of analysis.

Taken together, these studies use the quantitative techniques of those studies that compare many countries, but confine their comparisons to a smaller selection of countries. It is clear that the comparison over a smaller selection of countries produces different results, but in both examples, selection of the countries was not dependent on the outcome that is to be explained. Lerner (1958) uses his initial extensive comparison as a preliminary guide to his more intensive inquiry into the six case studies, but he maintains a large number of observations by using individual-level data. Neubauer's (1967) comparison across democracies and the time-series comparison of Latin American countries reveal no relationship between economic development and democracy. But are these results simply a product of the sample size, or are there theoretical and historical reasons for raising doubts about the association between economic development and democracy? The review of studies that compare few countries qualitatively seeks to provide some answers to this important question.

Comparing few countries qualitatively

The starting point for this group of qualitative macro-historical studies is to uncover the causal factors inside the 'black box' of the relationship between economic development and democracy (Rueschemeyer *et al.* 1992:29). While accepting some of the theoretical assumptions of the global comparisons, and arguing that at best the positive and significant statistical results they obtain are empirical generalizations (ibid.: 30), these studies seek to identify key intervening variables that help 'unpack' the relationship. These variables include the timing and nature of economic development, the strength and coalitions of different social classes, the strength and nature of the state, and important transnational factors in the form of wars and economic depressions. In this way, these studies emphasize the processes involved in the development of democracy over the *longue durée* (Rustow 1970). As these studies necessarily develop more complex and less parsimonious explanations than the global comparisons, they are discussed at greater length.

In *Industrialization and Democracy*, de Schweinitz (1964:7) argues that 'the rise of the democratic political community has been associated with industrialization and economic growth'; however, these must be seen as 'necessary but not sufficient' conditions for the emergence of democracy. For him democracy is 'a system in which the problems of government are resolved on the basis of an appeal to the preferences of autonomous individuals', through periodic use of a majority voting mechanism open to the adult population (ibid.: 14–15). This democratic system requires rational individuals capable of making appropriate choices and a general consensus on fundamental values in society (ibid.: 23), the cultivation of which depends highly upon high levels of education and income. The key question for de Schweinitz (ibid.: 34) is 'How may economic growth which is a process by which an economy passes from a subsistence to a high-income status economy democratize political systems which initially are nondemocratic?' The answer to this question lies in comparing the historical experiences with economic development and democratization in Britain, the US, Germany, and Russia.

The comparison begins with Britain, since it is seen as the first country to have undergone rapid industrialization and the development of democratic political institutions. Implicit throughout the comparisons is that the British experience somehow radiates out across Europe and North America, effectively offering the countries that comprise these regions a model for growth and governance. The key to explaining British success is the fact that the process of economic development was achieved autonomously, as opposed to being a state-led process. This process of autonomous growth resulted in the rise of the middle class, a well-tamed and well-managed and organized labour force, and the piecemeal installation of democracy, which 'did not have to be sacrificed at the altar of economic growth' (ibid.: 128). What is clear in the British case is that it was not fully democratic before the industrial revolution in the middle of the eighteenth century, but that the process of industrialization unleashed the necessary social forces to realize democracy by the middle of the nineteenth century.

The establishment of democracy in the United States had many factors in its favour that were absent in Britain. It possessed vast amounts of space, a favourable climate, and abundant natural resources, and perhaps most importantly, the American

Revolution meant that those pro-democratic forces in this new country did not have the vestiges of a feudal order with which to contend (de Schweinitz 1964:130 after Hartz 1955). In contrast to Britain, where democratization of the political process grew out of industrialization, the political institutions in the United States had to be created to restrain the democratic impulse while unleashing the forces of economic growth (de Schweinitz 1964:142). Like Britain, however, economic growth in the United States was produced autonomously and the period of rapid industrialization did not occur until after the Civil War. For de Schweinitz (ibid.: 148–152), there are several other conditions favourable to the establishment of democracy in the United States, including better working conditions for labourers, lower economic expectations and ethnic differentiation of immigrant groups, a strong political culture of individualism, and the overall size of the continental land mass, all of which helped overcome the 'welfare problem' created by the process of industrialization.

In contrast to the gradual installation of democracy in Britain and the relatively 'easy history' of the United States, de Schweinitz (ibid.: 159) argues that the German experience bore the heavy weight of history, which had created the need for a strong centralized state to unify its diverse political units in the latter half of the nineteenth century. By the First World War, Germany's rapid industrialization had outpaced that of Britain, but both the war and the subsequent rise to power of Hitler appear to have confounded the hypothesis about autonomous economic growth and democracy (ibid.: 184). This apparently deviant case is explained away with reference to a certain British 'exceptionalism'. At a comparable stage of development, Britain was not fully democratic but had over half a century of peace for democratic practices to flourish. Germany had a different historical legacy than Britain, which had created more formidable obstacles to democratization, and Britain was not as susceptible to political developments and crises on the continent. It is important to note that global comparisons treat deviant cases as a normal occurrence where they simply are outliers to a standard distribution of outcomes. In this comparison, de Schweinitz (1964) is at pains to explain why Germany did not achieve stable democracy by the dawn of the twentieth century. The difference between these two styles of analysis will be addressed further in the summary that follows.

The final case in this study is Russia, which was more underdeveloped and had less access to natural resources than the other cases, did not experience spontaneous and autonomous development, and was more open to foreign invasion. Moreover, the lack of growth of a middle class and the persistence of a system of serfdom further hindered any moves toward democracy. Although Russia achieved rapid industrialization towards the end of the nineteenth century, de Schweinitz (1964) argues that Marxist ideology became an important factor in shaping its subsequent history. Ultimately Russia forms a one-party state with no legitimate opposition. Paradoxically, there is no explanation for the Russian Revolution of 1917. Rather, it becomes a new factor that helps explain its lack of democracy. In the end, Russia and Germany had both late and less autonomous economic development, and either limited or no experience with democracy, while Britain and the US experienced autonomous economic development and the development of fundamental values that fostered the growth of democracy. These comparisons are summarized in Table 6.1.

Such qualitative comparison of a few countries allows de Schweinitz to concentrate on historical sequences and factors unique to the individual cases while

Table 6.1 A summary of de Schweinitz's (1964) *Industrialization and Democracy*

Case	Britain	US	Germany	Russia
Character of economic development	Early autonomous economic development	Autonomous economic development	Late industrialization, partly state-led	Late industrialization, not autonomous
Unique features	Isolated geographically	Space, climate, natural resources	Heavy weight of history	Limited access to natural resources
	Peaceful half century	No feudal past	Strong centralized state	Centralized state and persistence of serfdom
Social class development	Large middle class	Large middle class	Large but alienated middle class	No large middle class
	Strong labour movement	Weak labour movement	Strong labour movement	Small working class
Political culture	Liberal individualism	Rugged individualism	Lack of individualism	Marxist ideology
Outcome	Democracy	Democracy	Unstable democracy	No democracy

drawing larger inferences about the more general relationship between development and democracy. He stresses that his research design and method 'raise the possibility that a unique configuration of historical conditions relating to the availability of natural resources, the mobility of the population, ideology, and the locus and sequence of development, accounted for the emergence of the democratic political order' (ibid.: 269). Overall, the key obstacles to successful democratization are late development and state-centred growth. In drawing inferences beyond the confines of his four-country comparison, de Schweinitz (ibid.: 11) argues that the 'Euro-American route to democracy is closed' and that countries developing in the twentieth century must find other means for establishing democratic political institutions.

In *The Social Origins of Dictatorship and Democracy*, Barrington Moore (1966) extends the comparison of democratic and non-democratic outcomes found in de Schweinitz (1964) to a larger group of countries, including Britain, France, the United States, Japan, India, and China; he also makes implicit comparisons with Germany and Russia. Like de Schweinitz, Moore seeks to understand the relationship between processes of economic development and political form through comparing few countries. These comparisons 'serve as a rough negative check on accepted historical explanations. And a comparative approach may lead to new historical generalizations' (Moore 1966: xiii). Like de Schweinitz (1964), he believes that certain political outcomes are the product of discrete historical configurations, which may not be repeated. His comparisons reveal three 'routes to the modern world': (1) bourgeois revolutions and democracy, (2) revolution from above and fascism, and (3) revolution from below and communism. The central categories of comparison include economic development, state structures, and social classes.

The democratic route to modern society was achieved in Britain, France, and the United States. The Puritan Revolution (English Civil War), the French Revolution, and the American Civil War are seen as events that altered dramatically the developmental paths these three countries would take. The process of economic development was accompanied by a balance of power between the crown and the landed nobility. The development of commercial agriculture weakened the role of the landed upper classes, while building the ranks of the bourgeoisie, which for Moore (1966:418) was critical for the development of democracy: 'No bourgeois, no democracy.' There was no coalition between the landed upper classes and the bourgeoisie against the interests of peasants and workers. Finally, all three cases had a *revolutionary break with the past* (ibid.: 431). The Puritan Revolution altered forever the role of the monarchy in Britain, while the French Revolution abolished royal absolutism and established the political rights of modern citizenship.[5] While the American Revolution initially removed the role of the British crown, the American Civil War broke the landed upper classes and so paved the way for the continued growth of industrial capitalism. In this way, Moore (1966) argues that all three historical events were bourgeois revolutions, the conditions of which were made possible by economic development, and the resolution of which ultimately led to the establishment of liberal democracy.

The fascist and 'top-down' route to modern society is illustrated through a detailed analysis of Japanese history that is compared implicitly to that of Germany. In both countries, Moore (ibid.: 437) argues that the development of the commercial and industrial class was too weak and dependent to take power on its own and it therefore forged coalitions with the landed upper classes and royal bureaucracy, 'exchanging the right to rule for the right to make money'. This coalition against the interests of peasants and workers was supported by a strong state that provides trade protection and labour control. Any experiments with democracy soon disappeared as they were ultimately not to the liking of the landed upper classes and 'fascist repression is the final outcome' (Rueschemeyer *et al.* 1992:24).

The communist route in both Russia and China has four main causal factors. Both countries had a highly centralized state and a landed upper class, both of which repressed the labour force, which was the essential means of economic development at that time. The lack of commercial agriculture meant that only a weak bourgeoisie developed, which was not strong enough either to confront the strong land-owning class or the crown (as in Britain and France). Both societies had a mass peasantry that showed great potential for collective action. Thus, the 'absence of a commercial revolution in agriculture led by the upper classes and the concomitant survival of peasant social institutions' provided the social and political backdrop for communist revolution (Moore 1966:477). The failure of the landed upper classes to maintain institutional links with the peasantry and their continued exploitation of the peasants created the conditions by which the agrarian bureaucracies in Russia and China were ultimately overthrown.

Table 6.2 summarizes Moore's (1966) three routes to modernity, including the character of economic development, the nature of the emergent class coalitions, the role of the state, and the different political outcomes. Most striking is the fact that democracy is seen to be the product of a violent break with the past, not a gradual installation of a political form as the result of incremental advances in the process of economic development. The beheading of Charles I in Britain, the execution of Louis XVI in France, and the Union Army's defeat of the Confederates in the United States all serve as radical events that altered fundamentally the social,

Table 6.2 Moore's (1966) three routes to modern society

	I *Britain, France, United States (India)*	II *Germany, Italy, Japan*	III *Russia, China*
Character of economic development	Development of commercial agriculture	Development of commercial agriculture	No development of commercial agriculture
Class development and coalitions	Weakening of landed aristocracy	Strong land-owning class	Strong land-owning class
	Balance of power between crown and landed aristocracy (in Britain, France, and India)	Coalition of powerful land-owning class and weak, dependent bourgeoisie	Weak bourgeoisie
	Absence of aristocratic–bourgeois coalition against peasants and workers		Mass peasantry with capacity for collective action
Role of the state		Strong state that provides trade protection, manages industrialization, and controls labour	Centralized state and labour repression
	Revolutionary and violent break with the past		
Outcome	Capitalist parliamentary democracy	Capitalist fascism	Communism

Source: Adapted from Moore (1966)

economic, and political conditions that made democracy possible. Like de Schweinitz (1964), Moore (1966) is keen to point out that the constellation of events that led to these democratic outcomes was by no means inevitable, and that any one of these three societies (given a slightly different set of events), could have ended up taking one of the other two routes to the modern world.

In response to some of the limitations of both these two key qualitative studies and the quantitative global comparisons, Rueschemeyer *et al.* (1992) extend the analysis of the relationship between economic development and democracy. They accept that the global comparisons yield empirical generalizations, but like de Schweinitz (1964) and Moore (1966), they seek to examine the historical sequences that comprise the links between development and democracy. In contrast to de Schweinitz and Moore, they expand the number of countries to include smaller advanced countries of Europe, Britain's settler colonies, and countries in Latin America and the Caribbean. In contrast to Moore (1966), they emphasize the role of the working class and the importance of international factors, which they claim are lacking from his analysis. They thus focus on the meaning of democracy and its relation to social inequality, social class divisions, the role of the state, and transnational power constellations (Rueschemeyer *et al.* 1992:40). Due to the length and complexity of their study, the following review will sketch out in skeletal fashion the main points of the comparative analysis and subsequent argument.

The first part of the study compares the experiences with development and democracy in seventeen advanced countries, including Sweden, Denmark, Norway, Switzerland, Belgium, The Netherlands, France, Britain, the United States, Australia, Canada, New Zealand, Austria-Hungary, Spain, Italy, and Germany. The goal of the comparison is to identify the key variables that help explain prolonged periods of democracy, unstable periods of democracy, and authoritarianism in all these countries. All of them underwent some form of capitalist development, and most experienced the rapid development of industrial capitalism in the latter half of the nineteenth century.

Despite this similar set of starting conditions, some countries (Austria-Hungary, Spain, Italy, and Germany) were unable to sustain democracy through the inter-war years. Thus, the comparisons seek to explain these differences in outcome.

Like Moore (1966), the analysis stresses the importance of the strength of different social classes, including the agrarian elite, the bourgeoisie, and the working class. Except for Britain, the United States, and Australia, a strong agrarian elite stood as a key obstacle to democratization. In these exceptional cases, other important factors such as an autonomous state, a strong working class, and the legacy of British institutional practices in its former colonies helped attenuate this anti-democratic tendency within the *agrarian* elite. Elsewhere, a weak agrarian elite coupled with the presence of a strong bourgeoisie meant that the chances for sustaining democracy remained very high. The comparisons also reveal that historically it has been the working class that has been the main agent of democratization in the advanced countries. While certain elements in the middle class have supported democratic ideals, it has been the push for inclusion through the extension of rights by the working class that has made the key difference to the realization of liberal democracy in these countries (Rueschemeyer *et al.* 1992:97–98). Moreover, the inclusion in the comparison of the smaller democracies demonstrated that democracy is not dependent on a revolutionary break with the past as Moore (1966) maintained.

The authoritarian countries had a different set of experiences. They industrialized later than the democratic countries and had a strong agrarian elite. This elite formed a coalition with the bourgeoisie and the state that oversaw labour-repressive agricultural practices and the establishment of a certain authoritarian ideological hegemony, which manifested itself in fascist tendencies inimical to the development of democracy. Like Moore (1966), Rueschemeyer *et al.* (1992) suggest that the conditions for authoritarianism existed in countries that managed to avoid it. They insist that the United States was not fully democratic until the passage of the 1965 Voting Rights Act, which extended suffrage to African-Americans in the former Confederate states. In contrast to Moore (1966), they argue that the Civil War helped establish democracy in the north and the west, but the south was characterized by the re-institution of authoritarian practices dominated by a strong agrarian elite (Rueschemeyer *et al.* 1992:122–132, 148). These different historical trajectories are summarized in Table 6.3, including the nature of development, the strength of classes and class alliances, and the role of the state.

The comparison of the Latin American countries begins with the basic premise that they developed differently than the advanced countries in two major respects. The process of development was initiated much later than in the advanced countries and succeeded a period of growth that was highly dependent on the export of primary products particularly vulnerable to changing market conditions. The key determinants for the emergence of democracy in the first half of the twentieth century include the consolidation of state power, the nature of the export economy (mineral vs. agricultural), the strength and timing of the process of industrialization, and the agent of political articulation of the subordinate classes. Early consolidation of state power institutionalizes contestation among competing groups and ends overt challenges to the authority of the state. Mineral and agricultural export expansion developed different sets of social classes, which articulated their demands in different types of political party organizations; clientelistic parties developed in the agricultural countries while mass radical parties developed in the mineral countries. An early initialization of the process of industrialization breaks the landed classes and produces an active and strong subordinate class that can attract some middleclass support. The presence of two powerful political parties that seek to mediate competing interests in society helps foster democracy (Rueschemeyer *et al.* 1992: 197–199). Clientelistic parties that help channel the demands of the subordinate classes are seen as less threatening to elites. Taken together (see Table 6.4), these factors greatly enhance the chances of democratization in the region.

After the period of initial democratization, all of the countries in the comparison experienced breakdowns of democracy in one form or another. Some saw a collapse into civil war (Colombia and Venezuela), while others saw the rise of military authoritarianism (e.g. Brazil 1964–1985; Argentina 1966–1973, 1976–1983; Uruguay 1973–1984; and Chile 1973–1990). For Rueschemeyer *et al.* (1992: 216) the key to maintaining democracy and political stability is an institutionalized party system that protects the interests of elites (see Chapter 10). In addition to the weakness of party systems and the breakdown of democracy, they also stress the fact that the nature of the military and its relationship to the civilian world are different

Table 6.3 Conditions for democracy and authoritarianism in advanced countries

	Sweden, Denmark, Norway, Switzerland, Belgium, The Netherlands, France	Britain	United States, Australia	Canada, New Zealand	Austria-Hungary Spain Italy Germany
Development	Rapid development of industrial capitalism in latter half of 19th cent.	Rapid development of industrial capitalism in latter half of 19th cent.	Rapid development of industrial capitalism in latter half of 19th cent. in US only		Late industrialization
Classes	Weak agrarian elite Strong bourgeoisie Strong working class No labour-repressive agriculture	Strong agrarian elite Strong bourgeoisie Strong working class No labour-repressive agriculture	Strong agrarian elite Strong bourgeoisie Weak working class Autonomous state Labour-repressive agriculture	Weak agrarian elite Strong bourgeoisie Autonomous state No labour-repressive agriculture	Strong agrarian elite Strong bourgeoisie (except Germany) Agrarian elite–bourgeoisie–state alliance Labour-repressive agriculture
History	Revolutionary break from the past only in France	Revolutionary break from the past	Vast supplies of cheap land British colonial influence: representative government & suffrage Revolutionary break from the past (except Australia)	Vast supplies of cheap land British colonial influence: representative government & suffrage No revolutionary break from the past	Authoritarian ideological hegemony No revolutionary break from the past
Outcome	Democracy	Democracy	Democracy	Democracy	Authoritarianism

Source: Rueschemeyer et al. (1992: 79–154)

Table 6.4 Development and initial democratization in Latin America

	Uruguay, Argentina	Colombia, Ecuador	Brazil	Bolivia, Venezuela	Chile, Peru	Mexico	Paraguay
Development	Export expansion	Export expansion	Export expansion	Export expansion	Export expansion	Export expansion	No export expansion
	Agriculture	Agriculture	Agriculture	Mineral	Mineral	Mineral	Agriculture
	Non-labour-intensive	Labour-intensive	Labour-intensive				Labour-intensive
Mobilizing agent	Clientelistic parties	Clientelistic parties	State	Radical mass parties	Radical mass parties	Revolution	State
Industrialization	Before 1930	After 1945	1930–1945	After 1945	After 1945	Before 1930	After 1945
Initial democracy	Before 1930	1930–1945 Ecuador after 1945	1945–1964	1930–1945 Bolivia after 1945	1930; 1930–1945 for Peru		
Outcome	Full stable democracy	Restricted stable democracy	Restricted stable democracy	Full unstable democracy	Restricted unstable democracy	Authoritarianism	Authoritarianism
	> 12 yrs	> 12 yrs	> 12 yrs	< 12 yrs	< 12 yrs		

Source: Rueschemeyer et al. (1992: 159–199)

for Latin America, leading to frequent, and in some cases, long interventions into the political sphere. In sum, if the social and political forces unleashed by economic development are not channelled in such a way that the threat to elites is sufficiently minimized, the likelihood of democracy surviving during this period is very limited indeed.

This basic explanation for democracy holds in the comparisons of Central America and the Caribbean, with the added effects of the British colonial experience. Except for Costa Rica, the Central American cases have had difficulty in establishing organizations within civil society and representatives of the subordinate classes that are strong enough to counter an elite-dominated state, leading to a history of civil war, political instability, and repression (Rueschemeyer *et al.* 1992:259). Moreover, the heavy presence of US intervention has tended to strengthen the repressive apparatus of the state in these countries. In the Caribbean countries, the agrarian elite did not control the state during the period in which groups in civil society were forming, and by the time these countries achieved independence, both political parties and unions were well established (ibid.: 260).

It is clear from the examination of these various studies that the comparison of few countries offers different analytical opportunities for scholars. This method of comparison allows the intensive examination of individual countries and more focus on the differences between countries in order to explain the ways in which economic development may or may not foster democracy. A small number of countries allows the comparison to highlight historical sequences, and the importance of specific historical events on the subsequent chances of establishing democracy, including wars, revolutions, and economic crises. The difference in results between these studies and those that compare many countries regarding the relationship between economic development and democracy awaits final discussion, as it is important to consider a few single-country studies on this topic from the field.

Single-country studies

Clearly, there are likely to be as many (if not more) single-country studies as there are countries in the world that seek to explain paths of development and their relationship to democracy. From Tocqueville's classic study of democracy in the United States to the latest single-country studies of democratization, the field of comparative politics is replete with examples of such studies. As outlined in the previous chapter, among their many different functions single-country studies can confirm existing theories, infirm existing theories, or generate new hypotheses. Thus, this section presents some recent efforts to relate economic development and democracy at the single-country level that serve any or all of these comparative purposes. Moreover, they all in some way use the comparative categories and explanation found in the preceding studies. The studies in this section include Putnam's (1993) study of democratic institutional performance in Italy, Waisman's (1989) study of Argentina, and three case studies on Botswana, South Korea, and India found in Leftwich's (1996) *Democracy and Development*.

In *Making Democracy Work*, Putnam (1993a) offers a single-country study of Italy that compares democratic institutional performance across its twenty administrative regions using quantitative and qualitative research techniques. Putnam (1993a:63–82) establishes a measure of democratic institutional performance, which is an index at the regional level that combines twelve indicators of policy processes, policy pronouncements, and policy implementation. These indicators include cabinet stability, budget promptness, statistical and informational services, reform legislation, legislative innovation, the provision of daycare centres, the number of family clinics, industrial policy instruments, agricultural spending capacity, local health unit expenditures, housing and urban development, and bureaucratic responsiveness (ibid.: 65–73). This combined index then serves as the key dependent variable for the remainder of the study.

Geographically, the level of democratic institutional performance is higher in the northern regions of Italy than in the southern regions. Drawing on many of the same studies reviewed in this chapter, Putnam (ibid.: 83–86) initially posits that the level of socio-economic modernization accounts for the differences in institutional performance that he observes. A simple analysis that compares measures of economic development (per capita income, gross regional product, and agricultural and industrial shares of the workforce and value added) and institutional performance reveals that those regions with higher levels of economic development have higher levels of institutional performance (ibid.: 85). Moreover, these levels of economic development are higher in the north than in the south. Closer inspection of the figures, however, reveals that within either the north or the south, the relationship drops out. In other words, economic development goes some way towards explaining differences in institutional performance *between* regions, but it cannot account for differences *within* the north or the south.

Putnam suspects that the simple relationship between economic development and institutional performance is spurious, and the paradox identified for the north–south divide leads him to look for some other factor that may help explain institutional performance in Italy. The answer for Putnam lies in the history of civic involvement in Italy: a slow process of accumulation that begins in medieval times and extends to modern-day Italy (ibid.: 121–162). Civic involvement consists in

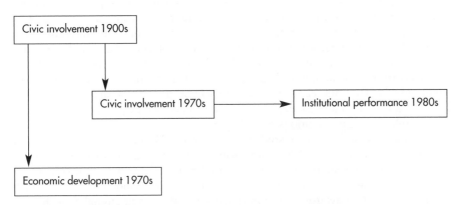

Figure 6.7 Explaining democratic institutional performance in Italy
Source: Adapted from Putnam (1993:157)

active participation in public affairs, the development of ideas of political equality, solidarity, trust, tolerance, and the formation of voluntary associations (ibid.: 86–91). When the effects of this additional factor are analysed, the direct relationship between economic development and institutional performance disappears. In its place, Putnam (ibid.: 157) specifies a model (see Figure 6.7) that establishes a link between past civic involvement (1900s) to civic involvement and socio-economic development in the 1970s. The level of civic involvement in the 1970s is related to democratic institutional performance in the 1980s.

Waisman's (1989:59) study of Argentina opens with a key question: 'Why did this country fail to become an industrial democracy?' He shows that between 1900 and the Great Depression, Argentina experienced growth rates in per capita GNP that were higher than growth rates in Sweden and France. On the eve of the Great Depression, per capita GNP was higher than that in Austria and Italy. And by the mid-1940s, the country had higher levels of urbanization than the United States and most of Europe (ibid.: 61–63). Throughout this period, Argentina saw the emergence of restricted liberal democracy with the beginnings of an institutionalized political party system, but by 1930 democracy collapsed and would only make fleeting returns from this year until its full re-emergence in 1983 (see also Chapter 9 in this volume). Between 1930 and 1983, the country saw six major military coups, 22 years of military rule, and 25 presidents, eighteen of whom were elected and subsequently overthrown between 1955 and 1983. The country's spectacular economic performance also collapsed by the middle of the century. Growth rates fell to 0.9 per cent in the 1950s, 2.8 per cent in the 1960s, 2.3 per cent in the 1970s, and negative levels in the 1980s, so that between 1950 and 1983, the country experienced only an average of 1 per cent growth (ibid.: 62).

To explain the fluctuations in the experience of democracy in Argentina, Waisman (1989) uses similar analytical categories to those found in Rueschemeyer et al. (1992). He argues that the emergence and stability of democracy in the first period (1900–1930) were due first to a high and sustained rate of economic growth. The expansion during this period allowed for the 'absorption of mass immigration, rapid urbanization and industrialization, expansion of education, and high standards of living for the lower classes'. Second, middle-class demands for participation and intense labour mobilization were absorbed by elites through inclusionary strategies (Waisman 1989:84). He argues that the subsequent periods of authoritarianism were largely due to the emergence of an autonomous developmental state and the presence of entrenched economic elites who opposed the interests of the subordinate classes as well as the representation of all interests through democratic political institutions (ibid.: 85–97). This study can be read alongside Hawkins' (2001) study of Cuba, since it too is a case of failure to make a transition to democracy given the presence of favourable economic conditions (see Chapter 5).

The three separate case studies of Botswana (Holm 1996), India (Kaviraj 1996), and South Korea (Moon and Kim 1996) show great variation in both economic development and experiences with democracy. Holm (1996) argues that Botswana has had a developing economy and an emerging democracy for over thirty years. From 1965 onwards, the country has seen 10 per cent annual growth rates based on a mineral economy that has diversified into producing coal, soda ash, and manufactured products. It has a hybrid presidential-parliamentary democracy and well-developed bureaucracy (due to the British colonial experience 1885–1965). In terms of free elections and the protection of political liberties, Botswana meets the criteria of a democracy as found in the global comparisons reviewed above (ibid.: 103). Despite this seeming association between economic development and democracy, Holm is keen to point out that Botswana still only has formal democracy, and that the society remains characterized by government secrecy and low accountability, weak opposition parties, and an underdeveloped civil society. For Holm (ibid.: 98, 107) the key intervening variable that lies between economic development and democracy is Tswana political culture, which maintains authoritarian and hierarchical patterns of organization, and tends to separate the activities of civil society and politics.

Like Moore (1966), Kaviraj (1996) argues that the temporal sequence of the relation between economic development and democracy is different for India than for the patterns observed in Europe. The secularization of politics, the individuation of civil society, and the development of a modern capitalist economy preceded the development of democracy in the West. In India these processes all happened at the same time. Thus, the development of democracy has altered but not displaced traditional identities based on the caste system and religious divisions. A formalized and 'modern' redefinition of the caste system has profound implications for the distribution of the economic goods of development as well as the definition of the proper activities for political and economic actors in society (ibid.: 132–133). Moreover, the case of India illustrates that both the process of economic development and democracy can raise expectations within a society as well as threaten political stability (ibid.: 133–134).

The final case of South Korea appears as the model of successful modernization. As in Botswana, it has maintained 10 per cent growth rates since 1965, a process of development which has also been accompanied by a reasonably equitable distribution of economic resources (Moon and Kim 1996:139). Politically, however, the country has seen the repressive Yushin regime in the 1970s, the quasi-military rule of Chun Doo Hwan in the 1980s, a period of democratic transition between 1988 and 1992, and its first free and fair elections only in 1992 (ibid.: 140). Thus, the successful model of economic growth has been accompanied by a long period of non-democratic rule. Moon and Kim (ibid.: 148) attribute the transition to democracy and the subsequent period of democratic consolidation to sustained economic growth, which has been mediated by two further important factors. Economic development has altered the distribution of power in society and this has favoured the emergence of democracy. Following Inglehart (1990), they argue that economic development has changed Korean political culture by replacing traditional conservative and authoritarian values with modern and participant values.

Summary

Table 6.5 summarizes the 'comparison of comparisons' on the relationship between economic development and democracy presented in this chapter. There appears to be a contradiction between the main findings of those studies that compare many countries and those that either compare a few countries or those that study one country. On balance, the comparison of many countries at one time or over time reveals a strong positive effect between the level of economic development and democracy. Some of these comparisons claim that the two phenomena are associated with each other, others argue that they are causally related, while others contend that the positive relationship is due to the fact that once established, wealthy democracies tend not to collapse. In contrast, the comparison of few countries and single-country studies claim that the relationship between economic development and democracy is mediated by other important factors, such as class structures, the nature of economic development, the role of the state, important historical events, political culture, and international factors.

The different conclusions reached by different methods raise an important question. Is there something wrong methodologically with each major type of comparison? The short answer is no. As Part I of this book argued, each method of comparison is useful for drawing inferences, and as the review of comparisons here demonstrated, scholars interested in this research question have used different methods precisely to redress problems of earlier studies, draw stronger inferences, and test different theories. A longer answer suggests that there are three factors inherent in these comparisons that account for the difference in result, including the role of historical time, the selection of cases, and the different emphasis put on similarities and differences between countries. This concluding section will discuss these in turn.

The global comparisons assume that all countries are on a common trajectory that extends from a 'traditional' end to a 'modern' one, which suggests that sooner or later, any country at any time will necessarily make this transition. Comparisons of many countries at one point in time imply this trajectory, since each country in their sample is located at a different point along this trajectory. Later global comparisons reacted to this criticism by comparing over time and space, and Bollen (1979) controlled for the effects of the timing of development. Studies that compare few countries argue that the inclusion of both time and the timing of development are not enough, since these factors still ignore the importance of history. These studies argue that specific historical events and the contingent concatenation of these events affect the nature of the traditional–modern trajectory implied by the global comparisons. In the 1960s, countries were undergoing the process of development after the Russian, Mexican, Chinese, and Cuban revolutions, all of which demonstrated different developmental trajectories than those assumed by the global comparisons.

The importance of historical time and the emphasis on historical sequences are necessarily related to the selection of cases, which is in turn related to the difference in results for the comparisons examined in this chapter. Thus, Neubauer (1967) compares only democracies, since he seeks to measure democratic development. Lerner (1958), Landman (1999, 2006a), and Mainwaring and Perez-Liñan (2003) compare countries that share geographical proximity and cultural similarities. Both de Schweinitz (1964) and Moore (1966) choose countries based on the key outcomes of democracy, fascism, and communism. Neubauer (1967), de Schweinitz (1964), and Moore (1966) all have problems with selection bias since the choice of cases is determined by the dependent variable (see Chapter 3). Lerner's (1958) study of the Middle East and the studies on Latin America do not have problems with selection

Table 6.5 Economic development and democracy in comparative perspective

Method of comparison	Number of countries	Exemplars	Result
Many countries	Between 48 and 135 either at one point in time or over time	Lipset 1959; Cutright 1963; Cutright and Wiley 1969; Dahl 1971; Jackman 1973; Bollen 1979; Helliwell 1994; Burkhart and Lewis-Beck 1994; Boix 2003; Boix and Stokes 2003	Weak version: democracy is associated with development; Strong version: development causes democracy
		Przeworski and Limongi 1997; Przeworski et al., 2000	Once established, wealthy democracies tend not to collapse
Few countries (quantitative)	Between 6 and 23 either at one point in time or over time	Lerner 1958; Neubauer 1967; Landman 1999, 2006; Mainwaring and Perez-Liñan 2002	For Lerner, modernity associated with democracy; for Neubauer, Landman, Mainwaring and Perez-Liñan no relationship exists
Few countries qualitative)	Between 4 and 37 countries over time	De Schweinitz 1964; Moore 1966; Rueschemeyer et al. 1992	Democracy is a product of discrete historical events that are not likely to be repeated in the future
Single-country studies	One country over time	Waisman 1989a; Putnam 1993a; Holm 1996; Kaviraj 1996; Moon and Kim 1996	Country-specific factors, particularly political culture, condition the relationship

bias since their choice of countries is not related to the dependent variable. In similar fashion, Rueschemeyer *et al.* (1992) avoid selection bias by comparing all the countries in each of their clusters (i.e. advanced countries, Latin America, Central America and the Caribbean). Indeed, by looking at the smaller democracies of the advanced world, they rule out a revolutionary break with the past as a significant explanatory variable for democracy. Even when selection bias is avoided, the selection of cases still helps explain the difference in results between the global comparisons and those that examine a smaller number of countries. The global comparisons concentrate their efforts on the regularities that hold across a large sample. Deviant cases are a natural occurrence in large samples, while the goal of the analysis is to demonstrate the commonality across the countries.

In contrast, studies that compare few countries place more emphasis on the differences across the countries. These studies demonstrate that the relationship between economic development and democracy does not hold for all countries. The global comparativists would not disagree; they would merely reply that the relationship does hold more often than not. Thus, the differences in results lie as much in the nature of the comparison as in the interpretation of the evidence. In sum, the different comparative methods should be seen as complements to one another. Global comparisons establish general patterns of co-variation, which can be examined further through the analysis of a smaller number of countries. Global comparisons allow for the specification of parsimonious explanations that are based on a small set of variables, while additional variables can be specified in studies that compare a few countries. Finally, both methods of comparison may identify deviant cases that can be examined further with a more intensive single-country study. In the case of the relationship between economic development and democracy, the evidence suggests that there is a stable positive association between the two, but as in many things, there are exceptions to the rule. The lesson for comparative politics is to determine whether these exceptions are important for the overall inferences that are drawn about the political world.

Notes

1   A corollary branch of comparative research inverts the relationship to examine whether democracies achieve better levels of economic development. See Helliwell (1994).
2   The comparison was made in 1971 with 1957 GNP per capita figures, when both the USSR and GDR existed.
3   The separate scales were originally developed by Raymond D. Gastil and since then have been maintained on an annual basis by Freedom House (see Foweraker and Landman 1997:55–56).
4   A similar style of analysis was carried out for Central America and arrived at similar results (see Seligson 1987).
5   Moore concedes that there were some conservative reversals with the Bourbon Restoration (1815–1848), but by 1830 the power of the old aristocracy had been effectively eliminated (Moore 1966:106).

Further reading

Boix, C. (2003) *Democracy and Redistribution*, Cambridge: Cambridge University Press.
    A new and interesting analysis of the relationship between economic development and democracy and a major proponent of the idea of *endogenous democratization*.

Lipset, S.M. (1994) 'The Social Requisites of Democracy Revisited', *American Sociological Review*, 59 (February): 1–22.
    This is a good overview of the entire topic of economic development and democracy.

Przeworski, A., Alvarez, M.E., Cheibub, J.A., and Limongi, F. (2000) *Democracy and Development: Political Institutions and Well-being in the World, 1950–1990*, Cambridge: Cambridge University Press.
  Comprehensive quantitative analysis of the relationship between economic development and democracy, and a major proponent of the idea of *exogenous democratization*.

Rueschemeyer, D., Stephens, E.H., and Stephens, J. (1992) *Capitalist Development and Democracy*, Cambridge: Polity Press.
  Chapter 2 of this book reviews the different efforts to examine the relationship between economic development and democracy.

Violent political dissent and social revolution

The quest to understand the individual, structural, and cultural motivations for violent domestic political dissent and the conditions for successful social revolution was in part stimulated by the process of decolonization in the post-World War II period. Concern over political violence and political instability is directly related to the establishment and maintenance of democracy. Seeking first to understand the origins of political violence and the conditions for revolution, scholars in this field ultimately hope to promote peace (Lichbach 1989:470), democratic stability (Huntington 1968; Sanders 1981:1–21; Cammack 1997), the protection of human rights (e.g. Poe and Tate 1994), and greater 'human security'. As in the many comparisons reviewed in the previous chapter, this chapter compares the research design and substantive findings of studies of many countries, few countries, and single countries in an effort to understand and explain this important research question. The 'comparison of comparisons' in this chapter examines the choice and number of cases, the time period of the studies, the types of measures and indicators each study uses to operationalize the theoretical concepts, and the different types of qualitative and quantitative techniques contained in each study.

The research problem

There are three interrelated research questions that form the basis for this field of inquiry in comparative politics:

1   Why do people rebel?
2   Which sectors of society are more likely to rebel?
3   What factors contribute to successful social revolution?

The first question concerns the individual, structural, and cultural factors that motivate people to rebel. These factors variously include 'relative deprivation' (Gurr 1968, 1970), general levels of inequality (e.g. Muller and Seligson 1987; Lichbach 1989), rational responses to changing economic conditions (e.g. Popkin 1979; Lichbach 1994), moral outrage at injustice (Scott 1976; Moore 1978), and the structural composition of primary export economies characteristic of lesser developed countries (Paige 1975; Wickham-Crowley 1993). The second question concerns the types of groups most likely to comprise the largest support for violent rebellions or revolutionary movements. Since many of the successful revolutions during the twentieth century occurred in countries whose economies were largely based on agriculture (Midlarsky and Roberts 1985:163–164), much comparative attention has been focused on the role peasants play in overall levels of political violence and revolutionary movements. Finally, the third question concerns the key explanatory factors for successful revolutions (Goodwin and Skocpol 1989), which in the history of the modern world are rare events.

    Those studies that compare many countries tend to focus on the motivational aspects of political violence, while those that compare few countries and single-country studies tend to concentrate on identifying the key groups and the necessary conditions for successful revolution while remaining cognizant of the individual motivations for rebellious activity. While the many-country studies focus most of their attention on the relationship between changing socio-economic conditions and political violence, few-country and single-country studies extend their analyses to examine the role of rebellious elites, revolutionary coalitions, the strength of guerrilla groups, the strength of the state, and other factors. Moreover, the many-country studies imply a link with revolution, while the few-country and single-country studies are more explicit in their attention to revolution. Thus, as in the comparisons that examine the relationship between economic development and democracy, the comparisons in this chapter show great variance in the factors that account for political violence and successful revolution. The discussion now turns to key examples from comparative politics that have examined these important questions.

Comparing many countries

As in the comparisons for economic development and democracy, the studies that compare many countries in this field of inquiry seek to discover the universal factors that account for political rebellion and political violence. They thus remain relatively high on the level of abstraction in order to include as many countries as possible (see Chapter 2). In this way, these studies identify a parsimonious set of factors that ought to explain 'why [individuals] rebel' (Gurr 1970). These studies assume that individuals and groups of individuals experience some form of grievance, and that this grievance ultimately manifests itself in violent political behaviour. Based on this assumption, these studies look for the micro and macro factors that may or may not lead to increased levels of grievance as manifested in political conflict.

This section considers six important studies from the literature that demonstrate the methodological issues encountered in the comparison of many countries. These studies include the comprehensive attention to general levels of political dissent found in Gurr's (1968) work on civil strife and Hibbs' (1973) *Mass Political Violence*; the examination of rural rebellion in Paige's (1975) *Agrarian Revolution*; and a subset of studies that focus primarily on the relationship between inequality and political violence, including Sigelman and Simpson (1977) and Muller and Seligson (1987). All five studies use quantitative methods to analyse a global sample of countries (49 $\leq n \leq$ 114) in order to identify the factors that account for political violence. The differences among them reside in the number of countries and time periods that each includes, the types of measures and indicators each employs, and the types of model each specifies.

As foreshadowed in the methodological discussions in Chapters 2 and 3, Gurr's (1968) search for conditions that cause 'civil strife' draws on a field of empirical inquiry in comparative politics that began with the publication of *Internal War* (Eckstein 1964). Gurr (1968:1109–1110) operationalizes the notion of relative deprivation through separate measures and indicators of persisting deprivation, short-term deprivation, the coercive potential of states, levels of institutionalization, the degree of political legitimacy, and general socio-structural conditions of facilitation. His variable for political dissent is the magnitude of civil strife, which is a combined measure of demonstrations, political strikes, riots, local rebellions, assassinations, coups, mutinies, plots, purges, and widespread revolts for the years 1961–1965. The data were coded from various primary news sources and individual country reports, yielding a total of 1,100 strife 'events' (ibid.: 1109). Through correlation and regression analysis, Gurr shows that all his indicators of deprivation are positively related to the magnitude of civil strife, even after controlling for the mediating effects of coercion, institutionalization, legitimacy, facilitation, and past levels of civil strife (ibid.: 1116–1117). His final model of civil strife is depicted in Figure 7.1.

The indices in this study operationalize the main theoretical concepts and the quantitative analysis shows how the variation in the magnitude of civil strife across 114 countries is explained by these different measures of relative deprivation. Figure 7.1 demonstrates that the two key independent variables (persisting and short-term deprivation) show significant positive effects on the magnitude of civil strife, while the analysis controls for the effects of the other independent variables. This study also shows that the comparison of many countries is an appropriate method with which to identify universal factors that account for civil strife. The large number of countries means that there are plenty of degrees of freedom to include the seven independent variables in the model. In other words, *there are enough countries to allow the variables to vary* (see Chapters 2 and 3). Moreover, the selection of countries was not determined by the outcome to be explained and thus *does not suffer from selection bias*. This study stands as one of the earliest and most comprehensive analyses of this research question using this particular comparative method.

Like Gurr (1968), Douglas Hibbs (1973:ix), in *Mass Political Violence*, seeks to examine the 'causal processes underlying differences across nations in levels of mass political violence during the post-World War II period'. He is quite clear in stating that he is willing to sacrifice both an examination of micro-political factors and the study of single countries in an effort to make generalizations based on global evidence. He develops two main indicators of mass political violence (the dependent variable). The first is *collective protest*, which comprises riots, armed attacks, political

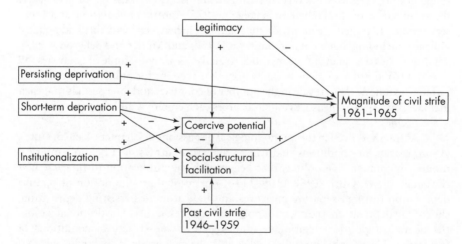

Figure 7.1 A causal model of civil strife

Sources: Adapted from Gurr (1968:1121) and Sanders (1995:71)

Note: Plus signs show positive effects and minus signs show negative effects strikes, political assassinations, deaths from political violence, and anti-government demonstrations. The second is *internal war*, which comprises armed attacks, deaths from political violence, and political assassinations. The components of each of these index variables were coded from newspaper sources and are reported in the *World Handbook of Political and Social Indicators* (Taylor and Hudson 1972). Both indices serve as the dependent variables used throughout the statistical analysis and serve as checks on each other as there is some overlap in their composition. The data are available for 108 countries and are grouped into two separate decades, namely 1948–1957 and 1958–1967.

Rather than establishing a well-developed theory of mass political violence, Hibbs (1973) engages in a comprehensive exercise of generating and testing hypotheses (see Chapter 1) before specifying a complex causal model. In testing hypotheses, Hibbs specifies over 25 different linear and non-linear relationships between his independent variables and his two indices of mass political violence. These relationships are grouped together in general categories including economic development, societal cleavages and separatism, state coercion and repression, and domestic politics. Table 7.1 summarizes in non-quantitative fashion the main findings of this hypothesis-testing exercise. Overall, Hibbs finds very little support for direct bivariate relationships between the various independent variables and his two dependent variables, although some of his findings are in the expected direction. For example, the level of political separatism in a society appears to be related to the level of internal war. Past levels of repression in the previous decade appear to inhibit mass political violence, while levels of repression in the same decade appear to encourage it. Finally, the presence of a communist totalitarian regime discourages political violence.

While direct bivariate relationships are by and large not supported by the data, Hibbs proceeds to use these findings to construct an elaborate multivariate causal model of political violence that takes into account the causal primacy of certain factors, which in turn determine the subsequent outcomes. Since the data are divided into two decades (1948–1957 and 1958–1967), Hibbs is able to construct models that examine the effects of values of some variables from the first decade on the same variables in the second decade, while estimating their overall effects on political violence. This complex model is depicted in Figure 7.2, from which it is possible to discuss the main conclusions of the study and highlight its strengths and weaknesses. Overall, Hibbs (1973) reports over 30 substantive findings from his statistical analysis, most of which refute popular propositions in the literature (Sanders 1981:19), and some of which are important for the present discussion. The key variables that emerge in the analysis to account for increased levels of political violence include past levels of political violence, the presence of societal cleavages, low levels of repression, and the absence of a Communist totalitarian regime. Thus, deeply divided societies tend to have higher levels of political violence either in the form of collective protest or internal war. Both forms of violence in the second decade are in part due to levels of violence in the previous decade. Violence also tends to be higher in countries without high levels of repression and in countries that are not controlled by a Communist regime.

The strength of the study is that Hibbs (1973) seeks to avoid the problem of 'omitted variable bias' (King *et al.* 1994:168–182) through the inclusion of a multitude of variables he thinks may (or may not) be related to political violence. Since he has two separate decades of indicators, he effectively doubles his sample size to 216 countries (108×2), which provides adequate degrees of freedom for the analysis; however, the use of ten-year aggregates has led some commentators to question his conclusions (see Sanders 1981:41–43). His conclusions adhere very closely to the statistical results and he is careful in specifying which effects are causally prior to others. Despite these strengths, no overarching theory of political violence

Table 7.1 Exploring the causes of political violence: a summary of hypothesis-testing in Hibbs (1973)

	Independent variables	Dependent variables	
		Collective protest (1948–1957)	Internal war (1958–1967)
Economic development hypotheses	Population	Positive linear	Positive linear
	Economic development 1 (static)	Inverted-U shape	Inverted-U shape
	Economic development 2 (dynamic)	Not significant	Not significant
	Urbanization	Not significant	Not significant
	Education	Not significant	Not significant
	Urbanization/development	Not significant	Positive linear
	Social mobility	Not significant	Negative linear
	Social mobility/expenditure	Not significant	Not significant
	Social mobility x expenditure	Negative linear	Negative linear
	Social mobility/welfare	Positive linear	Not significant
	Social mobility x welfare	Not significant	Negative linear
Cleavage hypotheses	Ethnic cleavages x social mobility	Not significant	Not significant
	Group discrimination	Positive linear	Positive linear
	Political separatism		Positive linear
	Post-war independence		Positive linear
Repression hypotheses	Internal security forces	Not significant	Inverted-U shape
	Repression (1958–1967)	Positive linear	Positive linear
	Repression (1948–1957)	Not significant	Negative linear
	Military coups	Positive linear	Positive linear
	Social mobility/institutionalization	Not significant	Not significant
Domestic politics hypotheses	Elite accountability	Not significant	Not significant
	Electoral turnout	Not significant	Not significant
	Political development (i.e. democracy)	Not significant	Negative linear
	Communist regime	Negative linear	Negative linear
	Left in parliament (% seats)	Negative linear	Not significant

Source: Adapted from Hibbs (1973:21–131)

is developed in the study; rather a series of interesting hypotheses are tested and separate models are variously constructed, effectively 'losing the forest for the trees'. In all the models, past levels of violence are taken as given, or *exogenous* to the overall system, and the significant effect these past levels have on current levels of political violence begs the question as to what accounts for the earlier levels of political violence. Finally, apart from one small reference, the analysis never examines the relationship between collective protest and internal war. Hibbs claims they are highly associated with one another, but neither is included as an independent variable in any of the models. Overall, the study stands as an example of an extreme form of quantitative cross-national comparison, which includes many more variables than Gurr (1968), yet the theoretical 'payoff' appears to be considerably less.

In *Agrarian Revolution*, Jeffrey Paige (1975) has a different scholarly goal than either Gurr (1968) or Hibbs (1973), but uses the same comparative method to achieve it. Like Gurr and Hibbs, he seeks to explain the incidence of rebellion and collective violence; however, he focuses only on rural rebellion in the agricultural sector, and he differentiates the dependent variable into reform, revolt, rebellion, and revolution.

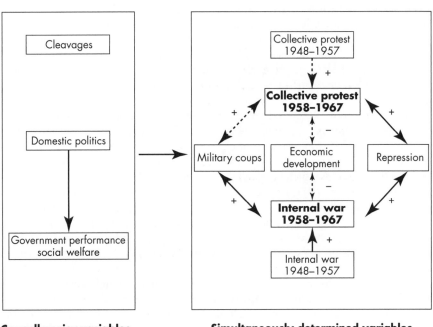

Causally prior variables   **Simultaneously determined variables**

Key: ────────▶ Unidirectional relationship
◀────────▶ Simultaneous relationship
◀-------▶ No significant relationship

Figure 7.2 A causal model of political violence
Source: Adapted from Hibbs (1973:135–153)

His empirical sample includes 135 different export sectors in 70 different developing countries for the period 1948–1970 (Paige 1975:72). In contrast to the psychological and individual theory of Gurr (1968) and the multitude of factors in Hibbs (1973), Paige focuses on the *structure* of the agricultural sector and its relation to collective violence. For Paige, there are two types of groups in this sector (cultivators and owners) with three sources of income (land, capital, and wages). Owners derive their income from land (plantations) or capital (commercial farms), while cultivators derive their income from land or wages. Different combinations of land, capital, and wages produce the following three different types of conflict between owners and cultivators: revolt, reform, and revolution. His structural theory contends that revolt should be more likely in agricultural sectors where the owners and cultivators earn their income from the land, while revolutionary behaviour is expected in agricultural sectors where owners earn their income from land and cultivators earn their income from wages.

Paige (1975:73) is keen to point out that studies such as Gurr (1968) posit individual-level motivations for political violence, but use national states as the units of analysis. His study of agrarian organization uses an appropriate unit of analysis, the agrarian sector itself, which is 'defined by the major producing regions for a given export crop within a given country' (Paige 1975:73). Thus, Paige avoids the problem of ecological fallacy (see Chapter 2) and minimizes problems of spuriousness in his statistical analysis. Having defined the unit of analysis, the study operationalizes both agricultural organization and collective behaviour from rural social movements. Each agricultural sector is categorized according to the organization of its labour force and the ownership of its agricultural enterprise (see Table 7.2). Social movements in general are defined as 'collective acts which take place outside the established institutional framework and involve participants who are united by some shared sense of identity' (Paige 1975:87, see also Chapter 8). Rural movement activities are coded from events reported in newspaper indices and regional press summaries and only if they are collective, non-institutional, involve solidary groups and are 'those actions which involved individuals who perform the physical work of cultivation' (ibid.: 90–91). Each event is coded using different categories, the most important of which is ideology, which allows the relationship between the type of rebellious activity and the structure of the agrarian sector to be examined.

Using correlation analysis, Paige (1975:104–105) finds strong support for a positive relationship between the structure of the agrarian sector and the type of rural social movement. Politically violent activities are carried out primarily by socialist or nationalist revolutionary movements, which are highly correlated with agrarian enterprises based on sharecropping and migratory labour. Thus, revolutionary action is most likely when cultivators derive their income from wages and owners derive their income from the control of land (ibid.: 120; see also Wickham-Crowley 1993:92). Paige's analysis demonstrates that it is the most vulnerable groups, namely sharecroppers and migratory labourers that are the most likely to rebel. Like Gurr (1968) and Hibbs (1973), the selection of cases in this study is not dependent on the outcome that is to be explained. The analysis is based on a full consideration of different export sectors in developing countries, which provides sufficient degrees of freedom to test the relationship, and the dependent variable includes revolutionary and non-revolutionary activity from rural social movements.

Like Gurr (1968) and in contrast to Hibbs (1973), the analysis identifies a parsimonious set of factors that account for the patterns of events that are observed.

Despite this strong pattern of correlation between agricultural organization and rural social movement events, Paige (1975:120) must complete a chain of inference that links the structure of the agrarian sector to collective political dissent. This chain of inference, however, is slightly shorter than the one required by Gurr (1968), since his unit of analysis is closer to the theoretical concepts he develops. In both types of agricultural systems where revolt and revolution are observed, landholders are dependent on the land as a source of income and power, while the cultivators have no strong ties to the land, making them more susceptible to revolutionary behaviour (Paige 1975:120–121). In addition to the cross-national evidence amassed for his theory, Paige 'triangulates' (Tarrow 1995:473–474) his study by comparing the three cases of Peru, Angola, and Vietnam – the discussion of which will follow in the next section of this chapter.

The studies that follow in the footsteps of Gurr (1968), Hibbs (1973), and Paige (1975) tend to focus on one explanatory factor – inequality – in an effort to explain political violence in the world. In general, there have not been a priori arguments for the type of relationship between inequality and political violence, rather this type of comparative work has attempted to provide evidence for four types of relationships, including positive linear, negative linear, U-shaped, or inverted U-shaped (see Briefing box 7.1).[1] Since the collection of cross-national studies on

Table 7.2 Types of agricultural organization

Type of organization	Definition
Commercial manor or hacienda	An individually owned enterprise which lacks power-driven processing machinery and is worked by usufructaries, resident wage labourers, or wage labourers who commute daily from nearby subsistence plots
Sharecropped estate	An individually owned enterprise which lacks power-driven processing machinery and is worked by sharecroppers or share tenants
Migratory labour estate	An individually owned enterprise which lacks power-driven processing machinery and is worked by seasonal migratory labourers
Plantation	An enterprise owned either by a commercial corporation or government body, or by an individual if the enterprise includes power-driven machinery, and worked by wage labourers resident for continuous terms of more than one year
Family smallholding	An individually owned enterprise worked by the owner and his family

Source: Adapted from Paige (1975:79)

Briefing box 7.1 Possible relationships between economic inequality and political violence

The relationship between economic inequality and political violence has received much scholarly attention since the seminal work of Ted Robert Gurr (1968, 1970) provided evidence for the link. Over the years, it has been posited that the relationship can assume four basic functional forms: (1) positive, (2) negative, (3) U-shaped, and (4) an inverted U shape (Lichbach 1989:436–440). Each of these functional forms is depicted below.

Figure 7.3 shows that as levels of economic inequality increase, levels of political dissent also increase while Figure 7.4 shows the opposite relationship. Figure 7.5 shows that the extreme ends of economic inequality are associated with high levels of political dissent, while Figure 7.6 shows the opposite relationship. Over the years, studies that compare many countries have sought to provide evidence in support of one of these basic models, the shape of which goes beyond the academy and can have policy implications for conflict resolution, peacekeeping, and securing peace agreements.

Figure 7.3 Positive relationship

Figure 7.4 Negative relationship

Figure 7.5 U-shaped relationship

Figure 7.6 Inverted U-shaped relationship

inequality and political violence is quite large (Sanders 1981; Lichbach 1989: 435–436), this section will concentrate on two key examples from the comparative literature. The differences between them reside in the different ways in which they conceive inequality (either land or income), the ways in which they measure political violence (internal war or deaths from political violence), and the ways in which they specify their various models.

Sigelman and Simpson (1977) compare indicators of inequality and political violence across 49 countries during the mid-1960s, while controlling for the effects of general levels of affluence, patterns of social mobility, degrees of socio-cultural heterogeneity, the rate of social change, and the size of the population. Affluence is measured by the per capita gross national product. The breadth of national educational enrolment represents social mobility. The degree of ethnic division represents sociocultural heterogeneity. The rate of social change is measured by the change in urban population between 1950 and 1960 (ibid.: 113–114). Inequality is operationalized as the distribution of income as measured by the Gini coefficient (see Briefing box 7.2). Political violence is measured using the Hibbs (1973) index for internal war (ibid.: 113–114). Thus, the measures of the various concepts are similar to those used by Hibbs (1973), but the study focuses on a smaller topic since it seeks to test only the relationship between income inequality and political violence.

Their comparative analysis tests the linear and non-linear forms of the relationship between income inequality and political violence. Their simple models include only income inequality and population as the independent variables and their results suggest that there is a positive linear relationship between income inequality and political violence. In other words, across the 49 countries in their sample, populous countries with high levels of income inequality have high levels of political violence; however, the curvilinear relationship receives no such empirical support. In addition to population and income inequality, their more complex models include the indicators for affluence, social mobility, socio-cultural heterogeneity, and the rate of social change. Again, a positive linear relationship is shown to exist between income inequality and political violence, while social mobility and affluence appear to have a negative effect, and socio-cultural heterogeneity have a positive effect. These results mean that while high levels of income inequality are associated with high levels of political violence, there is less political violence in affluent countries with opportunities for social advancement, and more political violence in countries whose societies are deeply divided.

Ten years after the publication of the study by Sigelman and Simpson (1977), Muller and Seligson (1987) re-examine the relationship between inequality and political violence. In contrast to the earlier study, they compare the effects of land inequality and income inequality on political violence. Both types of inequality are measured using the Gini coefficients for land and income distribution. Other independent variables in their model include the size of the agricultural labour force, the degree of landlessness, repression, governmental acts of coercion (past and present), political separatism, level of economic development, and past levels of political violence. In a departure from the earlier studies discussed in this section, Muller and Seligson (1987) use 'deaths from political violence' as their measure of political violence, excluding the measures of armed attacks and assassinations found in the Hibbs (1973) index of internal war. The analysis compares 62 countries during the 1960s and 1970s using simple and multiple regression techniques to examine the primary relationship between inequality and political violence. The findings are summarized in Figure 7.9, which shows that land and agrarian inequality matter only as they are mediated through general levels of income inequality. In other words, general levels of income inequality have a positive effect on the incidence of political violence. In addition, the authors find that the repressiveness of the regime contributes to political violence, as do government acts of coercion, past levels of political violence (compare Hibbs 1973), and the level of political separatism. It is clear that this study includes many of the independent variables found in Hibbs (1973) and combines them with the income inequality variable in Sigelman and Simpson (1977), while comparing the overall effects of land inequality.

Briefing box 7.2 The Gini coefficient as a measure of income inequality

Every country has a national income, known as either the gross national product (GNP) or the gross domestic product (GDP), which is the sum of all income earned in any given year. This national income is divided among those individuals who actually earned a share of it. Figure 7.7 illustrates this idea of national income and its distribution. The vertical axis represents the cumulative percentage of total income in a society, while the horizontal axis represents the cumulative percentage of the population that earned some portion of that national income. In a perfectly equal society, each percentage of the population earns precisely the same as the next. In an unequal society, some percentages of the population earn less than others. Thus, at point C in the figure, the lower 50 per cent of the population earn approximately

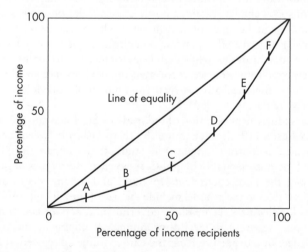

Figure 7.7 The Lorenz curve
Source: Adapted from Todaro (1997:141)

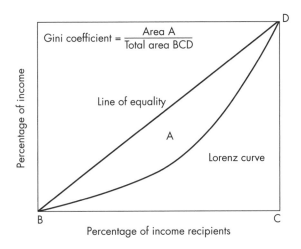

Figure 7.8 The Gini coefficient
Source: Adapted from Todaro (1997:146)

25 per cent of the national income, while at point F, the top 10 per cent of the population earn 80 per cent of the national income. This depiction of the distribution of income is known as the Lorenz curve (see Todaro 1997:141–142). In general, the more the Lorenz curve slopes away from the line of perfect equality, the more unequal the distribution of income.

The way in which to represent this state of inequality in income distribution is called the Gini concentration ratio or Gini coefficient. Figure 7.8 illustrates how this coefficient is calculated. It is the ratio of the area denoted A to the area denoted BCD, which represents the degree to which the Lorenz curve deviates from the line of perfect equality. The Gini coefficient ranges from 0 (no inequality) to 1 (perfect inequality). Thus, the higher the Gini coefficient, the more unequal is the distribution of national income. This measure is a popular measure in studies that compare many countries since it is a common measure that can be applied to all countries in the world.

Taken together, these studies represent a field of comparative inquiry dedicated to uncovering the universal factors that best account for political violence. The underlying assumption of all of them is that some form of grievance generated by some type of imbalance in society manifests itself in political violence, while the direct relationship between this imbalance and violence is mediated by other important factors. The strength of this type of comparison lies in the large number of observations and the full variance of the variables in the analysis. With the possible exception of Paige (1975), the main weakness of these studies is the choice of the nation state as the basic unit of analysis. While this choice is in part a function of data availability, the chain of inference required by the studies may lead many to

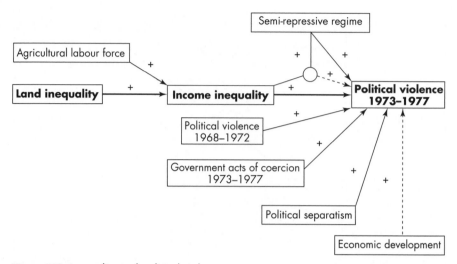

Figure 7.9 Inequality and political violence
Source: Adapted from Muller and Seligson (1987: 442)

question the overall strength of their conclusions since theoretically, the studies specify a set of relationships at the individual level yet test them with national-level data.

Comparing few countries

The comparison of few countries moves the analysis away from the identification of universal conditions for political violence and seeks to provide more holistic accounts of the groups that form revolutionary movements and the sequence and conjunction of events that lead to successful social revolutions. In stark contrast to the quantitative comparison of many countries, these studies seek to understand how '[t]he relations between army and party, between proletariat, peasantry, and middle class intellectuals are variably conjugated in different situations and not exhausted in simple formulas' (Wolf 1969:99). This section of the chapter considers Wolf's (1969) *Peasant Wars of the Twentieth Century*; the comparison of Vietnam, Angola, and Peru in Paige (1975); Scott's (1976) *Moral Economy of the Peasant*; Skocpol's (1979) *States and Social Revolutions*; Parsa's (2000) *States, Ideologies, and Social Revolutions*; Wickham-Crowley's (1993) *Guerrillas and Revolutions in Latin America*, and Brockett's (2005) *Political Movements and Violence in Central America*. In all these studies, a small number of countries are compared to examine the ways in which different groups have become mobilized, how they formed alliances, and how they were able to be successful (or not) in overthrowing the dominant political system under which they lived.

By comparing the history of revolutionary struggles in Mexico, Russia, China, Vietnam, Algeria, and Cuba, Eric Wolf (1969) seeks to identify the common factors that explain the outbreak of peasant wars and their role in fomenting successful revolutions. His 'master variable' is capitalist transformation, which introduced the logic of market mechanisms into agricultural communities historically founded on altogether different systems of production and existence. The commercialization of agriculture challenged the basic risk calculations peasants had been operating for centuries and broke traditional social ties and power relations that provided the basis for the subsistence economy. Wolf argues that all his cases (with the exception of Cuba) had the same starting condition of a large peasantry that was more or less bound to the land. The arrival of capitalism meant that increasingly landholders required more land, which with the growth of the population in each country led to perceptions of scarcity. Other significant variables for Wolf (1969:282–302) include the presence of a central state authority whose power base became rapidly eroded; the presence of middle and 'free' peasants able to be mobilized for revolutionary struggle; and violent peasant rebellion itself, which was carried out to preserve traditional forms of agricultural production.

Table 7.3 summarizes Wolf's (1969) comparison by listing the countries, the main independent variables, the outcome variable, and the main beneficiaries of these revolutions. The table shows that Wolf has adopted the most different systems design (MDSD) of comparison (see Chapters 2 and 4 in this volume), where the outcome is always present and the countries all share the main explanatory variables. His study has the problem of selection bias since the dependent variable (social revolution) is not allowed to vary. He does not, for example, compare instances in which peasant wars did not lead to social revolution. Thus, his inferences are less secure and confined to the countries in his study, even though one of his motivations for the study was to guide policymakers in the US to avoid more 'Vietnams' (Wolf 1969:x). Ironically, the main beneficiaries of these peasant wars and revolutions have not been the peasants but rather the middle classes, various revolutionary party organizations, and coalitions of the military and political parties. Nevertheless, like Barrington Moore (1966), his study stands as one of the first examples of comparative history that seek to identify common features across a very different set of countries in an effort to account for a similar set of outcomes.

Paige (1975) shows that the comparison of Peru, Angola, and Vietnam corroborates his findings at the global level. He chooses these three cases since each 'had experienced a particularly well-known and well-described movement and because each promised to provide detailed knowledge of the general principles linking types of agricultural organization and types of rural social movements' (ibid.: 123). His Peruvian case study compares the labour movements in the industrial sugar plantations and agrarian movements in the commercial hacienda systems. The Angolan case study examines the revolutionary nationalist movement in the settler-based coffee export sector. The Vietnamese case study considers the war as an example of a revolutionary socialist movement, which occurs in the sharecropping system of a rice export sector (ibid.: 123). Based on significant correlations between rural social movements and the particular structure of the agrarian sector in each of these cases, Paige (ibid.: 210) demonstrates that the 'primary determinant' of political conflict is the distribution of political and economic resources established by new forms of export agricultural organization. In each case, Paige is able to present evidence on the structure of the agricultural sector and the incidence of rural rebellion

Table 7.3 Conditions for peasant wars and revolution in the twentieth century

Variables	Mexico	Russia	China	Vietnam	Algeria	Cuba
Starting conditions	Land-bound peasantry	Land-bound peasantry	Land-bound peasantry	Land-bound peasantry	Land-bound peasantry	Sugar proletariat
Capitalist transformation	Yes	Yes	Yes	Yes	Yes	Yes
Mode of capitalist expansion	Violent expansion of farms	Entrepreneurs	Colonization of new land	Entrepreneurs	Violent expansion of farms	Entrepreneurs
Population growth	Yes	Yes	Yes	Yes	Yes	Yes
Central authority	Porfirio Díaz	Tsarism	Chiang Kai-shek	France	France	Batista
Vanguard supporters	Constitutional army	Russian Army peasant soldiers	Red Army			
Middle and free peasants	Yes	Yes	Yes	Yes	Yes	Yes
Peasant war	Yes	Yes	Yes	Yes	Yes	Yes
Outcome	Revolution	Revolution	Revolution	Revolution	Revolution	Revolution
Beneficiaries	Middle class	Communist Party	Communist Party	Communist Party	Middle class	Army–Communist Party

Source: Adapted from Wolf (1969)

to replicate the relationship he demonstrates in his global comparison of 135 export sectors.

James Scott (1976) provides a binary comparison of Burma and Vietnam in an effort to demonstrate how his theory of the 'moral economy' accounts for peasant revolutionary behaviour. Drawing on many of the ideas developed in Wolf's (1969) account, Scott develops a model, or portrait, of the peasant community and its basic organization that, when transformed by the arrival of market capitalism, contains the seeds for rebellion. The moral economy, as he calls it, develops from the particular nature of the peasant economy, which is organized to meet the basic subsistence of its inhabitants. For him, peasants are both 'risk-averse' and live so close to a basic line of subsistence that they establish community-based networks of support and norms of reciprocity that allow them to survive. His account centres on why peasants rebel rather than the reasons for successful social revolution, yet his analysis rests on similar arguments found in Moore (1966) and Wolf (1969). His master explanatory variable is market capitalism and his dependent variable is peasant rebellion. The intrusion of market capitalism under colonialism in Southeast Asia so transforms the basic 'subsistence ethic' of the moral economy that peasants rebel in an effort to preserve their centuries-old system of organization. Through a qualitative comparison of the history of colonial change and the introduction of market capitalism in Lower Burma and Vietnam, Scott (1976:157) demonstrates that 'structural change in the colonial period permitted elites and the state . . . to increasingly violate the moral economy of the peasantry and become more exploitative'.

In similar fashion to Wolf (1969), Theda Skocpol (1979) uses the comparative historical method to explain the social revolutions in France, Russia, and China. While her universe of countries is much reduced compared to Wolf (1969), her inclusion of the 'negative' cases of Japan, Prussia, and England is meant to address the problem of selection bias by 'checking' her structural theory of revolution (Skocpol 1979:37; Mahoney and Goertz 2004; see also Chapter 4 in this volume). She also draws a distinction between 'social' revolution and 'political' revolution. Social revolution involves a rapid and basic transformation of the state and class structures of a country, while a political revolution reforms the dominant political institutions of the day, but not the social ones (ibid.: 4). Like Wolf (1969), Paige (1975), and Scott (1976), Skocpol pays close attention to peasants as an important group for social revolution. In contrast to these studies, her master explanatory variable is the absolutist state and its subsequent collapse in the face of mounting international pressure, which provides the necessary political opportunity for revolutionary movements to be successful. In arguing against a purely Marxist account of revolution, Skocpol (1979:34–35) asserts that

> [c]ausal variables referring to the strength and structure of old-regime states and the relations of state organizations to class structures may discriminate between cases of successful revolution and cases of failure or non-occurrence far better than do variables referring to class relations and patterns of economic development.

Thus, Skocpol (1979) seeks to redress the gap in Marxist explanation with a direct analysis of changes in the patterns of state organization and their relationship to revolutionary movements. Her comparative method explicitly seeks to 'develop, test, and refine causal, explanatory hypotheses about events or structures integral to macro-units such as nation-states' (ibid.: 26). Her inclusion of 'positive' and 'negative' cases of social revolution thus combines the most similar systems design with the most different systems design in an effort to provide a comprehensive theory of social revolution. Table 7.4 summarizes the main evidence marshalled in support of her causal theory of social revolution. The comparison reveals that in addition to a crisis in state authority, relatively autonomous peasant communities and organized peasant protest play a key role in the breakdown of the absolutist states in these three cases. Moreover, the comparisons with Japan, Prussia, and England, reveal that the absence of these conditions led to political revolutions but not to social revolutions.

Having established similar causes of these revolutions, Skocpol (1979) turns her attention to the post-revolutionary period in each case to examine their outcomes. In this phase of her comparison, she compares only the three principal cases while dismissing the negative cases as no longer necessary. The comparison identifies five basic similarities across the post-revolutionary experiences in these countries, all of which Skocpol (1979) attributes to the way in which these revolutions unfolded. First, the so-called 'liberal option' remained closed for these states, while the dominant classes remained vulnerable and the subordinate groups remained susceptible to further mobilization. Her conclusion about France stands in contrast to that reached by Moore (1966), who argued that France is an exemplar of a 'bourgeois revolution' that led to liberal democracy (see Chapter 5 in this volume). Since her analysis extends beyond the revolutionary period (something Moore did not do), she claims that France experienced liberal phases that did not remain stable (Skocpol 1979:282).

Second, the economies of all three countries continued to be based on agrarian production characterized by a strong presence of peasants. Third, all three continued to be engaged in international competition. Fourth, the process of state-building featured mobilization of popular support against domestic and foreign opponents. Finally, the state itself established a greater presence in all three countries and replaced the landed classes as the pre-eminent and central authority. Overall, Skocpol's comparisons identify the causes and consequences of social revolution. She combines the two methods of comparison – most similar and most different systems design – and reaches some compelling conclusions about the causes, nature, and outcomes of social revolutions.

Parsa (2000) models his comparative study of revolution in Iran, Nicaragua, and the Philippines on Skocpol (1979), specifying structural variables of state strength and economic intervention, movement variables such as collective action, resource mobilization, and political opportunities, as well as consideration of the ideological composition of challenger groups. All three cases share a series of similar features, while the outcomes of the revolutions are different. Each country pursued broadly similar models of capitalist development, had authoritarian and exclusionary regimes that had survived earlier episodes of insurgent activities, did not suffer defeat in war nor experience the breakdown of their states, and enjoyed the economic, political, and military support of the United States (Parsa 2000:ix). Like Skocpol's (1979) portrayal of the cases of France, Russia, and China, the cases of Iran and Nicaragua

Table 7.4 Conditions for social revolution

	Positive cases			Negative cases		
	France	Russia	China	Prussia	Japan	England
Crisis conditions:						
Class	Landed commercial class + semi-bureaucratic absolutist monarchy	Weak landed nobility + bureaucratic absolutist state	Landed commercial class + semi-bureaucratic absolutist state	Weak landed nobility + bureaucratic absolutist state	No landed class + bureaucratic state	Strong landed class + no bureaucratic state
Economy	Growing non-capitalist	Extensive growth	No development breakthrough	Capitalist agriculture	Traditional with high productivity	Capitalist agriculture
External pressure	Moderate	Extreme	Strong	Strong/mild	Strong	Mild
Peasants:						
Class structures	Smallholders + opposition to seigneurial system	Peasants own/ rent. Strong community	Peasants own land, small plots, no community	Smallholders, labourers, no community	Communities dominated by rich peasants	Yeoman farmers + labourers, no community
Local politics	Autonomous villages + royal officials	Sovereign villages + tsarist bureaucracy	Landlords, usurers, literati dominate	Junker dominance	Bureaucratic control over local community	Landlords tied to monarchy
Outcomes	Breakdown of state + peasant revolts	Initial reforms; failed revolution 1905; collapse of state 1917	Breakdown of imperial state; agrarian disorder	Reforms and failed revolution	Political revolution + bureaucratic reforms	Constitutional monarchy
Social revolution?	Yes	Yes	Yes	No	No	No

Source: Adapted from Skocpol (1979:155–157)

experienced social revolutions, where the former regime was overthrown followed by a radical transformation of the society. As in Skocpol's (1979) cases of Prussia, Japan, and England, the Philippines only experienced a political revolution. Thus, the revolution in Iran established a theocracy led by the Ayatollah Khomeini, the revolution in Nicaragua uprooted the Somoza dictatorship and established a socialist state led by Daniel Ortega, and the political revolution in the Philippines brought to power a new elite faction after the ousting of Ferdinand Marcos.

Parsa's (2000) study is thus a comparison of cases with similar background conditions and different outcomes that need to be explained. His comparison focuses on the nature of the exclusionary and interventionist state in each of the countries, which alienated large sectors of the population and made the state vulnerable to large-scale mobilization and attack from challenging groups. The key variable that explains the difference in outcome (i.e. social vs. political revolution) is the nature of the broad coalitions that formed to overthrow the existing regime. Separate consideration is given to the mobilizational propensity of students, the clergy, workers, and capitalists who were in various degrees alienated and antagonized by the strong and exclusionary state. In the cases of Iran and Nicaragua, broad oppositional coalitions and large-scale disruption were made possible owing to the weakness of ideologically motivated challengers. Parsa (2000:240) argues that the presence of such ideological challengers divides the opposition, precludes the possibility of coalitions forming, and leads to a less radical outcome, demonstrated in the case of the Philippines. The absence of class coalitions and large-scale mobilization combined with a strong armed communist movement led to a political stalemate in the Philippines, which was only resolved through the ascendancy of a new elite faction that placed Corazon Aquino into power. Ironically, however, in the cases of Iran and Nicaragua, once the broad coalitions overthrew the Shah and Somoza respectively, more ideologically driven challengers assumed power. In Iran, a radical Islamist movement assumed power and in Nicaragua, a radical socialist movement (the Sandinista Front for National Liberation (FSLN)) assumed power.

Parsa's (2000) explanation thus combines states, movements, and ideology in order to account for the difference in outcome across the three cases. Like Skocpol (1979) his theoretical framework is meant to explain not only successful revolutions, but also unsuccessful revolutionary movements. He thus compares the successful periods with earlier unsuccessful movements in each of the cases. Like Skocpol's (1979) 'negative' cases of Prussia, Japan, and England, Parsa (2000) examines the failure of insurgency movements in the 1950s and 1960s in Iran, the 1960s and 1970s in Nicaragua, and the 1970s in the Philippines. The inability of these earlier insurgent movements to form broad-based oppositional coalitions prevented them from successfully overthrowing the regimes. This general account of revolutionary success and failure is meant to 'contribute to a comprehensive theory of social revolution in developing countries and a framework *within which to understand and explain other revolutions*' (Parsa 2000:5, emphasis mine). Parsa (2000) thus wishes to extend the inferences obtained from his own comparisons to other cases of revolution. Like many other few-country studies, however, the inferences that are drawn from this comparison are not particularly secure, since he has eight independent variables and only three cases. The summary table for his theory of revolution has the following independent variables: state power, state repression of moderate opposition, state intervention in the economy, popular opposition and collective action, class coalition, revolutionary challengers, transformations in the class structure, and transformations in the power structure (ibid.: 281). With the exception of state power, which is always 'exclusive/centralized', the other independent variables vary. Thus, the comparison suffers from an indeterminate research design (see Chapter 2 and Chapter 4 in this volume). Nevertheless, Parsa (2000) has added new insights into the nature of oppositional coalitions and the role of ideology in the process of revolution.

Wickham-Crowley's (1993) *Guerrillas and Revolution in Latin America* compares the relative fortunes of revolutionary movements in twelve Latin American countries during two successive historical 'waves'. Since all the countries come from the same region of the world, the study adopts a most similar systems design and seeks to identify both the sources of revolutionary behaviour and the conditions that favour successful revolution. While this study draws on the theoretical and operational insights of the many-country and few-country studies, the unit of analysis is the guerrilla movement itself. Wickham-Crowley seeks to strike a balance between the parsimonious identification of key variables found in the many-country studies with the attention to historical process and contingency found in few-country studies. The first set of comparisons examines the origins and fortunes of guerrilla movements in Cuba, Venezuela, Guatemala, Colombia, Peru, and Bolivia during the period 1956–1970. The second set of comparisons applies the same logic to movements in Nicaragua, El Salvador, Guatemala, Peru, and Colombia after 1970.

The comparison of guerrilla movements and revolutions across countries and historical waves reveals a common set of conditions that account for high levels of peasant support for revolutionary movements and the conditions that must be met for successful social revolution in the region. With regard to the first question, the comparisons reveal four important conditions for high levels of peasant support for revolutionary movements:

- the nature of the agrarian structure;
- disruption of the agrarian structure;
- the presence of rebellious cultures; and
- linkages between revolutionaries and peasants through well-established social networks.

The analysis goes beyond mere identification of these factors and demonstrates that it is the combination of these conditions that is important for explaining the proclivity of peasants to support revolutionary movements.

1   Peasant support came when conducive agrarian structures were combined with agrarian disruption in an area with substantial pre-existing linkages joining guerrillas to the peasantry.
2   Peasant support could also be obtained where conducive agrarian structures were joined to a historically rebellious peasantry, or
3   where such a rebellious peasantry was previously linked to the proto-guerrillas before the insurgency (Wickham-Crowley 1993:308–309).

With regard to the second question, since there were only two successful revolutions in the region after 1956, Cuba in the first wave (1959) and Nicaragua (1979) in the second, the comparisons reveal not only why revolutions succeed, but also why they fail. Table 7.5 summarizes the key variables that emerge in Wickham-Crowley's (1993:312) analysis, which shows a great frequency of guerrilla attempts to foment revolution (n=24) that spans the countries and periods outlined above. His 'truth table' (see Chapter 4) is organized into four basic groups:

1   those cases in which guerrilla movements were successful;
2   those in which guerrilla movements had many of the favourable conditions for revolution but were none the less unsuccessful;
3   those in which guerrilla movements never managed to garner support; and
4   those in which guerrilla movements never got off the ground.

While the fact that the cases of successful revolution contain all five conditions may appear unsurprising, the factors that determine the failure of revolution are an added dimension to the analysis. Indeed, the two variables that appear to be key for a successful revolution are the presence of a patrimonial praetorian regime and the loss of US support for that regime. In other words, a guerrilla movement in the region may have made an attempt, garnered significant support, maintained sufficient military strength, but did not mobilize against such a patrimonial praetorian regime, the result of which is the failure to overthrow the regime.

The final study to consider is Brockett's (2005) comparison of peasant mobilization and repression in El Salvador and Guatemala. Like Scott (1976) this is a good example of a binary comparison since it compares different outcomes across two very similar countries (see also Dogan and Pelassy 1990:126–134). Both countries are in Central America and experienced similar prolonged periods of social conflict in which relatively large numbers of people were killed, both in terms of the total number killed and as a proportion of the total population of these small states. The truth commission for El Salvador estimated that between 75,000 and 80,000 people were killed during the period of civil war from 1980 to 1991 (Wood 2003; Brockett 2005: 2; Landman 2006:110–111), while nearly 135,000 were killed in Guatemala between 1962 and 1996 (Ball et al. 2000; Landman 2006:110–111).

Brockett (2005) uses comparative historical analysis and an examination of time-series data on social protest and patterns of state repression in these two countries in order to examine the dynamic relationship between political movements and state violence. His study examines the paradox of cycles of protest under extreme threats from agents of the state, where progressive activists participated in strikes, demonstrations, factory and farm occupations, and sit-ins in public offices. The comparison of these two similar countries shows that in Guatemala, state repression virtually eliminated a popular rural movement, while in El Salvador, an urban movement 'persists in the face of great risk' (Brockett 2005: 3). His explanation for the difference in outcome across these two countries rests less on individual level grievance and more on the holistic notion of the 'configuration of political opportunities' (Brockett 2005: 325; see also Chapter 8 in this volume).

Overall, the comparison of few countries allows for closer attention to the role of historical contingency, the examination of class alliances, state strength and

Table 7.5 Conditions for social revolution in Latin America 1956–1990

	Favourable conditions for revolution					Revolution
	Guerrilla attempt	Peasant worker support	Guerrilla military strength	Patrimonial praetorian regime	Government loses US support	
Cuba 1956–1959	Yes	Yes	Yes	Yes	Yes	Yes
Nicaragua 1971–1979	Yes	Yes	Yes	Yes	Yes	Yes
Venezuela 1960s	Yes	Yes	Yes			
Colombia 1960s	Yes	Yes	Yes			
Guatemala 1960s	Yes	Yes	Yes			
Colombia 1970–1990	Yes	Yes	Yes			
Peru 1980s	Yes	Yes	Yes			
Guatemala 1975–1990	Yes	Yes	Yes	Yes		
El Salvador 1975–1990	Yes	Yes	Yes			
Argentina 1974–1978	Yes	Yes		Yes		
Brazil 1970s	Yes	Yes				
Argentina, *Montoneros*	Yes	Yes	Yes	Yes		
Mexico 1970s	Yes	Yes				
Uruguay, *Tupamaros*	Yes	Yes	Yes			
Argentina 1958–1963	Yes					
Peru 1965	Yes					
Bolivia 1967	Yes					
Nicaragua 1958–1963	Yes			Yes		
Dom. Republic 1963	Yes					
Ecuador 1962	Yes					
Haiti 1960s	Yes			Yes	Yes	
Paraguay 1958–1959	Yes			Yes		
Honduras 1965	Yes					
Brazil 1960s	Yes					
Costa Rica						
Panama 1959–1985						
Panama 1985–1989				Yes	Yes	
Paraguay 1960–1989				Yes		

Source: Adapted from Wickham-Crowley (1993: 312, Table 12–3). Copyright © 1993 by Princeton University Press. Reprinted by permission.
Note: *n* = 28

structures, political opportunities, and other important factors that are omitted from many-country comparative studies. Moreover, the use of history raises the number of observations and degrees of freedom for more variance in an effort to overcome the 'too many variables' problem (see Chapters 2 and 4 of this volume). The comparison of these few-country studies demonstrates the importance of case selection and the unit of analysis for drawing inferences. Wolf (1969) looks at positive instances of revolution, Paige (1975) and Scott (1976) examine confirmatory cases, and Skocpol (1979) and Wickham-Crowley (1993) use positive and negative instances of social revolution. Parsa (2000) compares social revolutions to political revolutions. For Wolf, Scott, Parsa, Skocpol, and Brockett, the unit of analysis is the nation state, for Paige it is the agricultural sector, while for Wickham-Crowley (1993), it is the guerrilla movement itself. It is clear that there are important trade-offs in terms of the types of inferences that can be drawn associated with both case selection and the unit of analysis, while all the studies invite replication using other samples of countries.

Single-country studies

Rather than compare a series of single-country studies on different politically violent and revolutionary periods in the world, this section of the chapter compares three seminal studies of violent political dissent and revolution in Mexico. Womack's (1969) *Zapata and the Mexican Revolution*, Nugent's (1993) *Spent Cartridges of Revolution*, and Harvey's (1998) *The Chiapas Rebellion* examine specific groups and events in Mexico. All three authors are insistent on the uniqueness of the 'story' they are recounting, yet use analytical categories developed in more comparative studies to make larger inferences about violent political dissent and the nature of revolutionary activity. Like the many-country and few-country comparisons, they examine the organization of the agricultural sector, the role of peasants in revolutionary processes, underlying economic transformations, as well as the role of the state and its relationship with the various subordinate groups. Womack (1969) focuses on the role of Emiliano Zapata and peasant support in the south central state of Morelos in the struggle for land during the heyday of the Mexican Revolution. Nugent (1993) traces the diachronic and dialectic relationship between state and community in the municipal area of Namiquipa in the northern state of Chihuahua as local cultivators resist repeated attempts to control their land. Harvey (1998) examines the contemporary rebellion led by the Zapatistas in the southern state of Chiapas, a struggle which reflects a larger historical political conflict over land and the cultural understanding of subordination that emerge from the interaction between macro- and micro-political processes. Together, land and who controls it feature prominently in each study as important comparative categories are drawn from the previous studies outlined above, and yet each of these studies focuses on specific cases (i.e. Morelos, Namiquipa, and Chiapas) within the broader context of Mexico as the evidentiary base of the main arguments that they develop.

Where these studies differ from the comparisons outlined above is in their insistence that they seek to provide a deeper and more meaningful understanding of political struggle in the Mexican context. Womack insists that his 'social history' is not an explanation or analysis of rebellious behaviour. Rather, it is 'a story because the truth of the revolution in Morelos is in the feeling of it, which I could not convey through defining its factors but only through telling of it' (Womack 1969:x). Similarly, Nugent (1993:28) seeks to examine the 'distinctive historical process in which the community [of Namiquipa] has formed in relation to the state . . . through struggles over land and labor or the production process'. While not ignoring the importance of objective conditions, systemic factors, and influences, he insists that

> [w]hile this specificity does not preclude the possibility of *making comparisons*, an analysis of these struggles in this pueblo [the town of Namiquipa] must focus not only on a series of actions by people on and in the world and relationships between groups and individuals and things, but also on the manner in which actions and relationships are organized by people both practically and conceptually.
>
> (Nugent 1993:29, emphasis mine)

In similar fashion, Harvey (1998:12) argues that he uses 'non-essentialist' categories of class, ethnicity, peasant, Indian, state, and citizenship and focuses his analysis on the processes of identity formation, political organization, and engagement with the state. By examining these fluid relationships, Harvey (ibid.: 11) does not seek to 'identify the factors that facilitate or hinder popular mobilization', but to 'grasp the political significance of popular struggle' in the context of Mexico and other authoritarian states. Thus, while all three emphasize the historical specificity of their case studies, they also seek to make larger inferences about the process of political struggle under adverse conditions, while at the same time avoiding a full commitment to providing explanations as is in previous studies considered here. Further consideration of each study will clarify this observation.

Womack's (1969:ix) study begins with the opening sentence, 'This is a book about country people who did not want to move and therefore got into revolution.' This sentence has a number of assumptions and conceptual categories built into it. It identifies the main group of the analysis as country people, a concept which is later qualified as *campesinos*, or people from the fields (ibid.: x).[2] It implies that some force beyond the power of these country people was changing the nature and possibly the organization of their community. It concludes that this change induced by the outside power resulted in the country people becoming involved in revolutionary activity. From this strong thesis statement, Womack tells an intriguing tale of the revolutionary activities of the common people of Morelos under the leadership of Emiliano Zapata in an effort to protect their land and way of life. The powerful outsiders are the emerging entrepreneurs under the pre-revolutionary period of Porfírio Díaz and then the various governing elites imposed by the revolutionary and post-revolutionary Mexican state. Womack's conclusion after detailing twenty years of complex revolutionary history is worth quoting at length:

> New attitudes, new policies, new laws, new agencies, new authorities – and of the plain country people of 1910, about three-fifths remained. They had won a victory too, simply in holding on as villagers, not in refuge in the state's cities or huddled into the haciendas but out where they felt they belonged, in the little

towns and pueblos and ranchos, still reeking at least of 'pacific Zapatismo'. In 1910 the bases of the only life they wanted to live had been breaking down. Although they wore themselves out, dutifully tilling their scattered patches of corn and beans, now and then trading a horse, a cow, for a few pesos, marketing eggs, tomatoes, onions, chiles, or charcoal, tending their scrubby orchards, desperately sharecropping on the planters' worst land, they had nevertheless lost the struggle to keep their communities going. In store for them then there had been only a long torment of grief and shame, to labor for a wage in steaming cane fields and rice paddies, to take orders from a boss, eventually to move into huts the boss's boss owned, to watch from a distance while old friends and neighbors and kinfolk moved away too, never to rest, and at the end to die in debt anyway. Now a decade later, two souls having disappeared for every three that stayed, they were still in their bases and back in the struggle. After all, the endurance in the pueblos counted more than the new government, the new champions, the new reforms. Those small communities burdened and threatened for centuries, had just survived the most vigorous, ruthless, and ingenious siege ever mounted against them, spoiling the best if not the last chance that usurpers would have to eradicate them.

(Womack 1969:370)

It is clear from this passage that Womack (1969) achieves much more than just telling a story. The conclusion is that country people, however defined, will resist change, whether induced through capitalist transformation of agriculture or the imposition of state-led reform projects, a conclusion that has strong resonance in the other studies of rebellion and revolution outlined in this chapter.

Nugent (1993) echoes this conclusion and perception of resistance by examining the dialectical history of community–state relations in Namiquipa. Like Womack (1969), Nugent is uneasy with the term 'peasant' and settles on *serranos*, which literally means 'hill people', who are more generally known as a type of free peasantry. He adopts a non-instrumental view of the state and a relational definition of ideology, which is seen to mediate between the *serrano* people and the state. Using these analytical categories, Nugent travels back and forth through history to unveil common themes in the political struggle for land, which is grounded in resistance to encroachment by 'outsiders'. These outsiders variously include the Apaches in the seventeenth century, the expansion of economic modernization in the nineteenth century, and the imposition of land reforms by the post-revolutionary Mexican state. Overall, his account focuses on questions of land, labour, identity, and revolutionary mobilization in which the key inference is that historically, similar struggles over similar types of grievance have been fought in this region, but the struggles do not follow some linear evolutionary path (ibid.: 151). Rather, he concludes that the relationship among land, labour, and politics is embedded in Namiquipa ideology, which responds to the ever-changing challenges from without, but also represents a constant in history that the peasantry, however defined, 'refuse to go away' (ibid.: 165).

Finally, Harvey (1998) examines the Zapatista rebellion, which began officially in January 1994 in the southern state of Chiapas. As its name suggests, the Zapatista rebellion draws on the history of struggle in southern Mexico and the leader from

Morelos Emiliano Zapata, but as Harvey contends, adds new dimensions to the older patterns observed. In tracing the history of violent political dissent from peasants, Harvey demonstrates that the Chiapas rebellion drew on the existence of new independent peasant organizations that had developed in the 1960s and 1970s, as well as a variety of networks at the national level. In addition to the demand for land reform in Chiapas, the protagonists of the rebellion demanded the full guarantee and protection of indigenous people's and women's rights, as well as democratization of the Mexican political system (ibid.: 199–200). This newest form of rebellion was brought about by a series of 'dislocations' in the region, including maldistribution of land, economic modernization (hydroelectric dam projects, oil exploration, logging, and ranching), shifts within the Catholic Church, education of bilingual teachers and catechists, post-1968 student activism, and the gradual liberalization of the Mexican political party system (ibid.: 228). For Harvey, the key outcome of the rebellion has been that the rights and culture of indigenous people have become an integral part of the process of democratization in Mexico.

Summary

As in the comparison of studies that examine the relationship between economic development and democracy, it is clear that there are important methodological trade-offs associated with the different types of comparison in this chapter. Table 7.6 summarizes the various studies outlined and compared in this chapter to demonstrate these trade-offs. The selection of studies is by no means exhaustive, but it shows how these different methods allow scholars variously to focus on different factors that help account for violent political activity and full-scale social revolution.

The quantitative comparison of many countries revealed common factors that account for variation in political violence that help guide the comparisons with few countries and the single-country studies. With the exception of the more specific relationship between inequality and political violence, for which there is still little agreement (see Lichbach 1989), the quantitative comparison of many countries revealed the importance of state strength and repression, past patterns of political violence, and the political composition of the current regime. Few-country studies draw on these insights and use macro-causal historical analysis to account for the incidence of rebellious activity and successful revolution, and demonstrate the ways in which key variables interact over time and limited space. Like the many-country studies, these few-country studies reveal the importance of state strength and repression. But they contribute further to our understanding of revolutionary processes through the additional consideration of rebellious histories, class conflict and class coalitions, the role of ideology, and external factors such as warfare and the influence of the United States.

Finally, the three studies of Womack (1969), Nugent (1993), and Harvey (1998) modify the categories and concepts from these other comparative studies to fit the particular context of Mexico, but they continue to provide similar analytical leverage for making inferences that stretch beyond the confines of the Mexican case. They draw on other comparative studies to refine what is meant by the term 'peasant'. They are cognizant of the types of relationships between inequality and violence that

Table 7.6 Violent political dissent and revolution in comparative perspective

Method of comparison	Number of countries	Exemplars	Result
Many countries	Between 49 and 114 countries either at one point in time or in different aggregated periods	Gurr 1968; Hibbs 1973; Paige 1975; Sigelman and Simpson 1977; Muller and Seligson 1987	Political violence is variously due to past political violence, patterns of deprivation and inequality, the presence of cleavages and political separatism, degrees of repression, and structural features of the economy, while the functional form of the relationship remains opaque
Few countries (quantitative)	Between 3 and 12 countries, while the number of observations remains large	Paige 1975; Wickham-Crowley 1993	The structure of the agricultural sector is a key determinant of the type of rural rebellion, while the main conditions for revolution include guerrilla organization and military strength, support for the guerrillas from other sectors of society, and an illegitimate dictatorial regime
Few countries (qualitative)	Between 2 and 6 countries	Wolf 1968; Scott 1976; Skocpol 1979; Parsa 2000; Brockett 2005	Key determinants of peasant rebellion are the economic and cultural nature of the peasant community, capitalist transformation of agriculture, a strong central authority, and changing configuration of political opportunities. The conditions for social revolution include peasant rebellion and an absolutist state facing external pressures; and the ability for challengers to form broad coalitions
Single-country studies	Mexico	Womack 1969; Nugent 1993; Harvey 1998	Peasant rebellion and participation in revolutionary activity are due to their resistance to various historical encroachments on their land and community

Note: Wickham-Crowley (1993) uses a variety of algebraic reductions to identify the key determinants of successful revolution in Latin America, a method that combines qualitative and quantitative techniques (see Chapter 4)

emerge from the quantitative comparison of many countries, and implicitly test whether these types of relationships are at work in the single country. The focus on a single country allows them to examine in closer detail the interplay between structure and agency and how that interplay shapes the historical process of political struggle. They are concerned with the defensive reaction of a particular social group to the encroachment of various outside forces that seek to disrupt their particular way of life.

Notes

1   A comprehensive review of quantitative cross-national comparisons that examines the relationship between inequality and political conflict concludes that the lack of clear formal modelling and theoretical reflection has led to inconclusive results, which are the product of the different operationalization of concepts and different specification of models (see Lichbach 1989).
2   Womack (1969:x) is uncomfortable with the term 'peasant' since it evokes a certain exotic quality he wishes to avoid.

Further reading

Gurr, T.R. (1970) *Why Men Rebel*, Princeton: Princeton University Press.
     This is Gurr's full theoretical and comparative statement on the motivation for violent political conflict.

Sanders, D. (1981) *Patterns of Instability*, London: Macmillan.
     A comprehensive review of quantitative cross-national studies of political violence.

Lichbach, M. (1989) 'An Evaluation of "Does Economic Inequality Breed Political Conflict" Studies', *World Politics*, 41:431–470.
     A comprehensive review of quantitative cross-national studies on economic inequality and political violence.

Skocpol, T. (1994) *Social Revolutions in the Modern World*, Cambridge: Cambridge University Press.
     A collection of Skocpol's essays on social revolution and macro-causal historical comparison.

Non-violent political dissent and social movements

In addition to periods of violent political dissent and social revolution, history is replete with examples of non-violent political dissent in the form of social movements. Ever since the emergence of the modern state (Tilly *et al.* 1975; Tilly 1978; Tarrow 1994), various forms of direct political action and political protest activities at the national level have challenged dominant political institutions in both the advanced industrial democracies the lesser-developed countries. Movements led by workers, students, women, peace activists, gays and lesbians, environmentalists and greens, as well as those led by religious fundamentalists, extreme radical right adherents, and ethnic minorities increasingly bring new issues to the political agenda through protests, demonstrations, marches, petitions, and lobbying efforts, all of which fall outside traditional institutional channels of interest inter-mediation. Comparative research sees these movements as different from those that espouse violent political dissent in terms of the groups they mobilize, the demands they make, and the goals they seek to achieve. Many of the insights from the literature on violent political dissent, however, continue to inform the study of social movements, including relative deprivation, economic transformation, state power and repression, and identity construction. As in the previous chapter, this chapter assesses key developments in the study of social movements by comparing many, few, and single-country studies in an effort to assess their methodological trade-offs and the answers that they provide to the substantive questions they raise.

The research problem

There are many research questions surrounding the topic of social movements. In general, scholars have sought to explain the emergence, strategies, shape, and success and impact of social movements in different political contexts. Comparative research has focused on *why* social movements arise in the first place, *how* they seek to achieve their ends, and *what* they actually achieve. Studies that examine why social movements arise in the first place focus their attention on the various sources of collective grievance and common identity that lead to popular mobilization and protest. Studies that examine how social movements successfully attract members and followers to participate in their activities focus on the role of social movement organizations and the mobilization of important resources necessary for sustained collective action, such as money, communications, and membership. These studies also examine the different strategies that social movements employ, given the different political systems and political opportunities for mobilization that they confront. Finally, studies that compare the relative success or impact of social movements focus variously on specific movement goals, the legal and institutional levels of impact, and the degree to which values and political behaviour have been altered by prolonged periods of social movement activity.

The study of social movements is often divided between those that examine mobilization from labour and those that examine other social movements. This division is in part a theoretical one. The labour movement is seen as an 'old' movement that articulates demands more closely associated with industrial capitalism and the material interests of those less fortunate groups in society, while other social movements (women, gays, greens, and peace) are seen as 'new', since they articulate demands that have more to do with lifestyle choices and less with material concerns; a shift made possible through the transformations induced by the transition to post-industrial capitalism. Many have argued that this distinction is overdrawn, since mobilization from such groups as women and greens is nothing new (Fuentes and Frank 1989; Foweraker 1995; Foweraker *et al.* 2003:147–165), and since the focus on new groups tends to neglect those groups located on the right side of the traditional left–right ideological spectrum. But some comparative studies have included the labour movement alongside consideration of other social movements (see Foweraker and Landman 1997), or have included movements from all aspects of the left–right spectrum (see Gamson 1975; Kriesi *et al.* 1995; Payne 2000). This chapter compares key examples from the literature and does not make the distinction between old and new movements, but seeks to reveal through the comparison of different studies the key factors that help account for the emergence, shape, and impact of social movements.

Comparing many countries

With the exception of studies that focus on the labour movement and in contrast to the two previous chapters, there are few studies that compare many countries in the field of social movement research. The studies included in this section are Powell's (1982) comparison of non-violent protest in 29 democracies in the 1960s and 1970s; Haas and Stack's (1983) comparison of labour strikes in 71 countries; Gurr's (1993) comparison of protest and mobilization from 227 different communal groups in 90 different countries; and Inglehart's (1997) and Inglehart and Welzel's (2005) comparison of the proclivity of individuals to support or participate in social movement activity across large number of countries. Together, these studies attempt to provide a parsimonious set of factors that account for either instances of social movement protest or the willingness of individuals to participate in protest activities.

In his comparison of 29 democracies, Powell (1982) provides various indicators for democratic performance across a range of political dimensions, including voting, socio-economic performance, constitutions, party systems, citizen involvement, and democratic stability. His analysis of citizen involvement (ibid.: 129–132) includes indicators of 'peaceful protest' taken from the *World Handbook of Political and Social Indicators* (Taylor and Jodice 1983). The indicator measures instances of protest coded from newspaper accounts for two separate decades (1958–1967 and 1967–1976). The author defines peaceful protests as 'organized events in which substantial numbers of citizens participate in an endeavor to win the support of others or of the authorities for a political cause' (Powell 1982:129). These protests are seen as different from riots since they are non-violent and require larger numbers of participants and greater amounts of organization. The nature of peaceful protests suggests that they will be more prevalent in the democratic countries with large populations and higher levels of economic development.

Across the democracies, Powell (ibid.: 131) finds that the likelihood of peaceful political protest is higher in countries with large populations, greater degrees of social heterogeneity, and higher levels of GNP per capita. More importantly, the analysis shows that democracies with multiparty systems tend to have lower levels of peaceful protest, while systems with strong support for extremist parties tend to have higher levels of peaceful protest. In short, the presence of political parties to absorb and channel the different interests of citizens and groups means that multiparty democracies tend to have lower levels of protest from social movements. This finding leads Powell (ibid.: 130) to make the larger inference that 'protest activity is very frequently an organized mass alternative to the electoral system, when the latter seems unresponsive or inaccessible'. From his sample of democracies, he concludes that protest in the United States is typical of a modernized country with a large population and few effective political parties to channel discontent (ibid.: 131).

For reasons of data availability, Haas and Stack (1983) limit their comparison to 71 countries with data on labour strike activity during the period 1976–1978. They are aware that the selection of countries may not constitute a representative sample, but they argue that the selection is still 'fairly large and seemingly representative of the market economies' (ibid.: 49). The selection, however, does cover the globe, including thirteen countries in Africa, sixteen in the Americas, fourteen in Asia, ten in Oceania, and seventeen in Europe. The dependent variable is the strike volume (i.e. the number of person-days lost per total working population) collected by the International Labour Organization (ILO) and is averaged in each country for the three years in order to reduce extreme fluctuation in the measure for some countries. The explanatory variables are similar to many of those used by Hibbs (1973) in his study of political violence (see Chapter 7). They include the level of economic development (per capita GNP), rate of economic growth, the rate of inflation, degree of unionization (union members as a proportion of the labour force), the degree of ethnic fragmentation, rural–urban migration, and the development of the mass media. In addition, the degree of political democracy is measured using Jackman's (1973, 1975) democratic performance index (see Chapter 6).

Initial correlation analysis across all the countries reveals a positive and significant association between the strike volume and the rate of inflation, the degree of unionization, and the development of mass media (Haas and Stack 1983:53). Further analysis of the comparative data using regression reveals that there is an inverted-U relationship between the level of economic development and the strike volume, suggesting that the 'strike volume increases through low levels of development, peaks out, and then decreases at high levels of development' (ibid.: 54). This curvilinear relationship holds even after controlling for the rate of economic development, the rate of inflation, the degree of unionization, mass media development, ethnic fragmentation, and rural–urban migration. Finally, further analysis demonstrates that the level of political democracy has a negative effect on the strike volume. Overall, the results support a 'liberal' perspective that strike volumes tend to be high in the early stages of economic development, while they tend to taper off in the later stages, owing to a separation between the ownership and control of large firms and general weakening of unionization (ibid.: 44–45).

Following his earlier work on political violence, Gurr (1993, 2000) has turned his attention to political protest from groups of individuals whom he labels 'minorities at risk', which comprise 'cultural and religious identity groups that do not have recognized states or institutionalized political status' (Gurr 1993: 161). His comparisons focus on more than 250 groups politically salient or active between 1945 and the 1990s, meeting two defining criteria. First, the group must collectively suffer or benefit from systematic discriminatory treatment. Second, the group is the focus of political mobilization in defence or promotion of its 'self-defined interests' (ibid.: 163). His sample of groups has expanded in size between the 1993 and 2000 publications and includes those that are subordinate plus those that are dominant yet who remain in the minority. Subordinate groups mobilize to attain new advantages and benefits, while dominant groups mobilize to maintain advantages and benefits. Overall, these groups include ethnic minorities, ethnic nationalists, indigenous groups, inter-communal contenders, and militant sects.

Like his work on violent political dissent, Gurr (1993, 2000) operationalizes notions of relative deprivation and group mobilization in order to uncover the key factors that account for both violent and non-violent political dissent from communal groups. Relative deprivation captures the motivation of political protest as a perceived gap between expected and actual achievement (see Chapter 5 and Gurr 1968, 1970, and 1993:167). Mobilization, on the other hand, examines the ways in which groups marshal resources in order to sustain collective action (see Gurr 1993:167; Lichbach 1995; Foweraker 1995). For the 1993 study, the two key dependent variables relevant for the present discussion are his measure of 'group protest in the 1980s' and 'mobilization for protest in the 1970s'. High values on both variables denote more protest participation and more organization for protest. As with the findings for violent political dissent outlined in the previous chapter, Gurr's (1993:179) preliminary analysis of the comparative data suggests that the level of protest is highest for communal groups that face certain economic disadvantages, including scarcity of land, high birth rates, and poor levels of health. In addition, certain political and cultural factors appear to be important determinants of non-violent political protest, including the historical loss of group autonomy and strong group identity (ibid.: 179). The analysis demonstrates that the correlates of political mobilization include: grievances expressed in terms of economic, social, and political demands; the loss of autonomy; group size; and group dispersion (ibid.: 180). His complete models estimate the group and systemic determinants of non-violent political protest, which include the demand for political rights, the demand for political autonomy, previous levels of mobilization, non-democratic forms of rule, and the scope of state power (ibid.: 186).

The newer study has a large number of groups and a longer time period for comparison, which necessarily yields more observations. Like its predecessor, the new study continues to focus on forms of relative deprivation or what he calls 'collective disadvantages' (Gurr 2000:163), which interact with the propensity of states to discriminate against minorities to increase the salience of group identity and raise the probability of political action (see Crighton 2003). Its descriptive analysis of trends in ethno-political conflict shows that toward the end of the 20th century, protest and conflict from communal groups has declined, a trend partly explained by increased democratization (see Chapter 9 this volume) and a lesser degree of discrimination in transitional societies.

In contrast to his earlier work on civil strife (see Gurr 1968 and Chapter 7), these two studies reduce the problem of ecological fallacy since they use communal groups themselves as the units of analysis rather then the nation state. Some problems of aggregation remain for the relative deprivation perspective, but the examination of groups works well for the mobilization perspective. Moreover, his analysis is able to determine in some degree what leads to mobilization in the first place, such as political and economic disadvantages that various groups face, particularly discrimination and poverty, which are in turn associated with group demands for the extension and protection of political rights (Gurr 1993, 2000). By including political variables, Gurr (1993:189) is able to make the more general statement that 'in long-established democracies the utility of non-violent communal activism is high, whereas the process of democratization provides opportunities that spur the mobilization of communal groups for . . . protest'. Nevertheless, the trends in the subsequent study show that in fact such protest was not as sustained as he first imagined.

The final comparisons of many countries examine individual-level data collected for up to 81 societies. Like Gurr, Inglehart has over the years increased the number of countries for which he collects individual-level data covering a range of values elicited through standardized opinion surveys. In *Modernization and Post-modernization* (1997) Inglehart examines, among other things, the cross-cultural proclivity for individuals to support or join protest movements. While he has data from a total of 43 countries, he only has data for both his time points (1981 and 1990) for 21 countries on four questions that probe non-conventional political activity. His countries are drawn from Europe, North America, Asia, and Southern Africa. His questions include whether the respondent had ever considered or actually joined a boycott, demonstration, unofficial strike, or building occupation (Inglehart 1997:308–315; Appendix 3, 384–385).

His comparison reveals a monotonic increase in all four forms of unconventional political activity. The percentage of respondents declaring that they had considered or had actually joined a boycott rose in fifteen of the 21 countries. The figures for demonstration rose in sixteen countries, for unofficial strikes in fourteen countries, and for building occupations for seventeen countries (ibid.: 313–314). This general increase in the individual proclivity to take part in unconventional political activity is seen to be in large part due to a pattern of economic modernization that has changed the underlying value structure of successive cohorts of individuals. The largest percentages for all four questions appear in the most advanced industrial democracies of the sample, lending support to Inglehart's (1990, 1997) more general theory of the rise of 'post-materialism' in the world (see Briefing box 8.1). In general, conventional forms of political activity such as voting and party activity have seen a decline in the most advanced countries, while less conventional political activity captured in part by his four questions has seen an increase.

In their follow-up study, Ingelhart and Welzel (2005) address similar sets of questions, and in reference to the topic of this chapter, turn their attention to the outcomes of collective action, which they understand to mean 'changing levels of formal democracy, and varying degrees of effective democracy' (ibid.: 224). They take such changes in democracy as a given outcome of collective action and then examine its cross-national variation against variation in the values of 'self-expression' (as opposed to values purely linked to survival), which in turn are linked to broader patterns of socio-economic modernization. The variation in self-expression values is highly correlated with both the level of formal democracy and an index of civil society (ibid.: 220–229), which they see as indicative of the public's capacity to carry out collective action (ibid.: 227).

Briefing box 8.1 Ronald Inglehart and post-materialism

Drawing on years of research based on mass surveys carried out first in advanced industrial democracies and then moving to countries from all regions of the world, Ronald Inglehart (1977, 1990, 1997, 1998), has consistently argued that there is a relationship between individual values and the level of economic development in a country. Inglehart has argued that as countries develop, there will be an overall shift in the value orientations of individuals and that these will be less concerned with the provision of immediate goods and resources (jobs, money, cars, mass consumption) and more concerned with lifestyle issues (clean environment, social justice, peace, and human rights). The former set of values he calls 'materialist' and the latter set of values he calls 'post-materialist'. Using a battery of questions to probe the value orientations of mass publics, he has been able to derive a scale that measures the degree to which individuals exhibit these 'post-material' values and, most recently (Inglehart 1997, 1998), use the scale across a selection of 43 different countries (see Table 8.1). To derive the scale, individuals are ranked according to the priority they assign to each indicator.

Table 8.1 The materialist/post-materialist scale

Materialist indicators	Post-materialist indicators
Maintain law and order	More say on the job
Fight against crime	Less impersonal society
Economic growth	Ideas count
Stable economy	More say in government
Strong defence	Freedom of speech
Fight rising prices	More beautiful cities

Source: Adapted from Inglehart (1998:65)

Theoretically, post-materialism can be seen as either a dependent variable or an independent variable. As a dependent variable, post-materialism is seen to be a symptom of economic modernization. For example, all modern and developed countries ought to exhibit a high percentage of individuals that adhere more closely to the core set of post-materialist values. As an independent variable, it is used to explain differences in the individual proclivity to carry out different forms of political action. For example, so-called post-materialists ought to be more likely to support the political activities of those social movements that issue demands for peace, equality, justice, and the protection of the environment than for those movements that make demands concerning job security and law and order.

Taken together, these comparisons of many countries represent various attempts to uncover the determinants of non-violent political dissent and social movement activity. The studies used different samples of countries, including democracies (Powell 1982), a selection of democracies and non-democracies (Inglehart 1997; Inglehart and Welzel 2005), and two global samples (Haas and Stack 1983; Gurr 1993). The studies also used different units of analysis, including nation states (Powell 1982; Haas and Stack 1983), communal groups (Gurr 1993), and individuals (Inglehart 1997; Inglehart and Welzel 2005). Despite these choices of countries and units of analysis, the studies reveal common determinants of non-violent political dissent. Powell (1982), Haas and Stack (1983), Inglehart (1997), Inglehart and Welzel (2005) and by implication, Gurr (1993) all demonstrate that socio-economic change accounts for some variation in protest activity, whether in the form of growth, level of development, or structural imbalances in the economy. Powell (1982), Haas and Stack (1983), and Gurr (1993) all show that social heterogeneity in the form of ethnic fragmentation or communal group mobilization are important factors that account for political protest. Haas and Stack (1983) and Gurr (1993) demonstrate that group organization is important for non-violent political protest. The key difference in these studies lies in their results for the effects of democratic forms of rule on political protest. For Haas and Stack (1983), democracy tends to inhibit labour strike volume, whereas for Gurr (1993), it tends to provide the necessary political opportunity for communal group mobilization. These and other differences surrounding the labour movement and other social movements form much of the basis of the comparative work on social movements in few countries to which the discussion now turns.

Comparing few countries

Controlled comparison of few countries yields important insights into the origins, shape, and impact of social movements since it allows a more detailed look at the dynamics of social mobilization and the features of the political contexts in which social movements seek to bring about change. This section considers five such studies: Kitschelt's (1986) comparison of anti-nuclear movements in France, Sweden, the United States, and West Germany; Dalton's (1988) comparison of individual-level protest data in the US, Britain, West Germany, and France; Kriesi *et al.*'s (1995) comparison of social movement dynamics in The Netherlands, Germany, France, and Switzerland; Foweraker and Landman's (1997) examination of citizenship rights and social movements in Brazil, Chile, Mexico, and Spain; and Bashevkin's (1998) comparison of the women's movement in Britain, the United States, and Canada.

Kitschelt (1986) argues that the anti-nuclear movement is suitable for comparison since it appeared in Europe and North America at roughly the same time, yet it experienced different fortunes in the four cases of his study (France, Sweden, the United States, and West Germany). He points out that single-country studies of the movement provide a 'wealth of descriptive detail, [but] individually they are not suited to the task of arriving at a generalized understanding of the factors that determine the dynamics of social movements' (ibid.: 57). Thus, his comparison of these four cases is meant to make larger inferences about the factors that shape the dynamics and impact of social movements. His key explanatory factor is the political opportunity structure, which is a configuration of resources, institutional arrangements, and historical precedents for social mobilization, where the difference in this structure across the cases either facilitates or constrains the development of protest movements (ibid.: 58). He argues that adopting this comparative framework can 'explain a good deal about the variations among social movements with *similar demands in different settings if other determinants are held constant*' (ibid.: 58, emphasis mine).

Kitschelt (ibid.: 60–61) carefully lays out his selection criteria and explains why his comparison is well suited to discovering the effects of institutional constraints on social mobilization. The four movements made similar demands for the end of nuclear power in terms of existing power stations, ongoing plant construction, and new projects. All four movements emerged from the local level to the national level at about the same time (1973–1974). All four movements shared the same 'subjective sense of deprivation and grievance' in terms of the social bases of the activists, which comprised three groups: professionals and public sector employees; affected farmers and property owners; and students and young radicals (ibid.: 61). Moreover, the governments in all four countries were similarly committed to developing the nuclear power industry.

The concept of the political opportunity structure is operationalized using a simple set of dichotomous categories that define a country's political input structures and its output structures. Input structures represent the relative openness and responsiveness of a country's institutions to groups making demands and are seen to be either 'open' or 'closed'. Output structures, on the other hand, represent the capacity of a country's institutions to satisfy group demands and redress their grievances through an appropriate policy response, and are seen to be either 'strong' or 'weak'. The combination of these two dimensions produces a 2×2 matrix, where the four cases of this study fit into each of the resulting boxes (see Figure 8.1). This fourfold typology of countries is then used to explain both the strategies and impacts of the anti-nuclear movement.

In terms of social movement strategies, Kitschelt (ibid.: 67–72) finds that movements in more open and responsive political opportunity structures (Sweden and the United States), adopted more 'assimilative' strategies, such as lobbying,

Political input structures

		Open	Closed
Political output structures	Strong	Sweden	France
	Weak	United States	West Germany

Figure 8.1 Political opportunity structure
Source: Kitschelt (1986:64)

petitioning, and political party activity. In contrast, movements operating in closed and less responsive political opportunity structures (France and West Germany) adopted more confrontational strategies, including public demonstrations and acts of civil disobedience. In terms of impact, movements achieved more procedural gains in the open and responsive political opportunity structures of Sweden and the United States, where greater access to formal decision-making had been made (ibid.: 74). Substantive movement impact such as the decommissioning of existing nuclear power plants, the slowing down of construction, and the cessation of funding for new plants, was much higher in the open and responsive political opportunity structures (ibid.: 77–82). The strength of green parties, which represent a structural impact of movements, is much higher in the least responsive political opportunity structures. In short, movement strategies, the degree to which they achieved their aims, and the legacies they leave behind are in large part determined by the types of political contexts in which they mobilize.

In *Citizen Politics in Western Democracies* Dalton (1988) compares individual-level data on social movement activity in the United States, Britain, West Germany, and France. The data are from a series of surveys that establish a scale of social movement activity ranging from the least confrontational and orthodox to the most confrontational and unorthodox (ibid.: 63–64). Using regression techniques, Dalton compares the effects of six important explanatory variables on the scale of social movement activity and finds consistent patterns across all four countries. For these countries, well-educated young men with strong political party identification, a personal sense of political efficacy, and overall dissatisfaction with government policies tend to engage in more confrontational social movement activity, including demonstrations, boycotts, and unofficial strikes (ibid.: 69–70). The patterns in these four democracies led Dalton to conclude that political protest is less likely among deprived and alienated individuals than among those that possess political and social resources.

Kriesi *et al.* (1995) use protest event data in their comparative analysis of four countries in Western Europe in order to examine the origins, nature, and to a limited degree the impact of the 'new' social movements in the context of larger patterns of mobilization from other social groups. They thus focus on the women's, student, peace, green, and gay movements in The Netherlands, Germany, France, and Switzerland, while comparing protest from right-wing groups. The protest event data are coded from a reading of the Monday issues of major newspapers in the four countries. This selection of events is not random, but the authors argue that it is representative and the most likely way to capture the majority of protest events while not requiring the vast time and resources to code everyday news coverage (ibid.: Appendix). Their analysis concentrates on the political opportunity structure these movements face in order to explain the observed differences across the four cases in their level of protest, magnitude of events, and types of strategies they employ.

The four key contextual factors important for explaining new social movement activity include the degree to which traditional cleavages have become pacified (see Briefing box 8.2), formal institutional structures, the left–right configuration of power, and the different policy areas addressed by movements. In an almost zero-sum fashion, new social movements appear to have more space to be politically active in those countries where traditional cleavages have been pacified such as

Germany and The Netherlands (Kriesi *et al.* 1995:25). Like Kitschelt (1986), the authors find a direct relationship between social movement activity and the institutional strength and responsiveness of the state in each country. On the one hand, countries with weak and inclusive states (such as Switzerland) exhibit high aggregate levels of social mobilization which are characterized by more conventional forms of political action. On the other hand, countries with a strong exclusive state (such as France) tend to have lower levels of social mobilization that is concentrated

---

Briefing box 8.2 Traditional societal cleavages

In examining the origins of group interests and the formation of political parties, Lipset and Rokkan (1967:1–64) identified four possible characteristics of countries which become key areas of difference in the process of economic modernization and nation state formation. These differences are labelled 'cleavages', since they can divide societies over national policy priorities. These cleavages include centre–periphery, state–church, land–industry, and worker–owner.

The centre–periphery cleavage developed in Europe during the sixteenth and seventeenth centuries and involves questions of national versus supranational religion (e.g. Church of England vs. Catholic Church), and national languages versus Latin. The state–church cleavage involves questions of secular versus religious authority over social policy such as mass education, marriage laws, baptism, abortion, etc. The land–industry cleavage involves questions of the proper economic balance between the agricultural sector and the industrial sector with regard to taxes, quotas, and tariffs. Finally, the owner–worker cleavage involves questions of labour exploitation and control over the means of production. After the Russian Revolution, it also involved questions of national versus supranational levels of worker identification and whether workers were committed to the international revolutionary movement (ibid.: 47).

While these four cleavages were born of historical developments that span from the sixteenth to the early twentieth century, they have a tremendous impact on the formation of political parties and their presence is still felt in the contemporary period. Religiously based political parties claim differences over the centre–periphery cleavage as well as the state–church cleavage. Liberal and conservative political parties claim differences over the state–church cleavage. Communist, socialist, and labour parties claim that more should be done for the plight of the worker under the throes of industrial capitalism and, in certain countries, post-industrial capitalism. Over time, it is argued, these traditional cleavages become less stark and more pacified so that new issues begin to create new cleavages. Thus, Kriesi *et al.*'s (1995:81) comparison of social movements in Western Europe shows that pacification of the owner–worker cleavage across the four countries has a direct impact on the degree to which social movements have supported the development of the new left. Indeed, the rise of post-materialism and the 'new' social movements (see Briefing box 8.1) is seen as the creation of a new cleavage in some countries.

into more confrontational forms of action (Kriesi *et al.* 1995:51–52). In countries where the 'old left' (i.e. socialist and labour-based parties) has been pacified, new social movements strengthen the new left within and outside established political parties (ibid.: 81). The different policy orientations of the various new social movements determine in part the type of response they receive from government. Movements that challenge high-profile policy issues (e.g. national defence, energy, immigration, and nuclear weapons) confront a more closed system while those that challenge low-profile policy issues (e.g. transportation, environment, and international solidarity) face a more open system (ibid.: 105–110).

Finally, their comparison of the dynamics of protest waves across the four countries reveals the importance of several factors for comparative social movement research. Descriptively, Germany and The Netherlands experienced well-developed protest waves which lasted more than half a decade and which exhibited large increases in the number and magnitude of protest events, increased involvement of social movement organizations, and the extension of protest nationally (ibid.: 116). In terms of protest activities, the waves in Germany and The Netherlands saw early periods with less violent protest give way to more violent tactics towards the end of the period (see discussion of Tarrow below). The role of organizations is also similar across the countries. Initial phases of protest are not led or accompanied by formal, professional social movement organizations owing to their difficulty in mobilizing quickly and their reluctance to get involved in activities that may not achieve desirable outcomes. Finally, a wave of protest ends with an increased level of institutionalization of movement organizations and patterns of political reform (ibid.: 136–137).

In shifting the focus away from the confines of welfare capitalist countries, Foweraker and Landman (1997, 1999) compare the mutual relationship between citizenship rights and social movements in Brazil, Chile, Mexico, and Spain. Their analysis traces the political origins and impact of social movement activity in terms of the protection of individual rights of citizenship. In order to raise the number of observations, the cases are compared over periods of political liberalization and democratic transition, comprising the period from 1964–1990 in Brazil, 1973–1990 in Chile, 1963–1990 in Mexico, and 1958–1983 in Spain ($n=99$). The authors argue that all four countries are 'instances of authoritarian regimes that have experienced a fluctuation in the guarantee of citizenship rights' and which 'exhibit a rise and fall of social mobilization over time' (Foweraker and Landman 1997:49), placing them in the 'mirror-image' of the most similar systems design (see Faure 1994 and Chapters 2 and 4 in this volume).

Like the quantitative comparative work on economic development and democracy (see Chapter 6 in this volume), the authors use various measures of political and civil rights protection to illustrate the contours of citizenship rights in the four cases. Rights 'in principle' are coded from a reading of the regimes' constitutions, decree laws, and institutional acts (Foweraker and Landman 1997:51–52). Rights 'in practice' are measured by combining a series of published abstract scales on rights protection (ibid.: 52–62). Both these rights measures are then used to derive a third measure that represents the difference between principle and practice (ibid.: 62–65). Social movement protest events from labour are gathered from the International Labour Organization, and events data from other social movements are coded using primary and secondary sources on activity from grass-roots groups, self-help groups, women's and peasant organizations, among others. Both measures of social mobilization are used to demonstrate the contours of social movement activity in the four cases. Both the rights and movements measures are then used to examine the direct relationship between rights and movements while controlling for underlying economic factors, including the growth rate, level of development, and inflation (ibid.: 172).

The initial comparisons reveal that the four cases show large fluctuations over time in their protection of the political and civil rights of citizenship, a general pattern that demonstrates their collective move away from authoritarianism towards democracy. These general similarities are contrasted to the differences in the nature of their democratic transition. Chile and Spain have 'rapid' transitions to democratic rule, and Brazil and Mexico experience 'protracted and incomplete' transitions (ibid.: xxiv). Moreover, the comparison shows the different ways in which the regimes in these countries protected rights in principle and rights in practice. The authors see this difference between principle and practice as critical to an understanding of the origins and impact of social movement activity (ibid.: 117–118), as well as a reflection of one aspect of the political opportunity structure (Foweraker and Landman 1999).

Using the protest event data, the authors show that similar waves of mobilization from labour and other social movements appeared in the four countries. Each wave has a distinct beginning, peak, and end where mobilization from the labour movement tends to precede mobilization from other social movements. This temporal primacy of labour mobilization suggests that it is the working class which leads a more general wave of mobilization under authoritarian conditions and is then complemented by mobilization from other social movements (Foweraker and Landman 1997:133–138). In all cases, the pattern of demands issued by social movements suggests that as a wave of mobilization builds, demands shift from material and economic concerns to the protection of basic political and civil rights (ibid.: 143–150).

Having described the contours of both citizenship rights and social movements, the comparison of the four cases uses correlation, regression, and a form of Boolean analysis to examine the ways in which rights and movements are related (see also Wickham-Crowley 1993). The authors posit unidirectional and mutually constitutive relationships between rights and movements (see Briefing box 8.3). The correlations are strongest between labour mobilization and rights protection, suggesting either that increased rights protection motivates movements or that movements achieve the extension of rights. The regression analysis confirms that there is indeed a strong, mutually constitutive relationship between rights protection and social mobilization in Brazil, a mutually conditioning but partial relationship in Chile, a relatively weak relationship in Mexico, and a highly concentrated relationship in Spain. In addition, the Boolean techniques show how the relationships differ across shorter moments within the overall time periods that are compared. Taken together, these various relationships suggest that the process of democratic transformation in these cases is characterized by the 'halting and contradictory' struggle for rights by social movements (ibid.: 232).

The final study in this section compares the fortunes of the women's movement in three countries with conservative governments: the Reagan and Bush (Senior)

Briefing box 8.3 Citizenship rights and social movements

Studies in history, sociology, and political economy variously specify the relationship between citizenship rights and social movements from three different perspectives: (1) the rights perspective, (2) the movement perspective, and the (3) dual perspective. The rights perspective suggests that the language of individual rights acts as a banner for social movements and as a common currency of social protest whereby individual rights elicit social movements. The movement perspective suggests that social struggles by poor, downtrodden, and excluded groups achieve the extension of individual rights in an incremental fashion over long periods of time whereby social movements disseminate a knowledge of rights as well as secure them for themselves. As its name suggests, the dual perspective argues that rights and movements actually encourage each other, acting as mutual catalysts. These three perspectives are pictured in Figure 8.2 and the comparative data analysis carried out by Foweraker and Landman (1997) on the cases of Brazil, Chile, Mexico, and Spain demonstrates empirical support for the dual perspective.

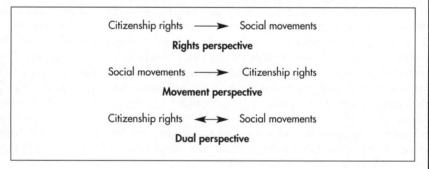

Figure 8.2 Three perspectives on the relationships between citizenship rights and social movements
Source: Adapted from Foweraker and Landman (1997:226–231)

administrations in the United States (1981–1992); the Mulroney premiership in Canada (1984–1993); and the Thatcher and Major years in Britain (1979–1997). Silvia Bashevkin (1998:3) begins *Women on the Defensive* with the following three important questions for comparative social movement research:

1   Whatever happened to the vibrant social movements of the 1960s and 1970s?
2   Were they swallowed up in the greedy good times of the 1980s?
3   Did the lean, mean 1990s spell final disaster, as more and more people adopted a 'me first' approach to life?

Her comparison of the same movement under similar governmental conditions seeks to answer these questions by focusing on the 'valley' of the women's movement after its 'peak' of the 1970s marked by the 1975 UN International Year of the Woman. In all three countries, the women's movement entered a period of retrenchment while their respective governments pursued social policies based on an extreme form of neo-liberal individualism, which paradoxically sought to limit women's freedom of choice with respect to their reproductive and other rights. The scope of her comparison includes an assessment of gains and losses before, during, and after these periods of conservative rule through an examination of the legislative–juridical record and over one hundred interviews with women activists. The study thus stands as an example of a most similar systems design that seeks to examine the particular case of the women's movement, while making larger inferences about social movement success in general.

The comparative assessment of legislative and juridical decisions concerning issues raised by the women's movement (see Figure 8.3) demonstrates that in Britain and the United States it suffered setbacks in formal terms, where the percentage of positive decisions declined for the periods of conservative governance. Only the Canadian movement saw gains during the Mulroney years, where the percentage of positive decisions increased dramatically. Of the three countries, the movement in

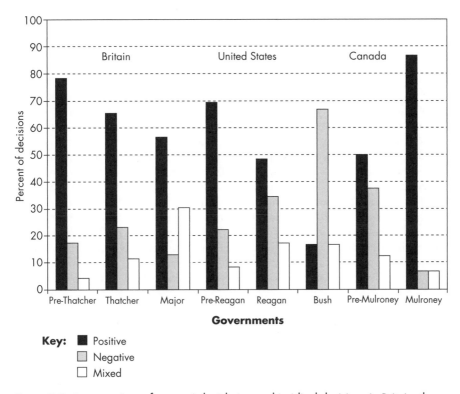

Figure 8.3 A comparison of women's legislation and juridical decisions in Britain, the US, and Canada

Source: Adapted from Bashevkin (1998:249–256)

the United States suffered the most setbacks, particularly during the Bush years where the percentage of negative decisions was higher than the percentage of positive decisions. Bashevkin (ibid.: 47) explains these cross-national differences in part by the presence of the European Court of Justice in the case of Britain, and the passage of the Charter of Rights and Freedoms in the case of Canada, both of which limited conservative politicians' ability to roll back pro-feminist legislation.

The qualitative comparison of activist women's discourse concerning the challenges they faced during conservative rule equally reveals the variety of experiences across these three political contexts. Activists in all three countries describe the difficulties they faced and the more defensive stance their various campaigns had to take while confronting the new conservative agenda. The movements in all three cases faced a concerted effort to divide them politically by exploiting lines of cleavage in the movements (ibid.: 165–166). Despite these similarities, activists in Britain framed their struggle in light of the dominant role of Margaret Thatcher as the leader of the Conservative party and as an ex-prime minister with continued influence in the Major government (ibid.: 161). In the United States, activists dealt with more decentralized political institutions that spanned the executive, legislative, and judicial branches of the federal government, as well as the organs of the state governments. They also benefited from a more highly developed set of interest groups, which led them to pursue pragmatic strategies involving coalitions, lobbying efforts, and non-confrontational campaigns (ibid.: 163). Finally, in Canada, activists were cognizant of a 'spillover of social and economic conservatism from the United States', while they saw that their overall 'progress during the Mulroney years was more in spite than because of the government' (ibid.: 163–164).

In contrast to the comparisons of many countries, the studies outlined here show that the number of observations can remain quite high while the analysis includes more complexity about the various aspects of social mobilization. Kitschelt's (1986) comparison illustrates how similar movements pursue different strategies and achieve different types of impact precisely because they face a different set of political opportunities. His study refines the notion of the 'political opportunity structure', his research design is a classic example of how certain features are held constant through controlled comparison, and his analysis invites extension to other political contexts and other social movements (see Tarrow 1994; McAdam *et al.* 1996; Imig and Tarrow 2001). Kriesi *et al.* (1995) confirm Kitschelt's (1986) finding concerning the importance of the political opportunity structure for movement dynamics. Foweraker and Landman (1997) operationalize the theoretical and analytical concepts necessary to examine the connections made between citizenship rights and social movements in contemporary authoritarian contexts. Finally, Bashevkin (1998) has advanced an important method for measuring social movement success and examined it by comparing similar movements confronting similar regimes while accounting for the remaining differences she observes.

Single-country studies

The three single-country studies in this section represent important examples of work that has advanced the comparative study of social movements by providing particularly useful analytical concepts and ways of measuring them despite only focusing on one country. Gamson's (1975) *The Strategy of Social Protest* compares 53 challenging groups in the United States to examine the strategy and success of social movements between 1800 and 1945. In *Democracy and Disorder*, Tarrow (1989) examines protest events from a variety of social movements to gauge their effects on Italian democracy between 1965 and 1975. Anne Costain's (1992) *Inviting Women's Rebellion* provides a comprehensive study of the women's movement in the United States that examines the relationship between protest events, legislation introduced and passed in the Congress, and patterns of public opinion. A comparison of these studies illustrates clearly their various contributions to the study of social movements.

Gamson (1975:19) identifies between 500 and 600 different 'challenging groups' (or social movement organizations) from the period 1800–1945 in the United States, of which he argues his sample of 53 is representative. His analysis 'explores the strategies they used and the organizational characteristics that influenced the success of their challenges' (ibid.: ix). A challenging group is a formal organization that is the 'carrier of a challenge to the political system' and that has the capacity to carry out actions necessary for realizing the challenge: 'holding meetings, planning events, issuing statements, calling demonstrations, and raising money' (ibid.: 14). His random sample includes ten socialist groups (19 per cent), six right-wing groups (11 per cent), seventeen reform groups (32 per cent), and twenty occupational groups (38 per cent). These various groups were most active in the 1830s, 1860s, 1880s, 1900s, and 1930s, which suggests a certain recurring and cyclical nature to their mobilization (ibid.: 21).

His notion of group success includes two dimensions. The first dimension concerns the degree to which the group gained acceptance by its main antagonists, which means that the group has experienced a change from 'hostility or indifference to a more positive relationship' (ibid.: 31), and is coded as 'full' or 'none' (ibid.: 28–29). The second dimension concerns the degree to which the group achieved new advantages for its members, which he divides into the categories 'many' and 'none' (ibid.: 29). The combination of these two dimensions produces a fourfold set of outcomes including full response, pre-emption, co-optation, and collapse. Figure 8.4 shows this fourfold classification and the number of groups that fall into each of the categories.

The figure shows that the largest portions of his sample either collapsed or achieved full response, 42 per cent and 38 per cent respectively. The remainder of the study seeks to explain these differences by examining the various group characteristics, strategies, and important historical factors.

Through a series of simple bivariate comparisons, Gamson identifies the key factors that account for high levels of success. In terms of group characteristics, large, bureaucratic, centralized groups with very little internal factionalism and high levels of outside sponsorship are more successful in achieving their aims. In terms of strategy, single-issue groups that do not seek to displace their antagonists and that offer selective incentives to their members are more successful. In addition, these same groups are more successful if they are willing to use violence and are able to avoid arrest by the authorities. Finally, in the light of the time period for his sample of groups, those that made challenges before the outbreak of the two World Wars

Acceptance

		Full	None
		Full Response	Pre-emption
New advantages	Many	20	6
		(38%)	(11%)
		Co-optation	Collapse
	None	5	22
		(9%)	(42%)

Figure 8.4 Outcomes of 53 'challenging groups' in the US, 1800–1945
Source: Adapted from Gamson (1975: figs 3.1 and 3.2)

and the Great Depression were more successful than were those that made challenges during these periods of international and national crisis.

These findings challenge much of the popular wisdom on social movements in the United States as well as other advanced societies in many important ways. First, they suggest that social movements are not an irrational response to an underlying failure of the political system, but organized, bureaucratic, and rational instances of group challenge. Second, collective action is most effective when groups offer 'selective incentives' to their members (see Briefing box 8.4). Third, the use of violence and the level of repression have a direct bearing on movement outcomes. In addition to these three developments, his findings have provided a fruitful number of scholarly paths of inquiry for subsequent studies on social movements in different time periods and in other countries. For example, the study of social movement organizations has continued to be important (see Zald and Ash 1966; Dalton 1994; Kriesi 1996) as well as comparative studies on policing of social movement protest activity (e.g. Della Porta 1996; Della Porter and Reiter 1998).

Sidney Tarrow (1989) examines how the boundaries of mass politics have been extended using the case of protest in Italy during the turbulent decade 1965–1975. During this period the country saw a wave of protest that started with organized strikes and university protests and spread to workers and high school students, doctors and patients, railroad men and commuters, bishops and priests, and rival regions and cities (ibid.: 5). His choice of Italy is defended on several grounds. First, its wave of protest started earlier, lasted longer, and affected its society more than other patterns in Western Europe. Second, the Italian case has long been ignored by other work on social movements and serves as a least likely case study (see Chapter 2 in this volume) since Italy, of all the systems in Europe, still managed to survive the disorders of this decade of mass protest (ibid.: 5–6). Third, according to Tarrow (ibid.: 7), the Italian case demonstrates that not only was it capable of surviving the crisis, but it emerged as a 'mature capitalist democracy'. Drawing heavily on previous

---

Briefing box 8.4 Mancur Olson and selective incentives

In *The Logic of Collective Action*, Mancur Olson (1965) develops a theory that raises a paradox concerning the propensity of individuals to join groups. First, he assumed that individual political behaviour is similar to individual economic behaviour, where it is rational for people to weigh the costs and benefits of choosing to follow some course of action. Second, he assumed that groups that mobilize around some common interest are providing a collective good, or a good that extends beyond the members of the group, such as environmental protection. Third, Olson argues that the provision of the collective good is not enough to make people join groups, since an individual does not have to join the group in order enjoy the benefits of its actions. Such an individual is known as a 'free rider', since he or she can enjoy the benefits of the group without enduring the cost of taking part in its activities. Fourth, if it is rational for individuals to be free riders, then, Olson argues, groups must provide certain goods only for those who participate. These goods are known as 'selective incentives' (ibid.: 51). Selective incentives can either be punishment for not participating or reward for participating. These are known respectively as negative and positive selective incentives (ibid.: 51). Only by offering such incentives can a group begin to mobilize supporters.

The idea of selective incentives is important for the study of social movements since it is not at all obvious that grievance alone is enough to bring people to action (see Foweraker 1995:15–16). Involvement in social movement activity is costly in terms of time, money, and other resources. In extreme cases, social movement activity can turn violent and thus threaten the physical well-being of movement participants. Formal social movement organizations such as environmental groups, or labour unions, women's groups, gay liberation groups, etc. must in some way provide a set of selective incentives in order to mobilize supporters. These incentives can come in many different forms, such as monthly newsletters, discounts on health or car insurance, reduced interest rates on credit cards, or more simple ephemera like bumper stickers, mugs, and shirts that send a signal to outsiders that members of the organization are in some way special.

---

work on social movements such as Gamson (1975), Tarrow (1989:7–8) focuses on forms of action, their evolution over time, the structure of their demands, and their interaction with antagonists in an attempt to understand the magnitude and dynamics of change in politics and society. Like Gamson and others, he sees collective protest as an 'outcome of a calculus of risk, cost, and incentive' (ibid.: 8).

One of the key contributions of this study for other comparative work on social movements is the notion of a 'cycle of protest' (see discussion of Kriesi *et al.* 1995 above, on pp. 132–133), which has the following identifiable features and trajectory:

> [A] cycle of protest begins with conventional patterns of conflict within existing organizations and institutions. As it gathers strength, new actors use expressive

and confrontational forms of action, demonstrating to others less daring than themselves that the system is vulnerable to disruption and that they have grievances in common. This expands the range of contention to new sectors and institutions, but without the confrontation or the excitement of the 'early risers'. Confrontation gives way to deliberate violence only towards the end of the cycle, as mobilization declines, repression increases, people defect to interest groups and institutions, and extremists are left to compete for support from a shrinking social base.

(Tarrow 1989:8)

He combines this notion of the cycle of protest with that of the political opportunity structure (see Kitschelt 1986) to account for the patterns of protest and decline that he observes in the Italian case.

Drawing on earlier studies of political violence and the comparison of social movement activity in many countries, the study uses the protest event as the unit of analysis. Like Tilly (1978) and Kriesi *et al.* (1995), the study gathers protest data using a detailed event-coding protocol that includes the type of event, its main actors, its target and direction, the type of organizations involved in the event, the direct outcomes of the event, and the various responses of government (Tarrow 1989: 349–356). These data are collected primarily from newspaper coverage of events (*Corriere della Sera*) and corroborated with other primary and secondary materials (movement documents, statistical records, and interviews) – a process which yields nearly 5,000 protest events for the Italian case (ibid.: 30–31, 360). The time-series analysis of the data is complemented with a qualitative focus on archetypal social movement organizations from the student, worker, and religious movements. Overall, the quantitative and qualitative evidence is used to provide descriptive accounts of this particular Italian cycle of protest, analytical statements about the origins, shape, and outcomes of social movements in Italy, as well as larger inferences about social movements and democracy.

Tarrow (ibid.: 58) argues that by the mid-1960s the post-war settlement that characterized the Italian political system began to show certain cracks due to 'the conflicts of a maturing capitalist society and the divisions in its political class'. These cracks created the political opportunity for mobilization by organized labour, newly emerging immigrant workers, and new middle-strata groups. Their demands and grievances centred on distributional claims that expanded to more general claims for new rights (ibid.: 138). The cycle of protest that Tarrow (ibid.: 62) describes reached its first peak in the spring of 1968, levelled off through 1969–1970 and then peaked again in 1971, and again in the middle of 1972, after which it declined until the end of the period. While the cycle of protest was largely characterized by 'classical forms of democratic public expression', the protests during the 1972 peak and decline saw a rise in more confrontational and violent forms of action, which were still in a distinct minority (ibid.: 81).

For the Italian case, Tarrow (ibid.: 323–324) concludes that the cycle of protest came to an end with the rise of violent protest and repression on the one hand, and political institutionalization on the other. These experiences with violence and institutionalization changed Italian political culture and gave ordinary people a new sense of autonomy and efficacy in contrast to earlier forms of paternalism (ibid.:

329). The cycle of protest introduced new actors into the political sphere who asserted new collective identities that erode traditional patterns of support for existing political parties (ibid.: 331). Finally, the cycle of protest led to real policy reforms across a range of new issues, such as abortion (ibid.: 335–336).

In addition to these conclusions about the Italian case, Tarrow draws larger inferences about the relationship between disorder and democracy. He argues that protest produces instability and even violence, but in the long run does not undermine democracy. Rather, 'democracy expands, not because elites concede reform or repress dissent, but because of the insistent expansion of participation that occurs within cycles of protest' (ibid.: 347–348). The limits of making inferences from a single-country study appear to be reached when Tarrow switches his focus to non-democratic systems. For him, cycles of protest under authoritarian and totalitarian systems are 'parenthetical' periods 'in a long dreary saga of repression and demobilization' (ibid.: 346). But this conclusion stands in stark contrast to the one reached by Foweraker and Landman (1997), whose comparison demonstrates that social mobilization is a critical component to regime liberalization and democratic transition, as well as a catalyst for greater participation. Moreover, Parsa's (2000) comparison of Iran, Nicaragua, and the Philippines shows that large-scale social mobilization is possible under authoritarian conditions (see Chapter 7) as does Hawkins's 2002 study of human rights mobilization under the Pinochet regime in Chile (see Chapter 11).

The final study in this chapter is on the women's movement in the United States from 1950 to 1985 (Costain 1992). Like Tarrow (1989) it is a single-country study of social movement activity in a mature capitalist democracy that uses the same protest-coding techniques and posits a relationship between changing political opportunities and patterns of protest. Like Gamson (1975), the study gauges the impact of the women's movement, and like Bashevkin (1998), it uses legislative decisions as a measure of movement success. Costain (1992) codes protest data from the *New York Times Index* and legislative events from the *Congressional Quarterly*. These data are supplemented with newspaper coverage of women's issues, individual-level data on support for the movement, interviews with lobbyists from major social movement organizations (e.g. the National Organization for Women, Women's Equity Action League, and the National Women's Political Caucus), and documents from these organizations.

For the latter half of the twentieth century, women's mobilization saw a decline through the late 1950s, a slight rise in the late 1960s, a peak in 1975, a decline and peak again in 1980, after which it saw a decline through the end of the period (ibid.: 9–10). For the twentieth century, the number of women's bills introduced and laws passed in the Congress rose sharply and peaked between 1919 and 1921. It peaked again between 1943 and 1944, while the highest peak in history was reached in 1973 and 1974 during the 93rd Congress (ibid.: 10–11). Throughout the remainder of the study, Costain (ibid.: 25) examines the relationship between the patterns of protest and lawmaking by focusing on the movement's mobilization of resources, the empowerment of supporters through consciousness-raising, and the ways in which government facilitates movement activities.

She argues that the structure of political opportunities changed significantly as the New Deal coalition began to break down in the late 1960s and early 1970s,

Table 8.2 Summary of comparative work on non-violent political dissent and social movements

Method	Number of countries	Exemplars	Origins	Results — Shape/strategy	Results — Impact
Comparing many countries	Between 29 democracies and 90 countries	Powell (1982); Haas and Stack (1983); Gurr (1993, 2000); Inglehart (1997); Inglehart and Welzel (2005)	Underlying economic change (growth, development, structural change), social heterogeneity, and group organization are important determinants of protest. Mixed results for the effects of political democracy		
Comparing few countries	Between 3 and 10 countries from North America, Europe, and Latin America	Kitschelt (1986); Dalton (1988, 1994); Kriesi et al. (1995); Foweraker & Landman (1997); Bashevkin (1998)	Movement supporters in Europe comprise well-educated, middle income, and professional people

Changing protection of political and civil rights can lead to increased mobilization | Different political opportunities can determine different movement strategies
Movements exhibit waves of mobilization with a distinct rise, peak, and decline
Early periods of protest are less violent than late periods
Labour mobilization tends to precede mobilization from other social movements | Political opportunities affect the type of movement impact
Mobilization can change public opinion about movement issues
Movements can make gains in 'lean' years
Social movements are a key component to the process of democratization |
| Single-country | Italy and the United States | Gamson (1975); Tarrow (1989); Costain (1992) | Government action can facilitate movement activity | Cycles of protest comprise early risers who are then joined by other sectors in a general peak of mass mobilization
Movement tactics change from more conventional to less conventional during a cycle of protest | Positive association between movements and legislative decisions
Cycles of protest enrich and strengthen democracy |

which in part explains the patterns in protest and legislation that she observes in the 1970s and 1980s (ibid.: xiv–xv). In addition, the changing opportunities for women with the advent of more effective birth control and the impact of them entering the workforce raised new issues and a new constituency for the women's movement that had not previously existed. To this coincidence of events was added the direct facilitation of the movement by the government initially signalled by John F. Kennedy's creation of the Presidential Commission on the Status of Women (ibid.: 23). By this time, the women's movement had the organizational capacity and an increasing willingness to seek collective solutions to women's problems in society (ibid.: 26).

With the aid of her time-series data, Costain chronicles the highs and lows of the movement as it struggled to bring about reform of America's dominant political institutions and culture. Rather than seeing a one-way flow of politics from movement to government, however, Costain paints a more nuanced picture of the mutually constitutive relationship among the movement, Congress, and public opinion. This relationship is neatly summarized in a statistical model in her Appendix and has been developed further in later work (see Costain and Majstorovic 1994). Beyond her immediate conclusions about the women's movement in the United States, Costain (1992) makes important inferences about the relationship between movements and governments. This relationship is not always an antagonistic one, and as Bashevkin (1998) also shows, many gains can be made within a political context that may be perceived initially as hostile to movement interests. Moreover, her study adds to the growing literature on social movements a series of effective methods for measuring and analysing the political nexus between movements and governments.

Summary

The comparison of comparisons in this chapter has pointed to a development in the social movement literature in terms of useful analytical concepts and the corroboration of important findings. The comparison of movements has refined the idea of a 'wave' or 'cycle' of protest that exhibits certain identifiable features and components, including the shape of mobilization, the participants, and the shifting pattern of strategies and demand-making. The political opportunity structure has proved a useful explanatory variable for movement strategy, shape, and impact. Finally, the idea of social movement organization (or SMO) is a useful category that appears to 'travel' quite well across different political contexts.

The comparisons variously demonstrated the explanatory importance of economic transformation, the social bases of protest groups and activity, collective identity, levels of organization, and political context. In terms of movement impact and outcomes, the studies have shown that the most likely result of protest is institutionalization, reform, the extension and protection of rights, and in many ways the public acceptance of political protest as a legitimate and alternative means for changing the dominant political institutions and culture. The comparisons have also revealed much about the relationship between protest and democracy, which may be further differentiated across movement sectors. Protest is more likely in democracies with less than three effective political parties. Political protest is likely to strengthen the ideal of democracy through increased political participation, which in turn may have important historical and cultural legacies. Finally, political protest is a critical component to political liberalization and democratic transition (see Table 8.2).

As Chapters 11 and 12 show, research on social movements has moved beyond the confines of the nation state to consider the different ways in which transnational social mobilization seeks to make changes through engagement with intergovernmental organizations such as the United Nations, the European Union and the Organisation of American States (Guest 1990; Weissbrodt and Bartolomei 1991; Risse *et al.* 1999; Imig and Tarrow 2001; Hawkins 2002; Bob 2005). Despite this move to look at movement emergence, trajectory, and impact at the international level, the analysis still very much relies on comparing the movements by the country within which they emerge and form links and against which they are mobilizing for change. Thus, despite this intentional foray into the traditional domain of international relations, this new work on social movements remained grounded in the kinds of comparative methods covered in this volume.

Further reading

Della Porta, D. and Diani, M. (1999) *Social Movements: An Introduction*, Oxford: Blackwell.
    A thorough review of social movement theory and research in advanced industrial democracies.

Foweraker, J. (1995) *Theorizing Social Movements*, London: Pluto Press.
    A comprehensive review of social movement theory and its ability to be used in contexts outside North America and Europe.

McAdam, D., McCarthy, J., and Zald, M.N. (1996) *Comparative Perspectives on Social Movements*, Cambridge: Cambridge University Press.
    This volume presents further developments in social movement theory and research.

Tarrow, S. (1994) *Power in Movement*, Cambridge: Cambridge University Press.
    This work traces the development of social movement theory and research.

Transitions to democracy

As the previous chapters have demonstrated, both the establishment and maintenance of democracy have long been a focus of comparative politics. Chapter 6 assessed the many comparisons of the relationship between economic development and democracy. Chapters 7 and 8 compared the ways in which scholars have analysed violent and non-violent challenges to political rule, as well as how those challenges are related to democracy. In addition to these research topics, the comparative study of democracy has also included a focus on critical historical moments of democratic transition. Democratic transitions increasingly became the object of comparative inquiry after the end of the Portuguese dictatorship in 1974, an event which ushered in the so-called 'third wave' of democracy in world history (Huntington 1991). The process of democratic transition that started in Portugal would spread to other authoritarian countries in Southern Europe, Latin America, Africa, Asia, and Eastern Europe such that by the beginning of the new millennium approximately 60 per cent of countries in the world are considered to have surpassed the minimum threshold for 'procedural' democracy (Diamond 1999:24–29; Zakaria 2003).

The global spread, pace, and process of democratization have become important topics for comparative politics and have led to the development of a sub-field in the discipline known as 'democratization studies' (Whitehead 1996a, 2002). While the bulk of democratization studies focus on the post-1974 transitions, some studies have sought to draw on the insights gained from researching earlier processes of democratization (Moore 1966; Therborn 1977; Rueschemeyer *et al.* 1992; Fischer 1996; Collier 1999). This chapter assesses key studies in this sub-field of comparative politics in an effort to demonstrate the different methods that have been used to answer a core set of common research questions surrounding the global proliferation of democratic rule.

The research problem

The comparisons outlined in this chapter variously seek to describe the global spread of democracy, to explain why, when, and where it happens, and to assess the future prospects for democracy in the world. Despite their different temporal and geographical foci, several defining research questions have remained the same. First, are there certain objective 'preconditions' for the establishment and maintenance of democracy (see Chapter 6 and Karl 1990)? Second, who are the 'agents' of democratization? Third, in reference to third-wave democracies, why have some countries that were initially thought to be 'doomed to endless authoritarianism', experienced democratic transitions (Levine 1989:377; Przeworski 1991:1)?[1] Fourth, what external factors help to promote democratic transitions? The studies included in this chapter have all sought to answer these questions; however, as in the previous chapters, the answers they provide are often a reflection of the comparative method they adopt.

Comparing many countries

As Chapter 6 demonstrated, the comparative literature is replete with examples of many-country studies that seek to explain democracy, but very few have focused on the process of democratic transition itself. The comparisons of democratic transition in this section include Huntington's (1991) qualitative global comparison of democratization; Jaggers and Gurr's (1995) description and classification of regimes during the third wave; Vanhanen's (1997) global comparison of democracy since the 1850s, and Doorenspleet's (2005) global analysis of democratization during the third and 'fourth' wave (i.e. post-1989 transitions). In each comparison the authors offer definitions of democracy and outline its different measures, while three of the studies examine a parsimonious set of explanatory factors for its appearance in time and geographical space.

In *The Third Wave*, Huntington (1991:15) defines a wave of democratic transition as a group of transitions from non-democratic to democratic regimes that occur within a specified period of time and that significantly outnumber transitions in the opposite direction during that period. He identifies three such waves in world history: the first was 1828–1926; the second 1943–1962; and the third 1974–1989. Each wave was punctuated by a period of democratic 'reversals' in which previously democratic regimes break down and authoritarian regimes are established. Since the first wave, both the number of countries and the number of democracies have increased to the extent that by 1990, Huntington (1991:26) considers 58 of the total 129 countries in the world to be democratic. The subsequent breakup of the Soviet Union added more independent countries to the world, a process that was accompanied by further democratization within the new Europe and in other regions as well (see the discussion of Doorenspleet below).

Figure 9.1 shows that the inter-war and war years saw a great reversal in democratization, while the immediate post-war years saw a dramatic increase in the number of democracies. More importantly, however, Huntington (1991) stresses that during the third wave the growth of democracy, expressed as a percentage increase, has been unprecedented in world history. His global qualitative comparison thus seeks to explain why and how countries became democratic during this period. The value of his study lies in his description of the third wave and less so in his explanation of it, which appears more as a series of possible factors that merit further comparative study (which subsequent studies have sought to test). For the methodological purposes of this book, this section examines his use of evidence in supporting his five propositions about why countries have become democratic during the third wave. The five explanatory factors for the democratic transitions between 1974 and 1990 are:

1   a developing crisis of legitimacy in the previous authoritarian regime;
2   high levels of economic growth in the 1960s;
3   changes in doctrine and practice within the Catholic Church;
4   a change in policies of important external actors; and
5   a general demonstration, or 'snowballing' effect across the globe (Huntington 1991:45–46).

He argues that there is no single cause of democratization and thus sees these five explanations as interdependent and cumulative (ibid.: 38). His study amasses various types of evidence in support of these five propositions, including aggregate statistics, anecdotal evidence, and informed personal impressions. Despite the comprehensive scope of the study, evidence is used to make qualitative comparisons that do not demonstrate the statistical significance of the patterns in democratization that are observed. Moreover, Huntington argues that a detailed comparison of the explanatory factors is beyond the scope of his study, particularly in reference to the role of legitimacy crisis, external actors, and demonstration effects. For example, he sees legitimacy as a 'mushy concept that political analysts do well to avoid' (ibid.: 46). In reference to external actors, he argues that the direct effects of the different foreign policies of the Carter and Reagan administrations on the process of democratization 'varied greatly from country to country and it would require extraordinary effort to evaluate the impact even in a single country' (ibid.: 95), where '[n]o definitive evaluation of the US role in third wave democratizations is possible here' (ibid.: 98). Finally, he suggests that '[to show] demonstration effects in individual cases is difficult and would require more intensive study than is possible here' (ibid.: 100).

In short, two of the five explanations for the third wave of democratization receive no more than impressionistic and anecdotal support, which perhaps is a good demonstration of the possible limitations of qualitative global comparisons, while pointing to future areas of research. For the two remaining factors (economic growth

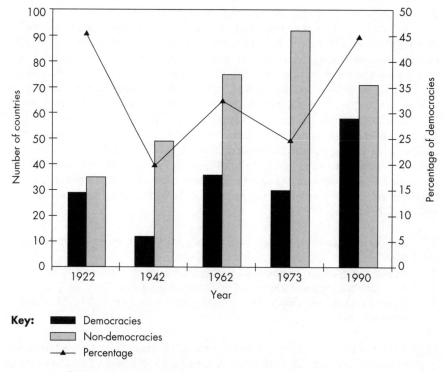

Figure 9.1 The growth and decay of democracy in the world
Source: Adapted from Huntington (1991: table 1.1)

and the impact of the Catholic Church), Huntington provides more robust evidence. For the post-1960 level of economic growth, virtually 90 per cent of the countries that experienced political liberalization or democratic transition reside in the 'middle range' of world per capita GDP, while half of the third-wave countries have incomes between US$1,000 and US$3,000 (ibid.: 63). While conceding that there is not a necessary relationship between economic development and democracy, he none the less implies that there is a positive association between the two such that economic development 'provided the basis for democracy; crises produced by either rapid growth or economic recession weakened authoritarianism' (ibid.: 59). He argues further that economic development involving significant industrialization unleashed a complex set of social forces which authoritarian regimes were unable to control, such as new values, education, better resources, trade liberalization, and the expansion of the middle class (ibid.: 65–66; compare Rueschemeyer *et al.* 1992).

For the role of the Catholic Church in fostering democracy, Huntington (1991:76) argues that nearly 75 per cent of the third-wave countries were Catholic. The wave started in Portugal and Spain, moved to Central and South America, the Philippines, back to Chile and Mexico (technically, Mexico did not experience its transition until 2000), and then to Poland and Hungary. Huntington claims there are several reasons for this 'Catholic effect'. First, traditionally poor Catholic countries experienced rates of growth that facilitated transitions to democracy (ibid.: 77). Second, the progressive turn of the Catholic Church at both the global and regional level led to increased grass-roots organizing and the mobilization of lay people in an effort to express grievances about conditions of poverty and repression. Third, a series of Papal visits to authoritarian countries encouraged regime liberalization. In sum, authoritarian regimes were pressured by the Catholic Church from above and below to initiate transitions to democracy (ibid.: 79–85).

In contrast to Huntington's (1991) qualitative comparison of the third wave, Jaggers and Gurr (1995) have employed the global and time-series Polity III data set[2] to 'track' the third wave descriptively across the globe and by region. The data set includes two measures of regime type – autocracy and democracy – which, when combined, give an overall measure of democracy in a given country at a specific time. The combined measure expresses the difference between the level of autocracy and democracy in a country across five main indicators, including the competitiveness of political participation, regulation of participation, competitiveness of executive recruitment, openness of executive recruitment, and constraints on the chief executive (ibid.: 472). Countries are awarded points on the democracy scale for high competitiveness of participation and executive recruitment, the absence of regulation, openness of recruitment, and restrictions on executive authority. Alternatively, countries are awarded points on the autocracy scale for having little or no competitiveness, high degrees of regulation, closed recruitment, and few constraints on executive authority (ibid.: 472).

Overall, the democracy minus autocracy measure ranges from positive ten for states that are purely democratic and negative ten for those that are purely autocratic (ibid.: 473). The score itself is highly correlated with other measures of democracy previously used in comparative studies of democratic performance (see Chapters 6 and 10), leading the authors to conclude that the measure of democracy is empirically valid (Jaggers and Gurr 1995:476). Beyond the quantitative aspects of the measure, it seeks to capture the idea that a country may have democratic and autocratic elements that co-exist at any one time. Descriptively, a time-series plot of the measure since 1960 shows that 'until the late 1970s, the post-1960 global trend was one of increasing autocracy in the international state system and a concomitant decline in the degree of democracy' (ibid.: 476). Only with the democratic transitions in Spain and Portugal, followed by those in Latin America, Eastern Europe, and parts of Asia and Africa, does this downward trend become reversed. Thus, by 1990, the 'degree of democracy in the international system surpassed the degree of autocracy' (ibid.: 476). These quantitative trends thus corroborate Huntington's (1991) description of the third wave.

These descriptive trends are analysed further in two ways. First, the authors examine the differences in the degree of democracy among five regions in the world: the Americas, Eurasia, Africa, the Middle East, and Asia and the Pacific. For the 1990s, only countries in sub-Saharan Africa and the Middle East have higher levels of autocracy than democracy. Second, they classify the globe into coherent and incoherent polities, which can be either democracies or autocracies. On the one hand, coherent democracies and coherent autocracies are located at the extreme ends of the combined measure (coherent democracies ≥ 7 and coherent autocracies ≤ -7). On the other hand, incoherent democracies and incoherent autocracies occupy the middle range of values ($-6 \leq$ incoherent autocracies ≤ 0 and $0 \leq$ incoherent democracies ≤ 6) (Jaggers and Gurr 1995:478–479). Conceptually, incoherent polities are most vulnerable to regime change either in a positive direction towards democracy or a negative direction towards autocracy. By 1994 the world (151 countries) is comprised of 18 per cent coherent autocracies, 50 per cent coherent democracies, 19 per cent incoherent autocracies, and 13 per cent incoherent democracies. These results suggest that 32 per cent of the world's countries may either move towards democracy or experience a reversal towards autocracy while a further 18 per cent await an initial impulse towards democracy (ibid.: 479).

This global comparison of regime type based on the difference between the level of autocracy and democracy in a country is useful for the descriptive patterns of the third wave, even though the authors have yet to identify the 'causes of these different patterns of regime change' (ibid.: 479). The global comparisons outlined in Chapter 6 that examined the relationship between economic development and democracy demonstrated one way in which these causes may be identified; however, these studies were not concerned with democratic transition *per se*. In contrast, the work of Tatu Vanhanen (1984, 1990, 1997, 2003) does seek to identify a causal explanation for democratization that holds across the globe (between 119 and 172 countries) and for all time (1850 to the present). This section of the chapter considers Vanhanen's comparative effort entitled *The Prospects of Democracy* (Vanhanen 1997), which builds on his previous work and differs little from his more recent study (Vanhanen 2003).

Rather than rely on subjective measures of the degree of democracy in a country using a series of ranked indicators, Vanhanen establishes an objective measure of democracy using two electoral indicators thought to capture the democratic principles of *competition* and *participation*. Competition is measured using the percentage votes cast in either presidential or parliamentary elections (or both) for the smaller political parties (i.e. 100 minus the share of the largest party).

Participation is measured by the percentage of the population who actually voted in the election (ibid.: 34). Assuming that both these principles are essential for democracy and that both are of equal value, an Index of Democratization (ID) is created by multiplying the measures of competition and participation together. Thus, high values denote a greater degree of democracy, while a zero on either component reduces the index to zero (ibid.: 35). This index of democratization serves as the dependent variable for the global comparisons, which Vanhanen carries out for the periods 1850–1979 (119 countries), 1980–1988 (147 countries), and 1991–1993 (172 countries).

The independent variable is a combination of six separate indicators that represent the distribution of power resources in a country. The six indicators include the number of university students per 100,000 inhabitants, the area of family farms as a percentage of the total area of holdings, the degree of centralization of non-agricultural economic resources, as well as the urban population, the non-agricultural population, and the literate population, all expressed as a percentage of the total population (ibid.: 42). In contrast to the studies outlined in Chapter 4 above, the index of power resources includes indicators of economic development as well as measures that capture the distribution of resources in a society. Thus, it leaves room for poor countries with well-distributed resources and rich countries with concentrated resource distributions. Vanhanen (ibid.: 155) argues that the distribution of power resources is the most important single causal factor to account for democratization in the world since 1850.

The remainder of his analysis uses correlation and regression to examine the relationship between the distribution of power resources and democratization for his three global samples of countries. The results of the statistical analysis show that the distribution of power resources explains 66 per cent of the variance in the degree of democracy for the total sample for 1850–1993, while it explains between 59 and 65 per cent of the variance for the sample from 1991–1993 (ibid.: 155). Using these findings over time and space, Vanhanen seeks to predict on a regional and country-specific level, the likelihood that democratization will take place. Table 9.1 summarizes his predictions for the regions of the world, predictions which appear to be upheld in three: (1) Latin America and the Caribbean (democracy), (2) sub-Saharan Africa (non-democracy), (3) East and Southeast Asia (non-democracy). His model is unable to account for the collapse of the Soviet Union and the democratic transitions in Eastern Europe. It failed to predict the maintenance of authoritarianism in North Africa, the Middle East, and East Asia, and did not foresee the process of democratization in South Asia and Oceania.

Renske Doorenspleet (2005) uses a modified version of the Polity data in her global comparative analysis to uncover the factors that account for democratization in the years after the Cold War (1989–2000). She labels this period the 'fourth wave' as it has some different features than the other waves of democracy described in Huntington (1991), and she tests a number of dominant propositions about the main explanatory factors that account for democracy. Her analysis is in agreement with Przeworski *et al.* (2000) in finding no support for an economic effect on demo-cratization, which is to say, authoritarian regimes in more developed countries are not any more likely to democratize than those in poor countries. She also finds that class structure has little to do with democratization. She does find that authoritarian countries with greater external economic links to core countries (see Chapter 6 in this volume) are more likely to democratize, and that international diffusion of democracy measured in terms of the number of democratic neighbours is an important factor (see Chapter 12 in this volume).

Global analysis of democratic transitions has not yet produced a series of consistent findings. On the one hand, as the analyses in Chapter 6 showed, the link between economic development and democratic transition has only really been sustained by the work of Carles Boix (see Boix 2003 and Boix and Stokes 2003). While Przeworski *et al.* (2000) rule out economic development as a main explanatory factor for democratization (something that Doorenspleet confirms), they do not provide a set of generalizations that apply across the experiences of democratic transition. Huntington (1991) and Jaggers and Gurr (1995) map the waves of democracy well, but again provide less in the way of explanation for the trends they observe. The contradictions in Vanhanen's results highlight the trade-offs associated with different methods of comparison. Like the comparisons in Chapter 6 above, a simple set of variables may account for regularities observed at the global level, yet the examination of the findings at the regional level become problematic, leading scholars to search for additional explanatory variables. To be fair, Vanhanen does not rule out other explanations for democracy such as political culture, external influences, and political institutions, but his comparative aspirations prevent him from operationalizing more context-specific variables. The comparative studies in the next section consciously examine a smaller number of countries in an effort to be sensitive to such context-specific factors while still attempting to draw larger inferences about the process of democratic transition.

Comparing few countries

In general, the sub-field of democratization studies emerged from the comparison of few countries as scholars responded to the first democratic transitions in Southern Europe and Latin America. Studies using this method of comparison tend to suffer from selection bias, since their focus is usually on countries that had experienced or were experiencing democratic transitions (compare the discussion of Wolf 1969 in Chapter 7 above). This section of the chapter examines three such studies, including O'Donnell *et al.*'s (1986a, 1986b, 1986c) *Transitions from Authoritarian Rule*, Peeler's (1992) comparison of elite settlements in Venezuela, Colombia, and Costa Rica, and Linz and Stepan's (1996) *Problems of Democratic Transition and Consolidation*. The O'Donnell *et al.* (1986a, b and c) volumes are collections of essays written by various scholars on fifteen countries of Southern Europe and Latin America and certainly stand as the origin of the current sub-field of democratization studies in comparative politics. Peeler's (1992) piece follows in the same tradition yet looks back in history to earlier transitions in Latin America, while Linz and Stepan's (1996) volume seeks to move beyond the study of democratic transition and makes larger inferences about the process of democratic consolidation in Southern Europe, Latin America, and post-communist Europe. These three studies are then contrasted to a comparative study of 'democratic experiments' in sub-Saharan Africa,

Table 9.1 Prospects for democracy in the world

Regions	Number of countries Total = 172	Prediction
Europe & North America	40	Prospects for democracy in North America are very high despite the serious problem of low electoral participation in the US Democracy likely to survive in Western Europe Collapse of socialist systems in Eastern Europe not predicted, yet the level of resource distribution is high enough to maintain democracy Democracy will survive in the new states of the former Soviet Union
Latin America and the Caribbean	29	The victory of democracy in Latin America in the 1980s was not unexpected from the perspective of resource distribution, and democracy will be more or less permanent in the region
North Africa, Middle East, and Central Asia	29	Democratization in the region has been much lower than expected, and the region shows the highest number of deviant cases for which alternative explanations are necessary
Sub-Saharan Africa	44	The region has the lowest level of democratization in the world, which is consistent with its equally low degree of resource distribution Despite the desire for democratization, the chances for establishing long-lasting democratic institutions are still very poor
South Asia	7	The degree of democracy was higher than expected Region demonstrates that democracy is possible in poor countries with a sufficient distribution of power resources
East Asia and Southeast Asia	16	The degree of democracy deviates very little from what was expected Popular pressures for democratization will be resisted by socialist and former socialist countries in the region
Oceania	7	The degree of democracy is higher than expected

Source: Adapted from Vanhanen (1997:106–154)

which compares the divergent paths to democratic transition across forty-two countries (Bratton and van de Walle 1997).

The scholars responsible for the four-volume set of studies of *Transitions from Authoritarian Rule* (O'Donnell *et al.* 1986) spent time together at the Wilson Center for International Scholars in Washington DC in an effort to explain and understand the democratic transitions in Southern Europe and Latin America. Volumes I and II contain thirteen single-country studies of democratization, and Volumes III and IV draw together the comparative findings across the cases. While conceding that transitions from authoritarian rule can lead to the 'instauration of political democracy, or the restoration of a new, and possibly more severe form of authoritarian rule', the thirteen studies focus primarily on processes of political liberalization and democratization (O'Donnell and Schmitter 1986:3–14).[3] The countries that comprise the studies in the volume include Italy, Greece, Portugal, Spain, Turkey, Argentina, Bolivia, Brazil, Chile, Mexico, Peru, Uruguay, and Venezuela. The authors accept the diversity of these contexts, yet their comparison searches for points of convergence across all the cases to help explain the process of democratization, while avoiding a 'test' of a specific theory of democratic transition (ibid.: 3).

To begin an assessment of this collection of studies, Table 9.2 summarizes the main explanatory factors and outcomes of each of the thirteen case studies in order to demonstrate the areas of convergence and divergence in the process of democratization across the countries. To some degree, the studies avoid selection bias since some of the countries have not experienced democratic transitions. Since the studies were written during the third wave, many of the political outcomes in the table are cases of no transition, yet the authors tried to anticipate the political changes that were to come in the future. Overall, the studies in these volumes establish the conceptual differences between liberalization, democratic transition, and redemocratization (O'Donnell and Schmitter 1986:2–14), while their comparisons reveal a common set of factors that help account for these different types of regime.

In the final volume to the series, O'Donnell and Schmitter (1986) draw tentative conclusions about the thirteen cases. They accept the inherent uncertainty of the outcomes, and this highlights a more general problem with the comparativist's 'preoccupation with the immediate, leading to a certain trendiness – a penchant for wanting to follow the events of the day' (Valenzuela 1988:78). Indeed, some of the non-democratic countries listed in Table 9.2 are now recognized as having undergone democratic transitions (Chile, Brazil, Bolivia, and Mexico), while others have seen a reversal of their transitions (e.g. Peru 1992–2000) (see Foweraker *et al.* 2003: 34–55). In most cases, the impulse for liberalization comes from within the authoritarian regime itself; from a conflict between 'hard-liners' who seek to maintain the authoritarian regime and 'soft-liners' who seek to initiate a process of liberalization in an effort to legitimize the regime (O'Donnell and Schmitter 1986:15–21). These two different groups of elites within the regime effectively weigh the costs of further authoritarianism (domestic and foreign opposition and loss of legitimacy) against the costs of liberalization (increased social and political instability).

In most cases, liberalization of the authoritarian regime is accompanied by the 'resurrection of civil society' (ibid.: 26–27, 48–56) in which increased social

Table 9.2 Transitions from authoritarian rule

Author	Country	Main explanatory factors	Outcome
Pasquino	Italy 1943–1948	Overthrow of dictator Allied liberation & Cold War Domestic forces (parties and resistance) Process of constitution drafting	Democratic transition
Maravall and Santamaria	Spain 1975	Pacts and negotiations between elites	Democratic transition
Maxwell	Portugal 1974	Decolonization Progressive military coup followed by popular mobilization Failure to liberalize	Democratic transition
Diamandouros	Greece 1974	Elite calculations Cyprus crisis General mobilization	Democratic transition
Sunar and Sayari	Turkey	Military dominated process Legacy of centralized state power	Liberalization
Cavarozzi	Argentina 1955–1983	Cycles of civilian–military regimes Failure of neo-liberal economic model Defeat in Malvinas/Falklands Radical Party leadership of Alfonsín	Democratic transition
Whitehead	Bolivia 1977–1980	General Banzer initiates transition Crisis in military–peasant pact Warring factions split authoritarian regime Inconclusive electoral results (3 elections) Absence of minimum alliance conditions	No, but weak democracy established in 1982

Table 9.2 continued

Author	Country	Main explanatory factors	Outcome
Martins	Brazil 1974–1985	Political liberalization initiated in 1974 End of economic miracle Military controls prolonged liberalization Increased social mobilization	Liberalization
Garretón	Chile 1980–1986	1980 referendum and constitution Regime crisis in early 1980s No opposition with alternative vision to military regime	No transition
Middlebrook	Mexico 1977–1986	Popular protest and repression in 1968 Alternative party formation Raise legitimacy of governing party	Liberalization
Cotler	Peru 1963 and 1977–1980	Intense social and political struggle Economic crisis in 1977 Elite bargain and 'transfer of office'	Democratic transition
Gillespie	Uruguay 1973–1984	Elite negotiation between dominant parties Public approval of liberalization pacts	Redemocratization
Karl	Venezuela 1958	Presence of petroleum Political pacts between two dominant political parties	Democratic transition

Source: Summary of O'Donnell et al. (1986a, 1986b)

mobilization creates pressure for democracy (see also Foweraker and Landman 1997; Bratton and van de Walle 1997). Despite this 'bottom-up' impulse for democrat- ization, the authors in this series tend to emphasize the important role played by elites in the democratic transition as they form 'negotiated pacts', which set out the 'rules governing the exercise of power' (O'Donnell and Schmitter 1986:37; see also Howarth 1998b). Finally, the moment of transition in most of the countries is accompanied by the announcement of elections either for a constituent assembly (as in the case of Peru) or for the first elections for some set of representatives (as in the case of Brazilian governors), or for both purposes. These elections serve to motivate both the political parties from before the authoritarian period and newly formed political parties to assume a more prominent role in the democratic transition, while the election itself is seen to be a founding event (O'Donnell and Schmitter 1986:57).

Adopting a focus similar to that of the previous set of studies, Peeler (1992) compares the historical experiences of Colombia, Costa Rica, and Venezuela, all of which have shown reasonable stability (until recently in the cases of Colombia and Venezuela) in their democratic institutions since the 1950s and serve as possible models for countries undergoing democratic transition during the third wave. While recognizing the differences between these cases, the comparative analysis examines how 'elite settlement' helps found the democratic regimes and how 'elite convergence' contributed to their survival (ibid.: 83; see also Briefing box 9.1). In addition, Peeler's study looks at the relationship between elite and mass behaviour at the moment of transition. He argues that democratic consolidation is more likely in countries where participation has been extended to all elites while some form of vertical control is established for channelling popular demands (ibid.: 83).

Table 9.3 summarizes the comparison with separate rows for prior conditions, crises, the moment of transition, and the period of consolidation. Colombia and Venezuela were important political and economic centres for the Spanish Empire whereas Costa Rica was isolated and offered nothing of interest to Spain. All three cases developed strong political classes and a coffee export economy. The years of crisis had similar origins that led to political conflict and violence between rival elites, and both Colombia and Venezuela experienced periods of dictatorship. In all three cases, the transition to democracy 'involved explicit pact making on the part of competing elites', which established 'competition within an agreed-upon framework of rules' (Peeler 1992:94). Finally, all three cases have withstood serious challenges to democratic rule from domestic and foreign sources where Costa Rica and Venezuela have fared the best in terms of democratic stability.

Linz and Stepan's (1996) comparison concentrates on countries in Southern Europe, Latin America, and post-communist Europe. Conducting their research after the third wave and during some of the fourth wave (i.e. post-1989), the authors are able to expand the scope of the comparison to the post-communist world and to extend their substantive focus to questions of democratic consolidation. The post- communist countries possess different 'starting conditions' and therefore face different constraints in the process of democratic transition and consolidation. For the countries from Southern Europe, there has been some time since their transitions, so the authors can make larger inferences about the key factors for successful democratic consolidation. They compare fifteen countries in total: three from Southern Europe, four from South America, and eight from post-communist Europe.

Briefing box 9.1 Elite settlement and elite convergence

The twin concepts of *elite settlement* and *elite convergence* have been used to explain the process of democratic transition and prospects for democratic consolidation from a perspective in which elites stop fighting with one another and essentially 'agree to disagree' within a peaceful framework of governance. An elite settlement is a political situation in which two warring factions of elites 'suddenly and deliberately reorganize their relations by negotiating compromises on their most basic disagreements' (Burton *et al.* 1992:13). Once the basic differences have ceased to cause violence between factions, they pave the way for open and peaceful competition and they may eventually lead to democratic consolidiation. In general, elite settlements stem from long periods of conflict and crises that threaten to rekindle widespread violence. Examples of elite settlements from history include England (1688–1689), Sweden (1809), Mexico (1929), Costa Rica (1948), Colombia (1957–1958), Venezuela (1958), and Spain and the Dominican Republic (1970s) (ibid.: 14).

Elite convergence occurs after an elite settlement and is isolated to unconsolidated democracies. It is characterized by a coalition of opposing factions within a disunified set of elites who are able to mobilize significant electoral majorities to dominant government executive power (ibid.: 24). Elite convergence progresses until the subordinate group of elites learns to beat the dominant group through the electoral process. This acceptance of the democratic rules of the game and the eventual sharing of electoral victories leads to democratic consolidation. In addition, competition over the middle set of voters necessarily means that the political spectrum becomes less polarized (ibid.: 25). Examples of elite convergence from history include: France from 1958 to the period of co-habitation in the 1980s; Norway and Denmark (1900–1933); and Italy, Japan, and Greece (1970s–1990s) (ibid.: 25).

The authors consider the first set to be 'completed consolidations' and the second set 'constrained transitions', while they argue the third set faces 'most complex paths and tasks' in order to consolidate democracy.

Their comparison seeks to develop a set of master variables that help account for different types of democratic transition and different modes of democratic consolidation. The set includes a total of seven variables: two macro-variables, two middle-range variables, and three contextual variables. The first macro-variable is 'stateness', which captures the degree to which a country is sovereign and has established a national identity and national cohesion (Linz and Stepan 1996:16–37). The second macro-variable is the type of regime that preceded the democratic transition, including authoritarian, totalitarian, post-totalitarian, and sultanistic (ibid.: 38–54; see also Briefing box 9.2). The middle-range variables include the leadership base of the previous regime (hierarchical military, non-hierarchical military, civilian, or sultanistic) and who initiates the democratic transition (civil society, regime collapse, armed revolution, non-hierarchical military coup, or

Table 9.3 Elite settlements and democratic transition

	Colombia	Costa Rica	Venezuela
Prior conditions	Colonial centre and strong creole upper class Strong Liberal and Conservative Parties Elections seen as a device for legitimation Coffee export economy (late)	Isolated, weak, and poor Individual politics and no development of parties Elections seen as a device for legitimation Coffee export economy (early) Development of public schooling	Colonial centre and strong planter class Liberal and Conservative parties, local boss rule Elections seen as a device for legitimation Coffee export economy (early)
Years of crisis	Great Depression and WWII Communist and populist parties Violence and dictatorship until 1958	Great Depression and WWII Communist and populist parties Personalist regime	Great Depression and WWII Communist and populist parties Dictatorship 1948–1958
Democratic transition	Explicit pact between competing elites National Front agreement and rotation of power	Explicit pact between competing elites Figueres–Ulate pact	Explicit pact between competing elites Three-way pact called Punto Fijo
Democratic consolidation	Deconsolidation and breakdown since 1974	Unbroken series of elections since 1953	Unbroken series of elections since 1958[†]

Source: Adapted from Peeler (1992:84–108)
Note: [†]Venezuela experienced a series of coup attempts in 1992 followed by the impeachment of Carlos Andres Perez (see Landman 1995) and Foweraker *et al.* (2003).

hierarchical state) (ibid.: 66–71). The three contextual variables are international influences, the political economy of regime legitimacy, and the environment in which the new democratic constitution is promulgated (ibid.: 72–83).

These seven variables are then examined across the fifteen countries in an effort to differentiate the experiences of democratic transition and to specify the degree to which democracy has been consolidated in each country. Table 9.5 summarizes the comparison by listing all fifteen countries in the first column followed by columns for the seven variables and a column for the outcome, namely democratic consolidation. Immediately apparent from the table is the problem of 'too many variables

Briefing box 9.2 Linz and Stepan's (1996) classification of prior regime types

A critical variable for Linz and Stepan's (1996) comparative project is the type of regime that precedes the democratic transition. They argue that the type of regime establishes constraints and determines in large part the paths to democracy. Like Aristotle and Finer (see Briefing Box 1.1), they use classification to define four basic types of modern non-democratic regimes, ranging from least to most authoritarian. These four types are *authoritarianism*, *totalitarianism*, *post-totalitarianism*, and *sultanism* (Linz and Stepan 1996:40–54). In addition, they specify three sub-types of post-totalitarianism, including early post-totalitarianism, frozen post-totalitarianism, and mature post-totalitarianism. Each of these prior regime types is categorized according to differences among their degrees of pluralism, their establishment and use of ideology, their capacity for popular mobilization, and their composition and style of leadership (ibid.: 44–45).

Following early work by Linz (1964) and O'Donnell (1973), Linz and Stepan argue that authoritarian regimes have limited forms of pluralism (particularly in the economic sphere), no overarching ideology, low levels of regime-led popular mobilization, and a small group of leaders who seek to incorporate sympathetic dominant elites. Totalitarian regimes have no pluralism, a hegemonic political party with a totalizing ideology and vision for social transformation, a strong capacity and tendency for popular mobilization, and often charismatic and arbitrary leaders with a committed, lower-level staff. Post-totalitarian regimes evolve from totalitarian regimes and have limited pluralism and possible parallel forms of opposition, a dominant party with a totalizing ideology and vision for social transformation that has begun to wane, less of a capacity and interest in popular mobilization, and less charismatic and more bureaucratic leaders. Sultanistic regimes have a low

Table 9.4 Modern non-democratic regimes

Regime type	Examples
Authoritarian	Argentina, Brazil, Chile, Spain, Portugal, Poland
Totalitarian	Soviet Union until Brezhnev period
Post-totalitarian	Soviet Union under Gorbachev; Russia, Estonia, Latvia after collapse of Soviet Union
Early post-totalitarian	Bulgaria
Frozen post-totalitarian	Czechoslovakia
Mature post-totalitarian	Hungary

Source: Adapted from Linz and Stepan (1996)

degree of pluralism that is subject to the arbitrary whims of the leader, a personalistic ideology that is not justified or strongly supported outside the inner circle of the leader, periodic regime-led popular mobilization, and a personalized, charismatic, and arbitrary leader. In addition to these four basic regime types, the authors specify a further three regime sub-types that lie on the continuum of post-totalitarianism. Early post-totalitarianism is the closest to totalitarianism, frozen post-totalitarianism is in the middle of the continuum, and mature post-totalitarianism is closest to making a transition to either authoritarianism or democracy (Linz and Stepan 1996: 294). These regime types and sub-types are summarized with modern examples in Table 9.4.

not enough countries' (see Chapters 2 and 4 in this volume), since seven variables each with several categories cannot fully vary across the fifteen countries. None the less, their comparison does yield tentative inferences that can be extended to those areas of the world that have not experienced democratic transitions or those that have yet to consolidate democracy. The two variables that have the most impact on successful democratic consolidation are *prior regime type* and the *initiator of the transition*. Previous civilian authoritarian regimes that had some form of 'pacted' transition appear to face fewer obstacles to democratic consolidation than any other combination of variables. Previous sultanistic and near totalitarian regimes with some form of regime-led transition appear to face the most obstacles to democratic consolidation. In addition, problems with stateness continue to hinder efforts at democratic consolidation in Hungary, Romania, Russia, Estonia, and Latvia.

For the authors, a consolidated democracy must have no problems with stateness, a 'free and lively civil society', a 'relatively autonomous and valued political society', the rule of law, and an 'institutionalized economic society' (Linz and Stepan 1996:7). In addition to historical evidence, they provide individual-level data on the degree to which citizens of these countries support the idea of democratic rule. Table 9.5 shows that of the fifteen countries, only four have consolidated their democratic regimes, and of those four, two are considered to be of 'low quality' (Greece) and 'risk prone' (Uruguay). Since the publication of this study, many of the cases have moved to achieve democratic consolidation, certainly in the case of Greece, Uruguay, Brazil, Argentina, Chile, Poland, Hungary, the Czech Republic, Bulgaria, Slovakia, Romania, Estonia, and Latvia.

Despite the somewhat pessimistic conclusions, most of which can now be seen as cautious, the study represents an advance on earlier studies in this field of inquiry. The expansion of the scope of countries in the comparison beyond Southern Europe and Latin America introduces new and important explanatory variables that have not been specified in previous studies. The notion of stateness is rarely specified (with the exception possibly of Spain) and serves as an important variable in the countries of post-communist Europe. In the past, little attention has been paid to the type of the prior regime, while more emphasis has been placed on the initiator and type of the democratic transition. In line with their earlier work on democratic breakdowns

Table 9.5 Democratic transition and consolidation in Southern Europe, South America, and post-communist Europe

Country	Stateness	Explanatory variables						Outcome
		Prior regime type	Base of leadership	Initiator of transition	International influences	Political economy	Constitutional environment	
Spain	Problematic	Civilian authoritarian	Civilian	Elites	European Community	Economic decline	Consensus not majoritarian	Democratic consolidation
Portugal	Not problematic	Civilian authoritarian + weak party	Civilian	Non-hierarchical military	US, EC, and European socialist parties	Strong economic growth	Military dominated process	Democratic consolidation
Greece	Problematic	Non-hierarchical authoritarian	Fragmented military	Hierarchical military	European Community	Weak economy	Military trials, contested constitution	Low quality democratic consolidation
Uruguay	Not problematic	Authoritarian	Hierarchical military	Military		Weak economy		Risk-prone consolidation
Brazil	Not problematic	Authoritarian	Hierarchical military	Military		Weak economy, inequality	Military constrained	Unconsolidated
Argentina	Not problematic	Authoritarian	Hierarchical military	External defeat, military	Malvinas/Falklands	Weak economy		Unconsolidated
Chile	Not problematic	Authoritarian	Hierarchical military	Military		Strong economy	Military constrained	Unconsolidated
Poland	Important factor	Authoritarian	Military, Com. Party	Regime	Perestroika, glasnost	Economic reform, debt		Unconsolidated
Hungary	Problematic	Mature post-totalitarian	Communist Party	Communist Party internally	Perestroika, glasnost	Economic reform, debt	Post-election amendment	Unconsolidated

Table 9.5 continued

Country	Stateness	Explanatory variables						Outcome
		Prior regime type	Base of leadership	Initiator of transition	International influences	Political economy	Constitutional environment	
Czechoslovakia†	Not problematic	Frozen post-totalitarian	Communist Party	Civil society, regime collapse	Perestroika, glasnost	Economic reform, debt	Used old federal design	Unconsolidated
Bulgaria	Not problematic	Early post-totalitarian	Communist Party	Regime	Perestroika, glasnost	Economic reform, debt	Tightly constrained	Unconsolidated
Romania	Problematic	Sultanistic-totalitarian	Ceauşescu	Civil society, internal purge	Perestroika, glasnost	Economic reform, debt	Tightly controlled	Unconsolidated
USSR/Russia	Very problematic	Post-totalitarian	Communist Party	Regime	Disintegration of USSR	Economic restructuring	No democratic procedures	Unconsolidated
Estonia	Problematic	Post-totalitarian	Communist Party	Regime	Russia and EU	Economic restructuring	Dominated by nationalism	Unconsolidated
Latvia	Problematic	Post-totalitarian	Communist Party	Regime	Russia and EU	Economic restructuring	Dominated by nationalism	Unconsolidated

Source: Adapted from Linz and Stepan (1996:87–458)
Note: †The 1992 breakup of Czechoslovakia into two independent republics is not seen as a problem either for the democratic transition or for democratic consolidation.

(Linz and Stepan 1978), they examine the interaction between the macro and micro levels of politics. In contrast to O'Donnell *et al.* (1986a, b and c), Linz and Stepan (1996) stress the importance of international influences, a point which is taken up in Chapter 12. Finally, apart from the problems of research design, their study offers an example of the *contextual description, classification* and *hypothesis-testing* functions of comparative politics (see Chapter 1 in this volume).

Finally, this section considers Bratton and van de Walle's (1997) comparison of democratization in sub-Saharan Africa. In contrast to most of the previous studies in this section, their study compares countries that have made successful democratic transitions (*n*=16), those that have 'flawed' transitions (*n*=12), those that have had 'blocked' transitions (*n*=12), and those that have had 'precluded' transitions (*n*=2) during the period 1988–1994 (Bratton and van de Walle 1997:120). Such a comparison has several distinct advantages. First, in contrast to extant studies on democratic transition, *the dependent variable varies*: some countries achieved democratic transition and some did not (see discussion of Collier 1999 in Chapter 2 of this volume). Second, the large number of countries allows for multivariate statistical analysis to complement their contextual historical analysis of neo-patrimonialism in the region. Third, like Landman (1999, 2006a) and Mainwaring and Perez-Liñan (2003), their countries all come from the same geographical region, making their comparison fit into the most similar systems design, which controls for shared cultural features and historical legacies while highlighting remaining differences. For example, in their review of neo-patrimonial rule in the region, they distinguish among five different 'modal regimes' that had existed by 1989: (1) plebiscitary one-party systems, (2) military oligarchies, (3) competitive one-party systems, (4) settler oligarchies, and (5) multiparty systems (Bratton and van de Walle 1997:79).

In order to explain the variation in democratic experience across their 42 cases, they construct a model that includes three main variables: (1) political mobilization and protest, (2) political liberalization and constitutional reform, and (3) founding democratic elections (their indicator of democratic transition). They dedicate separate comparative historical and multivariate analyses to account for the first two variables (Chapters 4 and 5, respectively), and then construct a complete model that incorporates the first two variables to account for the third (Chapter 6). In explaining the incidence of *political protest*, they find strong positive effects for political competition (measured by the number of trade unions permitted by the previous regime) and political participation (measured by the number of elections held under previous post-colonial regimes) (ibid.: 150–151). Together, these two variables alone explain roughly half the variation in political protest. Their analysis of *political liberalization* demonstrates the importance of a country holding a national con-ference on reform (a variable that is highly correlated with the incidence of political protest), as well as restricted forms of political competition (as measured by the size of largest parliamentary political party) (ibid.: 186–188). Finally, they combine the separate analyses of political protest and political liberalization to explain the variation in democratic transition. Their combined analysis shows very little effect for economic factors, while demonstrating how democratic transition is a highly *contingent political process* that is a function of the interaction between military actors and mass protesters, domestic political forces, and the institutionalization of the opposition. Moreover, those regimes that had limited previous experiences with political participation and political competition were more likely to undergo processes of democratic transition (ibid.: 221–225).

Taken together, their model of democratic transition is one that emphasizes the importance of domestic political actors and processes over international economic and political factors. Like Foweraker and Landman (1997), outlined in the previous chapter, their findings corroborate the importance of political protest for explaining democratic transitions, while their emphasis on previous experiences with political participation and competition fits well with Linz and Stepan's (1996) idea of 'prior regime type'. Even limited forms of participation and competition under otherwise authoritarian conditions raise the overall likelihood of successful democratic transition. What remains to be seen is whether and how these variables are important in single-country studies of democratic transition.

Single-country studies

The final section in this chapter examines three studies on democratic transition in Spain (Foweraker 1989), Poland (Colomer and Pascual 1994), and Portugal (Maxwell 1995), which show the various strengths and weaknesses of making inferences from a single country. In *Making Democracy in Spain*, Foweraker (1989) presents an in-depth analysis of the role played by the working class in Spain during the two decades that preceded the death of Franco in preparing the terrain for democratic transition. Colomer and Pascual (1994) examine the democratic transition in Poland using formal game theory techniques. In *The Making of Portuguese Democracy*, Maxwell (1995) offers an exhaustive account of the Portuguese transition which extends from the period of decolonization in Africa and the overthrow of the dictatorship by the Movement of the Armed Forces (MFA) to the final consolidation of democratic rule. In each study, contextual description is used in an effort to make larger inferences about the process of democratic transition.

In similar fashion to the studies by Womack (1969), Nugent (1993), and Harvey (1998) found primarily in Chapter 7, Foweraker (1989) examines the personal historical trajectories of key activists from the southern region of El Marco de Jerez and their struggle against the Franco regime in Spain. This 'case-study within a case-study' seeks to understand the ways in which grass-roots organizing and personal networks constructed the spaces necessary in a nascent and constrained civil society for the democratic transformation that took place over twenty years before the transition itself (ibid.: 9). In addition to 'telling the story' of these activists and their role in forging the terrain upon which the democratic transition would unfold, Foweraker (ibid.: 2) argues that 'the story of the struggle . . . has a political interest and potential application far beyond the boundaries of Spain itself'. The study thus has well-defined empirical (the activists), analytical (personal networks), and methodological (case study) components, all of which help make a larger statement about democratic struggle under authoritarian conditions.

The activists who feature in this study are drawn from the proletarianized rural working class with little initial political consciousness but with a history and personal experience with the Spanish Civil War, the terror that followed it, and the strong arm of the Francoist state. Without unnecessarily privileging the working class, Foweraker (ibid.: 6) argues that it was a crucial group that both 'spearheaded' and represented the 'standard bearer' of the democratic struggle. In terms of their organization, these activists were variously involved in the clandestine workers' commissions, the illegal Communist Party, or worked from within the official corporatist structure of Franco's Vertical Syndicate (ibid.: 5). From these different organizational bases, the activists pursued legal and extralegal strategies to address their basic grievances, which over time, evolved from purely economic demands to more political ones.

The setting of El Marco de Jerez has several important features for the study of democratic struggle. It had both an urban and rural working class, a strong commercial sector, a successful and unified bourgeois oligarchy, and it was the site of 'consistent and strategically sophisticated struggles' (ibid.: 3), all of which combined to make the region a 'microcosm of Spanish civil society' (ibid.: 60). The first part of the study examines the early lives and political memories of the activists, their clandestine activities of organizing the workers, as well as the political economy of the region and of the nation under Franco. The second part discusses the nature of corporatist labour relations under the Vertical Syndicate, and the ways in which the workers' commissions sought to serve the interests of the workers independently from the rule of the Vertical Syndicate. The Vertical Syndicate was designed to promote a total vision and ideology which eliminated the need for class struggle while providing organizational authority and control at the national, regional, and local levels (ibid.: 81). In contrast, the workers' commissions, whose birthplace Foweraker (ibid.: 91) traces to El Marco de Jerez, were a collective response to the lack of appropriate representation of worker grievances (i.e. wages and conditions of work) through the formal channels of the Vertical Syndicate. Far from providing a unified challenge to the Vertical Syndicate, however, the growth of workers' commissions at the regional and national levels proceeded in heterogeneous fashion (ibid.: 92–93). This part of the study concludes with a narrative account of the expansion of challenges grounded in the workers' commissions that culminated in a peak of protest in 1969 (ibid.: 125–129).

The third part of the study examines the three-way relationship between the workers' commissions, the Communist Party, and the regime over the twenty-year period. While both the commissions and the Communist Party sought an end to the Franco regime, they represented competing organizations in the struggle. While the Communist Party, by its own assertions and as the main target of the regime, has been seen as the key protagonist for the democratic struggle in Spain, its leadership was divided between those in exile and those in Spain, and its political practices were criticized for being heavy-handed and dogmatic (ibid.: 133–136). The study seeks to redress the elite bias to previous studies that privileged the role of party leaders and look to the everyday struggles of the workers. Foweraker (ibid.: 185) contends that the struggle for democracy during this period is best understood by the relationship that developed between the workers' commissions and the Communist Party. The study thus examines the evolving and contingent relationship between these two organizations in El Marco de Jerez in order to gain some insight into the overall development of the democratic movement at the national level. Far from being a unified and unidirectional movement pursuing a singular idea of democracy, Foweraker (ibid.: 198) is keen to stress that the 'democratic project contained and expressed the contingent outcomes of a specific political process' where the demo-cratic consciousness of the individuals in the struggle 'was formed through the complex choices they confronted within this *process*'.

Through induction (see Chapter 1 above), the final part of the study seeks to bring the empirical and the theoretical together in an effort to make a larger statement about the democratic transformation of civil society and its role in transitions from authoritarian rule. Figure 9.2 summarizes in graphical fashion the main steps of the argument drawn from the intensive study of El Marco de Jerez and its overall relation to both the level of the Spanish national political landscape and the conceptual level of democratic transformation. The arrows in the figure do not represent causality but the connections made between the various steps in the narrative discussion. The economic oppression in El Marco de Jerez and the political repression of the Franco regime did evoke the 'unquiet hearts' of the workers (ibid.: 13–28), which as mediated through their personal networks, found representation in the workers' commissions, the Communist Party, and in some degree through activities within the Vertical

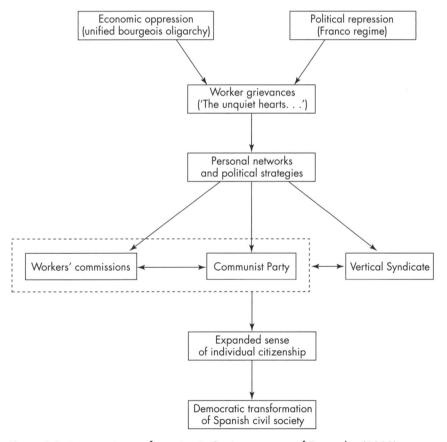

Figure 9.2 Democratic transformation in Spain: summary of Foweraker (1989)

Syndicate. The relationship between the workers' commissions and the Communist Party was not altogether harmonic, yet collectively, these two organizations stood in opposition to the Vertical Syndicate. Finally, the study concludes that over twenty years of incremental and piecemeal struggle, those involved in the political contestation expanded their sense of individual citizenship and so transformed Spanish civil society.

The second study in this section identifies the key political actors in the Polish democratic transition and seeks to model the strategic interaction between them during the 1980s using a popular analytical technique in political science called 'game theory' (see Briefing box 9.3). Colomer and Pascual (1994) argue that the Polish transition featured two important political actors: on the one hand, the Polish government, controlled entirely by the Communist Party, and on the other, the democratic opposition to the government, represented by the Solidarity movement. The authors argue that each of these two actors faced two choices concerning the political situation during the 1980s. The government either wanted to continue with the status quo (i.e. the maintenance of post-totalitarian rule) or reform the political system (i.e. legalize the opposition and implement political liberalization). In contrast, Solidarity either wanted to foment a radical break from the past (i.e. overthrow the government) or implement similar reforms envisaged by the government. The resulting combination of these two actors with two choices is depicted in Figure 9.4.

Briefing box 9.3 Game theory and political science

As Chapter 1 made clear, some political scientists prefer to analyse the political world from a micro-perspective by focusing on individuals. This perspective evolved from an examination of the psycho-sociological aspects of political behaviour to the specification of a rational model of political behaviour (see Cohen and Arato 1992; Lichbach 1995). The rational approach borrows a certain conception from economic theory that holds that individuals have a set of 'preferences' they pursue through the application of reason and instrumental action. Preferences in politics can include anything from higher wages, a cleaner environment, world peace, or the realization of democracy. In addition, individuals rank these preferences in a consistent and transitive manner. For example, someone who prefers Pepsi Max to Diet Pepsi and Diet Pepsi to regular Pepsi, also prefers Pepsi Max to regular Pepsi. The application of reason and instrumental action means that individuals intentionally choose the best strategy for achieving their ends (Cohen 1994:39).

Scholars using this approach examine the different ways in which such rational individuals interact with one another as they pursue their various political preferences. One such way to examine this interaction is to use 'game theory', which specifies a simple set of choices available to the individuals (players) and then models their interaction given their preferences. This game can involve many players with many choices; however, in order to reduce the complexity associated with a game with many players, it is common in political science to specify a two-player game, each with two choices, yielding a 2 x 2 matrix of possible outcomes. Given

Thief 2

	Confess	Do not confess
Thief 1 Confess	Both get 6 years	Thief 1 gets 2 years Thief 2 gets 12 years
Do not confess	Thief 1 gets 12 years Thief 2 gets 2 years	Both get 3 years

Figure 9.3 The Prisoner's Dilemma

the ranking of these outcomes by the two players, certain 'pay-offs' or rewards can be assigned to the players. By knowing the preferences and pay-off structures, the political scientist can examine all possible combinations of choices by the two players. In addition, the players can engage in a single interaction with one another, or multiple interactions with one another.

A popular game in game theory is that of the 'Prisoner's Dilemma', which formalizes an interaction of two players made popular in police and crime pro-grammes. In this common scenario, two thieves have been arrested by the police for the same crime, are locked away in two separate cells in the county jail, and are unable to communicate with each other. Each thief has two choices, either to confess to the crime or not to confess to the crime. The police use the fact that the two thieves are separated to their advantage by giving the thieves a range of options. If one thief confesses to the crime and the other does not, the thief that confesses gets a sentence of two years while the thief that did not confess gets twelve years. If both thieves confess to the crime, they get a sentence of six years. If both thieves do not confess to the crime, they both get a sentence of three years. This simple situation is depicted in Figure 9.3. For each thief, the dilemma rests with the expectation of what the other thief will choose while both know that it is rational to minimize their prison sentences. Since neither can trust the other, the rational solution to the dilemma is for both to confess, which gives them both a six-year sentence. While the sentence is not the least or the greatest number of years, it is the best outcome given the nature of the game.

The task of the political scientist using game theory is to identify the actors in the game and specify their choices as well as their preferences so as to model their strategic interaction. The most important aspect of game theory is that none of the outcomes is certain, but *contingent* upon the actions of both (or many) players. The basic form of the 'Prisoner's Dilemma' (and many other types of games) has been used throughout political science, including the modelling of trench warfare (Axelrod 1984), the basis for a liberal theory of society (Gautier 1986), the reform of bureaucracies in Latin America (Geddes 1991), the breakdown of democracy in Chile and Brazil (Cohen 1994), transitions to democracy (Colomer 1991; Przeworski 1991; Colomer and Pascual 1994), and research problems in comparative politics more generally (Tsebelis 1990).

Communist Party
(Government)

	Continue regime	Reform
Radical break	I Continue vs. break Open confrontation	II Reform vs. break Worst for the government
Reform	III Continue vs. reform Worst for Solidarity	IV Reform vs. reform Agreement

Solidarity movement (Opposition) is labeled on the left-hand side, with **Radical break** beside Cells I and II, and **Reform** beside Cells III and IV.

Figure 9.4 Game theory and the Polish democratic transition
Source: Adapted from Colomer and Pascual (1994:279–280)

The Communist Party (government) is at the top of the figure and the Solidarity movement (opposition) is on the left-hand side of the figure. The four cells represent the strategic interaction, or 'game' between these two actors. Each cell represents a particular outcome, which either actor ranks from least-preferred to most-preferred. Cell I illustrates the situation where the government chooses continued hard-line rule and the opposition openly confronts the government. Cell II shows the situation where the government chooses reform and the opposition a radical break. This outcome is considered worse for the government since it means that it has 'caved in' to the opposition. Cell III shows the situation where the government chooses to continue with the status quo while the opposition seeks reform. This outcome is considered worse for the opposition since it means that it has 'caved in' to the government. Finally, Cell IV demonstrates the situation where both the government and the opposition choose reform. These four outcomes are not predetermined but are logical combinations resulting from the different choices available to the two actors.

With this basic framework in place, the authors examine the historical sequences surrounding the Polish democratic transition, including the open confrontation, initial agreement, and declaration of martial law in 1981, as well as the Round Table and final agreement in 1989. For the early 1980s, the authors argue that Solidarity most preferred the outcome where the government caves in to its open challenge (Cell II). These preferences are followed in decreasing order by the outcomes in Cells IV, I, and III, respectively. In other words, if Solidarity could not get the government to cave in, it then preferred a mutual agreement, followed by open confrontation, and lastly giving in to the government. The first preference for the government during this period was to continue with its post-totalitarian rule while Solidarity caves in (Cell III). This preference was followed by the outcomes in Cells IV, I, and II.

By formalizing the choices and preferences of the two actors, Colomer and Pascual (1994) are able to model the sequence of historical events. In 1980, the initial state of play is represented in Cell III in which the post-totalitarian government dominates the opposition (compare Linz and Stepan 1996 in Table 9.5). The 1980 strikes led by Solidarity represent the first move in the game in which the opposition confronts the government openly and shifts the interaction to Cell I. In the second move, the government and the opposition reach an initial agreement (Cell IV); however, claims of betrayal on both sides led to a shift back to open confrontation and the declaration of martial law in 1981. Since the opposition continues to confront the regime during the period of martial law, Colomer and Pascual (1994) argue that the outcome is represented by Cell I. Thus, the sequence of historical events in the early 1980s modelled as a game shows how the two actors made a series of choices that ultimately yielded a stable but confrontational outcome.[4]

During the period of martial law, a number of important events occurred, such as Gorbachev's implementation of *glasnost* and *perestroika*, which made the government change its order of preferences while the opposition maintained the same order of preferences as in the early 1980s (ibid.: 284). Given this new state of affairs, the government in 1989 had a strong preference to implement reforms that would legalize Solidarity, allow nominal representation in the Polish parliament (the Sejm), while maintaining its overall political control. In this case, the government preferred the outcome in Cell IV, followed by the outcomes in Cells I, III, and II (ibid.: 286). Thus, the start of play is Cell I, the condition that was sustained for the balance of the 1980s. The first move occurred when the Minister of the Interior, General Kiszczak, began negotiations with Lech Walesa, the leader of Solidarity. As the Round Table negotiations developed, the order of play shifted from Cell I to Cell IV, where ultimately Solidarity was legalized and participated in the first elections for the Sejm (ibid.: 284–291).

The final single-country study in this section seeks to link together the historical and international influences surrounding the Portuguese democratic transition in 1974. In developing a *fuller* argument about the Portuguese case than in the O'Donnell *et al.* series (see Table 9.2), Maxwell (1995) presents an exhaustive account of the Movement of the Armed Forces (MFA) that overthrew the dictatorship, the immediate problems of post-dictatorial rule that confronted the new regime, and the subsequent consolidation of democracy. Maxwell (ibid.: 1–2) stresses the need to take a longer view on the democratic transition and emphasize the unique features of the Portuguese case so as not to homogenize it into a larger comparative framework. The account begins with the rise of the Portuguese Empire in the fifteenth century and ends with democratic consolidation and membership of the EU in the 1980s. The uniqueness of the Portuguese case centres on the non-hierarchical and radicalized military officers who put an end to the Salazar dictatorship (compare Linz and Stepan 1996 in Table 9.5), a historical process that was couched in an international environment dominated by the United States, the Soviet Union, and the European Community (later European Union).

The challenge for Portugal during the transition period was to come to terms with the end of its empire in Africa and to tame the radicalized lower echelons of the military, whose initial period of rule sought to revolutionalize and transform the political system. While the military revolt overthrew a right-wing authoritarian regime, throughout the late 1970s and early 1980s, it threatened to replace it with a left-wing one (Maxwell 1995:160). Indeed, the success of the period was the marginalization of the radical military and the appropriation of the 'gains of the revolution' (land expropriations, socializing clauses in the 1976 constitution) by the Socialists (ibid.: 2). Like Foweraker (1989), Maxwell (1995:3, 182) argues that Portuguese democracy was born of struggle, but it was a struggle that was ultimately won by the civilian politicians whose moderate position led them to oppose the radical military. This moderate solution was supported financially and encouraged diplomatically by foreign powers.

In concluding this section, it is important to compare the chain of inferences each of these single-country studies is constructing in terms of the distance between the unit of analysis and the final conclusion. Foweraker (1989) begins with the detailed account of the individuals in El Marco de Jerez in the 1950s, who through personal struggle experienced the expansion of their own sense of citizenship. The experiences in this one region are extrapolated to all of Spain, and the political process that he describes is then applied to the general case of democratic struggle under authoritarian conditions. Colomer and Pascual (1994) focus on two (collective) actors over ten years of history and use their interaction to develop an abstract model of democratic transition, where the Polish case serves to confirm their general theory. Maxwell (1995) begins with the Portuguese Empire, proceeds to the period of decolonization, the radicalization of the MFA and its role in the democratic transition, and ends with the period of democratic consolidation. He links this long historical process, however, to the beginning of the third wave, the end of the Cold War, and the collapse of the Soviet Union (ibid.: 180). For the Spanish and Polish studies, the final inference is limited to democratic transitions in similar cases, while the Portuguese study extends its inferences to a series of events well beyond the scope of the original study. None the less, in following Eckstein (1975), each succeeds in generating hypotheses, confirming theories, and providing fruitful areas for further research.

Summary

In contrast to the research topics of the three preceding chapters, the study of democratic transitions was initially carried out through the comparison of few countries and then as the universe of democratic countries increased, comparative efforts sought to become more comprehensive. Thus, the study of transitions followed the history of the third wave while trying to make larger inferences about the process of democratization by comparing within the current experiences as well as comparing between the current and older experiences. Broadly speaking, the literature has either focused on the role of elites and the nature of pacts that are formed between them (see Howarth 1998b), or has focused on the role of members of civil society and the ways in which they struggle for democracy. As in the comparisons in the previous chapters, the few-country and single-country studies include a deeper focus on the specific events, factors, and contingencies associated with democratic transition, while the many-country studies seek to identify common features that help account for democratization.

Table 9.6 summarizes the main findings of the studies that have been outlined in this chapter, where it appears that there is not a broad consensus on the main factors that help explain democratic transitions. These differences are due to several important factors concerning the study of democratic transition. First, apart from the studies that use some form of rational choice and game theory (e.g. Colomer and Pascual 1994), the comparative study of democratic transitions has been and continues to be largely an inductive process through the examination of an increasing number of countries that have made transitions. While Linz and Stepan's (1996) comparison advances the study of democratic transition by classifying prior regime type and linking the classification to challenges of transition and consolidation, the multiple paths to democracy they identify threaten to be filled by only single countries. A clear exception to this generalization is the study by Bratton and van de Walle (1997) who apply the logic of inference from global quantitative comparative studies to the region of sub-Saharan Africa. Second, and perhaps more importantly, there has not been a clear definition of the dependent variable in the field of democratization studies (see Whitehead 1996a: 354). For some, the outcome is democracy while for others it is the process of democratization, which includes liberalization, democratic transition, and democratic consolidation. Defining a dependent variable as a process and then seeking to identify a range of important explanatory variables is difficult (ibid.: 361–366). Linz and Stepan (1996) establish thresholds for determining in which phase of democratization a country resides (liberalization, transition, or consolidation), but since their study has too few countries for the number of variables, the strength of the inferences about them is necessarily limited.

In sum, the challenge for democratization studies in comparative politics lies in better classification and definition of the object of inquiry, and better research design (Przeworski 1991:3; Whitehead 1996a, 2002). There are still problems with the definition of democratic consolidation. As Diamond (1999:65) rightly observes, it risks becoming tautological unless it 'rest[s] on conceptual foundations other than what we hypothesize to be its principal consequence: the stability and persistence of democracy'. If a consolidated democracy is a political situation in which democracy has become 'the only game in town' (Przeworski 1991; Linz and Stepan 1996:5), then it is plausible to argue that no country has a consolidated democracy. Indeed, as the previous two chapters have demonstrated, democracies continue to be threatened by a range of challenges and challengers who may not see democracy as the only game in town. Moreover, many countries that would fall into the category of a consolidated democracy (e.g. Chile before 1970) experienced military coups and long periods of authoritarian rule. In terms of research design, the study of democratization ought to adhere to the methodological principles outlined in Chapters 2 and 4: namely, if the number of explanatory variables increases, the number of countries in the study must also increase so as to avoid an indeterminate research design.

Table 9.6 Transitions to democracy in comparative perspective

Method of comparison	Number of countries	Exemplars	Result
Many countries (qualitative)	30 countries over time	Huntington 1991	Transitions due to legitimacy crisis, economic growth, Catholic Church, international influences, and democratic diffusion
Many countries (quantitative)	151 to 172 countries over time	Jaggers and Gurr 1995; Vanhanen 1997; Doorenspleet 2005	For Jaggers and Gurr, a measure of democracy maps the contours of the third wave and shows that the world is constituted by 50% coherent democracies For Vanhanen, democracy is a function of the distribution of power resources, although certain regions contradict expectations about the level of democratization; Doorenspleet shows support for international structural dimensions and diffusion of democracy
Few countries (qualitative)	Between 3 and 13 countries over time	O'Donnell et al. 1986; Peeler 1992; Linz and Stepan 1996	For O'Donnell et al., democracy is an uncertain outcome, largely due to impulses from within the authoritarian regime, and a negotiated pact between elites For Peeler, democracy is the outcome of elite pacts; For Linz and Stepan, the likelihood of democratic consolidation depends on the prior regime type, the initiator of the transition, and problems with stateness
Few countries (quantitative)	42 sub-Saharan countries	Bratton and van de Walle 1997	Democratic transition is a highly contingent political process involving political protest, regime leaders, institutionalized opposition, and previous forms of limited political participation and competition
Single-country studies	One country over time	Foweraker 1989; Colomer and Pascual 1994; Maxwell 1995	For Foweraker, Spanish democracy is made from the long struggle for individual citizenship For Colomer and Pascual, Polish democracy is the product of a strategic game between the government and opposition For Maxwell, Portuguese democracy is the result of the collapse of empire, the radicalized military, and the triumph of civilian moderate politicians

Notes

1   This third question applies equally to the military authoritarian regimes of Latin America as well as to the communist 'totalitarian' regimes in Eastern Europe. Indeed, one line of inquiry concluded that the location of some dependent capitalist countries of Latin America necessarily meant that they would undergo prolonged and necessary periods of authoritarianism (O'Donnell 1973), while another line of inquiry suggested that totalitarian regimes were the least likely to experience democratic transitions (Kirkpatrick 1979).

2   The polity project seeks to measure and document regime types in the world from 1800 to the present and has produced four editions (*Polity I*, *Polity II*, *Polity III*, *Polity IV*).

3   The fourth volume, *Tentative Conclusions about Uncertain Democracies*, was written by Guillermo O'Donnell and Philippe Schmitter, while the other three volumes were edited by O'Donnell, Schmitter, and Whitehead.

4   It is stable since neither actor would shift from the choices that constitute this particular outcome. It is confrontational since the choice of each actor is the furthest from mutual agreement.

Further reading

Diamond, L. (1999) *Developing Democracy: Toward Consolidation*, Baltimore: Johns Hopkins University Press.
     An extension of Huntington's (1991) *Third Wave*, which argues that the third wave of democratization extends in the 1990s, but that the new democracies tend to be *electoral* democracies and not fully fledged *liberal* democracies.

Hadenius, A. (1997) *Democracy's Victory and Crisis*, Cambridge: Cambridge University Press.
     A collection of essays on the political, economic, and cultural aspects of democratization.

Rustow, D.A. (1970) 'Transitions to Democracy: Toward A Dynamic Model', *Comparative Politics* 2:337–363.
     A definitive and concise statement on democratic transition and consolidation with contemporary relevance and applicability.

Shin, D.C. (1994) 'On the Third Wave of Democratization: A Synthesis and Evaluation of Recent Theory and Research', *World Politics*, 47 (October): 135–170.
     A review of the main studies of the third wave, including theory, method, and research design.

Whitehead, L. (1996) *The International Dimensions of Democratization: Europe and the Americas*, Oxford: Oxford University Press.
     A collection of essays on various international aspects of democratization.

Whitehead, L. (2002) *Democritization: Theory and Experience*, Oxford: Oxford University Press.
     Good overview of democritization studies, theories of democritization, and key institutional challenges for successful democritization.

Chapter 10

Institutional design and democratic performance

This chapter examines the comparative study of institutional design and democratic performance. Institutional design involves the actual choice and set of institutions within a country that both link the citizens to the government and shape the relationship among its various branches. Institutions are related to democratic performance since they embody the representative and accountability functions of democracy and structure the ways in which political conflicts under democratic rule are mediated, and the ways in which distributional questions are settled. In this sense, they are linked to both the intrinsic (representation, accountability, and rights) and extrinsic (resource allocation and distribution) dimensions of democracy. Different combinations of institutional arrangements and their relationship to democratic performance are particularly relevant for scholars and politicians alike who have an interest in the stability and survivability of third and fourth-wave democracies (Mainwaring 1993; Jones 1995; Foweraker and Landman 2002).

The comparative study of institutions is not new in political science. Indeed, the early 'public law phase' of political science (Valenzuela 1988:65–66) involved the largely descriptive cross-national comparison of constitutions, which examined the similarities and differences in the powers of governmental branches. While the 'behavioural revolution' in political science in the 1950s (Eulau 1996:95–106; Goodin and Klingemann 1996a: 10–11) led scholars away from such static comparisons of constitutions, the renewed interest in institutions in the 1980s and 1990s produced an increasing number of studies that not only compare the similarities and differences in institutions, but gauge the effects of these differences (March and Olsen 1984; Mair 1996:311). Both the comparison of institutions and the linking of institutional design to democratic performance thus bring comparative politics back in a full circle to its origins, but with the added insights and additional analytical techniques that have been developed in the interim (see Chapter 14 in this volume).

As in the previous chapters, this chapter reviews key comparative studies that examine the nature and effects of institutional design on democratic performance. The main aim of these studies moves beyond the search for objective preconditions of democracy to a focus on the best institutional arrangements for the maintenance of democracy and in some cases, the realization of its normative aspirations. Again, the different comparisons and the selection of cases that constitute them often have a direct bearing on the types of inferences that these studies are able to draw about the relationship between institutional design and democratic performance. In addition to the selection of countries, the differences in results are also due to the types of institutional questions each study examines and the ways in which they operationalize the notion of democratic performance.

The research problem

For the purposes of this chapter, the comparative study of institutional design involves three types of institutions that are of greatest importance for democracy, including executive–legislative arrangements, the electoral system, and as a consequence, the political party system. Executive–legislative arrangements concern the relative power given to the executive and legislative branches of government both in terms of the way each is constituted and the powers that each possesses with respect to the other. Typically, the comparative work in this area specifies three basic types of executive–legislative arrangements, including pure presidentialism, pure parliamentarism, and some hybrid between the two (see Briefing box 10.1). The electoral system provides the rules and formulas through which the votes of the electorate are converted into support for popularly elected executives and members of the representative assemblies. Like executive–legislative arrangements, the electoral system assumes three forms, including majoritarian (also known as plurality, first-past-the-post, or single-member district), proportional, and some hybrid between the two (see Briefing box 10.2). The party system is seen to be closely related to the electoral system and includes those parties that are successful in achieving enough electoral support in the electoral arena to hold power in government. In all democracies, the party system consists of two or more parties.

It is clear from the specification of these different elements of institutional design that countries comprising comparative analysis in this research area must meet some minimal procedural definition of democracy. For example, 'a political system where multiple political parties compete for control of the government through relatively free and fair elections' (Foweraker 1998:651). Without such a political system, the key components of institutional design would not be in place or have any particular meaning, nor could the question of democratic performance be examined. Beyond this minimal definition, however, modern democracies vary a great deal in terms of their capacity to deliver both intrinsic democratic goods (e.g. political and civil liberties, minority rights, due process, representation, political equality) and extrinsic public goods (political stability, economic growth and stability, social welfare, national security, physical quality of life) to their citizens. The boundaries drawn around these intrinsic and extrinsic goods are also a function of the definition of democracy itself, such as procedural, liberal, and social democracy (see Landman 2005c). Thus, the comparative study of institutional design seeks to uncover the ways in which different combinations of the main components of institutional design affect the intrinsic and extrinsic aspects of democratic performance.

Briefing box 10.1 Executive–legislative relations

A key aspect of any institutional design for new or old democracies is the formal relationship established between the executive and the legislature. This set of arrangements not only guides the formation, passage, and implementation of public policy but also influences the day-to-day functioning of modern democratic government. In general, there are three types of formal executive–legislative relations: (1) pure presidentialism, (2) pure parliamentarism, and (3) some mixed system. The key distinction between pure presidentialism and pure parliamentarism lies in the degree of dependence or independence between the executive and the legislature. Pure presidential systems have independent sources of democratic legitimacy for the executive and the legislature since both branches of government are elected separately, while prime ministers in pure parliamentary systems are dependent on the confidence of the majority in the legislature, which is elected in a single election. Presidents can be dismissed by a lengthy impeachment procedure, while prime ministers can be dismissed with a vote of no confidence from the legislature. Presidents cannot dissolve legislatures, while prime ministers (usually in conjunction with the head of state) can dissolve the legislature and hold new elections. Table 10.1 summarizes these different types of executive–legislative relations, the key features that make them distinct, and provides examples of each type.

Table 10.1 Types of executive–legislative relations

Type	Main features	Examples
Pure presidentialism	Mutual independence of executive and legislature	United States Colombia Venezuela
	Executive is elected by the people for a fixed term and has its own source of democratic legitimacy	Costa Rica
	Legislature is elected by the people for a fixed term and has its own source of democratic legitimacy.	
Pure parliamentarism	Mutual dependence between executive and legislature	United Kingdom The Netherlands Belgium
	Executive depends on confidence of the majority (or coalition) in the legislature	Germany Norway Sweden
	The executive can dissolve the legislature (usually in conjunction with the head of state)	Italy Iceland Denmark
	There are not separate elections for each executive and legislature	
Mixed system	Generally combines key features of both systems	France (president and prime minister)
	Executive is elected by the people for a fixed term and has its own source of democratic legitimacy	Portugal (president and prime minister)
	Prime minister requires confidence of a majority in the legislature	

Source: Stepan and Skach (1993); Sartori (1994)

These different combinations and comparisons raise a series of important research questions for political science. For example, are presidential systems more or less stable than parliamentary regimes? Does the combination of a presidential regime with a proportional electoral system signal the worst prospects for democratic longevity? Are the protection of rights and the maintenance of political stability better under presidential two-party systems or parliamentary multiparty systems? Do presidential multiparty systems have more problems with legislative impasse than do parliamentary multiparty systems? Do majoritarian or consensus democracies provide greater economic and political stability? In each case, the research question seeks to link the configuration of the different components of the institutional design

---

Briefing box 10.2 Electoral systems

In addition to the various types of executive–legislative relations (see Briefing box 10.1), the electoral system itself is an important dimension of institutional design. In general, countries have proportional systems, majoritarian systems, or some mixture of these two systems. Proportional systems (called PR for proportional representation) award seats in the legislature according to the proportion (or percentage) of the popular vote that parties receive in elections. Examples of countries with proportional systems include Austria, Italy, Greece, Iceland, and Belgium, and all of Latin America (Jones 1995; Foweraker 1998). Majoritarian systems (called SM for single-member districts) award seats in the legislature to the single party that wins the highest percentage (majority or plurality) of the popular vote. Examples of majoritarian systems include the United States, Britain, India, and Canada (Lijphart 1994a). For any given electoral district, proportional systems can have many seats in the legislature, while districts in majoritarian systems by definition have only one seat. Mixed systems combine some features from both the proportional and majoritarian systems. Typically, a mixed system may elect some representatives through majoritarian means and then add a 'top-up' list of parties (as in Germany and Scotland). Studies of the relationship between votes and seats demonstrate that on balance, proportional systems tend to have a larger number of parties in the legislature than majoritarian systems and mixed systems (e.g. Lijphart 1994a; Sartori 1994).

In addition to these main differences between the systems, there are variations among proportional systems that award the seats differently. In the purest proportional systems, voters number candidates in order of preference and the seats are distributed accordingly, taking into account the redistribution of votes for the least-preferred candidates. This system is known as the single-transferable vote (or STV). Other variants include the 'largest remainder' method, the 'highest average method' (also known as D'Hondt), and the Saint Laguë method, all of which use different mathematical formulae to convert the vote share into the seat share in the legislature (Sartori 1994: 8). Overall, these various proportional systems achieve a greater or lesser degree of proportionality in representation.

to some key aspect of democratic performance. As in the previous chapters comprising this part of the volume, this chapter compares how many-country, few-country, and single-country studies have sought to answer these important questions.

Comparing many countries

The recent spread of democratization across the world has provided a new opportunity to investigate the relationship between institutional design and democratic performance since the increase in the number of democratic countries allows both institutional design and democratic performance to vary considerably over time and space. As Part I made clear, the increase in the number of observations enhances the strength of the comparative inferences that can be drawn about this research area. In response to the proliferation of democratic transitions in the world, scholars have endeavoured to compare many countries in an effort to examine the various questions surrounding institutional design and democratic performance. Far from there being a dearth of empirical evidence on questions of institutional design (Przeworski 1991), comparative work in this area has blossomed since the early 1990s. This section considers Shugart and Carey's (1992) *Presidents and Assemblies*, Stepan and Skach's (1993) global comparison of democratic stability, and Lijphart's (1994a) *Electoral Systems and Party Systems*. Each study examines the effects of a specific configuration of some or all of the components of institutional design on democratic performance.

In *Presidents and Assemblies*, Shugart and Carey compare up to 46 different countries at different time periods in order to examine a range of important questions surrounding presidential forms of government and democratic performance. They are interested in key aspects of presidential democracies, including the election of the president and assemblies, the formation of cabinets, the legislative power of the president, and the ways in which electoral systems produce different party systems (Shugart and Carey 1992:272). Each of these concerns is linked to two key aspects of democratic performance. First, they examine the extent to which different presidential systems are likely to experience democratic breakdown. Second, they demonstrate how different presidential systems produce a trade-off between the principles of democratic *efficiency* and democratic *representation*. Efficiency is the principle that voters ought to be able to assess the responsibility of and exercise control over the incumbent government. Democratic representation is the principle that voters ought to have a large 'menu of partisan choices' so as to maximize the articulation of different interests across the executive and legislative branches (ibid.: 273).

The question of democratic survivability is first examined through a comparison of democratic countries grouped into three categories – parliamentary, presidential, and other – and then compared across those that experienced democratic breakdown and those that did not. For the whole sample, the comparison reveals that presidential democracies are more likely to break down than parliamentary democracies. Isolating the comparison to Third World countries shows that parliamentary regimes are more likely to break down than presidential regimes (ibid.: 40–41). These simple comparisons obscure important differences among the presidential democracies that may have a bearing on democratic survival. Using a list of ten legislative and non-legislative powers of the president (see Table 10.2), the authors examine whether the differences in presidential power are related to democratic survival. A comparison across a sample of 44 presidential democracies reveals that those systems with a vast number of presidential legislative and non-legislative powers are more likely to have problems with democratic breakdown (ibid.: 154–157). Thus, it is not presidentialism *per se* that is the problem for democratic survival, but strong presidentialism, since countries with these systems are more likely to have more extreme conflicts between presidents and assemblies. In contrast, systems with strong assemblies are better for resolving conflicts and reaching compromises (ibid.: 165). These findings provide the foundation for their further work on why and under which conditions executives use what they call 'executive decree authority' (see Shugart and Carey 1998).

Using the four indicators from the list of non-legislative powers outlined in Table 10.2, Shugart and Carey (ibid.: 158–165) draw a further distinction between presidential regimes based on the president's control over the cabinet and the relative independence of the assembly. The resulting typology reveals four 'ideal' types. Pure presidential systems have strong presidential power over the formation of cabinets and separation of powers between the president and assembly. On the other extreme, premier–presidential regimes require assembly oversight in the formation of cabinets while the president has authority to dissolve the assembly. In between the two extremes are hybrid regimes – president parliamentary and assembly-independent – in which either the president has increased authority over cabinets or restricted ability to dissolve the assembly (ibid.: 158–160). While the countries in their sample variously cluster into one of these four ideal types, the authors point out that these differences have a direct effect on democratic performance. Their analysis suggests that instability is most likely in systems where the authority for cabinet formation is shared between the president and the assembly, since it is not clear who 'owns' the ministers in the cabinet (ibid.: 165).

Their next set of comparisons assesses the relationship among presidential systems, electoral systems, and party systems. For party systems, the authors devise

Table 10.2 Legislative and non-legislative powers of popularly elected presidents

Legislative powers	Non-legislative powers
Package veto/override	Cabinet formation (exclusive or controlled)
Partial veto/override	Autonomy from legislative censure
Decree laws	Cabinet dismissal
Exclusive introduction of legislation	Dissolution of assembly
Proposal of referenda	
Budgetary powers	

Source: Shugart and Carey (1992:150)

a scale that measures whether the party leadership controls its rank and file members, where a higher score represents stronger party leadership (ibid.: 176). Through a comparison of seventeen countries from their sample of presidential democracies, the authors examine the relationship between the strength of party leadership and the strength of presidential legislative power. The comparison reveals that countries with strong presidential powers tend to have weak party leadership while those with weak presidential powers tend to have strong party leadership. Moreover, those systems with strong presidents and weak parties have experienced more problems with breakdown than those systems at the other extreme, a finding that adds a further dimension to the relationship between strong presidentialism and democratic failure. The electoral system, on the other hand, is seen to be the key factor that links the presidential system to the party system. Following Duverger (1951, 1954, and Chapter 1 this volume), the authors demonstrate that systems with plurality electoral systems tend to have fewer 'effective parties' than those systems with proportional electoral systems (see Briefing box 10.3). The different electoral systems also affect the selection of the president. Plurality electoral systems tend to produce two identifiable blocs while majority run-off elections tend to produce more fragmented support. In addition, the timing of elections can also affect the structure of power within presidential democracies. Systems in which both the president and the assembly are elected at the same time (concurrently) tend to have fewer problems with 'divided government' or 'co-habitation' than those systems in which both offices are elected at different times (not concurrently). Divided government occurs in pure presidential systems when a different party than the party of the president controls the assembly (e.g. the United States from 1994–2000). Cohabitation occurs in premier–presidential systems when the president is from a different party than the prime minister, which has been a fairly common occurrence in France since 1986.

Taken together, different combinations of presidential, electoral, and party systems can have profound effects on democratic performance. The comparison of presidential regimes demonstrates that more difficulties arise in systems with strong presidential powers, a large number of weak parties, and non-concurrent elections for the president and assembly. These difficulties are due to the conflicts that arise between both institutions that lay claim to democratic legitimacy. Since the president and the assembly are elected separately, and depending on the strength of party support that a president may enjoy, the resolution of political conflicts becomes problematic, which in extreme cases may threaten the stability of the democratic regime. Overall, Shugart and Carey (1992:287) do not seek to prescribe a particular institutional design to ensure better democratic governance. Their comparisons do reveal, however, that presidentialism is far from a monolithic regime type; it can vary in terms of the president's overall powers as well as the degree of support in the assembly, given differences in both the electoral and party systems. Thus, the lesson for new democracies is that the choice of institutions is directly linked to the challenges of democratic consolidation.

Stepan and Skach (1994) focus on how key differences between pure presidentialism and pure parliamentarism affect democratic performance, which is operationalized using a variety of measures. In addition to democratic survival, the authors compare the relationship between institutional design and the following variables: the number of effective parties; Vanhanen's democracy prediction residuals (see Chapter 9 and Briefing box 1.3); a scale of political rights; the susceptibility to military coups; the likelihood of legislative majorities; and cabinet stability. Across all these measures, pure parliamentary regimes perform better than pure presidential regimes. A brief discussion of each measure and the results of the comparisons illustrate how these findings were obtained.

First, for the 43 countries that had continuous democracy between 1979 and 1989, pure parliamentary regimes are associated with a large number of parties in their legislatures, while pure presidential regimes are not associated with a large number of political parties. From this difference in the number of effective parties, the authors infer that presidential democracies are unable to draw on the conflict-reducing function of multiparty systems (Stepan and Skach 1994:121). In contrast, using the logic of the arguments found in Shugart and Carey (1992), it is possible to

---

Briefing box 10.3 Counting the effective number of parties

Political parties are a central element of modern representative democracies. For comparative political scientists, the number of political parties in a given political system has been an important variable for research. Counting the number of parties, however, has not been a straightforward exercise, since there are more parties in the political system than actually succeed in gaining seats in the national legislature. Thus, political scientists have devised different ways of counting the number of political parties. Drawing on the pioneering work of Douglas Rae (1967), a consensus has emerged within the discipline that counting the number of 'effective parties' (i.e. those that actually have seats in the legislature) is the best way to represent a particular party system. Laakso and Taagepera (1979) have developed the most popular and widely accepted formula (see below) for calculating the effective number of parties, expressed either as the vote share or seat share that a party receives. Either measure is derived by squaring each party's share of seats (or votes), summing these squares, and taking the reciprocal of the resulting number. The final number expresses the effective number of parties in the political system, weighted according to their size (see Lijphart 1994: 68–69; Mainwaring and Skully 1995: 28–29). The effective number of parties has become a standardized measure that 'travels' well to new democracies and features prominently in comparative studies of institutional design and democratic performance.

Vote share	Seat share
$\dfrac{1}{\Sigma\,(Vote\,\%)^2}$	$\dfrac{1}{\Sigma\,(Seat\,number)^2}$

Figure 10.1 Counting the effective number of parties
Source: Laakso and Taagepera (1979)

---

suggest that those presidential regimes with multiparty systems were unable to maintain continuous democracy over the period. Second, using Vanhanen's residuals, whose positive and negative values capture democratic 'over-achievers' and 'under-achievers', the comparison of 59 deviant countries in Vanhanen's analysis reveals that presidential regimes are over three times as likely to be democratic under-achievers. In other words, countries with presidential systems tend to have lower than expected scores on Vanhanen's index of democratization, given the distribution of their power resources (Stepan and Skach 1994:123). Thus, institutional design appears to be an important intervening variable between socio-economic variables and democratic performance.

Third, using a sample of 53 non-OECD countries to control for the effects of economic development, the authors demonstrate that pure presidential regimes were less likely to maintain continuous democracy during the period 1973–1989, and were twice as susceptible to military coups over the same period (ibid.: 124–125). Fourth, using the same sample of non-OECD countries, presidential systems were almost half as likely to have legislative majorities that support the executive. Fifth, of the 93 countries that became independent between 1945 and 1979, none with presidential regimes experienced continuous democracy for the period 1980–1989. Finally, using data on the duration and reappointment of cabinet ministers, their comparisons of countries in Europe, the United States, and Latin America show that presidential regimes experience less frequent reappointment of cabinet ministers with a shorter duration in office (ibid.: 127).

Taken together, these comparisons across different samples of countries using different measures of democratic performance seek to demonstrate what Linz (1990) has called the 'perils of presidentialism'. At their most extreme, the perils produced by the mutual independence of the president and the assembly include the tendency for minority governments, executive violation of the constitution, and support for military intervention in political affairs (Stepan and Skach 1994:128). Since their comparisons are isolated to either new countries or new democracies (or both), the authors are concerned with the tendency of countries to adopt presidential regimes, an observation and concern equally raised by Shugart and Carey (1992). While Stepan and Skach (1994) are pessimistic about the prospects of democratic performance under pure presidentialism, Shugart and Carey argue that all presidential regimes are not alike and that certain types of electoral and party systems may exacerbate the problems of presidentialism.

In *Electoral Systems and Party Systems*, Lijphart (1994a:1) examines the 'operation and political consequences of electoral systems' with respect to the ways in which individual votes are converted into seats in the assembly and the structure of the party system. To that end, his study compares 27 democracies from 1945 to 1990 using basic properties of electoral systems, including the electoral formula, the district magnitude, the electoral threshold, and the size of the assembly. The electoral formula refers to plurality, proportional, or hybrid systems (see Briefing box 10.2). The district magnitude is the number of representatives that are elected per district or constituency. The electoral threshold concerns the minimum amount of electoral support that a party needs in order to obtain seats in the assembly (see Briefing box 10.4). The size of the assembly simply refers to the number of seats in the lower chamber of the representative body in a bicameral system or the representative body in a unicameral system. The selected countries in the comparison are all examples of long-standing democracies (i.e. continuous democracy for more than twelve years) from Western Europe, Southern Europe, Scandinavia, North America, Latin America, Asia and the Pacific, and the Middle East.

The *electoral system* serves as the unit of analysis instead of the individual countries, while elections under the same electoral system are the repeated observations (Lijphart 1994a:7). Electoral systems are defined as 'sets of essentially unchanged election rules under which one or more successive elections are conducted' (ibid.: 7). The use of the electoral system gives the comparison enough degrees of freedom (in this case 70) for quantitative analysis. Moreover, using the most similar systems design, Lijphart can compare different electoral systems within one country to examine the effects of change in the electoral system while all other factors are held constant. The fact that some electoral systems in certain countries have changed means that the cases are not independent, but Lijphart (ibid.: 7–8) seeks to control for these changes by using a reduced sample of 53 electoral systems. This section will concentrate on Lijphart's (ibid.: 95–117) comparisons that use the full data set of 70 electoral systems across 27 democracies over 45 years in an effort to show the relationship between a key aspect of institutional design on democratic performance.

The first three comparisons gauge the effects of the electoral system variables, including the degree to which the system is proportionally representative, the number of effective parties, and the generation of majorities in the assembly. The first comparison reveals that plurality systems have a higher degree of disproportionality, a lower number of effective parties, and more frequent majorities in the assembly than proportional systems. In terms of democratic performance, this means that plurality systems aggregate the interests of citizens into larger, more inclusive blocs, which may obscure differences and lead to the under-representation of certain groups, but they produce the majorities in the assembly necessary for governance. Comparing across the systems using the effective threshold does not change the main difference in these effects between plurality and proportional systems, but does allow Lijphart (ibid.: 100) to discriminate among the proportional systems. For the most part, proportional systems with a lower effective threshold for parties to obtain seats in the assembly tend to have lower disproportionality, a higher number of effective parties, and less frequent majorities. In this way, representation is improved but governance is made more problematic. Finally, comparing only those countries with proportional systems reveals that the size of the assembly is associated with lower degrees of dispro-portionality, but has only a weak relation to the number of effective parties and the generation of majorities (ibid.: 100–102).

Using regression analysis and a combined model, Lijphart (ibid.: 107–114) is able to compare the independent effects of the various aspects of the electoral systems on his main indicators of disproportionality, the effective number of parties, and the frequency of majorities. Disproportionality is most often explained by the difference in electoral systems and the most important explanatory factor is the effective threshold, which when combined with effects of the assembly size, explains 63 per cent of the variance in disproportionality. The effective threshold explains between 8 and 42 per cent of the variance in the effective number of parties and the frequency of majorities in the assembly. These findings hold across a smaller sub-set of countries to eliminate the problem of influential cases. Overall, Lijphart's cross-sectional and

---

Briefing box 10.4 Electoral threshold

In all political systems there are minimum and maximum percentages of the vote that parties need in order to gain representation in the legislature. The lower threshold is the minimum percentage needed to make it possible for a party to win a seat, while the upper threshold is the maximum percentage where a party is guaranteed to win a seat. Imagine a majoritarian electoral system (see Briefing Box 10.2) with ten candidates competing. The winning candidate need only win slightly over 10% of the vote if all the other candidates evenly split the remaining 90% of the vote (i.e. all other candidates receive less than 10%). This 10% is the lower threshold. The upper threshold is 50%, since in a race with two strong candidates, the winning candidate must garner more than 50% of the votes (i.e. 50% plus one vote). Thus, both the lower and upper thresholds for parties are a function of the size of the electoral district (number of representatives elected per district), the electoral formula (proportional, majoritarian, or mixed), and the number of political parties that compete with each other. Lijphart (1994: 27) has devised a way to calculate the effective threshold for political parties in any given electoral system, which is expressed as the sum of the average of the lower and upper thresholds. Formally, the effective threshold (T_{eff}) is as follows:

$$T_{eff} = \frac{50\%}{(Magnitude + 1)} + \frac{50\%}{2 * (Magnitude)}$$

For political science research, the effective threshold is a measure of the relative difficulty for parties to get represented in the legislature, and by extension, the 'representativeness' of the political system.

---

within-case comparisons (not reported here) demonstrate that the effective threshold is the single most important factor that helps determine the disproportionality of the electoral system. In other words, for new democracies and those democracies seeking to alter their electoral systems, manipulation of the effective threshold is a useful method of changing the degree to which citizen votes are accurately converted into representative seats in the assembly.

This section of the chapter has demonstrated that the global proliferation of democracy has provided a robust set of countries and periods of time with which to examine the relationship between institutional design and democratic performance. The studies that were considered show great variation across all components of institutional design and each has shown various ways in which to operationalize key elements of democratic performance. The large number of countries available for comparative analysis has made this research question, like those in the previous chapters, susceptible to quantitative analysis in an effort to uncover generalizations that hold across a large part of the sample. The next section will illustrate how the results of these studies can be examined using a smaller sample of countries.

Comparing few countries

This section considers three examples of studies that investigate the relationship between key aspects of institutional design and democratic performance using a smaller sample of countries, all of which fit within the most similar systems design of comparative method. Lijphart (1994b) compares the intrinsic and extrinsic democratic performance of eighteen established democracies across a range of indicators. Jones (1995) compares the performance of sixteen Latin American presidential democracies. Finally, Mainwaring and Scully (1995) compare the party systems of Latin American democracies. In each study it is assumed that the comparison controls for similarities such as the level of economic development, culture, and history, while the remaining differences expressed in the various independent variables account for the variation in the dependent variables used to operationalize democratic performance.

In contrast to his comparison of electoral systems, Lijphart (1994b) examines the democratic performance of countries across one primary difference: whether they have a majoritarian or proportional electoral system. He operationalizes both intrinsic and extrinsic aspects of democratic performance using several indicators. For intrinsic performance, he uses women's representation, voter turnout, and Dahl's democracy score (see Chapter 6). For extrinsic performance, he uses measures of innovative family policy, income distribution, riots, deaths from political violence, economic growth, inflation, and unemployment. He divides his sample of eighteen countries into parliamentary plurality systems, parliamentary proportional systems, and other systems (e.g. presidential and hybrids). His comparisons reveal that those countries with proportional systems do better across all indicators of intrinsic democratic performance and *no worse* across the indicators of extrinsic performance. For example, women's representation, which is a proxy measure for minority rights, is higher among the proportional systems, while there are no statistical differences between the systems for levels of political violence and macro-economic performance. These findings are corroborated by a further comparison using a refined index that differentiates between majoritarian and proportional systems. Overall, the comparisons of eighteen democracies suggest that proportional systems are 'to be preferred over plurality since [they offer] both better representation and at least as effective public policy-making' (Lijphart 1994b:8).

Lijphart (1994b:12–15) makes some important methodological points concerning his study which necessarily limit the types of inferences that can be drawn from it. The most similar systems design shows that for the eighteen countries, proportional systems outperform the others, but his analysis invites replication using a different sample of countries (see Foweraker and Landman 2002). The original sample contains long-standing and well-established parliamentary democracies, such as Austria, Belgium, Denmark, Finland, Germany, Italy, The Netherlands, Norway, and Sweden; it therefore ignores the important intervening variables of economic development and political culture. In other words, most of the countries with proportional systems have well-established welfare states, which tend to promote equality of representation and have developed a certain democratic civic culture. Thus, the superior performance of these countries may have less to do with their electoral systems than with the development of the welfare state and an egalitarian political culture. While Lijphart (1994b:11) excludes the Nordic countries from the analysis to control for these effects, a comparative study using a different sample of countries that lie outside the confines of the old democracies may add new insights to his findings. As outlined in Chapter 3 of the present volume, however, the addition of new and more dissimilar countries to the analysis may lead to the problem of conceptual stretching, and having noted these problems, Lijphart (ibid.: 12–13) remains cautious in his recommendation that proportional systems offer the greatest benefits for new and emerging democracies.

In *Electoral Laws and the Survival of Presidential Democracies*, Jones (1995) draws on the comparative analysis found in Shugart and Carey (1992) but limits his comparisons to sixteen Latin American countries, placing his study squarely within the most similar systems design. All of these countries have presidential systems and by limiting the comparisons to Latin America, Jones (1995:65) is able to control for such intervening factors as religion, colonial history, and culture. He argues that '[b]y restricting the analysis to a relatively small set of nations, there is a greater opportunity to conduct an informed contextual analysis which is enhanced by a developed understanding of the culture and history of the region' (ibid.: 65). Moreover, to triangulate his study, he compares the performance of 28 different provincial systems in the single case of Argentina. His study seeks to demonstrate that successful performance among presidential democracies relies on the degree to which the electoral system produces legislative support for the president. Through a series of comparisons across the region, Jones links the problems of governance to the absence of legislative support for the president, which is a function of the difference in electoral laws.

His analysis begins by demonstrating the problems of democratic governance at the global level. A comparison of stable democratic countries from 1945 to 1994 shows that with the exception of Chile (1932–1973), countries that have not produced a legislative majority or near-majority for the president have experienced democratic failure (ibid.: 35–39). Such a global comparison, however, may contain a possible spurious relationship between this aspect of institutional design and democratic performance, a problem which can be minimized by his 'intra-presidential system comparison' (ibid.: 38). In the light of these considerations, Jones limits the scope of his comparison to Latin America and refines a measure of democratic performance, which he relates to the degree of legislative support for the president.

His refined measure of democratic performance is the percentage coverage of executive–legislative conflict in the *Latin American Weekly Report* over the period 1984–1993 (ibid.: 41–43). Presidential support is operationalized with two different measures. The first represents the percentage of seats the president's party controls in the lower chamber of the legislature. The second is a dichotomous variable indicating whether the president has a majority or near-majority of seats in the lower chamber (ibid.: 44). In addition to examining legislative support for the president, his comparison includes four additional explanatory variables, including the percentage of the president's term that has been completed, the power the president has over the legislature, the capacity the legislature has to censure the cabinet, and the amount of presidential control over the presidential party legislators (ibid.: 44–48). His analysis uses presidential years as the unit of analysis to compare across fourteen countries spanning the terms of 31 presidents over the period, which yields a total of 99 presidential years.

The comparison uses regression analysis to determine the independent effects of each of these explanatory variables on the level of executive-legislative conflict. The results demonstrate that both measures of presidential legislative strength have a significant effect on the level of conflict, which means that the less legislative support a president enjoys, the more conflict there is between the two branches. In addition to this key finding, his analysis shows that the level of conflict decreases with the amount of time the president has been in office, and tends to be lower in systems where the legislature does not have the power to censure the cabinet. Taken together, his initial comparisons across Latin American democracies show that countries with low levels of legislative support for the president are more prone to conflict and, by extension, to democratic failure.

But what are the sources of low legislative support for the president? The answer lies in the level of multipartism in the legislature, which is a function of the electoral system. Systems with a large number of parties in the legislature necessarily create problems in generating legislative support for the president (Jones 1995: 75–86), and certain key features of the electoral system tend to produce a large number of parties. Thus, in the remainder of his study, Jones (ibid.: 76–154) seeks to examine the relationship between elements of the electoral system and the number of political parties in the legislature. These elements include the formula to elect the president (plurality or majority run-off), the timing of executive and legislative elections (concurrent or non-concurrent), the effective magnitude of electoral districts, the system for converting votes into seats, and whether the legislature contains a single chamber (unicameral) or two chambers (bicameral).

The comparative analysis reveals that of all these aspects of the electoral system, the timing of elections and the formula for electing the president have the most effect on the number of parties in the legislature. Both concurrent elections for the president and the legislature and plurality electoral formulas for selecting the president tend to reduce the number of parties and therefore increase the likelihood of presidential support. The path of the comparative evidence and the substantive argument is summarized in Figure 10.2. First, the regression analysis established positive relationships among the various aspects of the electoral system and multipartism, the strongest of which are the majority run-off formula for electing presidents and the non-concurrent timing of elections for both branches. Second, multipartism leads to problems of support for the president. Third, low presidential legislative support, expressed in terms of seats and majorities, and controlling for legislative censure, has a negative effect on democratic performance in terms of both executive–legislative conflict and democratic survival. The lesson for new democracies is to formulate electoral laws in order to reduce the number of political parties and make the legislature more compatible with successful presidential government (ibid.: 160).

The final study in this section concerns the relationship between party systems and democratic performance and also uses a sample of Latin American countries, the comparison of which adds two further dimensions to the conclusions reached by Jones (1995). Mainwaring and Scully (1995:1–2) argue that beyond the problem of multipartism for presidential democracy, both the degree to which a party system is institutionalized and its level of ideological polarization are critical for its smooth

Electoral laws

    Majority run-off presidential elections
    Non-concurrent elections
    High effective district magnitude
    Proportional representation
    Bicameralism

+ ↓

Multipartism

+ ↓

Low presidential legislative support   —→   Democratic performance

    Low percentage of seats   High executive-legislative conflict
    Absence of majority or near-majority   Low democratic survival rate
    Legislative censure of cabinet

Figure 10.2 Electoral laws and democratic performance
Source: Summary of Jones (1995)

functioning as well as the process of democratic consolidation. An institutionalized party system has four important characteristics: stable interparty competition; parties with stable roots in society; the acceptance of parties as institutions for determining who governs; and party organizations with stable rules and structures (ibid.: 1). Party polarization refers to the ideological 'distance' between political parties on the left–right spectrum (ibid.: 2). Their comparison of twelve Latin American countries over the period 1970–1993 examines the degree to which the party systems have become institutionalized and the level of ideological polarization – a two-dimensional scheme of classification that is linked to democratic performance.

    Table 10.3 shows how the presence of each characteristic determines a rough classification of the party systems in the twelve countries (listed in the second column of the table), which is then linked to aspects of democratic performance, including legitimacy, accountability, corruption, and the quality of governance. By definition, institutionalized party systems have all the characteristics, while inchoate party systems are deficient across most of the characteristics, and hegemonic party systems fall somewhere in between. Both inchoate and hegemonic party systems are problematic for democratic performance. Inchoate systems provide weak forms of representation, suffer problems of accountability, and make governance difficult since the political process is not well structured. Hegemonic systems provide effective governance since they control the political process, but they fail to represent interests. In addition to the institutionalization of the party system, Mainwaring and Scully (1995) examine the number of effective parties (see pp. 229 above and Briefing Box 10.3) and the level of ideological polarization. Across the twelve countries, there is a positive association between the number of effective parties and the level of ideological polarization. Countries with a small number of effective political parties (e.g. Paraguay, Costa Rica, and Colombia) have low levels of ideological polarization, while those countries with a larger number of effective parties (e.g. Chile,

Ecuador, Brazil, and Peru) have high levels of ideological polarization (ibid.: 31). The combination of multipartism and a high level of ideological polarization creates problems for democratic performance. Indeed, those countries from the region that have long-standing experiences with democracy have fewer parties and low levels of ideological polarization, while those that have had problems with democracy have the opposite combination (ibid.: 32).

Overall, these comparisons demonstrate that a low level of institutionalization in a multi-party system with high levels of ideological polarization produces problems of governance that threaten the stability and maintenance of democratic rule. Moreover, the authors claim that these inferences can be applied to countries beyond the confines of the Latin American region to the emerging party systems of Eastern and Central Europe, Africa, and elsewhere (ibid.: 6). Like the other studies in this chapter, this systematic comparison of key components of institutional design across a selection of countries yields important inferences for the architects of the new democracies about which arrangements are most likely to sustain democracy and promote effective governance (ibid.: 34).

Table 10.3 Party institutionalization and democratic performance

Party system type	Countries	Democratic performance
Institutionalized		
Stable competition	Venezuela	Compromise and coalitional governance
Deeply rooted	Costa Rica	Political process is structured
Accepted institutions for	Chile	High levels of legitimacy
determining who governs	Uruguay	Provides accountability
Strong organization	Colombia	Less corruption
	(Argentina)	Effective governance
Inchoate		
Unstable competition	Bolivia	Erratic politics
Less deeply rooted and	Brazil	Weak representation of interests
personalistic	Peru	Low level of legitimacy
Less accepted as institutions	Ecuador	Problems with accountability
for determining who governs		More corruption
Weak organization		Ineffective governance
Hegemonic		
Very little competition	Mexico	No full expression of interests
Deeply rooted	Paraguay	Weak representation
Little acceptance as institutions		Effective governance
for determining who governs		
Strong organization		

Source: Mainwaring and Scully (1995:6–28)

Single-country studies

This final section examines the United States, whose institutions were intentionally designed to provide separate powers to three branches of government and electoral mandates to two branches of government. Its combination of pure presidential system with a plurality electoral system and two dominant political parties may produce a degree of conflict between the executive and the legislature. American history has experienced various periods in which a political party different from the party that controlled the executive has controlled the legislature, a phenomenon known as 'divided government'. During the post-war period in the United States, periods of divided government have been more prevalent than periods of unified government. Indeed, roughly 20 per cent of the period 1900–1968 experienced divided government, while the figure for the period 1968–1992 has been over 80 per cent (McKay 1994:517), while both the Clinton and Bush Jr. administrations have endured periods of divided government. Given the rise in the frequency of divided government, scholars have sought to examine both its origins and consequences. Since this chapter is concerned with the relationship between institutional design and democratic performance, it necessarily focuses on the consequences of divided government in the United States.

In contrast to the studies examined in this chapter that use other countries in their comparisons, democratic survival has never been a serious concern in the United States since the end of the Civil War in 1865. Thus, political scientists have concentrated on other key aspects of democratic performance to examine its relationship with institutional design. Three such studies include Mayhew's (1993) analysis of legislative output from 1946 to 1990, Peterson and Greene's (1993) analysis of executive-legislative conflict from 1947 to 1990, and Fiorina's (1996) assessment of additional indicators of democratic performance. Each study compares periods of divided government to periods of unified government in an effort to see if divided government has a negative effect on democratic performance. The inferences drawn from the United States have implications for the comparative study of divided government in other democracies (Fiorina 1996:112). Thus, in keeping with the argument put forward in Chapter 2, this section demonstrates that the study of institutional design and democratic performance in a single country can have comparative merit that extends beyond its borders.[1]

In *Divided We Govern*, Mayhew assembles a time-series data set of 267 significant pieces of legislation that were passed during the period 1946–1990. Significant pieces of legislation were identified through a comprehensive reading of reports in the *New York Times* and the *Washington Post* as well as retrospective judgements in various policy studies (Mayhew 1993:37–50). In addition, he examines 30 significant instances of congressional investigation and harassment of the executive (ibid.: 8–33). Both these sets of data are seen as key indicators of executive–legislative co-operation, where the latter measures congressional oversight of the president, and the former measures the political output (performance) of US government (McKay 1994:526). The time period was chosen to provide a good and even contrast of divided and unified periods of governance, a long enough length of time to make strong generalizations, and a 'natural modern unit' (Mayhew 1993:5). Somewhat surprisingly to those commentators who viewed divided government as a problem for democratic performance (e.g. Sundquist 1988), the comparisons over time demonstrate that periods of divided government make very little difference both in terms of congressional investigations (Mayhew 1993:32) and the volume of legislative output (ibid.: 51–99). During periods of divided government, 12.8 legislative acts per Congress (two-year sessions) were passed, while during periods of unified government, thirteen legislative acts per Congress were passed. With regard to congressional investigations, fifteen such investigations occurred under unified government while fourteen occurred under divided government. Thus, Mayhew's (ibid.: 4) study demonstrates that unified as opposed to divided government has not made an important difference in the incidence of high-publicity investigations or important legislation.

Like Jones (1995), Peterson and Greene examine the level of executive–legislative conflict over the period 1947–1990, which is measured as the conflict that arises when executive branch witnesses are questioned by congressional committees and subcommittees (Peterson and Greene 1993:38). The potential quantity of such interactions is so large that the authors use a random sample of committees across five important policy areas (agriculture, armed services, finance, foreign policy, judiciary), and their total sample consists of 11,000 observations (ibid.: 41). In addition to their selection procedure, they ensured further variation across two dimensions: the degree to which the policy area was foreign or domestic, and the degree to which the issue area had local or national impact (ibid.). Apart from demonstrating different levels of executive–legislative conflict for the different committees and across the policy dimensions, their analysis shows more importantly that for the whole period 1947–1990, executive–legislative conflict actually *declined*. For the four decades, the level of conflict dropped from an average of 38.8 per cent to 26.7 per cent, even after controlling for the increased volume of congressional committee activity during the period (ibid.: 46). Combined with the fact that the incidence of divided government has increased over the same period, their results suggest, in line with Mayhew's (1993) findings, that divided government does not adversely affect democratic performance in the United States.

Finally, Fiorina (1996) summarizes the main findings of Mayhew (1993) and Peterson and Greene (1993), while adding further indicators of democratic performance from the US case. Like the two previous studies, Fiorina (1996:95–102) examines executive–legislative relations, but adds some new measures, including the Senate confirmation of presidential appointees (for executive offices and the judiciary), the signing of international treaties, and the use of presidential vetoes. His analysis demonstrates that divided government makes no difference for the confirmation of executive and judicial appointments, nor does it affect the president's ability to sign treaties. The only effect of divided government that is demonstrated by Fiorina (ibid.: 102) is that presidents who face a Congress controlled by the opposition are more inclined to veto unfavourable legislation.

Taken together, these studies provide a systematic analysis of the phenomenon of divided government in the United States. Each study raises the number of observations within the single country through an analysis of the time-series trends in key indicators of democratic performance while gauging the effects of divided government. With the exception of the use of the veto power, all three studies conclude that divided government in the United States does not have an effect on democratic performance. Methodologically, Mayhew (1993) has been criticized both for his definition and sources of 'significant' legislation, as well as his measure of legislation, which represents its supply rather than its demand (see Kelley 1993; McKay 1994:527; Fiorina 1996:88–89). Yet, Peterson and Greene's analysis, which uses a different measure of democratic performance, corroborates his results. For both studies using different measures of performance over the same period, divided government does not make a difference. Despite this corroboration, some scholars remain sceptical about the findings and still believe that divided government is at least a problem of perception as much as a problem of performance, which may ultimately erode the legitimacy of democratic institutions (McKay 1994:532).

Beyond the basic conclusion that divided government does not affect performance, what comparative inferences can be drawn from these studies of the United States? Fiorina (1996:111–124) argues that divided government in a presidential system is similar to coalition government in a parliamentary system, both of which are capable of sustained democratic performance. For him, what really needs to be addressed is the practice of split-ticket voting, which produces divided government in the first place. But by confining his comparative inferences to parliamentary and (mostly) European democracies, Fiorina fails to consider other presidential systems, for example those promulgated in the new democracies of Latin America, Africa, and Asia. While the two-party presidential system in the United States may produce conditions similar to coalition government in Europe, multiparty presidential systems in Latin America, as the comparisons outlined above have demonstrated, are fraught with problems of governance that may threaten democracy. Moreover, there may be 'exceptional' factors about the United States that have allowed its conflict-prone political system to continue to function.

Summary

Summarizing the results and conclusions of all the studies in this chapter shows a remarkable degree of consensus (see Table 10.4). The first conclusion is that parliamentary systems tend to perform better, both in terms of democratic survival and other aspects, than presidential systems. But this simple dichotomization between these two basic forms obscures the great variation among presidential systems and neglects the interaction among the electoral system, the party system, and the set of executive–legislative arrangements. Among presidential systems, it is those with strong presidents combined with weak and ideologically polarized parties that are the most problematic. They are more prone to conflict, have a greater tendency to use extra-constitutional means to achieve policy objectives (e.g. Iran-Contra in the US or the *autogolpes*[2] in Peru and Guatemala), and in certain cases, a greater propensity to encourage military intervention (Stepan and Skach 1994).

Thus, for new democracies seeking survival and stability in the long run, certain lessons can be drawn from the comparison of comparisons presented in this chapter. If possible, new constitutions and institutional arrangements ought to establish parliamentary forms of rule. If, for reasons of culture and history, new democracies favour the establishment of presidential systems (see Foweraker 1998), then the electoral systems ought to be designed so as to minimize the worst qualities of

Table 10.4 Institutional design and democratic performance in comparative perspective

Method of comparison	Number of countries	Exemplars	Result
Many countries	Between 27 and 93 countries over time	Shugart and Carey 1992; Stepan and Skach 1994; Lijphart 1994a	Overall, parliamentary systems appear to perform better than presidential systems; however, among presidential systems, the most problems occur in those with strong presidents facing weak party systems elected through non-concurrent elections
			For Lijphart, the effective threshold is the key aspect of the electoral system that can be manipulated to produce more proportional representation
Few countries	Between 12 and 18 countries	Lijphart 1994a; Jones 1995; Mainwaring and Scully 1995	For Lijphart, proportional systems are better at providing the intrinsic goods of democracy and no worse at providing the extrinsic goods
			For Jones, certain features of the electoral system can produce multipartism, which translates into low legislative support for the president and problems with democratic performance
			For Mainwaring and Scully, low levels of party institutionalization and high levels of ideological polarization threaten the stability of Latin American presidential democracies
Single-country studies	United States	Mayhew 1993; Peterson and Greene 1993; Fiorina 1996	Across many measures of democratic performance, including executive–legislative conflict, the production of legislation, and the signing of treaties, divided government does not have a negative impact. Only the use of executive vetoes increases under conditions of divided government

multiparty systems. But these prescriptions must be viewed with a degree of caution. First, an examination of certain outliers has shown that manipulation of electoral and party systems can have unintended consequences. Second, more comparative research is needed on the coalitional behaviour within presidential multiparty systems, since many do exist and as yet have not experienced democratic breakdown since the advent of the third wave.

Notes

1   Although American politics constitutes a vibrant and comprehensive sub-field in political science, the United States is, after all, simply another country in the world and many of its research questions are applicable to other countries. It thus can be incorporated quite easily under the comparative umbrella.
2   In 1992 in Peru and 1993 in Guatemala, the presidents of both countries sought extra-constitutional means to pursue their political objectives. President Fujimori in Peru shut down the Congress with the support of the military, and President Serrano sought to do the same in Guatemala. The term 'autogolpe' means 'self-coup'.

Further reading

Foweraker, J. (1998) 'Institutional Design, Party Systems, and Governability – Differentiating the Presidential Regimes of Latin America', *British Journal of Political Science*, 28:651–676.
   A comprehensive review of institutional design and democratic performance in Latin America.

Foweraker, J. and Landman, T. (2002) 'Constitutional Design and Democratic Performance', *Democratization*, 9(2):43–66.
   An extension of Lijphart's (1994b) comparison of eighteen established democracies, which shows the superiority of parliamentary systems and unitary systems across a range of performance indicators *intrinsic* to liberal democracy, while controlling for regional, cultural, and developmental differences.

Lijphart, A. (1999) *Patterns of Democracy: Government Forms and Performance in Thirty-Six Countries*, New Haven, CT: Yale University Press.
   A combination of his earlier work (1994a and 1994b), this study compares democratic performance across a range of political dimensions, including party systems, cabinets, executive–legislative relations, electoral systems, interest groups, federal and unitary systems, bicameral and unicameral systems, and macro-economics.

McKay, David (1994) 'Review Article: Divided and Governed? Recent Research on Divided Government in the United States', *British Journal of Political Science*, 24:517–534.
   A comprehensive review of the origins and consequences of divided government in the United States.

Sartori, G. (1994) *Comparative Constitutional Engineering: An Inquiry into Structures, Incentives, and Outcomes*, London: Macmillan.
   A theoretical and empirical exploration of institutional design and its effects.

Human rights

239

This chapter is concerned with the global variation in the protection of human rights. The defeat of fascism in Europe ushered in a new period of international concern and awareness that a global system of institutions, legal guarantees and mechanisms should be established to promote and protect individual and collective rights. These desires found expression in the creation of the United Nations system and its key documents for the promotion and protection of human rights: the 1945 United Nations Charter and the 1948 Universal Declaration of Human Rights. These two documents were soon followed by two more legally binding instruments, promulgated in 1966 and entered into force in 1976: the International Covenant on Civil and Political Rights (ICCPR) and the International Covenant on Economic, Social, and Cultural Rights (IESCR) (Davidson 1993:39–45; Donnelly 1989, 1998:18–35; Forsythe 2000:28–52).

These two international legal instruments and those that followed (see Briefing box 11.1) have set an ideal standard of achievement for the promotion and protection of human rights. Countries that sign and ratify these instruments are legally obliged to uphold their commitment to protect human rights as set out in the instruments. As of 2000, there were between 122 and 190 countries that were signatories to these various instruments (see Table 11.1). Yet, global evidence suggests that 'there are more countries in the world today where fundamental rights and civil liberties are regularly violated than countries where they are effectively protected' (Robertson and Merrills 1996:2).

This disparity between official proclamations and actual implementation of human rights protection is a fruitful area for comparative political science research. The gap between so-called 'rights in principle' and 'rights in practice' (Foweraker and Landman 1997) can be compared across any number of countries to uncover key explanatory factors that may account for this difference. As in the previous chapters in Part II, this chapter examines important many-country, few-country, and single-country studies that seek to explain this variation in human rights protection. The chapter addresses the problems of defining and measuring human rights, identifying key independent variables that help account for their continued violation, focuses

---

Briefing box 11.1 International human rights instruments

The United Nations system and its key documents for the promotion and protection of human rights – the 1945 UN Charter and the 1948 Universal Declaration of Human Rights – formed the basis of the international human rights legal regime. These two documents were soon followed by two more legally binding instruments, promulgated in 1966 and entered into force in 1976: the International Covenant on Civil and Political Rights and the International Covenant on Economic, Social, and Cultural Rights (Davidson 1993:39–45; Donnelly 1989; Donnelly 1998:18–35; Forsythe 2000:28–52). Further treaties addressing specific human rights concerns (racial discrimination, discrimination against women, prohibition of torture, and the rights of the child) have entered into force since 1976. Table 11.1 lists these various international human rights instruments, the dates that they were open for signature, and the number and percentage of states parties to the treaties. The Convention on the Rights of the Child has the largest number of states parties, while the Second Optional Protocol to the International Covenant on Civil and Political Rights has the lowest. In addition to these legal instruments, there are monitoring bodies attached to each treaty that examine the degree to which states are fulfilling their legal obligations under the terms of each treaty (Alston and Crawford 2000). Taken together, these human rights instruments and the monitoring bodies form an international legal regime that seeks to limits state behaviour in order to protect and promote human rights.

Table 11.1 The main International human rights instruments, dates, and membership

Name	Date when open for signature	States parties 2000 n and %
International Covenant on Civil and Political Rights (ICCPR)	1966	146 (75.6)
International Covenant on Economic, Social, and Cultural Rights (ICESCR)	1966	142 (73.6)
Optional Protocol to the International Covenant on Civil and Political Rights (OPT1)	1976	95 (49.2)
Second Optional Protocol to the International Covenant on Civil and Political Rights (OPT2)	1989	44 (22.8)
International Convention on the Elimination of all Forms of Racial Discrimination (CERD)	1966	156 (80.8)
Convention on the Elimination of All Forms of Discrimination against Women (CEDAW)	1979	164 (85.0)
Convention against Torture and other Cruel, Inhuman, or Degrading Treatment or Punishment (CAT)	1984	122 (63.2)
Convention on the Rights of the Child (CRC)	1989	190 (98.4)

Source: OUNHCHR (Sept. 2000), *Status of Ratification of the principal International Human Rights Treaties*, www.unhchr.ch/pdf/report.pdf and International Service for Human Rights (January 2000), *Info-Pack*, pp. 46–50. See also Bayefsky (2001:11).

on the politics of human rights in post-authoritarian countries, and shows how comparative politics has much to contribute to this important area of research.

The research problem

What are human rights? Why do countries violate human rights? How can human rights be better promoted and protected? These three inter-related questions have motivated scholars from many disciplines in the field of human rights, while there has been renewed attention to them in political science. Rights and rights discourse have long been a concern of political theory and political science, but attention to human rights has increased since the advent of the 'third wave' of democratization (see Chapter 7 this volume) and the end of the Cold War. Normative political theory has struggled to find the foundations that justify the existence of human rights, while empirical political science has sought to define, measure, compare, and improve their protection worldwide. There remain unresolved problems with the ontological and epistemological status of human rights that transcend political theory, philosophy, and anthropology (Landman 2005a). However, within these disciplinary communities, many scholars argue for minimal and pragmatic understandings of human rights as the respect for human dignity and protection from the permanent threat of abuse, whether that understanding is in terms of Western-derived concepts of rights or their 'homeomorphic' equivalents.[1] Today, there are three broad categories of human rights, including (1) civil and political rights, (2) economic, social and cultural rights, and (3) solidarity rights (see Briefing Box 11.2).

Empirically, the task of comparative politics is to explain and understand the global variation in the promotion and protection of human rights. In addition, the accumulation of information on human rights protection in the world and the results of comparative analysis can serve as the basis for the continued development of human rights policy, advocacy, and education (Rubin and Newburg 1980; Claude and Jabine 1992). In contrast to some sceptics (e.g. MacIntyre 1971; Freeman 2001),

---

Briefing box 11.2 Categories of human rights

At the turn of the twenty-first century, there exists a collection of human rights that has increasingly become the object of protection in international law (see Briefing box 11.1). This collection of human rights draws on a longer tradition of rights from philosophy, history, and normative political theory and now includes three sets of rights: (1) civil and political rights, (2) economic, social, and cultural rights, and (3) solidarity rights. Civil and political rights uphold the sanctity of the individual before the law and guarantee his or her ability to participate freely in the political system. *Civil rights* include such rights as the right to life, liberty, and personal security; the right to equality before the law; the right of protection from arbitrary arrest; the right to the due process of law; the right to a fair trial; and the right to religious freedom and worship. When protected, civil rights guarantee one's 'personhood' and freedom from state-sanctioned interference or violence. *Political rights* include such rights as the right to speech and expression; the rights to assembly and association; and the right to vote and political participation. Political rights thus guarantee individual rights to involvement in public affairs and the affairs of state. In many ways, both historically and theoretically, civil and political rights are considered fundamental human rights for which all nation states have a duty and responsibility to uphold (see Davidson 1993:39–45; Donnelly 1998:18–35; Forsythe 2000: 28–52).

The second set of rights includes social, economic, and cultural rights. *Social and economic rights* include such rights as the right to a family; the right to education; the right to health and well-being; the right to work and fair remuneration; the right to leisure time; and the right to social security. When protected, these rights help promote individual flourishing, social and economic development, and self-esteem. *Cultural rights*, on the other hand, include such rights as the right to the benefits of culture; the right to indigenous land, rituals, and shared cultural practices; and the right to speak one's own language and to receive bilingual education. Cultural rights are meant to maintain and promote sub-national cultural affiliations and collective identities, and protect minority communities against the incursions of national assimilationist and nation-building projects. In contrast to the first set of rights, this second set of social, economic, and cultural rights is often seen as an aspirational and programmatic set of rights that national governments ought to strive to achieve through progressive implementation. They have thus been traditionally considered less fundamental than the first set of rights (Davidson 1993; Harris 1998:9; see also Foweraker and Landman 1997:14–17).

The third set of rights comprises what are usually called *solidarity rights*, which include rights to public goods such as development and the environment. This collection of rights seeks to guarantee that all individuals and groups have the right to share in the benefits of the earth's natural resources, as well as those goods and products that are made through processes of economic growth, expansion, and innovation. Many of these rights are transnational in that they make claims against rich nations to redistribute wealth to poor nations, cancel or reduce international debt obligations, reduce environmental degradation, and help promote policies of sustainable development. Of the three sets of rights, this final set is the newest and most progressive and reflects a certain reaction against the worst effects of globalization (see Chapter 14), as well as the relative effectiveness of 'green' political ideology and social mobilization around concerns for the health of the planet. The distinction between these sets of rights follows the historical struggle for them (Marshall 1963; Claude 1976; Barbalet 1988; Davidson 1993), the appearance of the separate international instruments that protect them, the philosophical arguments concerning their status, and the methodological issues surrounding their operationalization (Claude and Jabine 1992; Foweraker and Landman 1997: 46–65). With the 1993 Vienna Declaration and Programme for Action, however, human rights scholars have begun to reassert the indivisibility of all human rights, effectively abolishing such distinctions (Boyle 1995; Donnelly 1999; Landman 2006b).

comparativists studying human rights accept that valid comparisons can be made between and among different countries to examine empirically the universal claims for human rights that are made normatively.[2]

Carrying out such comparisons involves the use of comparable indicators and measures of human rights performance that operationalize their content as laid out in the international legal instruments, identifying key explanatory factors that account for their variation, and drawing valid inferences in order to prescribe solutions to improve their protection in the future. The various comparisons examined here include global studies of personal integrity rights violations, the diffusion of international human rights norms and the change in domestic human rights policy, the role of truth commissions in post-authoritarian countries, and the single-country studies of Argentina during the 'dirty war' (1976–1983) and its subsequent processes of democratic transition and consolidation.

Comparing many countries

Global studies of human rights protection draw on the longer tradition of comparative research examined in Chapter 6 on the 'pre-requisites' of modern democracy. Like these studies on democracy, human rights research in this area begins by measuring the protection of human rights in a way that is comparable across a global selection of countries and then examines the explanatory factors that account for its cross-national variation. While the reporting of human rights violations in various parts of the world suggests which areas may have the most problems, establishing equivalent measures is often problematic for ethical, methodological, and political reasons. Ethically, it can be dehumanizing to use statistics to analyse violations of human rights (Claude and Jabine 1992) and it is difficult to judge the relative weight of one type of violation over another, thereby committing some form of moral relativism. Methodologically, raw numbers of violations are continuous without an upper limit, which can make them intractable for comparative purposes (Spirer 1990), while the level of available information on violations ranges from an ideal of full information to only those violations that are reported by the international press (Bollen 1992:198). Politically, international government and non-governmental organizations (NGOs) refuse to rank the countries for fear of recrimination and loss of credibility. Indeed, the United Nations Development Programme (UNDP) came under strong political criticism for its 1991 *Human Development Report*, which used a measure of human rights that ranked all UN member states (see Barsh 1993). For these reasons, NGOs such as Amnesty International refuse to rank the countries in their *Annual Reports*.

While cognizant of these concerns, global comparisons start from the assumption that human rights can be 'more or less' protected in nation states, and that this 'more or less' can be measured in some fashion. Accepting the tentative nature of these measurements, comparative human rights scholars using statistical methods agree with Strouse and Claude's (1976:52) argument that 'to forswear the use of available, although imperfect, data does not advance scholarship'. To date, global comparisons tend to concentrate on a narrow conception of human rights that includes more salient violations such as torture, extrajudicial killings, political imprisonment, and disappearances.[3] These categories, considered to comprise life integrity violations, are coded on a standard scale (e.g. Mitchell and McCormick 1988; Poe and Tate 1994; Poe *et al.* 1999; Zanger 2000; Carey and Poe 2004; Abouharb and Cingranelli 2007).

One popular measure is known as the 'political terror scale' (see Gastil 1980; Gibney and Dalton 1996), which scores a country according to the frequency of these violations, and ranks countries from low protection of rights (i.e. frequent violations) to high protection of rights (no violations).[4] Most studies treat the components of the political terror scale as having equal value, while some argue that violations of these rights are sequentially ordered from least to most egregious (see McCormick and Mitchell 1997; Cingranelli and Richards 1999). Whatever the case, the components are aggregated into a single score, which serves as a dependent variable for which a variety of independent variables are specified and tested using advanced statistical techniques. The key explanatory variables identified in these studies include socio-economic factors such as wealth, the pace of development, and population size, and political factors such as the form of government (democracy, autocracy, transitional, leftist, or military), previous levels of repression, and involvement in international or domestic conflict.

Some studies examine the relationship between these explanatory variables and the protection of human rights by comparing a selection of countries synchronically (e.g. Strouse and Claude 1976; Mitchell and McCormick 1988; Henderson 1993), while others compare across space and time (e.g. Poe and Tate 1994; Poe *et al.* 1999; Zanger 2000; Carey and Poe 2004). Overall, their results demonstrate that democracies (or those countries moving toward more democratic forms), wealthy countries, and those that have become developed are less likely to violate personal integrity rights. On the other hand, those countries involved in international and civil warfare, countries with a large population, the presence of an authoritarian regime, previous levels of repression, and those that have undergone a transition to either 'anocracy'[5] or autocracy are more likely to violate personal integrity rights. One study shows that the benefits of democracy with respect to the protection of personal integrity rights come into effect within the first year of a democratic transition (Zanger 2000:229). Finally, there are mixed effects for leftist governments that depend on whether the terror scale is coded using the US State Department reports or the Amnesty reports, a difference which may uncover possible biases against leftist regimes by the US State Department (Poe and Tate 1994:866; cf. Innes 1992).

In addition to the global comparative studies in the general determinants of human rights violations, another series of studies identify additional sets of economic and legal-institutional variables that may be related to human rights protection. The additional economic variables include direct foreign investment as a measure of the presence of multinational corporations (Meyer 1996, 1998, 199a, b; Smith *et al.*, 1999), and overseas aid from the United States, the United Kingdom, the European Union, and the World Bank and International Monetary Fund (Poe 1990, 1992; Zanger 2000; Abouharb and Cingranelli 2004, 2007; Barratt 2004). The additional legal-institutional variables include various measures of state participation in the international regime for the protection of human rights (Keith 1999; Hathaway 2002; Landman 2005b; Neumayer 2005; Hafner-Burton and Tsutsui 2005, 2007).

The analysis of direct foreign investment examines whether such investment helps or hurts the protection of human rights; the analysis of foreign aid examines whether human practices form the basis for aid allocation; and the analysis of international law examines whether state ratification of international human rights treaties makes a difference for human rights protection. In this way, human rights protection is specified as the dependent variable for the examination of the impact of direct foreign investment and international law, while serving as an independent variable for the examination of foreign aid allocation. Thus apart from human rights being specified in these different ways, all of the studies use the same basic research design and similar measures of human rights as in the previous set of studies.

To date, the results for all these analyses are mixed. Using one set of measures for the presence of multinational corporations, the statistical analysis shows a strong positive association between direct foreign investment and the protection of civil, political, economic, and social rights (Meyer 1996, 1998, 1999), while studies using another set of measures show that such results cannot be upheld (Smith *et al.* 1999). For foreign aid, a large number of studies show no significant relationship between US foreign aid and human rights protection across different samples of recipient and non-recipient countries, while one study finds a positive relationship and another finds mixed results (Poe 1990). The study on European Union aid finds no relationship between foreign aid and human rights protection (Zanger 2000; Carey 2007), while the study on the United Kingdom shows that aid to rights-abusive countries is reduced only for those states that do not have significant economic value (Barratt 2004). For structural adjustment lending, it appears that in addition to using economic criteria for awarding loans to needy countries, both the World Bank and the IMF exercise some political judgement and do not lend disproportionately to rights-abusive governments, while the IMF does not discriminate against democracies (Abouharb and Cingranelli 2004). The structural adjustment process associated with lending, however, has been shown to be detrimental to some rights protections (Abouharb and Cingranelli 2007). It thus seems thus there is a mismatch between the rhetoric of governments and IFIs in claiming an importance for good governance, the rule of law, and human rights protection in their aid allocation decisions and the available evidence provided in these studies. Indeed, Barratt's (2004) study provides a realist explanation for this apparent contradiction, since her analysis shows that aid allocation as a function of human rights practices interacts with the relative economic value of the recipient country.

Finally, for some studies on the importance of international law (Keith 1999; Hathaway 2002; Neumayer 2005; Hafner-Burton and Tsutsui 2005, 2007), bivariate analysis shows a positive and significant relationship between treaty ratification and rights protection, while for multivariate analyses that control for the other independent effects of democracy, wealth, conflict, population, among other variables, the relationship drops out. In contrast, Landman (2005b) replicates the bivariate findings, but specifies a non-recursive, or 'two-way' model that sees both treaty ratification and rights protection primarily as a function of democracy, development, and interdependence. His results show that there is a significant but limited effect of human rights law on human rights practices, while the timing of democratization accounts for differences in treaty ratification and rights protection, such that late democratizing states tend to ratify more treaties with fewer reservations but such states are less able to protect human rights. This apparent discrepancy in results is explained by differences in model specification in the multivariate analysis and the underlying theory of state behaviour that each study adopts.

By extending the analysis of the first set of studies on the determinants of human rights protection, these additional studies by and large maintain the original research design, but include additional variables and in the case of foreign aid allocation, specify human rights protection as an independent variable. Foreign aid, the penetration of multinational capital, and the proliferation of human rights norms sit squarely in contemporary debates about policy measures that may be useful for the promotion and protection of human rights. The mixed results that are obtained in these additional studies are the product of different measures of the key variables (e.g. those used to measure the presence of multinational corporations), different samples of countries (e.g. different sets of recipient and donor states in the studies on foreign aid), and different model specifications (e.g. recursive versus non-recursive in the studies on the impact of international law), which flow from the ways in which empirical relationships between and among the variables have been theorized and estimated. It is clear that additional studies that test these different measures and models against one another would make a valuable contribution to moving this particular research agenda forward.

These results are summarized in Figure 11.1, but as in previous chapters, they must be seen as empirical generalizations that hold for more of the countries than not, where exceptions to the overall patterns identified will necessarily appear. Global comparisons identify the regularities that hold across the selection of countries in order to make general claims, and these general claims should be of interest to human rights scholars and practitioners (Poe and Tate 1994:867). The empirical results help reinforce arguments about associations and relationships made in normative and legal studies, and they provide support for important prescriptions for the

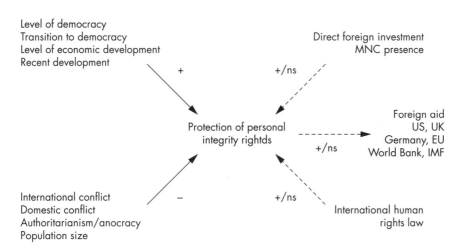

Figure 11.1 Summary of many-country studies of human rights
(Adapted from Landman 2003:208, 2005a:566; 2006:103).

international community to reduce the violation of personal integrity rights. These prescriptions include the promotion of economic development and democracy, the reduction of international war and prevention of domestic conflict, and focusing more attention on the political problems inherent in more populous countries.

The more robust results are shown on the left side of the figure and the mixed results are shown on the right side of the figure. While there have been both positive and non-significant findings for multinational capital, foreign aid, and international law, there is little disagreement that democracy (level and transition) and economic development (level and recent) have a positive impact on personal integrity rights protection, while international and domestic conflict, prolonged periods of authoritarianism (and unstable anocracies), and population size (not change) have a negative impact on personal integrity rights protection. This consensus is based on the fact that across the two sets of studies, there is robust statistical support for these relationships, which have been replicated for slightly different selections of countries and years but which have achieved similar magnitude, direction, and significance in their estimations.

Despite the effort to measure personal integrity rights, the strong inferences about key explanatory factors for their global variation, and the important policy prescriptions drawn from their conclusions, there are many areas in these studies that remain problematic. First, it is not clear that the types of generalizations made possible by the global comparisons are necessarily universal. It may be the case that, for particular regions and groups of countries, the strong relationships between the explanatory factors and the protection of human rights simply cannot be upheld (see Chapter 6 in this volume and Landman 1999, 2006a; Mainwaring and Perez-Liñan 2003). Second, the conception of human rights is effectively isolated to civil rights, while the protection of political rights (i.e. the presence of procedural democracy), and the realization of economic, social, and cultural rights are either not operationalized, or are specified as explanatory variables.[6]

Thus, the presence of procedural democracy and levels of economic development are seen to *explain* the protection of personal integrity rights, while it is entirely possible to specify these relationships in different ways. Third, there may be omitted variable bias where key explanatory variables have not been specified. Such variables may include the strength of the state, the location of the country in the world capitalist system (Burkhart and Lewis-Beck 1994; Foweraker and Landman 2004), the type of economic development (Brohman 1996), the presence of social mobilization (Foweraker and Landman 1997), and perhaps most importantly, the effectiveness of the international and regional human rights regimes to which countries are a party (see Weissbrodt and Bartolomei 1991 below). Finally, the set of research questions that global comparisons can answer are quite limited since many topics in human rights research either cannot be operationalized for this kind of analysis, or require different levels of analysis and techniques.

Comparing few countries

It is precisely these types of omissions and lacunae identified in the global comparisons of human rights that have led many comparativists to examine a smaller selection of countries. While similar research questions are posed to those in the global comparisons, the smaller number of cases allows deeper investigation into the similarities and differences that are observed. The smaller selection of cases also allows human rights research to move beyond the questions posed by the global comparative studies and examine key questions that are more intimately linked to the cultural and political specificities of the countries under comparison. This section of the chapter examines a collection of analyses on the diffusion of international human rights norms (Risse *et al.* 1999), a comparison of truth commissions (TCs) in fifteen countries (Hayner 1994), and a further comparison of TCs in Uruguay and Chile (de Brito 1997). Each comparison demonstrates how a smaller selection of countries allows for the examination of more detailed processes and relationships between institutions, states, individuals, and international and national human rights NGOs.

Transnational advocacy

In *The Power of Human Rights*, Risse, Ropp, and Sikkink (1999) and their contributors present a series of paired comparisons (and one single-country study) of liberalizing authoritarian regimes in order to examine the degree to which 'transnational advocacy networks' contribute to the diffusion of international human rights norms and promote domestic policy change. Such networks are seen to create both 'top-down' and 'bottom-up' pressure on authoritarian regimes to undergo political transformations necessary for the full institutionalization of human rights protection. The paired comparisons provide evidence in support of a 'spiral model' of norms diffusion. The model depicts a progression from initial international consciousness-raising about human rights violations in the target country, followed by regime denial of the atrocities (which is in itself an acknowledgement of human rights norms), concessions by the state to improve the situation, and the ultimate institutionalization of human rights norms through changes in domestic policy and state behaviour (Risse *et al.* 1999:17–35). In short, the model shows how the international human rights regime can have an impact on state behaviour, while the inferences from the comparison of the eleven countries remain 'generalizable across cases irrespective of cultural, political, or economic differences' (Risse and Sikkink 1999:6). In addition, the model is advanced as providing a superior account for domestic policy change in the area of human rights than either 'realism' or 'modernization' (see Briefing box 11.3).

Like the many-country comparisons, the analyses in *The Power of Human Rights* focus on a very narrow set of human rights, including the right to life (free from extra-judicial killings and disappearances), the prohibition of torture, freedom from arbitrary arrest, and detention. These 'basic rights of the person' are seen as a central core of rights that ought to have the most impact internationally since there is larger consensus around their content and protection (Risse and Sikkink 1999:3; cf. Foweraker and Landman 1997:14–17). In a variation on the idea of a 'crucial case study' (see Chapter 5 this volume), the study argues that if no progress has been made on this core set of rights, *then* it is highly unlikely that progress could be made on a less consensual set of rights. Thus, the paired comparisons ought to show

Briefing box 11.3 Realism, modernization, and human rights

Realism

Realism is a theoretical perspective popular in international relations that sees the world as comprised of self-interest maximizing states in pursuit of power. The prime motivation for state action in international affairs, whether carried out unilaterally, multilaterally, through alliances, peaceful negotiations, or warfare, is to maintain or enhance political power relative to other states. From Thucydides (1982), through Machiavelli (1952), Hobbes (1985), Morgenthau (1960), and Waltz (1979), realists have used this set of assumptions about human nature to model and explain state behaviour in international affairs, where the system of states is described as anarchic without a single authority. Variants on realism, such as balance of power theories and hegemonic stability theory, argue that a small number of powerful states dominate world affairs, contribute to long-term patterns of stability, and may guarantee the enforcement of certain norms of international behaviour (see Viotti and Kauppi 1999; Donnelly 2000). In the field of human rights, traditional realism argues that state concessions to international human rights norms are a way for states to gain short-term benefit and raise international legitimacy while counting on weak sanctions and largely unenforceable legal obligations. Thus, a realist would argue that China stands to gain in international legitimacy for agreeing to sign and ratify the two international covenants on human rights, while being able to avoid any sanctions for continued violations of human rights. In an application of hegemonic stability theory, Stephen Krasner (1993:143) argues that the relative power and interests of states best explain the variation in success of human rights protection. He shows that the slave trade in the nineteenth century would not have been abolished without the naval dominance of Great Britain (ibid.: 152), while the protection of minorities in Central Europe in the late nineteenth and early twentieth centuries was a failure since the dominant powers of the day were not 'willing to enforce the norms and rules which they had themselves initially imposed' (ibid.: 166).

Modernization theory

Building on the original arguments found in Rostow's (1961) *The Stages of Economic Growth*, modernization theory claims that as countries save and invest at appropriate levels that help enhance their infrastructure and social institutions, liberal democratic institutions will flourish as a natural response to the functional imperatives of society, and supply the best form of governance. The development of social institutions enhances the level of education of the population, improves its social and spatial mobility, and promotes the political culture that supports liberal democratic institutions. In short, modernization theory assumes that the process of socio-economic development is 'a progressive accumulation of social changes that ready a society to its culmination, democratization' (Przeworski and Limongi 1997:158). Extending the theory to human rights means that broad socio-economic changes would lead to a natural and inevitable improvement in the protection of human rights, especially civil and political rights. Indeed, in the Vienna Declaration and Programme for Action 1993, paragraph 8 states that 'democracy, development, and the protection of fundamental freedoms are interdependent and mutually reinforcing', suggesting that modernization theory is broadly correct. As Chapter 6 in this volume shows, however, many-country studies on the relationship between economic development and democracy support modernization theory, though recent work questions the interpretation of the robust statistical findings. In similar fashion, many-country studies on human rights find a positive relationship between economic development and the protection of personal integrity rights (see Figure 11.1).

progress on the protection of this core set of rights that is the result of transnational advocacy networks diffusing human rights norms and changing state behaviour. A positive result to the analyses means that for this core set of rights, the international human rights regime and its associated transnational networks of activists can be effective in bringing about improvements in the protection of human rights.

With the exception of the single-country analysis of South Africa, the paired comparisons include (1) Kenya and Uganda, (2) Tunisia and Morocco, (3) Indonesia and the Philippines, (4) Chile and Guatemala, and (5) Poland and Czechoslovakia. In all the cases, the authors claim that progress has been made in the protection of the core set of rights. But it is the variation in rights protection and the relationship with activities carried out by the actors that form part of the transnational networks that is of central interest to the analyses. In applying a variant of the 'most different systems design' (see Faure 1994; Chapters 2 and 4 this volume), the analyses compare countries from a variety of geographical regions with different cultural and historical backgrounds. The final phase of the spiral model ('rule-consistent behaviour') is achieved in Chile, South Africa, the Philippines, Poland, and Czechoslovakia, while the penultimate phase ('prescriptive status') is achieved in Uganda, Morocco, Tunisia, and Indonesia (Risse *et al.* 1999:259). Table 11.2 summarizes the analyses by listing the authors of the case comparisons, the cases and years, and the inferences drawn from the qualitative and narrative evidence. The various country accounts span the period beginning in the 1960s in South Africa to the 1990s in Eastern Europe. These comparisons are considered in turn.

The worst atrocities in Uganda occurred a decade (1970s) before the increase in violations in Kenya (1980s), and were the result of different factors, but both countries drew the attention of international groups and both made improvements in their overall protection of human rights. Uganda has seen domestic trans-formations to the point of reaching prescriptive status, while Kenya is only at the stage of making tactical concessions, which are more likely to remain sustainable (Schmitz 1999:40). The struggle against Apartheid in South Africa does much to support the spiral model, and has served as an inspiration for the further development of human rights transnational advocacy networks. But the issue of racism, which the other cases in the collection did not have to confront, tempers the generalizability of the processes in South Africa (Black 1999). The human rights situation in both Morocco and Tunisia activated transnational advocacy networks, which were more

Table 11.2 Summary of Risse, Ropp, and Sikkink (eds) (1999) *The Power of Human Rights*

Authors	Countries and years	Region	Outcomes and qualifications
Schmitz	Kenya (1980s–1990s) Uganda (1970s–1980s)	Africa	Transnational networks play a crucial role in both countries, Uganda's human rights abuses occurred earlier so the international human rights regime was less responsive.
Black	South Africa (1960s–1990s)	Africa	Early internationalization of human rights struggle puts top-down and bottom-up pressure on the Apartheid regime, although domestic changes were further tempered by anti-racism policies of Eastern Bloc countries and post-Apartheid governments have emphasized civil and political rights over economic and social rights.
Gränzer	Tunisia (1980s) Morocco (1980s–1990s)	Arab world	Transnational networks lead to institutional reforms and rights improvements in Morocco, while early tactical concessions in Tunisia lead to the collapse of the network and deterioration of human rights situation.
Jetschke	Indonesia (1970s–1990s) Philippines (1970s–1980s)	East Asia	Improvement in human rights situation is greater in the Philippines than in Indonesia, while the timing of the improvements is explained by the legacies of colonialism and nationalism.
Ropp and Sikkink	Chile (1970s–1990s) Guatemala (1970s–1990s)	Latin America	Substantial improvement in human rights situation in Chile, while Guatemala experiences difficulty in institutionalizing human rights protection.
Thomas	Poland (1970s–1980s) Czechoslovakia (1970s–1990s)	Eastern Europe	Early success in both countries after Helsinki Act of 1975 held in check by Soviet hegemony, which gives way in 1989, ushering in domestic transformations that institutionalize human rights protection.

effective in Morocco than in Tunisia, a difference in outcome that is explained by the different strength of the networks, and early tactical concessions in Tunisia that demobilized the networks (Gränzer 1999:110–111). The cases of the Philippines and Indonesia also show differences in outcome, with greater improvements in the former than the latter, a difference that is explained by varying legacies of colonialism and the effects of nationalism (Jetschke 1999:135). For Latin America, Chile emerges as a country that has achieved rule-consistent behaviour, while the situation in Guatemala is 'uncertain and still in flux' (Ropp and Sikkink 1999:172) even though both cases received wide international attention for their abuse of human rights. Finally, the comparison of Poland and Czechoslovakia demonstrates the influence of the Helsinki Final Act of 1975, which established the importance of 'human rights as a norm binding on all the states of Europe, and as a legitimate issue in relations between them' (Thomas 1999:205).

But are these accounts superior to realist accounts? And is the spiral model the best way to capture the dynamic process of norm diffusion? It is with the last two paired comparisons that some limits to the inferences drawn in the volume are evident. First, the cases of Poland and Czechoslovakia both show that any initial attempt to get tactical concessions from the Communist regimes were unsuccessful owing to the hegemonic presence of the Soviet Union. Indeed, it is not until Gorbachev initiates the processes of *glasnost* and *perestroika* that new opportunities are made available for transnational advocacy networks and domestic opposition groups to put pressure on the two states to change their practices. As Colomer and Pascual's account of democratic transition in Poland shows in Chapter 9, it is precisely this change in *external power relations* that changed the game that was being played between elites in the regime and leaders of the opposition. Realist accounts would argue that unless the dominant power in the region (in this case the Soviet Union) changes, such reforms would not be possible, a point which challenges the spiral model's claim to explanatory superiority.

Second, the analysis of Chile and Guatemala (Ropp and Sikkink 1999) never mentions the Chilean state of siege declared in 1985 after two years of recurring 'days of national protest' (Foweraker and Landman 1997:xxii–xxiii, 246–247). The state of siege was infamous for its gross violations of human rights, including the immolation of two students from the opposition in the streets of Santiago. Such renewed violation of human rights and regression in the general pattern of 'concession' suggests that transnational advocacy networks were not successful in changing the behaviour of the Pinochet regime during this period. Instead, the authors focus on the 1988 plebiscite and subsequent transition to democracy and claim that these domestic changes are clear evidence of the spiral model at work. By comparison, the analysis in Foweraker and Landman (1997:238) demonstrates that the relationship between domestic social mobilization and the protection of rights is not inevitably progressive, but can be 'uneven, fragmented, and contradictory', an account which does include the state of siege. By extension, is the fact that many of the cases considered do not reach the final phase of the spiral model (rule consistent behaviour) a problem for the conclusions that are reached? In a sense, the accounts may be assuming progress in the rights protection that cannot yet be upheld by the comparative evidence.

Truth commissions

The role of truth commissions is another area in the field of human rights that is particularly appropriate for few-country comparisons. These formal bodies have included international tribunals like those used in Nuremberg after World War II, the International Criminal Tribunal for the Former Yugoslavia (ICTY) in the Hague and the International Criminal Tribunal for Rwanda (ICTR) in Arusha; and they have included domestically-based (although in some cases internationally run) truth commissions, commissions for historical clarification, truth and reconciliation commissions, and community-based justice programmes (e.g. the *gacaca* system in Rwanda). They also include larger projects on historical memory and lustration processes for former agents of the authoritarian state apparatus. In each case, the establishment of such a formal body fundamentally puts down a marker to acknowledge that past wrongs must be addressed in some way and to recognize that ignoring such past wrongs is to leave open the possibility of them happening again.

To date, there have been more than 30 such commissions that have spanned the regions of Central and South America, the Caribbean, Africa, Europe, and South East Asia and the Pacific (see Table 11.3 for a list of the most notable ones). While these commissions have been established for different purposes with different legal mandates and under the auspices of different authorities, they share a number of common features: (1) they focus on the past, (2) they do not focus on specific events, but seek to discover a broader picture, (3) they are temporary, (4) they have the authority to access all areas to obtain information (see Hayner 1994:604; 2002:14), and (5) they have a legal mandate to 'clarify', 'establish the complete picture', 'investigate serious acts of violence', 'establish the truth', and 'create an impartial historical record'. The proliferation of truth commissions and the similarity in their basic features, purpose, and work has led to a burgeoning social science literature that examines their establishment, impact, and the 'essentially contested' (Gallie 1956) nature of the truth that they uncover (see e.g. Hayner 1994, 2002).

Hayner (1994) compares fifteen countries with such bodies to uncover patterns in their political genesis, mandates, resources, levels of authority, and lasting impact. She defines truth commissions as 'bodies set up to investigate a past history of violations of human rights in a particular country – which can include violations by the military or other government forces or by armed opposition groups' (Hayner 1994:600). Of the countries listed in Table 11.3, Hayner's (1994) fifteen cases include Uganda (1974), Bolivia (1982–1983), Argentina (1983–1984), Uruguay (1985), Zimbabwe (1985), Uganda (1986–), Philippines (1986–1987), Chile (1990–1991), Chad (1991–1992), South Africa (1992), Germany (1992), El Salvador (1992–1993), South Africa (1993), Rwanda (1993), and Ethiopia (1993).

Her descriptions and comparisons of these truth commissions reveal that no one model predominates; however, she reaches some important general conclusions about the minimum standards for operating such bodies, as well as key insights that account for the regional differences she observes. First, she argues that truth commissions should meet a set of minimal standards including impartiality, political independence, significant financial resources, access to information, immediate post-conflict formation, limited duration, and immediate publication of findings. Second, her comparisons reveal key differences between Africa and Latin America, the two

Table 11.3 Truth commissions around the world

Country	Date of commission	Dates covered
Uganda	1974	January 25, 1971–1974
Bolivia	1982–1984	1967–1982
Argentina	1983–1984	1976–1983
Uruguay	1985	1973–1982
Zimbabwe	1985	1983
Uganda	1986–1995	December 1962–1986
Nepal	1990–1991	1961–1990
Chile	1990–1991	September 11, 1973–March 11, 1990
Chad	1991–1992	1982–1990
South Africa	1992	1979–1991
Germany	1992–1994	1949–1989
El Salvador	1992–1993	January 1980–July 1991
South Africa	1993	1979–1991
Sri Lanka	November 1994–September 1997	January 1, 1988–November 13, 1994
Haiti	April 1995–February 1996	September 29, 1991–October 215, 1994
Burundi	September 1995–July 1996	October 21,1993–August 28, 1995
South Africa	December 1995–2000	March 1, 1960–May 10, 1994
Ecuador	September 1996–February 1997	1979–1996
Guatemala	August 1997–February 1999	1962–1996
Nigeria	1999–2000	1966–May 28, 1999
South Korea	October 2000–2003	'past authoritarian regimes'
Panama	January 18, 2001–April 2002	1968–1988
Peru	June 2001–August 2003	1980–2000
Ghana	January 2002–	March 6, 1957–January 6, 1993
Sierra Leone	2000–2001; 2002–2005	1991–1999
East Timor	July 2001–July 2005	April 25, 1974–October 25, 1999
Liberia	February 2006–present	1974–2003

Source: Adapted from Landman 2006b:108. Additional material from International Centre for Transitional Justice (www.ictj.org)

regions in the world that have had the most truth commisions to date. On balance, the Latin American TCs have had more funding, better staff, less politicization, and are more likely to publish their findings. More importantly, she argues that since the nature of conflict in these two regions is different, the outcomes of the truth commissions will be different. The pattern of human rights abuse in Africa is borne of ethnic, religious, and group conflict, where civilian elites are primarily responsible for the gross violations. In contrast, the pattern of abuse in Latin America finds its genesis in an ideological struggle between forces of the left and right, where the military is responsible for the majority of the abuses. She argues these two differentiating features make reconciliation more likely in Latin America than Africa (Hayner 1994:653).

In *Human Rights and Democritization in Latin America*, de Brito (1997:1) compares Uruguay and Chile in order to examine the 'political conditions which permitted, or inhibited, the realization of policies of truth-telling and justice' under the new regimes that emerged after long periods of authoritarianism. Her comparison of the two cases is meant to move beyond truth and reconciliation and show how systematic attention to accountability can add to our understanding of the larger process of democratization. Her selection of cases is based on the model that the Southern Cone set for the rest of the world to follow, where Chile and Uruguay serve as 'formative examples of attempts to deal with a fundamental aspect of the politics of transition and democratization' (ibid.: 4). In this way, she adopts a most similar systems design that identifies the factors that account for the differences she observes across the two cases. The key features that are addressed across the two cases include the nature and the strength of the human rights movement, the amount of international support for the process, the relative autonomy of state institutions, the inherited constitutional legislation, and the judicial precedents for prosecution. Moreover, there are key features of democratic transition that need to be taken into account. These include the relationship between opposition parties and the human rights organizations, the legal and constitutional setting, the nature of the military and its relationship with the new civilian regime, the role of the Catholic Church, and the ways in which human rights violations are articulated by the main political actors (ibid.: 33–34).

The comparison of these two cases across all these factors reveals that the process of truth and reconciliation is inextricably linked with the legacy of authoritarian rule and the politics of the democratic transition, as well as the balance of political forces in the new democratic period (ibid.: 213). Arguably, the Chilean military has maintained far more reserve domains of power than in the Uruguayan case, and the detention and extradition proceedings against General Pinochet in the United Kingdom demonstrate the precarious nature of truth-telling and reconciliation. While total truth and justice are not possible, the process itself is an important symbolic dimension for consolidating democracy as it appeals to principles of accountability and to 'more fundamental intuitions about the just treatment of all citizens in a civilized society' (ibid.: 8).

Single-country studies

The field of human rights research is full of single-country studies that serve the different comparative functions outlined in Chapter 2. By definition, they focus on countries with particularly problematic human rights records and include official reports from international governmental and non-governmental organizations, domestic commissions and NGOs, journalistic and descriptive accounts, and research monographs. The *Nunca Más* (CONADEP 1984) report from Argentina and the *Nunca Mais* (Dassin 1986) report from Brazil are classic examples of such descriptive accounts of human rights abuse under conditions of authoritarianism, and as mentioned above, truth commissions often publish their findings for the general public.[7] On balance, however, these descriptive accounts are not grounded in any one discipline, nor do they seek to make larger inferences from intensive examination of the individual case. The descriptive accounts can, however, serve as the foundation for research monographs which are grounded in one or more disciplines and which seek to make larger inferences about human rights.

While the plethora of single-country studies is simply too large to treat in this chapter, it is possible to compare a few examples of such studies from political science to illustrate the type of contribution that they can make to our understanding of human rights promotion and protection. Instead of comparing a disparate set of case studies, this section focuses on the case of Argentina, which offers a good example of a 'most likely' case study for the field of human rights. In 1976, the Argentine military ousted civilian President Maria Estela Martinez de Peron and established a 'bureaucratic-authoritarian' regime, which aimed to suppress leftist subversion and 'reorganize' the Argentine political, economic, and social system. A key element in this 'Process of National Reorganization' was the systematic elimination of political opposition through the use of torture, execution, and disappearance.[8] The pattern of human rights abuse continued throughout the regime, while the practice of disappearance began to subside in 1979. British defeat of Argentina over the disputed Malvinas (or Falklands) Islands brought the downfall of the regime and subsequent democratic transition in 1983.

The Argentine example is a 'most likely' case study since the military regime presented the world with a stark pattern of gross human rights violations, precisely of the kind that the international and regional human rights mechanisms and organizations, albeit young, are meant to respond to. Success in such a case bodes well for the international law of human rights, while failure demonstrates the limits to the full implementation of international human rights law. The comparison of three studies of this period in Argentina's political history demonstrates the different dimensions of the human rights issues at stake. In his account of the 'Dirty War' conducted by the Argentine military, Guest (1990) considers the challenge the regime offered to the United Nations, while examining the conflict between the United Nations and the United States over the case during the shift from the Carter to the Reagan Administration. Weissbrodt and Bartolomei (1991) analyse the effectiveness of international human rights pressure by comparing the activities of the Inter-American Human Rights Commission, the then-named UN Subcommittee on

Prevention and Protection of Minorities, international NGOs, and domestic NGOs. Finally, Brysk (1994a) examines the success and limitations of the domestic human rights movement and its resistance against the military regime. What is important to this chapter is that each study seeks to make larger inferences about different aspects of the politics of human rights protection based on a consideration of a particularly acute case of abuse.

In *Behind the Disappearances*, Iain Guest (1990) offers an exhaustive account of the Argentine case that extends from the military coup of 1976 and the first reports of disappearances to the new democratic regime of President Raúl Alfonsín. Beyond a mere journalistic reporting of events, Guest (1990:xiii) strives to convince the reader that the United States should not mistrust the United Nations, nor should the UN be construed as having a politicized human rights machinery that is used selectively, but one that is particularly useful and important. Despite his plea for the UN, his study demonstrates that without the support of the US, UN effectiveness in the area of human rights protection is limited. In the end, the UN system responded, albeit belatedly, to the gross violations in Argentina during the Carter administration (1976–1980), which had explicitly formulated its foreign policy around the promotion and protection of human rights.

Any gains that were achieved during this period, however, were quickly stifled with the inauguration of President Reagan in 1981, whose foreign policy was guided by more geo-strategic concerns, where Argentina was perceived as a tolerable bulwark against the possible advance of communism in the region.[9] The defeat and subsequent transition brought with it a commitment to seek truth and reconciliation, where former military officers were put on trial for abuses committed during the period. This most likely case offers hope that, even in the most coup-prone nation in Latin America, democracy has taken root, and since 1985 has not been reversed. As for the United Nations, Guest (1990) argues that it should reassert its role as human rights advocate and openly confront governments for their abuses.

Like Guest (1990), Weissbrodt and Bartolomei (1991) examine the effectiveness of human rights pressure on the Argentine military regime, but they broaden their inquiry beyond the UN and United States to include the Inter-American Commission, as well as important international and national human rights NGOs. Overall, the primary aim of the NGOs and INGOs was to document and publish human rights abuses for the attention of international governmental organizations and media.[10] The Inter-American Commission for Human Rights responded in part to the increasing number of reports coming out of Argentina and by 1978, asked for permission to carry out an on-site visit, which was reluctantly granted[11] and ultimately led to the Commission publishing a highly critical report on the situation. The Commission did not follow up with any significant action following the publication of the report. The UN Sub-Commission on Prevention of Discrimination and Protection of Minorities, under the auspices of Economic and Social Council (ECOSOC) Resolution 1235, adopted a resolution expressing concern over the situation in Argentina. This resolution was followed up by the confidential procedures for the investigation of human rights abuses stipulated in ECOSOC resolution 1503.

Despite the efforts of the NGOs, INGOs, and the Inter-American Commission, Weissbrodt and Bartolomei (1991:1029–1031) demonstrate that the UN Sub-Commission could not establish a consensus to take action against the military regime. Key obstacles to successful action included a delay in initiating proceedings until after the NGOs published their findings, a savvy Argentine ambassador who used UN procedures to block any action, strong allies within and outside the region, and the presidential succession of Ronald Reagan. Like Guest (1990), their study demonstrates the political vulnerability of the United Nations, relative effectiveness of the Inter-American Commission, and the ultimate reduction of abuses as a result of a complex combination of multilateral and bilateral pressure on the regime. More importantly, they conclude by arguing 'the lessons of this case study must be tested in cases involving other countries and time periods to determine whether more general lessons can be drawn from this single case' (Weissbrodt and Bartolomei 1991:1034).

The final case study of Argentina considers the power of the domestic human rights movement in challenging the repressive apparatus of the regime, negotiating within a complex set of relationships among state, society, and international system (Brysk 1994a:xi). Drawing on analytical categories from social movement research (see Chapter 6 this volume), Brysk (ibid.: 2) chronicles the origin, trajectory, strategies, and impact of a movement comprised of ordinary citizens 'who were protesting to defend traditional, legitimate values like the right to life, the rule of law, and the sanctity of the family'. Like Foweraker and Landman (1997) and Bratton and van de Walle (1997), Brysk's (1994a:2) account demonstrates that social movements can and do prosper under conditions of authoritarianism and democratic transition, and that in this particular case, the human rights movement was able to 'produce unexpected social change . . . by unleashing symbolic challenges to regime legitimacy'.

Her study traces the background of the military regime and the emerging pattern of abuses, the emergence of the human rights movement under extreme conditions of repression, and the strategy of symbolic protest against regime legitimacy. The account demonstrates that the movement achieved real changes, including international delegitimation of the regime, the establishment of governmental commission on disappearances and the Subsecretariat of Human Rights, trials of the former military rulers and officers, new legislation to safeguard civil liberties, and the introduction of new social norms and institutions in civil society (ibid.: 2–3). Beyond the Argentine case, Brysk (ibid.: 166–170) argues her study provides important lessons for the politics of human rights and transitions to democracy. First, rapid post-transition political reform is vital for democratic consolidation that may be lost if the new democratic leadership procrastinates. Second, establishing a causal link between a human rights movement and real human rights reform requires a controlled comparison of Argentina with other cases without such movements that did or did not achieve such reforms. The Argentine case demonstrates the importance of such explanatory variables as the interaction between the movement and the international system, the role of the judiciary, and the overall legitimacy of the protesters. Finally, the case shows that international learning and diffusion of human rights discourse across national boundaries are possible.

Summary

This chapter has shown how comparative political science has been actively studying the importance of human rights in the world, a process that has recognized the growth in the international human rights legal regime while considering its political implications. Table 11.4 summarizes the main findings of the various exemplars of human rights research considered in this chapter. Global comparisons focus on establishing a series of general statements about key explanatory variables that account for the variation in human rights protection, such as economic development, form of government, and involvement in conflict. The few-country studies show that apart from these important variables, scholars must take into account the increasing role of the diverse groups that comprise so-called 'transnational advocacy networks', which seek to put pressure on states to transform their practices. Moreover, the few-country examples here also show the complexities involved in the search for truth about past wrongs, and the politics of providing reconciliation for the victims of such past abuses of human rights. Finally, the single-country studies of Argentina demonstrate the political limitations to international human rights law and the mechanisms established for its enforcement, a point which will be discussed further in Part III.

Complementing these various research findings are the remaining challenges and lacunae in the field of human rights research. It is clear that from all the studies reviewed in this chapter that there continues to be a narrow focus on the protection of political and civil rights, which are seen to form the core set of human rights. Such an omission of other human rights is partly due to the history of the discipline (see Chapter 14) and partly due to the quest for commensurability of measures across disparate cultural contexts. First, political science has traditionally been interested in the design, analysis, and evaluation of political institutions that best realize the 'good life' through the establishment and protection of fundamental political and civil rights, while concerns with social welfare could be considered over the long term. Thus, comparative politics has always been concerned with forms of governance based on the protection of such rights. Second, methodologically, it has proved easier for political scientists to establish standards-based scales and coding strategies for measuring political and civil rights, while benchmark measures of social and economic rights remain problematic. Recent research in this field has begun to establish ways to operationalize social, economic, and cultural rights for systematic comparative analysis (see Hertel *et al.* 2007; and www.humanrightsdata.com).

The field of comparative politics thus has much to offer to the field of human rights research. The notion of universality inherent in human rights discourse and law necessarily implies the need for cross-national comparison, and this style of analysis complements other disciplines in the field of human rights, particularly law. Such comparisons can help explain the gap between what is claimed in principle and what is observed in practice. It accepts that international, regional, and domestic bodies of law represent an expression of consensus achieved in the various public fora in which such laws are promulgated. Yet, it sees these agreements and acts as an important starting point for political analysis. In this way, both the theories and methods of comparative politics provide a useful set of tools to examine the precariousness of international, regional, and national human rights regimes, while suggesting important prescriptions for strengthening them in the future.

Table 11.4 Comparative methods and the politics of human rights

Method of comparison	Number of countries	Exemplars	Results
Many countries	Up to 120 countries over 20 years	Mitchell and McCormick (1988); Henderson (1993); Poe and Tate (1994, 1999); Poe et al. (1999); Zanger (2000); Meyer (1996, 1998, 1999); Keith (1999); Smith et al. (1999); Zanger (2000); Hathaway (2002); Abouharb and Cingranelli (2004, 2007); Barratt (2004); Landman (2005b); Neumayer (2005); Hafner-Burton and Tsutsui (2005, 2007); Carey (2007).	Personal integrity rights are protected better in developed, peaceful, democratic countries First year of a democratic transition has real benefits Threats include internal conflict, poverty, authoritarian regimes Ambiguous relationships for multinational capital, foreign aid, and international law
Few countries	11	Risse et al. (1999) Kenya, Uganda, South Africa, Tunisia, Morocco, Poland, Czechoslovakia, Chile, Guatemala, Indonesia, Philippines.	Transnational advocacy networks can help diffuse international human rights norms and bring about domestic policy change across a wide range of different political contexts.
	Up to 15	Hayner (1994) Uganda (1974), Bolivia (1982–83), Argentina (1983–84), Uruguay (1985), Zimbabwe (1985), Uganda (1986), Philippines (1986–87), Chile (1990–91), Chad (1991–92), South Africa (1992), Germany (1992–), El Salvador (1992–93), South Africa (1993), Rwanda (1993), and Ethiopia (1993). De Brito (1997) Uruguay and Chile	Truth and reconciliation is more likely in Latin America than Africa Truth and reconciliation depends on the legacy of the prior authoritarian regime and the balance of political forces in the new democratic period
Single-country studies	Argentina	Guest (1990)	Conflict between UN and US can confound efforts to halt gross violations of human rights
		Weissbrodt and Bartolomei (1991)	Inter-American commission is more effective than UN bodies. 1503 procedures are too laborious and vulnerable to political influence
		Brysk (1994)	Domestic human rights movement achieved a symbolic and political victory over the military government

Notes

1   Such homeomorphic equivalents in anthropology are akin to 'functional equivalents' in political science (see Renteln 1988; Dogan and Pelassy 1990; Mendus 1995 and Chapter 2 this volume).

2   The term 'normative' is understood in two ways: (1) as legal norms that maintain a certain objectivity of law that is free from political and social construction, or influence, and (2) as moral and ethical norms in political theory, which inform larger statements about how political systems ought to be organized (see Glaser 1995; Steiner and Alston 1996:50–52; Hutchings 1999).

3   Strouse and Claude's (1976) pioneering work in this area is a notable exception, which uses the political and civil liberties measure devised by Raymond D. Gastil, and later taken over by Freedom House.

4   One version of the political terror scale ranges from 1 to 5, while a more recent coding scheme uses a scale of 0 to 2 for each separate violation. The former scale uses both the US State Department *Country Reports* and Amnesty International's *Annual Reports*, while the latter relies exclusively on the Amnesty reports (see Poe and Tate 1994, 1999; Cingranelli and Richards 1999:409–410).

5   Zanger (2000) uses the category of 'anocracy' to include those incoherent regimes that have both democratic and autocratic features, outlined in the discussion of Jaggers and Gurr (1995) in Chapter 7 in this volume.

6   New developments in this style of research that are exceptions to this more general observation include measures of women's human rights to political participation and economic equality (see Poe *et al*. 1997).

7   For example, the Reittig Commission in Chile published its findings about the Pinochet regime in 1991, shortly after the democratic transition (see Comisión Nacional de Verdad y Reconciliación 1991).

8   A total count of those disappeared during the military period 1976–1983 will never be established (Brysk 1994b). Of the 8,960 known cases, 30 per cent were blue collar workers, 21 per cent students, 18 per cent white collar workers, 11 per cent professionals, 6 per cent teachers, 5 per cent self-employed, and the remaining percentages comprised the self-employed, housewives, military conscripts, journalists, actors, and members of the clergy (Manzetti 1993:53–54).

9   The underlying logic to the Reagan Doctrine was that right-wing authoritarian regimes were inherently more capable of political liberalization and democratic transition than left-wing authoritarian regimes, a view voiced most prominently by Jeane Kirkpatrick, Ambassador to the UN at the time. In this perspective, US support for the Argentine military regime in the short run was seen as vital to US interests in the long term.

10 The key NGOs included the Madres de la Plaza de Maya, the Permanent Assembly for Human Rights, the Argentine League for the Rights of Man, the Ecumenical Movement for Human Rights, the Committee of Families of Persons who have Disappeared or Been Detained for Political Reasons, the Centre for Legal and Social Studies, and the Argentine Commission for Human Rights. The most important INGOs included Amnesty International, International Federation of Human Rights, and the Lawyers' Committee for Human Rights. While not exhaustive, this list represents the key human rights NGOs that were present during the Dirty War. The Argentine Commission for Human Rights consisted of those Argentineans who had managed to leave their country, and had representatives in Geneva, Madrid, Mexico City, Paris, Rome, and Washington DC (Weissbrodt and Bartolomei 1991:1015–1016). The National Commission on the Disappearance of Persons (CONADEP), which published the *Nunca Más* report, was not formed until 1983 by President Alfonsín (Brysk 1994a:175).

11 The authors argue that perhaps US political and economic pressure led the Argentine military to accept a visit from the Commission, a point that corroborates Guest's (1990) argument about the diplomatic power of the United States.

Further reading

Baehr, P. (2001) *Human Rights: Universality in Practice*, London: Palgrave.
> Excellent overview of human rights and their practical implications.

Davidson, S. (1993) *Human Rights*, Buckingham: Open University Press.
> A good overview and introduction to human rights.

Falk, R. (2000) *Human Rights Horizons: The Pursuit of Justice in a Globalizing World*, London: Routledge.
> Excellent overview and examination of the tension between the international law of human rights and the geopolitics of world order.

Forsythe, D. (2006) *Human Rights in International Relations*, Cambridge: Cambridge University Press.
> Introduction to human rights as a challenge to state sovereignty and realist approaches in international relations.

Jones, P. (1994) *Rights*, London: Macmillan.
> Excellent overview of different categories of rights, including human rights.

O' Byrne, D. J. (2003) *Human Rights: An Introduction*, London: Longman.
> Comprehensive introductory text on the theory and practice of human rights.

Robertson, A.H. and Merrills, J.G. (1996) *Human Rights in the World*, 4th edn, Manchester: Manchester University Press.
> A summary of human rights and how they are protected in international law.

International relations and comparative politics

Research problems

Across the preceding chapters in Part II of this volume, we have seen instances in which comparative research has addressed how political processes and events at the domestic level have significant implications for politics at the international level, and we have seen many studies include significant variables drawn from attention to the state behaviour, state interaction, and other factors at the international level that have an impact on domestic political developments. Studies on economic development and democracy often take into account the mediating effects of the structural division of labour in the world economy (Burkhart and Lewis-Beck 1994; Foweraker and Landman 2004; Li and Reuveny 2003) and the impact of constellations of power in the international sphere on socio-political developments at the domestic level (Rueschemeyer *et al.* 1992). Studies of violent political protest and social revolutions pay attention to external factors that may weaken states and contribute to their collapse (Skocpol 1979; Wickham-Crowley 1993), while policy makers worry about the potential for civil strife to move beyond borders and threaten international stability. New research on social movements and non-violent social protest has turned its attention to the transnational nature of mobilization, for example, against the forces of globalization, for the promotion and protection of human rights, and in a response to international events (e.g. Risse *et al.* 1999; Imig and Tarrow 2001; Bob 2005; Tarrow 2005; Inglehart and Welzel 2005).

The studies on democratic transitions initially focused on domestic actors for political transformation but increasingly examined the importance of transnational processes of 'contagion' (Huntington 1991; Whitehead 2002) and diffusion (Gleditsch 2002). Increasingly, international donor organizations and OECD countries are taking into account the institutional arrangements and quality of governance of recipient states in their decision to allocate development assistance, which is based on new comparative research linking good governance to economic performance (see World Bank 2002; Knack 2003; Abouharb and Cingranelli 2007). Finally, it is clear that human rights form an important nexus between the international sphere and the domestic sphere since the promotion and protection of human rights relies heavily on the mechanisms (however weak) of inter-state treaties and international law to govern the relationship between states and citizens (Landman 2005a, 2005b).

Traditionally, theories and research in international relations focused on some domestic variables as important determinants of international state behaviour while discounting or completely ignoring other variables. For example, the realist perspective takes into account 'material' variables, such as economic power, military capability, size of the population, and geographical location (e.g. distance and contiguity) (see Morgenthau 1961; Waltz 1979; Mearsheimer 1994–1995, 2001), while ignoring regime type, institutions, values, norms, and dimensions of 'soft' power (Wendt 1999; Nye 2004) as either largely inconsequential or as having no independent effect on state behaviour in the international sphere (Legro and Moravcsik 1999; Mearsheimer 1994–1995; 2001). The liberal (and liberal republican) perspective in international relations has argued that domestic institutional arrangements do matter for explaining international behaviour (see e.g. Putnam 1988; Moravcsik 1997, 2000), while the neo-liberal institutionalist perspective argues that international law, institutions, and regimes can have additional 'constraining' effects on states at the domestic level (Keohane 1984, 2001, 2002; Raustiala and Slaughter 2002). While studies in comparative politics have paid more attention to domestic variables, there has been a much greater tendency within the sub-field to incorporate international variables in the kinds of ways that have been evident across the previous chapters in this part of the book.

The stylized way of representing the main research questions motivated by the overlap between international relations and comparative politics is illustrated in Figure 12.1. It is clear from the figure that many research questions and associated research designs are concerned with examining the relative significance and impact of key domestic variables on state behaviour in the international sphere. But they are also concerned with addressing the different ways in which international variables have an impact on domestic politics. Methodologically, empirical studies in international relations often use similar comparative research designs to analyse substantive research topics, including the comparison of many countries, the comparison of few countries, and single-country studies. Where the methods in international relations differ is the use of comparing 'dyads' of politically relevant states across time, but even then, many of the variables that differentiate one state from another in the dyad are domestically based, such as the level of democracy, development, and other features of the kind examined in the previous chapters.

With this brief introductory background in mind, this chapter continues to use the architecture of the preceding chapters to examine studies that compare many countries (including dyads), few countries and single countries across a range of substantive topics to illustrate the ways in which international factors have an impact on domestic politics and how domestic characteristics of states have an impact on their behaviour in the international arena. The first section looks at two main studies: Li and Reuveny's (2003) many-country comparison on the impact of globalization has on democracy and Russet and O'Neal's (2001) study on the 'democratic' peace and the Kantian 'tripod'. The latter study compares dyads of states over time to test general propositions drawn from Kant's (1795) prescient argument in *Perpetual Peace* on the pacific benefits of increased economic interdependence, participation in international organizations and institutions, and so-called 'civic republican' systems of governance. The second section considers Bob's (2005) market-based analysis of the success and failure of domestic insurgent groups in Nigeria and

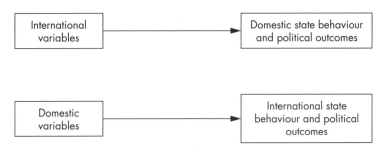

Figure 12.1 Linking international relations and comparative politics

Mexico for attracting international financial and moral support, and Moravcsik's (2000) comparison of the impact of nascent democratic institutions on the establishment of the European human rights regime in the aftermath of World War II. The final section uses the case of Chile to demonstrate how actors from the international human rights community created the opportunity for an internal dynamic that liberalized Pinochet's Chile (Hawkins 2004 and Chapter 5 this volume) and how the developments surrounding Pinochet's legal status as a former of Head of State provided firm support for the notion of 'universal jurisdiction', which is a bedrock legal doctrine for the International Criminal Court in the Hague established in 2002 (Kornbluh 2003; Hawkins 2002; Sands 2005).

Comparing many countries

This section starts by considering a study that compares many countries in order to examine the impact of key economic and cultural features of globalization on democracy. Drawing on the research design and findings in the field on economic development and democracy covered in Chapter 6, Li and Reuveny (2003) compare 127 countries between 1970 and 1996 across a range of domestic and international variables. Their analysis tests a variety of claims about the relationship between globalization and democracy, where they summarize seven main arguments for a positive relationship (Li and Reuveny 2003: 32–35), seven arguments for a negative relationship (ibid.: 35–38), and three main arguments on an ambiguous relationship (ibid.: 38–39). The dependent variable is democracy and the four globalization variables are trade openness, foreign direct investment flows, portfolio investment flows, and the spread of democratic ideas across countries. Democracy is measured using the Polity III combined score for democracy (see Jaggers and Gurr 1995; and Chapter 9 this volume). Trade openness is total imports and exports as a percentage of GDP, foreign direct investment is the net inflow of investment as a percentage of GDP, portfolio investment is the net inflow of investment as a percentage of GDP, and like Doorenspleet (2005) the spread of democratic values is measured by counting the number of democracies in the region from which a country comes.

These four globalization variables are proxy measures for the degree to which countries are integrated into the world economy and the flow of ideas with a particular normative commitment to democracy. Higher scores on any one of the measures indicate a greater degree of integration, while lower scores indicate a greater degree of isolation from these larger processes of globalization. In addition to the main variables, they also include GDP per capita, economic growth (i.e. the annual percentage change in GDP), the annual rate of inflation, and lagged values of the dependent variable to control for democratic inertia and possible omitted variables. To control for other features of their data (see Chapter 3 in this volume), they use lagged values of the independent variables, separate estimations of the relationship for different decades comprising their sample (1970s, 1980s, and the 1990s), and the White estimator to control for the possible confounding effects of heteroscedasticity (i.e. non-uniform variance in their disturbance terms) (Li and Reuveny 2003: 39–41).

Cognizant of the fact that the mature industrialized democracies of the world have achieved democratic stability and have a higher degree of integration into the world economy, their comparisons are carried out for all the countries in their sample and for a sample of countries that excludes the developed countries (ibid.: 39). This methodological move is consistent with the discussion in Chapter 6, where different analyses of the general relationship between economic development and democracy compared countries at a particular level of development or for a particular region in the world. Across the different country samples and time periods, their analyses find that trade openness and portfolio investment have a negative relationship with democracy, where the negative effect of portfolio investment increases over time. Foreign direct investment has a positive relationship with democracy that weakens over time, while the spread of democratic values has a persistently positive relationship with democracy over time (ibid.: 30, 43–52).

Their main conclusion is that 'the economic aspects of integration into the world economy are beginning to cause a decline in national democratic governance' (ibid.: 53); a finding that creates a tension between two larger policy goals: greater economic efficiency versus better democratic governance. They argue that governments in lesser developed countries lack the capacity to manage their economies in the face of increased capital mobility and the flippancy of international investors who remain largely unaccountable to the people residing in the countries seeking inward investment. Moreover, the general positive trend in democratization illustrated in Chapter 9 may well become eroded as the nascent democratic institutions within transitional societies become undermined by those factors associated with processes of economic globalization. Overall, this study adds value to the comparative literature on economic development and democracy in recognizing the truly international character of processes of economic development, particularly those that have unfolded during the third and fourth waves of democratization.

Our second study in this section focuses on the relationship between particular domestic and international variables that for a long time did not receive attention from international relations scholars as having a bearing on the probability of conflict between states. This field of research has become known as the 'democratic peace' since it focuses on how domestic regime types have an effect on inter-state conflict, specified as either full-blown warfare or as 'militarized disputes' (Russet and O'Neal 2001: 94–96). As Chapter 1 already pointed out, 'the closest thing we have to a law in international politics' is the fact that democratic countries rarely, if ever, fight each other (Levy 1988). The logic of the proposition is simple and the research design to test the proposition is fairly straightforward. First, there is a normative argument that political elites within democracies adhere to democratic norms, which in turn lead them to prefer non-violent conflict resolution and negotiation to violent conflict. This general normative orientation is then shared by democracies that develop greater trust for one another and leads any two democracies to forgo violent conflict with one another (Rosato 2003: 586). Second, there are several institutional logics at play involving the inherent element of accountability within democracies that constrains leaders from engaging in warfare or conflict, including public constraints on leaders, interest group constraints, the difficulty in mobilizing the public for war, the inability for surprise attacks, and the relative availability of information within the public domain (Rosato 2003: 586–587).

Both the normative and institutional logics inherent within democracies suggests that they would be less likely to go to war with one another and that the presence of a democracy in any one dyad of states would lower the probability of inter-state conflict. The methods for testing the proposition and extending it to other liberal variables have evolved over time from the original studies by Babst (1964, 1972) with the development of increasingly complex data sets of all the politically relevant dyads between the late nineteenth century and the late twentieth century (see, for example, Bremer 1992 and 1993; Dixon 1994; Doyle 1983, 1995, 1996, and 1999; Farber and Gowa 1995; Owen 1994; Russett 1993a, 1993b, and 1995; Russett and O'Neal 1999, and 2001; Small and Singer 1976). Of these various studies, Russett and O'Neal's (2001) study tests both the democratic peace proposition and the larger Kantian 'tripod', which adds examination of the pacifying effects of economic interdependence and participation in international organizations.

Methodologically, Russett and O'Neal (2001) compiled a database of politically relevant dyads from 1886 to 1992. Since the politically relevant dyad is the basic unit of analysis, they have a much larger number of observations (dyad-years $\approx 40,000$) than is typical for many-country studies of the kind considered in this volume thus far. Their main dependent variable is the militarized dispute, which is an international interaction that includes all instances when one state threatened to use force, made an expression of force, or actually used military force against another state. The dispute variable is dichotomous (the dyad was in conflict or not). In order to present a fair test of the Kantian Peace proposition at the global level, they specify a series of liberal and realist independent variables. The liberal variables include democracy, economic interdependence (trade dependency and trade openness), and international institutions (joint IGO membership). The realist variables include contiguity and distance, power ratio, and alliances.

The fairness of the test comes from the fact that they are testing for the statistical significance of the liberal variables alongside the realist variables. The large number of observations allows for this kind of statistical control to be introduced, where all the liberal variables are significant, even in the presence of the realist variables. The quantitative results show that even after controlling for the realist variables and the pacifying effects of interdependence and joint membership of international organizations, 'two democracies are 33 percent less likely than the average dyad to become involved in a militarised dispute', which they argue is a conservative estimate of the 'pacific benefits of democracy' (Russet and O'Neal 2001: 275). Their various analyses show further that not only are democracies less likely to fight one another, but they are even less likely to become involved in disputes than autocracies (ibid.: 276). If the effects of all the liberal variables are taken into account, then the probability of dispute falls by 71 per cent, a finding they argue means that peace in the world is becoming more likely since both the number of democracies and the degree of interdependence is increasing (ibid.: 282).

Figure 12.2 is a stylized graphical depiction of how the dyads are examined and how the different combination of countries with different regime types (i.e. democracy or autocracy) affect the probability of conflict between any two states. The first dyad comprises two democratic states, which has a lower probability of conflict. The second dyad comprises one democracy and one autocracy, which also has a lower probability of conflict, particularly if the level of democracy in the democratic state increases over time. The third dyad comprises two autocracies, which has a higher probability of conflict. The analysis then compares multiple dyads over long periods of time to determine the kind of probabilities that are summarized above. Overall, the analysis provides robust statistical evidence of the pacific benefits of democracy and serves as a particularly good example of a many-country comparative research design that examines the relationship between domestic variables and state behaviour at the international level.

Recent studies have queried the robustness of these types of findings for democracy in several ways. From a regional perspective, democratic peace theory (and its Kantian counterpart) can be seen as ethnocentric since it articulates a prescription for peace based on Western liberal democratic values (see, e.g., Chan 1984). In fact, 90 per cent of purely democratic dyads have been confined to two geographical regions: Western Europe and North America (Rosato 2003), which suggests that the discovery of a statistically significant and substantive impact of the Kantian variables at the global level may well be a reflection of the Western experience with democracy, trade, and international institutions. Thus, the basic research design may suffer from a form of selection bias and spuriousness. Second, democratizing countries or states 'in transition' may actually be more war-prone than mature democracies, since they lack fully developed and 'coherent political institutions needed to manage intensified domestic political competition and to prevent it from provoking international conflicts' (Mansfield and Snyder 2005:21; see also Ward and Gleditsch 1998).

While grounded primarily in questions of theory and methodology, these criticisms have substantive importance that go well beyond the academy, since much of the Cold War foreign policy of the United States has been based on democratic peace theory; policy prescriptions that were raised to high relief with the 2003 US-led invasion of Iraq. Moreover, the debates between the supporters and detractors of democratic peace theory have implications for whether some sort of democratic 'sequencing' is required, which places more emphasis on the development of state institutions than on encouraging founding elections (see Mansfield and Snyder 2005

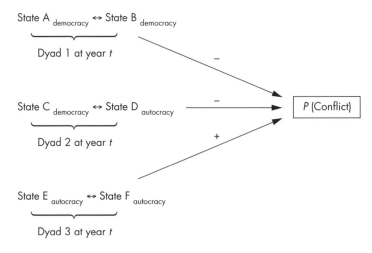

Figure 12.2 Different dyads and the probability of conflict

and Carothers 2007). Indeed, as Kopstein (2006) argues there have been different understandings of how democracy comes about that have had profound implications for different foreign policies pursued by the United States and countries in Europe.

Comparing few countries

The previous section showed how different aspects of globalization can have a different impact on democracy and how democracy both in its normative and institutional understanding might well have an influence on the international behaviour of states. A comparative research design comprising many countries over time has been a typical way to address these two research topics. This section considers another set of comparative studies concerned with relationship between domestic and international variables. In *The Marketing of Rebellion*, Bob (2005) compares the fortunes of four instances of insurgent groups in Nigeria and Mexico to show how some movements are more successful than others in attracting international attention, material resources, and advocacy on their behalf from international NGOs and transnational advocacy networks. Moravcsik's (2000) study compares the new democracies of the second wave (i.e. European democracies of the immediate post-World War II period) in an effort to show how concern over the future prospects of democracy led these countries to establish a supranational regime in the area of human rights, which has developed into the most developed of the regional human rights regimes (see Donnelly 1989, 1998). The first study is an example of how the demand for support from groups mobilized at the domestic level interacts with the supply of support at the international level, while the second study shows how domestic institutional arrangements and concern over the survival of democracy led to the creation of a set of international institutions designed to constrain the behaviour of states.

Bob (2005: 2) begins his study with three simple questions:

1   How and why do a handful of local challengers become global *causes célebres* while scores of others remain isolated and obscure?
2   What inspires powerful transnational networks to spring up around particular movements?
3   Most basically, which of the world's myriad oppressed benefit from contemporary globalization?

He adopts a most similar systems design (MSSD) of 'unlikely' movements that suddenly vaulted to national and international prominence (ibid.: 10). He focuses on one successful and one unsuccessful movement in Nigeria and Mexico to examine their different strategies to attract international support. In Nigeria, he compares the relatively successful efforts of the Ogoni people in the Niger River Delta to attract significant international support for their cause as against the unsuccessful efforts of other minorities in the region to attract the same kind of attention and support. In Mexico, he compares the success of the Zapatista Army of National Liberation (EZLN) in the southern state of Chiapas (see Chapter 7 this volume), which 'galvanized advocacy and solidarity activists worldwide' to the failure to do the same by the Popular Revolutionary Party (ibid.: 11). His study thus compares two movements in two countries (n=4) which he argues share similar international and domestic features. Movements in both countries faced a similar international context in terms of the number of NGOs, institutional setting, dominant ideologies and technical development, while at the domestic level, they faced similar state structures and leaders, social groups and attitudes, and processes of economic development and change (ibid.: 12). In short, he compares different outcomes across similar countries.

To explain these differences in outcome, Bob develops a model based on the simple logic of the market. Domestically based challengers *demand* various forms of international support to raise awareness of their plight and bring about social and political transformations in their own governments to provide redress of their grievances. Internationally based inter-governmental and non-governmental organizations *supply* the much-needed support in material and moral terms, but the supply is necessarily limited (the principle of economic scarcity) and thus the market for such support is necessarily highly competitive. In other words, demand for support is much higher than the supply of the support and movements need to compete against one another in this market, which is characterized by the classic features of power, exchange, and marketing. Drawing on social movement literature, Bob (2005:22–46), argues that the two main sets of variables responsible for successful attraction of international support include: (1) movement strategies for raising awareness and framing their struggle in terms that match the goals, culture and ethics of international supporters; and (2) structural factors of the movements (e.g. status, contacts, material resources, and leadership) and their opponents (e.g. identity and reactions to mobilization).

The qualitative analysis of the four groups shows that in both the cases of the Ogoni people and the Zapatistas, movement strategies were more effective in raising awareness and matching the goals of their supporters than in the cases of other minority groups in the Niger Delta and the Popular Revolutionary Party. Despite some differences between the movement in terms of the use of force, direct lobbying, diffuse international consciousness-raising, and support from advocacy and solidarity groups, both the Ogoni and the Zapatistas shared fundamental features, including their marketing approach, factors driving the approach, and the motivations of the supporters which were ultimately in tune with the grievances of these two groups. His findings challenge the popular view that international advocacy and solidarity networks represent an unlimited supply of material resource and good will for the downtrodden, which when tapped, will spring into action and put pressure on states to implement necessary reforms that address the needs of the movement (Risse *et al.* 1999). Rather, there are oppressed groups everywhere who need to mobilize their resources and market their message in ways that match the main aims and objectives of transnational advocacy networks who are ultimately quite selective in who they support.

Our second study in this section examines how particular sets of domestic variables affect the international behaviour of states. Moravcsik (2000) seeks to explain the creation of the European human rights regime through the passage and enactment of the 1951 European Convention on Human Rights (ECHR). The establishment of such a mechanism with the power of enforcement appears counter-intuitive from many perspectives in international relations, most notably realism. Moravcsik (2000:219) asks:

> Why would any government, democratic or dictatorial, favour establishing an effective, independent international authority, the sole purpose of which is to constrain its domestic sovereignty in such an unprecedentedly invasive and overtly non-majoritarian manner?

Drawing on the insights of Putnam's (1988) 'two-level' game (see Briefing box 12.1) and combining them with variants of democratic peace theory (see above), Moravcsik (1997, 2000) develops a theory of 'liberal republicanism', which makes explicit reference to democratic forms of rule and how such domestic systems will have an influence on a country's propensity for making international agreements. He argues that making international agreements can 'lock in' and consolidate democratic institutions, thereby enhancing their credibility and stability in the long run against possible threats from non-democratic forces. In echoing realist language, he argues that states will make such agreements when the benefits of reducing future uncertainty outweigh the costs of membership in an international regime (Moravcsik 2000:220). He argues further that this argument only really applies to newly established democracies since they face more immediate uncertainty which regime membership tempers. Thus, like Russet and O'Neal (2001), he argues that domestic political processes and institutions associated with democracy are important for explaining international behaviour, but further specifies the argument to address the processes and institutions for newly established democracies.

To test his main proposition, he compares national preferences for the establishment of the human rights regime in 1950 across seventeen European countries during the post-World War II period, including the 'old' democracies, new democracies, and semi-democracies and dictatorships. These preferences are measured according to the relative willingness of states to accept compulsory jurisdiction of the regime and for all individual petitions to be filed against states for breach of the human rights obligations. A vote for both provisions indicates support for a 'reciprocally binding' regime that establishes supranational authority over the domestic affairs of states (Moravcsik 2000:231). His group of old democracies (i.e. democratic from before 1920) includes Belgium, Denmark, Luxembourg, The Netherlands, Norway, Sweden, and the United Kingdom. His group of new democracies (i.e. those that became established between 1920 and 1950) includes Austria, France, Italy, Iceland, Ireland, and West Germany. His group of semi-democracies and dictatorships (i.e those countries not fully democratic by 1950) includes Greece, Turkey, Spain and Portugal, even though the latter two were not involved in the negotiations to establish the regime.

He adopts a most similar systems design since he compares different outcomes (i.e. support for the enforcement of the European Convention on Human Rights) across seventeen similar European countries. While his comparison controls for those features common to the countries, his main independent variable is regime type, which varies across his groups of old democracies, new democracies, and semi-democracies and dictatorships. Table 12.1 shows the results of his comparison across these different groups of countries. It is clear from the table that there is a distinct

---

Briefing Box 12.1 The two-level game

International relations scholars have focused on the structure of state interaction and how that may account for outcomes such as war, peace, trade, and security, while comparativists have remained focused on the structure of individual interactions in larger processes of economic development, democratization, and conflict, among many other topics. The exception to this observation has been the work on 'two-level' games (Putnam 1993), which brings the convergent views in international relations and comparative research together. Putnam (1993:459) observes that '[t]he most portentous development in the fields of comparative politics and international relations in recent years is the dawning recognition among practitioners in each field of the need to take into account entanglements between the two'. Any engagement of a state in international relations reflects the domestic array of social and political forces, including key actors and institutions (Putnam 1993: 435). The politics of such a two-level game is summarized as follows:

> At the national level, domestic groups pursue their interests by pressuring the government to adopt favourable policies, and the politicians seek power by constructing coalitions among those groups. At the international level, national governments seek to maximize their own ability to satisfy domestic pressures, while minimising the adverse consequences of foreign developments.
>
> (Ibid.: 436)

While there may be different 'rational' strategies available at either level of the game, Putnam (1993:473) argues that 'there are powerful incentives for consistency between the two games.' What is absent from the formulation of the two-level game is any consideration of the type of government that is in place, although it appears that Putnam implies some form of representative government and most of his empirical examples are of advanced industrial democracies. Indeed, liberal democratic states are simply more open to and reflective of competing claims from domestic groups than authoritarian states. Nevertheless, as the elite-centred work on democratic transitions demonstrates (e.g. see Przeworski 1991; Colomer 2000 and Chapter 10 in this volume), authoritarian regimes are susceptible to competing demands within the authoritarian coalition as well as from groups in civil society, however repressed they may be. It is thus possible to think in broader terms about how the games played at the domestic level (whatever type of government is in place) will be important for state interaction at the international level, thereby giving the notion of the two level game universal applicability (see Czempiel 1992: 257–258).

---

relationship between the type of regime and support for the enforcement of the ECHR. The second column in the table shows that among the old democracies, only Belgium supported the enforcement provisions, while all others opposed it. This is in stark contrast to the new democracies, where all of them supported the enforcement provisions. The final column shows that like most of their democratic counterparts, the semi-democracies and dictatorships also opposed the enforcement provisions.

Table 12.1 Support for the European Convention on Human Rights

Support for enforcement of the European Convention on Human Rights (ECHR)	Old democracies (democratic since before 1920)	New democracies (democratic between 1920 and 1950)	Semi-democracies and dictatorships (not yet democratic by 1950)
Yes	Belgium	Austria France Italy Iceland West Germany	
No	Denmark Sweden Netherlands Norway United Kingdom Luxembourg		Greece Turkey (Spain) (Portugal)

Source: Adapted from Moravcsik (2000:233)

These results provide compelling comparative evidence of the propensity for new democracies to desire the establishment of a supranational regime in the area of human rights, and they lend support to Moravcsik's liberal republican theory. He concludes his analysis by suggesting that his findings may apply to other human rights regimes (e.g. the UN system, the International Criminal Court, the Inter-American System, and the African System) and other issue areas, such as international trade and the environment. Other scholars have suggested that regime membership, particularly for human rights, may well be a function of democracy in general rather than isolated to new democracies (see Zacher 1992:94; and also Vincent 1986), and subsequent analysis of the growth and effectiveness of the international human rights regime shows that fourth wave democracies were more likely to ratify more international human rights instruments with fewer reservations than third wave and old democracies (see Landman 2005b:88–92).

Single-country studies

The previous two sections have shown how the comparison of many countries and the comparison of few countries can uncover the different ways in which domestic variables and international variables interact. This final section shows how single-country analysis can add to this kind of research agenda by examining the case of Chile under Pinochet. There are many countries that become the centre of the world's attention for both negative and positive reasons. Indeed, the world has been fixated on events such as the Soviet crackdowns in Budapest and Prague, the Soweto violence in South Africa, the Chinese crackdown on dissidents in Tiananmen Square, and the plight of detainees in Guantanamo Bay and Abu Ghraib. But it has been equally fixated on the dramatic turn towards democracy since the Portuguese transition in 1974, the fall of the Berlin Wall and the collapse of the Soviet Union, the dramatic release of Nelson Mandela and the subsequent transition in South Africa, among many other good news stories of the latter half of the twentieth century.

The case of Chile falls into both categories and its political developments between 1973 and 1998 provide a good illustration of the different ways in which international developments have an impact on domestic developments and how the domestic factors have an impact on international events. The period began in 1973 with a military coup that overthrew the democratically elected president Salvador Allende and ended with the arrest, detention, and return of Augusto Pinochet, the dictator who emerged from within the junta to rule Chile through coercion and repression for nearly eighteen years. Studies on the Chilean case have shown that international factors led to the overthrow of Allende (e.g. Kornbluh 2003), the development of significant opposition to the dictatorship (Hawkins 2002), and the arrest and detention of Pinochet in London (Sands 2005), while domestic factors led to the defeat of Pinochet in a plebiscite (Constable and Valenzuela 1993) and his eventual house arrest for crimes against humanity. Chile thus sits at the nexus of international and domestic concerns over democracy, dictatorship, atrocity, and accountability.

As Chapter 5 outlined, Hawkins' (2002) careful analysis of internal com-munications, international and domestic mobilization from NGOs, and 'process-tracing' of decision making within the military regime itself shows that fissures developed within the ruling junta that ultimately favoured some form of political liberalization. The democratic transition was prolonged and convoluted throughout the period beginning with the 1980 constitution to the 1988 national plebiscite and 1990 democratic elections. In contrast to some analyses (see Ropp and Sikkink 1999 and Chapter 11), Hawkins (2002) shows that these developments did not take place in linear fashion but involved mobilization against the regime, regime crackdown (particularly during the 1985 state of siege), and eventual capitulation after Pinochet's failure to win a majority in the plebiscite (see also Foweraker and Landman 1997).

The post-authoritarian period in Chile has been equally convoluted with respect to accountability and impunity for the crimes against humanity that were committed during the years of the regime. Pinochet managed to establish certain 'reserve domains' (Foweaker et al. 2003) for the military and claimed immunity for his crimes on the basis of being a former head of state. Chile has also had two truth commissions with the mandate to establish a record of the human rights abuses that took place during Pinochet's rule (see Hayner 1994, 2002 and Chapter 11). On a visit to London in 1998, Pinochet found himself arrested by the British authorities acting on an application for extradition by a Spanish judge, and after much debate in the House of Lords, which ultimately decided Pinochet could not claim immunity, was released on the grounds of ill health and returned to Chile in 2000. Emboldened by these international developments, groups seeking justice mobilized the Chilean legal system to seek his prosecution. He was stripped of domestic immunity in 2005 and placed under house arrest in 2006. He subsequently died of heart failure.

Summary

This chapter is slightly different than the preceding chapters in Part II since it does not focus on one particular research topic. Rather it has sought to demonstrate how the fields of international relations and comparative politics have significant areas that overlap. There are numerous ways in which international variables have been and should be taken into account when seeking to explain domestic political developments, events, and outcomes. Equally, there are numerous domestic variables

Table 12.2 Summary of studies that examine the nexus between domestic and international variables

Method of comparison	Number of countries	Exemplars	Result
Many countries	127 countries between 1970 and 1996	Li and Reuveny (2003)	Trade openness and portfolio investmen have a negative relationship with democracy; negative effect of portfolio investment increases over time. Foreign direct investment has a positive relationship with democracy that weakens over time; spread of democratic values has a persistently positive relationship with democracy over time.
	40,000 dyad-years between 1886 and 1992	Russett and O'Neal (2001)	Joint democracy, economic interdependence, and participation in international institutions lowers the probability of inter-state conflict.
Few countries	Nigeria and Mexico	Bob (2005)	Movement strategies for awareness raising and framing struggle to match international NGOs garner successful support for domestic struggle
	17 post-World War II European countries	Moravcsik (2000)	Uncertainty within new democracies leads them to establish supranational institutions to lock in future generations to democracy.
Single-country studies	One country	Kornbluh 2003; Hawkins 2004; Sands 2005	International pressure provokes fissures within domestic ruling faction and leads to democratization; international arrest and detention of Pinochet fortifies doctrine of universal jurisdiction and emboldens domestic actors to prosecute former head of state.

that need to be taken into account when seeking to explain international state behaviour. This chapter has made it clear that there are numerous examples of both these main points in the studies covered in the previous chapters, while the studies considered here (see Table 12.2 for a summary) are particularly good examples for demonstrating the overlap between the international level and the domestic level. Moreover, this chapter has shown that the studies that incorporate this kind of analysis benefit from the kind of comparative methods examined throughout this book.

Further reading

Legro, J. and Moravcsik, A. (1999) 'Is Anybody Still a Realist?' *International Security*, 24 (2): 5–55.
> Good analysis of the main tenets of realism.

Morgenthau, H.J. (1961) *Politics among Nations: The Struggle for Power and Peace*, 3rd edn, New York: Alfred A Knopf.
> Classic realist text.

Schmidt, B.C. (2002) 'On the History and Historiography of International Relations', in W. Carlsnaes, T. Risse, and B. Simmons, (eds) *Handbook of International Relations*, London: Sage, 3–22.
> Good summary of the field of international relations.

Part III

COMPARATIVE METHODS AND NEW ISSUES

This final section of the book summarizes the studies in Part II (Chapter 13) and discusses the new issues and challenges that will confront the field in the future (Chapter 14). Chapter 13 reviews the studies in Part II with respect to the ways in which they have highlighted the methodological trade-offs associated with different comparative methods and the contributions they have made to build theories in political science. In this way, the comparative architecture of Part I is brought to bear on the issues and methodological discussions in Part II. The key factors that are important for comparative research that emerge from this analysis include case selection (both number and type), the limitation of inferential aspirations, and the practice of good theorizing and adequate research design.

Chapter 14 explores the new issues and challenges that will confront comparative politics in the twenty-first century. The chapter summarizes briefly the developmental path that comparative politics has taken and where it is likely to lead in the years to come. It examines new developments in method and analytical software that will help the field to evolve as well as to break down traditional barriers in the discipline. It discusses the key challenges to comparative politics in the future. Finally, it shows how systematic comparative analysis makes contemporary political science relevant to politicians and policy makers addressing the crucial political issues and problems that confront the world today.

Common themes and different comparisons

The chapters in Part II demonstrate clearly that comparative politics is an exciting, dynamic, and developing field in the social sciences both in terms of its substantive topics and methodological techniques (Mair 1996:309). Comparative politics as a field is not merely defined in terms of its primary activity – comparing countries – but as a broad research community that seeks to provide individual, structural, and cultural explanations for observed political phenomena (Lichbach 1997:240–241). Each of the research topics in Part II has been examined using comparative methods, while the review of the specific studies illustrates that some have been more systematic in their comparisons than others. This 'comparison of comparisons' identifies similarities and differences among the studies with respect to the operationalization of key concepts, overall research design, choice of countries, and types of comparative inferences they are able to make.

With respect to the chapters in Part II, the research questions address common themes that are best examined using some form of comparison. The themes include the emergence of democracy (both in the past and more recently), violent and non-violent challenges to its institutions, the institutional configurations that may facilitate its long-term survival, the fundamental rights that it ought to protect (Apter 1996:373), and its relationship with international peace. The research questions were posed in such a way that comparison provided the best method for making substantive inferences. Whether searching for the objective preconditions of democracy, the individual and structural correlates of rebellion, the origins, trajectory and impact of social movements, the conditions for democratic transition, the institutional arrangements for successful and effective democratic rule, the reasons for human rights violations, or the different relationships between domestic and international variables, systematic comparison of one or more countries helped to provide answers. Such systematic comparison includes comparing many countries, few countries, and the intensive examination of single countries using both quantitative and qualitative techniques.

This chapter discusses these common themes and different comparisons to achieve several objectives. First, the issues and methodological concerns raised in Part I are brought to bear on the methods and substantive results in Part II in order to illustrate the methodological trade-offs associated with comparative politics. These trade-offs include those between the scope of countries and the types of inferences that can be drawn; generalizations based on the comparison of many countries and the presence of outliers, and different levels of analysis. In so doing, it identifies the methodological sources for the different substantive results obtained by the studies compared in Part II, including units of analysis, the selection of cases, and the inferential aspirations of the different studies. Second, the chapter summarizes the studies from Part II and examines how each has contributed to building individual, structural, and cultural theories of politics. Finally, the chapter outlines the key lessons scholars ought to draw from these observations.

Methodological trade-offs

Comparing many countries

The comparison of many countries provides statistical control and reduces the problem of selection bias; it gives extensive comparative scope and empirical support for general theories, and identifies deviant cases that warrant closer comparative examination. The many-country studies in Part II make important generalizations about the key issues identified in each chapter. Those in Chapter 6 identified important socio-economic correlates of democracy, some of which suggest that economic development actually causes democracy. For political violence (Chapter 7), the studies identify a bundle of explanatory factors, while their different results are more due to their different theoretical conceptualizations and model specifications than to the method they have adopted. The studies in Chapter 8 identify broad socio-economic changes and organizational factors as important explanations for social movement origins, while largely ignoring the trajectory, shape, and political impact of movements.

For democratic transition (Chapter 9), Huntington's (1991) qualitative study argues that a crisis of legitimacy in the authoritarian regime, high levels of economic development, the national and international presence of the Catholic Church, other international influences, and the diffusion of democratic ideas all help account for the global spread of democracy since 1974. The quantitative studies either map descriptive attributes of the 'third wave' of democratic transition (Jaggers and Gurr 1995), or identify the importance of key socio-economic variables that lie behind it (Vanhanen 1997; Doorenspleet 2005). The global evidence on institutional design and democratic performance presented in Chapter 10 demonstrates that parliamentary systems tend to perform better and break down less frequently than presidential systems. In Chapter 11, we learn that while economic development and democracy are associated with a greater protection of personal integrity rights, the global comparisons showed that resolving inter- and intra-state conflict is crucial to reducing the violation of such rights. Finally, Chapter 12 showed how there is a significant crossover of concerns between the field of comparative politics and international relations, where comparative politics has been slightly more amenable to include international variables than international relations has been in accepting that domestic variables other than material resources and features may also have an impact on state behaviour.

What is clear from these studies is the identification of a parsimonious set of explanatory factors and sufficient degrees of freedom to allow for great variance in the variables, as well as the inclusion of control variables to rule out rival hypotheses. Of the issues in Part II, the most frequently verified empirical generalization is for the positive relationship between economic development and democracy. The second strongest generalization to emerge from these studies is the superior democratic performance (however measured) of parliamentary systems. There is less academic consensus, however, on the explanation for political violence, a dearth of many-country studies on social movements, few quantitative global comparisons of democratic transition (but see Boix 2003; Boix and Stokes 2003; Doorenspleet 2005), a continued focus on a narrow set of human rights, and a rise in the number of studies looking at the interaction between variables at different levels of analysis.

These problems in the global comparative literature illustrate the key weaknesses of this method. For political violence, many of the theories posit relationships that exist at the individual level, yet the tests for them use the nation state as the unit of analysis. Indicators for social movement activity such as protest event data are difficult to collect for a large number of countries. Similarly, measures of human rights beyond civil and political rights have presented a great challenge, although some advance is being made (see www.humanrightsdata.com; and Hertel *et al.* 2007). Democratic transitions tend to be operationalized in dichotomous terms, while theoretically transition is often thought to be a *longer political process*, which makes its cross-national study more difficult (see Whitehead 1996a). Thus, for the many-country comparisons to provide more valid and reliable inferences, better specification and measurement of the key variables are needed. Given the advances in communication and information technologies, however, the collection and sharing of global data on a variety of social, economic, and political indicators will continue to be easier. Moreover, the establishment of an ethos of replication and data-sharing within the scholarly community will aid in this goal for improving global analysis (see Chapter 14).

Comparing few countries

The weaknesses associated with comparing many countries and the discomfort scholars may have in specifying parsimonious models of politics have led many to compare a smaller set of countries. As Part I made clear, this method of comparison also provides control through use of the most similar or most different systems design (or both). It uses concepts and variables that may be more sensitive to the nuances of the particular political contexts under investigation. It allows for historical and intensive examination of cases not possible in studies with a large sample of countries. Together, the strength of few-country studies lies in their lower level of abstraction and their inclusion of historical and cultural factors. While many of these studies do not seek universal aspirations for their inferences, they do seek to extend their generalizations beyond the immediate scope of the countries included in the analysis.

For economic development and democracy, few-country studies introduce a broader set of variables and, using a historical perspective, not only 'unpack' the simple bivariate relationship between development and democracy but also uncover the sequences through which countries have (or have not) become democratic. While the few-country studies do not dispute the generalizations of the global comparative literature, they are keen to point out that there are exceptions to every rule. Thus, the global comparative studies focus on the similarities across the sample, while the few-country comparisons focus on the differences. Both strategies of comparison are equally valid but will necessarily yield different results. Similarly, the studies on political violence introduce a broader set of explanatory variables and historical sequences, as well as the inclusion of full revolution as a dependent variable. These studies focus on the structure of the agricultural sector, capitalist transformation, the cultural and community features of key groups most likely to exhibit violent and revolutionary behaviour, group organization and support, the strength and legitimacy of state power, and the role of international actors. Rather than identifying a mono causal explanation, all these studies seek to demonstrate the configuration of different explanatory factors and their likely association with political violence and revolution. Some of these studies select countries on the basis of having had a revolution (e.g. Wolf 1969), while others select a larger sample of countries to include positive, negative, and mixed cases of revolution (e.g. Paige 1975; Skocpol 1979; Wickham-Crowley 1993). Those that provide greater variance in the dependent variable through this type of selection necessarily can make stronger inferences from their comparisons.

Few-country studies of social movements move beyond explaining their origins to questions of their trajectory, shape, strategies, and political impact. They identify new sectors of the population that support movements, the changing political opportunities that allow for the emergence, shape and impact of movements, the differences between the so-called 'new' and 'old' social movements, as well as the different strategies they employ. The changing political opportunities include the level of repression in a political system, the variable provision of individual rights, and different sets of elite alignments. These studies use both quantitative and qualitative techniques to marshal the comparative evidence on movement activity. Overall, more comparative work on the nature and impact of social movement activity is needed, as this alternative form of politics will continue to be important.

Initially, democratization studies compared few countries and focused on uncertain outcomes of elite manoeuvring at critical moments of crisis during periods of authoritarian rule. More recently, studies have taken into account the nature of the prior regime, fundamental questions of 'stateness' (Linz and Stepan 1996), the political economy of the transition, and important international influences. Like the early studies of political violence and revolution, many of these studies suffer from selection bias as they focus on those countries that have made a democratic transition rather than comparing them to those that have not. While Linz and Stepan (1996) seek to redress this problem by looking at clusters of transitions and non-transitions, they introduce many other explanatory variables that create the problem of indeterminacy. In other words, their study does not quite overcome the problem of 'too many variables not enough countries' (see Chapters 2 and 4). As in the study of political violence and revolution, it is important to compare successful transitions to unsuccessful transitions across a sufficient number of cases to identify the key factors that help explain the process of democratic transition. Clearly, Bratton and van de Walle (1997) adopt just such a strategy within the geographical region of sub-Saharan Africa. By comparing 42 countries that experienced successful, unsuccessful, and flawed democratic transitions, they are able to combine historical analysis with quantitative analysis to draw larger inferences about the domestic political factors that help account for democratic experiments in the region.

The few-country studies on institutional design and democratic performance do not conflict with the global comparisons, but complement their findings with a more intensive examination of the features of presidential systems that may or may not inhibit their overall performance. These comparisons provide a differentiation of presidential systems themselves to demonstrate that both strong presidential systems and those with multiple political party systems tend to have more problems than those with significant limits on presidential power and a small set of strong political parties. Thus, the generalizations made by the many-country comparisons warrant further investigation with a smaller set of countries. In this regard, Jones' (1995) study complements the global comparisons in examining the key differences among the presidential systems of Latin America. His study uses the most similar systems design since he compares countries with similar cultural and historical legacies and similar institutional arrangements. The many- and few-country comparisons of electoral systems complement one another since the general rule that proportional electoral systems tend to have multiparty systems identified by the global comparisons also holds in the comparisons of a smaller sample of countries. Moreover, it is precisely these types of electoral system that produce some of the major problems for the presidential systems examined in the few-country studies.

The comparative study of human rights protection using a smaller selection of countries allows scholars to focus on different topics of research such as transnational influences on state behaviour and the relative successes of truth commissions. Paired comparisons of problematic countries showed to some degree that pressure from above and below can change state behaviour and lead to greater protection of human rights as a rule-consistent culture and a new set of rights-protective institutions become established. Despite the noble impulse for establishing truth, the process of truth-telling is fraught with political complexities involving the negotiated withdrawal from power of military elites in the case of Latin American TCs and ethnic or racial tensions in the African TCs, and more comparative research is needed on why countries adopt truth commissions, and if they do, why particular models of truth commissions are used.

Finally, the few-country comparisons on the market for rebellion and the quest for supranational constraints on state behaviour show that domestic actors frequently look to the international system to provide solutions to their problems. Bob's (2005) study is consistent with the resource mobilization perspective in the literature on social movements, which argues that grievance is everywhere, the key question is to examine how social movements make *their* particular grievance the one that becomes taken up by supporters. Using this logic and applying it at the international level shows that movement entrepreneurs do not need to isolate their strategies within the domestic context. By using strategies of awareness raising and framing that match the aims of objectives of international organizations, social movements and insurgencies can garner much needed international support. Equally, Moravcsik (2000) shows how those domestic actors who worried about the sustainability of their nascent democratic institutions demonstrated a strong set of preferences for a supranational regime of human rights with provisions for enforcement in ways that were different from those actors in more secure democracies or in dictatorships and semi-democracies.

Methodologically, the biggest weakness in few-country comparisons is the problem of selection bias, particularly when the choice of countries relies on the outcome that is to be explained. For example, by including more countries from Europe in their study of capitalist development and democracy, Rueschemeyer *et al.* (1992) find that a violent break with the past is not an important factor for democracy, which contradicts Moore's (1966) findings. In addition, the extension of their study beyond Europe into Latin America and the Caribbean reveals that it is the working class, and not the bourgeoisie as Moore (1966) contends, that is the key agent for democracy. Whether the inclusion of Moore's (1966) cases of China and Japan would have altered the conclusions of Rueschemeyer *et al.* (1992) remains an empirical question; however, it appears that the inclusion of more countries in similar regions provides different substantive conclusions about the relationship between capitalist development and democracy.

Similar selection effects are apparent in the studies on violent political dissent and revolution. Skocpol (1979), Wickham-Crowley (1993), and Parsa (2000) variously include positive, negative, and mixed instances of revolutionary activity at different periods of time in providing more robust accounts of revolution than offered by Wolf (1969). Indeed, the most Wolf does is to identify the presence of a single explanatory factor across six countries that have experienced revolution. In contrast, Wickham-Crowley (1993) and Parsa (2000) demonstrate the key factors for successful revolution as well as account for the failure of many revolutionary attempts in their cases. Thus in both research areas, Moore (1966) and Wolf (1969) select countries based on values of the dependent variable, while Rueschemeyer *et al.* (1992), Skocpol (1979), Wickham-Crowley (1993), and Parsa (2000) select countries based on other criteria. Moore (1966) chooses particular examples of democratic, fascist, and communist outcomes, while Wolf (1969) chooses instances of revolutionary outcomes only. Rueschemeyer *et al.* (1992), Skocpol (1979), Wickham-Crowley (1993), and Parsa (2000) choose countries on regional, cultural, and historical similarity while the outcome they are trying to explain – democracy or revolution – varies. Brockett (2005) adopted a similar strategy in comparing mobilization under repressive conditions in Guatemala and El Salvador. Bob (2005) compares successful and unsuccessful cases of challenger groups and Moravcsik (2000) compares countries that supported the European regime with enforcement provision to those that did not.

Single-country studies

By definition, there is great variation in results among the single-country studies. Part I argued that such studies are useful for comparative analysis if they make explicit use of comparative concepts or generate new concepts for application in countries beyond the original study. Such studies can generate hypotheses, infirm and confirm existing theories, allow for the intensive examination of deviant cases identified by larger comparisons, and be a useful way for conducting process tracing and uncovering causal mechanisms implied by the results of studies with a larger number of countries. Single-country studies, however well intentioned and well designed, have serious difficulty in making generalizations that are applicable at the global level. Two of the studies in Part II clearly establish a relationship between economic development and democracy (Argentina and South Korea), while three of them (Italy, Botswana, and India) find political culture to be an important intervening explanatory factor for the development of democracy. Thus for Italy, a certain 'civicness' explains good democratic performance. In Botswana, the presence of Tswana political culture inhibits the development of democracy beyond its formal components. The persistence of the caste system in India has meant that modern democracy is still embedded in traditional identities. Thus, closer attention to the historical and cultural specificities of individual countries enriches the understanding of the relationship between economic development and democracy, which may be lost in larger comparisons.

The three case studies on rural rebellion in Mexico show a certain consensus that, among other factors, the historical encroachment on land and lifestyle by outside agents has spurred on rebellious activity from the period of the Mexican Revolution to the latest peasant-based uprising from the Zapatistas in the southern state of Chiapas. Like the studies that compare many countries, the inference from these studies is that the encroachment and displacement of people whose livelihood is derived from land increase the likelihood that they will participate in rebellious and revolutionary activity. This inference is in line with Paige's (1975) comparison of agricultural sectors in 70 countries and it fits well with the types of explanation for rural rebellion offered by Wickham-Crowley (1993). Future single-country studies on rebellion and revolution can test whether the inferences from the Mexican case can be upheld in other contexts.

The single-country studies on social movements demonstrate how changing political opportunities interact with movement activity, as well as how the time-dependent dynamics of social movements can be described as a 'cycle of protest' (Tarrow 1989). The studies of social movements in the United States (Gamson 1975; Costain 1992) both show that protest activity can win concessions from the state. To compensate for some of the limits of the single-country study, both authors, like Tarrow (1989), raise the number of observations to provide greater variance (see Chapter 3). Gamson (1975) compares the activities and outcomes of over 50 social movement organizations, while Costain (1992) uses time-series indicators of social movement activity, government activity, and shifting patterns of public opinion. This greater variance allows both authors to make important inferences about social movement activity and political impact from a single country.

The quest to understand democratic transition has in large part been driven by studies of individual countries that have undergone such processes since 1974. Two of the studies compared in Part II demonstrate elite and popular struggle perspectives on transition. Colomer and Pascual (1994) develop a game theory model of transition, which is applied to the Polish case. The history of the transition is seen as a series of sequential games 'played' by the key political actors of the period. The strength of the analysis lies in the identification of all the outcomes possible from a combination of 'moves' by the players. Democratic transition is thus seen not as an inevitable outcome, but as one of many outcomes. In the Polish case, the authors demonstrate that democracy was indeed the outcome, yet their model is specified in such a way that it can be applied to other countries. Foweraker (1989) offers a more comprehensive analysis of the democratic transformation of Spanish civil society that preceded the moment of transition. Less attention is paid to elite political actors as the study focuses on the everyday activities of workers as they attempt to contest power through various representative organizations. Like Colomer and Pascual (1994), Foweraker's inferences concerning incremental struggle under conditions of authoritarian rule have application to countries other than Spain, but we saw that the inferences made to the end of the Cold War in the Portuguese study were slightly overdrawn.

Finally, the exclusive focus on the problem of divided government in the United States shows that across a range of conflict and legislative measures, the simultaneous control of the presidency and Congress by different political parties does not appear to make a difference. Even though the post-war period in US political history has seen more years of divided government, the volume of legislation and level of conflict between the executive and legislature have remained unchanged. The global comparison of presidential and parliamentary democracies reveals a certain democratic weakness in presidential democracies and the few-country studies demonstrate that strong presidentialism combined with multiple political parties is particularly problematic. The case of the United States appears to be an outlier to the general rule established by the global comparisons and falls well within the expectations of the few-country comparisons. It is one case where a presidential system does not seem to inhibit democratic performance and it is one case where strong presidentialism combined with a weak two-party system functions.

The single-country studies on human rights in Chapter 11 and Chapters 12 reveal many things about the strengths and weaknesses of the various regimes for the protection of human rights. The case of Argentina in Chapter 11 showed the limits of the UN and Inter-American systems at the time to address the grave concerns over gross human rights violations carried out during the 'dirty war' (1976–1982), while at the same time showing the resilience of civil society within Argentina to bring about significant transformations before and after the democratic transitions. The case of Chile in Chapter 12 showed that mobilization from global actors aligned with domestic actors brought about a certain capitulation among the hardliners in the regime to begin a process of political liberalization, while the Pinochet case itself illustrates how international actors seized the political opportunity in the late 1990s to invoke the principle of universal jurisdiction to seek extradition of a former head of state to face a foreign court for crimes against humanity. The impact of the arrest, detention, and return of Pinochet to Chile in many ways emboldened his domestic opponents, whose legal actions resulted in a stripping of immunity and his eventual death under house arrest.

Building theory

The book has throughout intentionally avoided a direct and full discussion of empirical political theory since it has sought to examine how different comparative methods contribute to theory-building. It also takes the view, contrary to some authors, that there is not a distinctive set of comparative theories (see Chilcote 1994). Rather, there is a collection of research problems that is best addressed through some form of comparison, which in turn helps build our theoretical understandings of the world. Cumulatively, the studies in Part II make contributions to theories that span a wide range of different perspectives. In a seminal piece on the contribution of comparative politics to social theory, Mark Lichbach (1997) delimits the following three broad theoretical perspectives and 'research communities' that have emerged in the field of comparative politics: (1) rationalist, (2) structuralist, and (3) culturalist. Each of these approaches has different assumptions about how the world 'works' and which aspects of the world deserve attention in order to understand and explain observed political phenomena. A short outline of each of these approaches is warranted before considering the ways in which the studies in Part II have contributed to them.

Rationalist perspectives concentrate on the actions and behaviour of individuals who make reasoned and intentional choices based upon sets of preferences, or interests. Those who adhere to the rationalist perspective are 'concerned with the collective processes and outcomes that follow from intentionality, or the social consequences of individually rational action' (Lichbach 1997:246). Moreover, rationalists in political science believe 'that "bed rock" explanations of social phenomena should build upwards from the beliefs and goals of individuals' (Ward 1995:79). The development of the rationalist perspective followed earlier individual theories that emphasize the non-rational aspects of human behaviour such as grievance and relative deprivation (see the discussion of Gurr 1968 in Chapter 7). In contrast to these earlier individual theories, rationalists claim that grievance alone is not enough to explain political action and that real choices at the individual level must be examined. While both perspectives concentrate on individual political behaviour, rationalists look for the intentional and 'means-ends' features of individual choice.

In contrast to the rationalist (and other individual) perspective(s), culturalist perspectives seek an understanding of political phenomena by focusing on the broader holistic and shared aspects of collectivities of individuals. Single individual interests and actions cannot be understood in isolation, but must be placed in the context of the shared understandings, inter-subjective relationships, and mutual orientations that make human communities possible (Lichbach 1997:246–247). These shared meanings and understandings form broader cultures and communities that can be grouped together and analysed as whole units. Such cultures and communities are held together by certain social rules that are emblematic of the identities of both the individuals and the groups themselves (ibid.: 247). Identifying the boundaries of these cultural units and separate identities remains problematic for systematic comparative research; however, scholars have tried to examine the world-views, rituals, and symbols that provide 'systems of meaning and the structure and intensity of political identity' across different geographical regions of the world (Ross 1997:43–44). Structuralists also focus on the holistic aspects of politics, but unlike the culturalists, they focus on the interdependent relationships among individuals, collectivities, institutions, or organizations. They are interested in the social, political, and economic networks that form between and among individuals. Adherents to this perspective insist that structures that have become reified over time constrain or facilitate political activity so that individual actors are not completely free agents capable of determining particular political outcomes (Lichbach 1997:247–248). Rather, individuals are embedded in relational structures that shape human identities, interests, and interaction. These relational structures have evolved owing to large historical processes such as capitalist development, market rationality, nation state building, political and scientific revolutions, and technological progress (Katznelson 1997:83). These large historical processes, it is argued, provide both possibilities and limits for human action.

Together, these three perspectives have variously sought to account for political phenomena in the world by emphasizing and examining key explanatory factors that adhere to the assumptions of their theories. Thus, rationalists focus on the interests and actions of individuals, culturalists focus on the ideas and norms of human communities, and structuralists focus on the institutions and relationships that constrain and facilitate political activity. These theoretical perspectives are not mutually exclusive, however, since scholars have examined the ways in which the interaction between and among the three perspectives helps explain certain outcomes. There are only very rare instances of work in comparative politics that rely exclusively on one of the three perspectives.[1] The comparative methods in this book have all been used to marshal evidence in support of these perspectives virtually across the range of research topics. With the exception of Chapter 10 on institutional design and democratic performance, which by definition focuses exclusively on the functions and effects of democratic institutions, the studies in all the other chapters contribute to individual, structural, and cultural theories of politics.

Moreover, the discussions in Chapters 11 and 12 address rational, structural and cultural theories of international relations. The chapter on human rights shows how the normative principles of human rights have been embodied through international law, which uses the inter-state treaty system to govern state–citizens relations at the domestic level, and that the force of the law and the 'power of human rights' (Risse *et al.* 1999) challenges the main tenets of realism, which is in effect a rationalist account of state behaviour in the international arena. Indeed, while rational choice theory has been branded 'methodological individualism' (Przeworski 1985) at the domestic level, realism has been branded 'methodological nationalism' at the international level (Zürn 2002). The democratic peace found in Russett and O'Neal (2001) and liberal republicanism in Moravcsik (2000) focus our attention on democratic institutions and democratic values in ways that demonstrate their impact on inter-state relations. While these variables would be labelled structuralist and culturalist at the domestic level, the international relations literature uses the terms neo-liberal institutionalist and social contructivist, respectively (see e.g. Wendt 1999; Keohane 2001; Carlsnaes, Risse and Simmons 2002; Landman 2005b).

Table 13.1 summarizes the studies in Part II with reference to their location across individual, structural, and cultural theories of empirical political science and international relations. The first column in the table lists the research topics of each chapter while the remaining columns represent the three theoretical perspectives. Individual theories include the older theories that focus on grievances and deprivation as well as the newer rational choice theories that focus on preferences and interests, and also the realist perspective in international relations. The structuralist column refers to the presence of broad socio-economic changes, the development of key institutions, the relational structures in which individuals are embedded, and supranational institutions. The culturalist column concerns the importance of ideas, shared understandings, and accepted norms and rules for behaviour at the domestic and international levels. The arrows between the main columns capture the notion that many studies seek to examine the interplay between these different theories.

The studies on the relationship between economic development and democracy are located in the cells extending from the structuralist to the culturalist approaches. The studies focus on the broad socio-economic changes and processes of modernization that were accompanied by changes in class structure, class alliances, the nature and power of the state, as well as the impact of transnational structures

Table 13.1 Empirical theories of political science and international relations: topics and examples from Part II

Topics	Individual/states (interests and actions)	↔	Structuralist (institutions and relationships)	↔	Culturalist (ideas and norms)
Chapter 6 Economic development and democracy	Boix (2003) Boix and Stokes (2003)		Lipset (1959) Cutright (1963) Moore (1966) Neubauer (1967) Cutright & Wiley (1969) Dahl (1971) Jackman (1973) Bollen (1979) Waisman (1989) Helliwell (1994) Burkhart & Lewis-Beck (1994) Przeworski et al. (2000) Rueschemeyer et al. (1992) Landman (1999) Mainwaring and Perez-Liñan (2003)		Lerner (1958) De Schweinitz (1964) Putnam (1993a) Holm (1996) Moon & Kim (1996) Kaviraj (1996)
Chapter 7 Violent political dissent and social revolution		Womack (1969) Gurr (1968) Hibbs (1973) Sigelman & Simpson (1977) Muller & Seligson (1987) Nugent (1993) Parsa (2000) Brockett (2005)	Wolf (1969) Hibbs (1973) Paige (1975) Skocpol (1979) Parsa (2000) Brockett (2005)		Hibbs (1973) Scott (1976) Wickham-Crowley (1993) Nugent (1993) Harvey (1998) Harvey (1998) Parsa (2000)
Chapter 8 Non-violent political dissent and social movements	Gamson (1975)	Dalton (1988) Tarrow (1989) Costain (1992) Gurr (1993) Foweraker & Landman (1997) Bashevkin (1998)	Powell (1982) Haas & Stack (1983) Kitschelt (1986) Kriesi et al. (1995)		Gurr (1993) Inglehart (1997) Inglehart and Welzel (2005)
Chapter 9 Transitions to democracy	Colomer & Pascual (1994)	O'Donnell et al. (1986a–c) Foweraker (1989) Peeler (1992) Maxwell (1995) Linz & Stepan (1996)	Jaggers & Gurr (1995) Linz & Stepan (1996) Vanhanen (1997) Bratton and van de Walle (1997)		Huntington (1991) Linz & Stepan (1996) Doorenspleet (2005)

Table 13.1 continued

Topics	Individual (interests and actions)	↔	Structuralist (institutions and relationships)	↔	Culturalist (ideas and norms)
Chapter 10 Institutional design and democratic performance		Bratton and van de Walle (1997)	Doorenspleet (2005) Shugart and Carey (1992) Mayhew (1993) Peterson & Greene (1993) Stepan & Skach (1993) Lijphart (1994a) Lijphart (1994b) Jones (1995) Mainwaring and Scully (1995) Fiorina (1996)		
Chapter 11 Human rights		Hayner (1994, 2002) Risse et al. (1999) De Brito (1997) Guest (1990) Weissbrodt and Bartolomei (1991) Brysk (1994a)	Strouse and Claude (1976) Mitchell and McCormick (1988) Poe and Tate (1994) Poe et al. (1999) Zanger (2000) Hayner (1994, 2002) Risse et al. (1999) De Brito (1997) Guest (1990) Weissbrodt and Bartolomei (1991) Brysk (1994a)		Hayner (1994) Risse et al. (1999) De Brito (1997) Brysk (1994a) Keith (1999) Hathaway (2002) Landman (2005b) Hafner-Burton and Tsutsui (2005, 2007) Neumayer (2005)
Chapter 12 International relations and comparative politics	Russet and O'Neal (2001) Bob (2005) Moravcsik (2000) Hawkins (2002)		Li and Reuveny (2003) Russet and O'Neal (2001)		Li and Reuveny (2003) Russet and O'Neal (2001) Bob (2005) Moravcsik (2000) Hawkins (2002) Sands (2005)

of power. In addition these studies imply, or in some cases state explicitly, that the development of democracy also depends on the formation of a sustainable political culture that emphasizes tolerance and promotes democratic norms. While earlier studies suggested that this political culture would be fomented by an emerging middle class, later studies recognize the importance of the working class in its role as an agent for democratic inclusion. In either case, these studies examine the interaction between broad structural changes and the development of political culture.

The studies on violent political dissent and revolution are located around the middle columns of the table since they seek to explain these political phenomena with a combination of individual and structural theories on the one hand and structural and cultural theories on the other. For example, Wolf's (1969) study shows that capitalist transformation of agriculture is a structural change that produces grievance among a particular set of rural cultivators who then become involved in revolutionary activity. Scott (1976) argues that similar structural changes transformed the moral economy and the culture of reciprocity that had become a key feature of the peasant communities in Burma and Vietnam. Parsa (2000), on the other hand, is quite explicit that structural variables alone cannot account for the differences between social and political revolution that he observes across Iran, Nicaragua, and the Philippines. Hibbs' (1973) comprehensive set of explanatory variables captures a whole range of individual, structural, and cultural concepts. Brockett (2005) relies primarily on the concept of political opportunity structure, which as its name implies, is a structural variable that helped explain the different patterns of peasant mobilization across his two countries.

The comparative studies from Chapter 8 are equally located in the middle columns as they seek to explain the origins, trajectory, and impact of social movements. All three theoretical perspectives have been used to explain the origin of social movement activity. Rationalists examine the key incentives that may or may not lead individuals to join a social movement. Structuralists look at long-term socio-economic fluctuations and the changing set of opportunities for social protest and political transformation. Culturalists are concerned with the changing nature of collective identities and how these identities provide the shared understanding and common will necessary for sustained political mobilization. The studies that combine these rational and structural theories (column four) look at how individual and collective behaviour in social movements is facilitated or constrained by broader structural changes, while those that combine structural and cultural theories (column five) examine how new values and identities form from broader structural changes.

The initial quest to understand democratic transition centred on the strategic interaction of elites and thus primarily adopted a rationalist perspective. Colomer and Pascual's (1994) application of game theory is a classic example of a strong rationalist effort to explain the democratic transition in Poland. Other elite-centred accounts such as those found in O'Donnell *et al.* (1986a, 1986b) examine the ways in which changing structural conditions lead to opportunities for 'hard-liners' and 'soft-liners' within the authoritarian regime to manoeuvre for political advantage. Popular struggle perspectives, on the other hand, are concerned with the opportunities for social mobilization and democratic transformation that are provided by changing structural conditions. Thus, Bratton and van de Walle's (1997) study of Africa and Foweraker's (1989) study of Spain equally examine the relationship between structure and agency in accounting for democratic transition. Finally, studies that adopt culturalist explanations examine patterns of democratic 'habituation' and the acceptance of rules and democratic norms, as well as the cross-national diffusion of democratic ideas. The global studies on democratic transition identify a variety of structural and cultural variables, including Huntington's (1991) economic development and 'Catholic' effects and Doorenspleet's (2005) economic and democratic diffusion variables.

As mentioned above, the studies on institutional design and democratic performance necessarily ground themselves in structural explanations since they examine the ways in which formal institutions of democracy (e.g. parties, electoral systems, presidential versus parliamentary systems) structure the activities of key political actors. This structuring of action has immediate implications for democratic performance. The studies in Chapter 10 suggest that the nexus between structure and agency can have direct effects on governance. For example, strong presidents facing multiple parties in the legislature may find it difficult to bring about new legislation or may face recurring governmental gridlock, which can have adverse effects on democratic performance, particularly in new democracies. Indeed, Stepan and Skach (1993) argue that presidents facing such constraints may flout the constitution, seek extra-constitutional means to achieve their objectives, and even encourage military intervention, particularly in countries with a past history of such intervention.

Finally, even though the study of human rights is inspired by normative concerns for human well-being and human dignity, global comparisons in this research area are very similar to the studies on economic development and democracy in identifying broad structural factors that help account for the protection of human rights. While they do control for regional differences and historical legacies such as British colonial influence, the primary focus is on socio-economic variables and differences in political institutions. But as the studies move down the level of abstraction, greater attention is paid to the interaction between structure and agency, as well as the importance of the diffusion of human rights norms transmitted by transnational advocacy networks. Thus the few-country and single-country studies on human rights incorporate a wider range of theoretical concepts from the rationalist and culturalist perspectives while remaining sensitive to the structural and institutional constraints faced by states.

The chapter on human rights crosses over all the theoretical traditions and addresses those at the international level in some degree. The global comparative studies by and large included an array of socio-economic and structural variables to explain the cross-national variation in the protection of human rights, while the latter set of studies on the impact of international law examined the role that international institutions play in constraining the actions of states at the domestic level. The few-country comparisons, in particular the paired comparisons found in Risse *et al.* (1999) address the rational, cultural, and structural dimensions of domestic and international mobilization surrounding violations of human rights. The spiral model itself combines attention to the ways in which the socialization of norms can have an impact on state behaviour, especially when those norms are combined with agency at the domestic and international levels.

Finally, it is clear that the studies in Chapter 12 illustrate similar kinds of cross-over of these theoretical perspectives at the domestic and international levels. The analysis of the impact of globalization on democracy included both the structural aspects of globalization (flows of trade, capital, and finance) as well as its cultural dimension in terms of the diffusion of democracy (see also Doorenspleet 2005). The democratic peace is a proposition informed by structural and cultural theories of politics. As Rosato (2003) aptly points out, the underlying causal logic of the democratic peace proposition involves the normative and institutional constraints on democracies in their ability to wage war, which arguably reduces the probability of democracies fighting one another and other states. The mobilization of challenger groups in search of international support is rational in terms of the market analysis, but also cultural in its attention to raising awareness, framing, and matching the aims and objectives of potential international supporters. Finally, it is clear that the Chilean case in all its complexity reveals the interplay between international norms, political opportunities, and rational calculation at the domestic and international level.

Conclusion: drawing the lessons

This review of over 80 comparative studies across a range of different methods, techniques, and substantive topics shows both the trade-offs associated with conducting comparative research as well as the valuable contribution to theory that such studies can make. From this review and analysis, the following four key factors are important for scholars to bear in mind when embarking on comparative research: the research problem, case selection, inferential aspirations, and theorizing. First, since there is no one comparative method that is superior to another, it is important to remember that in most cases, the research problem is intimately linked to the method adopted. Second, case selection significantly affects the answers that are obtained to the research questions that are posed (cf. Geddes 1990). Both the actual countries in the sample and the number of countries that comprise it can lead to different results. In order to make stronger inferences, the rule of thumb for political science method is to raise the number of observations (King *et al.* 1994), which for comparative politics means either a larger sample of countries or more observations within a smaller sample of countries.

Third, the substantive conclusions and inferential aspirations of a particular comparative study should not go too far beyond the scope of its sample. A single-country study of democratic transition may provide some important inferences that can be examined in countries with a similar set of circumstances but it does not provide a universal set of inferences for democratic transition in general. A study of social mobilization under authoritarian rule can make inferences relevant to social mobilization in other countries under similar conditions of authoritarian rule. On the other hand, a study of social movement activity under democratic rule cannot make inferences about such activity under authoritarian rule (see Chapter 9). Many-country studies may have universal aspirations yet must remain sensitive to the fact that there are exceptions to every rule. In short, comparative scholars must recognize the limits of their own enterprise in making generalizations about the political world they observe.

Finally, comparativists ought to spend more time on careful theorizing and research design. Once the assumptions of a theory are established and the observable implications of that theory are identified, then the research can be designed in such a way to provide the best set of comparisons given the available resources. Careful theorizing about political events and political outcomes will lead scholars to compare similar outcomes in different cases, or different outcomes in similar cases. The differences and similarities that are identified through comparison help provide an explanation for the outcomes themselves. Together, problem specification, case selection, self-limiting inferential aspirations, and careful theorizing provide the foundation for comparative politics. What remains to be examined are the new issues, new methods, and new challenges that are confronting the field. It is to these issues that the final chapter turns.

Note

1   There are exceptions to this rule for each perspective. For the rationalist perspective, see for example Bates' (1989) study of the political economy of Kenya, Tsebelis' (1990) study of European political behaviour, and Geddes' (1991, 1994) work on state reform in Latin America. For the structural perspective, see Luebbert's (1991) study of regime origins in inter-war Europe and Poulantzas' (1976) study of dictatorships in Greece, Spain, and Portugal. For the cultural perspective, see Scott's (1985) study of peasant resistance in Malaysia and his comparison of Burma and Vietnam (Scott 1976) as examined in Chapter 7.

Further reading

Hay, C. (2002) *Political Analysis* London: Palgrave
    An excellent overview of conducting political analysis, including foundations for political science, theory, and methods.

Lichbach, M. (1997) 'Social Theory and Comparative Politics', in M. Lichbach and A. Zuckerman (eds) *Comparative Politics: Rationality, Culture, and Structure*, Cambridge: Cambridge University Press, 239–276.
    A concise model of rational, structural, and cultural theories and how comparative politics has contributed to their development.

New challenges for comparative politics

This book has consistently argued that the systematic comparison of countries is an effective method for making inferences about the political world we observe. The basic methods of comparative politics (many-, few-, and single-country studies) and its basic unit of analysis (the independent nation state) will not change for the foreseeable future, despite some of the more extreme pronouncements about the disappearance of the state in the new era of globalization. Comparative politics as a field and a method fits squarely in the 'evidence-inference methodological core' of political science (see Chapter 1 of present volume; cf. Almond 1996:52), and the application of comparative methods to real-world problems will continue to play a valuable role in the incremental accumulation of knowledge in this field. Indeed, for many, comparative politics is seen as the central concern of political science, as well as a central feature in helping us to understand current affairs in the world (see Peters 1998:212; Pennings *et al.* 1999:2–3). This chapter addresses these claims and examines the way in which the field has evolved and is likely to evolve, the continuing challenges the field faces, and the ways in which it can adapt to our rapidly changing and increasingly global political environment.

Full circle

In many respects, comparative politics has come full circle since its early days as a new field in the social sciences (Mair 1996:315–316). Rather than simply returning to earlier research questions and methods, however, the field has evolved, effectively retaining key developments, rediscovering problems not addressed thoroughly in the past, and enhancing the robustness of systematic comparative methods. In this way, the field has mirrored the history of political science more generally. Described as an 'eclectic progressive' development, the discipline started with formal legal and institutional comparisons, moved to an almost exclusive focus on individuals (the 'behavioural revolution'), rediscovered the importance of institutions (the advent of the 'new institutionalism'), while continuously struggling with the question of culture (see Almond 1996; Mair 1996). In response to patterns of globalization, comparative politics has become even more explicit in its attention to international variables, while international relations has paid more attention to the role that domestic variables play in shaping international behaviour. While the substantive foci, inclusion of variables, and theoretical perspectives with which to examine them are more eclectic and open to change than ever before, the importance of systematic comparison and the need for inferential rigour (Almond 1996:89), despite attempts to argue otherwise, has remained constant (see e.g. Flyvbjerg 2001; Schram and Caterino 2006).

The evolution in method, detailed throughout this book, also mirrors the substantive evolution in the field. Earlier 'legalistic' and formal institutional comparisons were carried out on a small sample of countries usually isolated to the United States and Western Europe, or to areas such as Latin America (see Valenzuela 1988). The relegation of formal institutional comparisons in favour of more general comparisons was accompanied by the increase in the number of countries in the sample, aided by the advent of computer technology and a commitment to providing comparable indicators of politics. A certain disillusionment with large-scale comparisons and the 'rediscovery' of institutions (particularly the state) led to an increase in few-country studies, and in some corners of the discipline, a definitive call for a conscious return to few-country studies (ibid.: 86). But significant developments in all three methods of comparison mean that the contemporary era of comparative politics includes many-country studies, few-country studies, and single-country studies, all of which comprise the methodological universe of the field and all of which are devoted to providing explanation and understanding of observed political phenomena in the world.

Table 14.1 summarizes the evolution of comparative politics in terms of its substantive foci and dominant comparative methods. This evolution has in part been reflected in the chapters that comprise Parts I and II. On the one hand, large questions addressed in Part II including the establishment and maintenance of political institutions, patterns of violent and non-violent political behaviour, the relationship between institutions and political performance, the variable protection of human rights, and the interplay between domestic and international variables map onto the history of the field detailed in column two of the table. On the other hand, the chapters in both parts have demonstrated the evolution towards a more inclusive set of comparative methods. Contrary to the observations of some comparative scholars (e.g. Mair 1996; Peters 1998), all three methods of comparison are valid and continue to be employed by scholars in the field (see Gerring 2006). The period of 'new eclecticism' recognizes and even celebrates the plurality of topics, theories, and methods in comparative politics. But this eclecticism and claim of methodological pluralism does not mean 'anything goes'. Rather, as Part I has made clear, the method adopted and the research design that is formulated are a function of both the type of research question that is being addressed and the theoretical perspective that has been adopted. There is not a unity of method in comparative politics, but as in more general developments in the philosophy of the social sciences, there is now the practice of 'cognitive instrumentalism', which applies the necessary theoretical and methodological tools to a series of important and challenging political puzzles (Gordon 1991:624–634; Grofman 2001). But as new issues emerge and new research questions are posed, the key for comparative politics in providing sound answers to such new puzzles is systematic analysis that follows the general guidelines outlined in this volume.

New methods

In addition to the many strengths and weaknesses of the different comparative methods outlined in this book, there are several new developments in the field that will continue to improve its ability to make strong inferences about the political world. These include important issues of data collection and analysis, the transcendence of traditional boundaries in the field, and the development of new analytic software and comparative techniques. Each of these developments relates directly to the concerns raised throughout the book, but in particular, to those in Part I. At the height of the behavioural revolution, there was a sanguine view about the ability to collect meaningful indicators on global samples of countries in an effort to make universal generalizations about politics and political events.

Table 14.1 Evolution of comparative politics: substantive foci and dominant methods

Period	Substantive focus	Comparative method
Public law phase Inter-war period	Institutional design and political order	Few- and single-country studies
	Objects of inquiry: presidential vs. parliamentary regimes, federal vs. unitary systems, political party organizations, legal and legislative instruments, democratic, fascist, and socialist regimes	Descriptive history Formal and configurative analysis Basic unit of analysis: individual countries (mostly in Europe and North America)
Behavioural revolution 1940s–1960s	Political behaviour Explaining patterns of political development, including democracy, political instability, and political violence Objects of inquiry: interest groups, parties, elections, decision making, rules of the game, the military, peasants, students, and workers	Many-country comparisons Cross-national indicators Quantitative analysis Search for covering laws and universal generalizations Basic unit of analysis: individuals and individual countries (global and regional samples)
Institutional revival 1970s and 1980s	Relationship between institutions and political actors Objects of inquiry: democracy and democratic transition, revolution, economic and political dependency, political protest, public policy mechanisms and outcomes, and the welfare state	Few-country comparisons Qualitative and quantitative techniques Inferences limited to similar countries outside scope of comparison Basic unit of analysis: individuals and individual countries (global and regional samples)
New eclecticism 1990s until present	Individual, institutional, and cultural foundations of politics Objects of inquiry: democratic transition, institutional design, social movements, globalization (economic, political, and cultural dimensions), transnational networks, political and cultural diffusion, terrorism, human rights, international law, environment	Many-, few-, and single-country studies Qualitative and quantitative techniques Universal generalizations, as well as regional and country-specific inferences Basic unit of analysis: individuals and individual countries (global and regional samples)

Sources: Valenzuela (1988); Erickson and Rustow (1991); Rustow and Erickson (1991); Mair (1996); Apter (1996); Lichbach (1997); Brady and Collier (2004), George and Bennett (2005), Schram and Caterino (2006).

Many criticized this optimistic view of the 'new' comparative politics (Apter 1996), yet now, more than ever, the global collection of meaningful data is possible. The tremendous advance in information and communication technologies (ICTs), have made the production, collection, and analysis of global data much easier than in the past. On-line data availability has made large-scale comparative analysis so much easier as has the increase in processing power of computers. But the increase in data availability has also led to a new demand for accountability and replicability in the field, since data sets that provide the evidence base for journal articles and research monographs can (and should) be shared between and among scholars.

The demand for sharing, replication, and accountability means that scholars need to develop more systematic ways of collecting, documenting, and diffusing data. Scholars need to explain the sources, coding, problems, and potential areas for error in their data collection efforts. These need to be fully documented in the accompanying codebooks. Moreover, the field, and political science more generally, needs to develop an ethos of replication and data-sharing. Once data have been collected, documented, and analysed, scholars should make them available through the direct or indirect means mentioned above. Replicating and performing secondary analysis on published articles and books provides corroboration, incremental advancement in knowledge, and an excellent way to teach future generations of comparativists. Overall, technology now allows to a greater extent than ever before the development of a networked comparative research community.

The benefits of better data collection and diffusion are not isolated to many-country comparisons using quantitative analysis. They apply equally to other comparative methods. Global indicators put regional comparisons, other few-country studies, and single-country studies in a broader comparative perspective. Likewise, comparative studies with a smaller sample size can demonstrate the limits of the global data and increase our understanding of political processes and events at the local level. In addition, as Part I made clear, the term 'data' is a broad one that includes all empirical information marshalled for systematic comparative analysis. Thus, in echoing the call articulated by King *et al.* (1994), the improvement in data collection and diffusion practices ought to extend to non-quantitative evidence. Comparative histories and single-country studies using qualitative methods should provide details and documentation of their collection of evidence.

The advent of new analytic techniques and computer software supports this general call for data improvement. New advances in qualitative data software allow new types of analysis that seek to provide structures and clusters of meaning from texts collected through traditionally qualitative means, such as in-depth interviewing, participant observation, or published official statements by political elites and policy makers. In this sense, texts themselves provide the data from which inferences can be drawn. The new computer software can draw connections, perform word counts, develop typologies and classification schemes, and calculate word, phrase, or sentence frequencies for more advanced analysis. In the past, this type of work has often been completed by hand. For example, Ian Budge and his collaborators (Budge *et al.* 1987, 2001; Klingemann *et al.* 1994) have coded political party manifestos published since World War II into thematic categories in an effort to compare policy and ideological positions of political parties in Europe and North America. The entire data set is now available on CD-ROM. New developments in the field of human rights have meant that complex narrative data collected by truth commissions and other organizations can be deconstructed quantitatively and then used in macro analyses of political conflict (see Ball *et al.* 2000; Ball *et al.* 2003; Brockett 2005). In addition, new advances in text and qualitative analysis software packages allow for more systematic comparative studies that adopt discursive approaches to politics more generally (see Beer and Balleck 1994; Howarth 1995, 1998a; Howarth *et al.* 2000; Dryzek and Holmes 2002; Franzosi 2004).

For quantitative analysis, new software and techniques are being developed to handle new types of data. Typically, cross-sectional data analysis of the kind performed on a large sample of countries at one point in time (see, for example, the earlier many-country studies outlined in Chapters 6 and 7), was a relatively straightforward exercise. Time series data, 'event count' data such as protest events, and dichotomous data collected on such events as wars, coups, and revolutions require more advanced kinds of analysis to overcome some of their inherent biases. Skewed distributions (i.e. some countries with particularly high or low values), 'ceiling' problems (i.e. no events in one year followed by 4,000 events in the next), and 'either-or' outcomes require different kinds of analytical techniques to avoid drawing erroneous inferences. Moreover, many variables in comparative politics change very slowly over time or rarely change at all, and methods of estimation have been developed to take account of these 'time-invariant' variables (Plümper and Troeger 2007). Developments in this area of quantitative comparative analysis continue to be made to deal with these new indicators and forms of data.

In addition, new techniques for combining quantitative and qualitative methods have been developed to offer more holistic explanations for political outcomes. Wickham-Crowley's (1993) comparison identified necessary and sufficient conditions for successful revolution in Latin America. He used Boolean algebra to eliminate those conditions that did not appear to be important for revolution while retaining those that did (see Chapter 7 and Table 7.5, and also Chapter 4). The values of these supportive conditions were derived in qualitative fashion through a deep reading of the events surrounding these (non) revolutionary moments in Latin American history. In this way, he combines the strengths of a 'variable-oriented' study with the strengths of a 'case-oriented' study to reach substantive conclusions about social revolution (see Ragin 1987; Peters 1998:162–171). Other comparative studies have used the 'either-or' categories of Boolean analysis (see De Meur and Berg-Schlosser 1994; Foweraker and Landman 1997: Chapter 7) to reduce the complexity of qualitative information while harnessing the strengths of logical analysis. As in other areas of political methodology, this type of analysis has been aided by the development of computer software (Qualitative Comparative Analysis, or QCA), which reduces the burden of calculating the key conditions by hand (see Drass and Ragin 1991).

Future comparative studies may want to adopt this strategy, which strikes a balance between quantitative and qualitative approaches while remaining systematic. In *Fuzzy Set Social Science*, Ragin (2000) argues that many of the categories used in conventional quantitative analysis are actually the product of qualitative distinctions that may create homogenizing tendencies in the analysis. He argues that case-oriented qualitative research demonstrates that individual countries may share different 'sets' of distinguishing features that belie simple classification (see Chapter 1 this volume) and that require a more flexible understanding of the diversity and heterogeneity of cases. Thus, 'fuzzy set' approaches use a 'configurational approach' (cf. Cioffi-Revilla 1981; Wickham-Crowley 1993) to social and political phenomena 'viewing cases as specific configurations of aspects and features' (Ragin 2000:5).

Such attention to configurations of events and features, combined with a concern over the uncertain and probabilistic nature of political phenomena is examined comprehensively in Cioffi-Revilla's (1998) *Politics and Uncertainty*. While firmly grounded in the epistemological position that political events are observable and measurable, Cioffi-Revilla (1998) argues that political science must move beyond deterministic explanations to consider probabilistic explanations. Such explanations focus on uncertain (but not haphazard) behaviour of macro-political variables and the uncertain occurrence of micro-political events, each of which has an underlying causal structure that can be ascertained through systematic analysis (Cioffi-Revilla 1998:25). For example, using archaeological data on the Mayan city states of Ancient Meso-America, Cioffi-Revilla and Landman (1999) analyse the probabilistic distributions of city-state duration to support a new theory of the collapse of the Mayan Empire and a new periodization of Maya political evolution. Other applications of probabilistic causal explanation include the formation and failure of government cabinet coalitions (Browne *et al.* 1986; Cioffi-Revilla 1984), international alliances, domestic violence, and international warfare (Cioffi-Revilla 1998:282–287). Taken together, these advances in methods, techniques, and software strengthen our ability to conduct systematic comparative research and help to break down traditional barriers that exist within the discipline. No longer should qualitative practitioners be pitted against their quantitative colleagues. Rather, the insights of both communities can inform each other. Regionally based comparative studies that traditionally inhabit the faculties of area studies programmes (e.g. Latin America, Africa, and Asia) can contribute to more general theories and research communities in political science (see Foweraker *et al.* 2003). Many of the regionally based studies reviewed in this book either developed new concepts and theories applicable to contexts outside the scope of the original comparison, or used particular parts of the world as natural 'laboratories' to test theories and ideas developed elsewhere. Wickham-Crowley's (1993) comparison of successful and unsuccessful social revolutions in Latin American and Bratton and van de Walle's (1997) comparison of democratization in Africa provided inferences applicable well beyond the confines of the regions originally compared. There thus must be an ongoing intellectual conversation among the practitioners of different comparative methods, across different levels of analysis, and across different theoretical perspectives, as well as across different parts of the world.

Maintaining relevance

The preceding discussion on the evolution of the discipline demonstrates that political science, and systematic comparative analysis in particular, continues to address real-world problems and provides solutions and policy prescriptions based on the best evidence available. Ironically, at a time when world events call out most for unbiased, systematic, rigorous political science analysis, there continues to be significant disagreement in some quarters of the discipline about how political science can maintain its relevance. The 'Perestroikan' movement primarily based in the United States, criticizes the discipline's over-emphasis on method and mathematical sophistication, leading the profession to lose sight of political puzzles and problems and/or providing answers that are largely unintelligible to policy makers and practitioners (Bennett 2002; Smith 2002; Schram and Caterino 2006). The main charge of the movement is that the discipline has become highly 'technicist' and 'statistical', where method is given greater weight than substance (Bennett 2002; Smith 2002).

The movement argues that more weight should be given to substance over method, effectively loosening the rules of inquiry and the logic of inference, while providing 'distinctive insights into substantive political questions' (Smith 2002:10). Flyvbjerg (2001, 2006) proposes a way of recapturing the substance of politics and making political science 'matter'. Flyvbjerg challenges fundamentally the desire and attempt within the social sciences to emulate the natural sciences (i.e. its appeal to observable events and the logic of inference advocated in King *et al.* 1994). He draws on a short passage in Aristotle's *Nichomachean Ethics* on the 'chief intellectual virtues' to build a framework for conducting more holistic social scientific analysis that pays greater attention to the rich complexity of context, while offering a deeper understanding of politics that moves beyond the narrow techno-rationalism of certain dominant strands in contemporary political science.

In particular, he uses Aristotle's virtues of knowledge (*episteme*), craft (*techné*), and practical wisdom (*phronesis*) to build what he sees is a more complete approach to studying social phenomena. Where *episteme* refers to abstract and universal knowledge (e.g. the rational individual) and *techné* to the specific 'know-how associated with practicing a craft' (e.g. multivariate regression analysis or the use of MDSD and MSSD), *phronesis* comes from an 'intimate familiarity with the contingencies and uncertainties of various forms of social practice embedded in complex social settings' (Caterino and Shram 2006:8). Of course, many have referred to this idea more colloquially as 'getting your feet wet in the mud' through knowing your cases and the political contexts in which you are working. *Phronesis* is thus 'situated practical reasoning' (Caterino and Schram 2006:8) and for Flyvbjerg, it ought to be at the centre of social science research. While he does not seek to displace *episteme* and *techné* altogether, which he sees as the essential features of the natural-science model of social inquiry, he does want to recapture *phronesis* and place it on an equal footing to these other two elements.

While not abandoning methodological concerns altogether, this proposition for political science and complementary arguments put forth more generally by the Perestroika movement argues that political science research 'may not be metho-dologically innovative, unusually precise, or indeed mathematical, but [it must] nonetheless [provide] fresh empirical evidence and well-reasoned arguments sufficient to judge some positions on important issues to be more credible than others' (Smith 2002:B10). In this sense, the movement is making a call to re-balance the discipline away from an emphasis on *explanation* towards a greater emphasis on *under-standing*. This duality between explanation and understanding, much like other dualities in the social sciences (e.g. universality and particularity, qualitative analysis and quantitative analysis, nomothetic deductivism and hermeneutic interpretivism, methodological unity and methodological pluralism, value-free and value-laden political science, and method-driven and problem-driven political science research programmes) may be overdrawn for rhetorical purposes, and if taken too far, could steer political science in a dangerous and unhelpful direction.

It appears that there are three positions available to the discipline. The first, which the Perestroikans charge is no longer tenable, is that method takes precedence over substance. The second, which many within the Perestroikan movement advocate, is that substance ought to take precedence over method. The third position, which this volume advocates, is *that method is the substance* (see also King *et al.* 1994:9). Without careful specification of the research problem, the identification of observable implications of the theory, careful collection and presentation of the evidence, and logical drawing of inferences, political science research will never be more than speculation and conjecture. While it is empirically true that a large number of political science publications debate the finer points of methodology, causal inference, and quantitative techniques, without such debates the quality of our inferences and the usefulness of our research are necessarily limited. This point can be illustrated through the quantitative and qualitative examples from this volume.

Chapter 6 examined the relationship between economic development and democracy. The global quantitative studies from Lipset (1959) to Boix (2003) and Boix and Stokes (2003) tested the relationship using the best available data and quantitative techniques. Early studies made synchronic 'snap-shot' analyses of the relationship, the positive results of which fed directly or indirectly into US foreign policies such as Kennedy's Alliance for Progress, Reagan's Caribbean Basin Initiative, and Clinton's Summit of the Americas (Landman 1999:626; Chilcote 1994; Cammack 1997). The Alliance for Progress invested public funds into Latin America in an effort to promote economic development and democracy, while preventing social revolutions of the kind that occurred in Cuba. The Reagan and Clinton initiatives sought closer economic ties within the Americas, while ostensibly strengthening support for democracy. Such links between development and democracy have found expression in the Inter-American Democratic Charter, ratified in Lima on September 11, 2001 by the Organization of American States (OAS). Moreover, current policy debates on the 'sequencing' of democracy against the backdrop of the interventions in Afghanistan and Iraq revisit the classic arguments made on the basis of these findings about the economic correlates of democracy (Carothers 2007a, 2007b; Mansfield and Snyder 2005, 2007; Fukuyama 2007; Berman 2007a, 2007b).

Subsequent studies tested the relationship across space and over time, the results of which show a robust relationship between development and democracy, but one that is less so for developing countries. But doubts remained, and new methods using different measures of democracy and different selections of countries showed the limitations of the inferences from the earlier studies. Landman (1999), Mainwaring and Perez-Liñan (2003), and Przeworski *et al.* (2000) show that democracy is not the inevitable outcome of economic development in the world, and in Latin America, in particular. Moreover, the results of their analyses have influenced debates within the United Nations Development Programme, which have been published in the *Human Development Report 2002* (UNDP 2002:56). Without an ongoing debate and refinement of comparative quantitative methods, such an evolution in the inferences about the relationship between development and democracy would not have been possible.

On the qualitative side, Barrington Moore (1966) compared the developmental histories of six countries and concluded that the emergence of liberal democracy was explained by a violent break with the past led by forces from the bourgeoisie. In contrast, Rueschemeyer *et al.* (1992) expanded the number of cases on methodological and theoretical grounds. They found that a violent break from the past was not a necessary and sufficient condition for the emergence of liberal democracy and that it is the working class, not the middle class that is seen to be the main agent of democratization. Thus, the methodological advance represented by the latter study shows that precisely the kind of insights into real political problems that the Perestorikan movement calls for can be the direct result of methodological considerations and innovations. Similar arguments can be made in comparing Wolf's (1969) study of six peasant revolutions to Wickham-Crowley's (1993:312) comparison of 28 cases of revolutionary 'winners', 'also-rans', 'losers', and 'non-starters'. The methodological developments between the two different studies allowed Wickham-Crowley (1993) to think more carefully about how case selection would influence the results of the study (see also Mahoney and Goertz 2004).

These examples demonstrate that methodological dialogue and debate in political science matters and that the substantive inferences drawn from comparative studies have practical relevance to policy makers. Another final example serves to make this point more forcefully. In the 1980s, there emerged within the US policy community on international development what became known as the 'Washington Consensus' (see e.g. Drazen 2000:619), based on a reinvigoration of ideas found in neo-classical economics. Economists and political scientists began to call for supply-side macro-economic policies that reduced the size of the state through privatization and liberalized the economy through deregulation and the encouragement of private sector competition (Todaro 1997:86–90). These policies were originally adopted in the United States and the United Kingdom during the Reagan and Thatcher years, but policy makers in the World Bank and IMF soon turned their attention further afield and prescribed such 'neo-liberal' ideas for developing countries. The evidence for the success of such policies, the neo-liberals argued, came from careful analysis of East Asia.

Methodologically, however, the evidentiary base for making such prescriptions was flawed for three reasons. First, in a classic example of selection bias, the original comparisons of East Asian economic success only focused on successful countries (e.g. Taiwan, Japan, Singapore, and South Korea) (see Chapters 2 and 4 in this volume; Geddes 1990). Second, the neo-liberals only examined the period of economic development during which export-promotion policies were adopted, and wrongly concluded that such policies were appropriate for other countries (Wade 1992). They ignored the fact that most of these countries underwent long periods of import-substitution industrialization, which relied heavily upon state intervention in the economy. Only after such periods of state-led growth could these countries afford to liberalize their economies. By comparing the period of export-promotion in East Asia to import-substitution in Latin America, where the liberalization of their economies was less politically feasible, the neo-liberals wrongly concluded that their polices would have to be enacted in Latin America (Brohman 1996:84). Third, any evidence that contradicted the assumptions of neo-liberalism was either ignored or seen as unimportant (Wade 1992). Indeed as Stiglitz (2002:x) argues, ideological and political motivations within the World Bank and the IMF clouded sound analysis of evidence from the developing world and maintained the neo-liberals' hegemony in this policy area.

Finally, the many-country, few-country, and single-country architecture developed and applied in this volume appears particularly apt for considering the new wave of studies on international terrorism that has emerged since the attacks on New York City and Wasington DC on September 11, 2001. Many-country studies of global terrorism analyse the social and political determinants of terrorism as well as patterns in the frequency, severity, and targets of terrorist attacks (see, e.g. Enders and Sandler 2006). A debate is emerging surrounding the generalization that democracies are more likely to be targets of terrorist attacks, or whether democratic countries that are allies of the US or the UK (or both) suffer a disproportionate number of terrorist attacks (see Li 2005). This debate has been crucial in trying to understand and explain the response to terrorism in few-country and single-country studies of mature democracies (see Brysk and Shafir 2007; Lustick 2006; Landman 2008). For example, does the greater probability of terrorist attacks on democracies necessarily mean that democracies face a trade-off between an expected level of terrorist damage and the curbing of civil liberties (Enders and Sandler 2006:24–51)? Or, does a significant curbing of liberties have the perverse effect of mobilizing individuals and groups to commit terrorist acts (see Campbell and Connolly 2006; Landman 2008)? Lustick's (2006) careful analysis of the war on terror within the United States reveals a remarkable dearth of evidence on a real terrorist threat and quite a lot of evidence on the patterns of expenditure and mismanagement within the federal government.

Summary

The examples and discussions in this final chapter demonstrate that the future for comparative politics is indeed bright. The proliferation of new issues and the examination of old ones continue to provide an ample supply of research topics for systematic comparative analysis. The accretion of comparative methods that has developed over the years provides scholars with a rich 'tool-chest' to examine and explain observed political phenomena in the world. Continued developments in information and communications technology will make the world a smaller place and ought to encourage an ethos of replication, develop a network of shared knowledge, build a stronger comparative-research community, and for certain research areas, promote links with the field of international relations. As in the many other examples detailed throughout this book, careful and systematic comparative analysis as well as dialogue between scholars that conduct studies using different comparative methods is the sensible approach to adopt when addressing such a timely issue as international terrorism. Global analysis can be used to tease out general relationships, while careful few-country and single-country analysis can examine in much greater detail and depth some of the more problematic assertions made on the basis of global analysis. Dialogue, transparency, and intellectual honesty about the links between research questions, methods, and inferences in comparative politics will provide the basis for a thriving and fruitful discipline. It is hoped that this book will make scholars more careful in their choice of countries, their collection of evidence, and their substantive conclusions about the particular research questions that have motivated them, while not losing sight of the importance of the work that is to be done.

Note

1   While Keck and Sikkink (1998a, 1998b) focus on a collection of advocacy groups that comprise a broad leftist agenda for rights and social justice, the radical right has shown itself to be equally adept at global mobilization of its main constituencies.

Further reading

Erickson, K.P. and Rustow, D.A. (1991) 'Global Research Perspectives: Paradigms, Concepts and Data in a Changing World', in D.A. Rustow and K.P. Erickson (eds) *Comparative Political Dynamics: Global Research Perspectives*, New York: Harper Collins, 441–459.
   An excellent summary of new directions for the field of comparative politics.

O'Neil, P. (2007) *Essentials of Comparative Politics*, 2nd edition, New York and London: W. W. Norton.
   Comprehensive introduction to concepts and methods in comparative politics.

Glossary

aggregate statistics Any quantitative indicators collected at the country level. Examples include per capita gross domestic product (GDP), inflation, income inequality, population size, number of riots, and the number of televisions per capita. Also referred to as official statistics.

anocracy An incoherent regime with both democratic and autocratic characteristics.

behaviouralism A period (1950s and 1960s)/methodology of political science that concentrates on the analysis of observed political phenomena in the search for universal laws of politics. Post-behaviouralism concedes that the collection of indicators and subsequent analysis may not be free of value biases of the researcher, nor are the resultant inferences necessarily universal.

binary comparison The comparison of two countries, which can either be 'most similar' or 'most different'. Greater analytical leverage is achieved through the comparison of two 'most different' countries that have a similar outcome that is to be explained. This is sometimes called the 'contrast of contexts'. See also **most similar systems design** and **most different systems design**.

bivariate relationship A significant relationship between two variables, such as economic development and democracy. Theory specifies which variable is dependent and which is independent. See also **dependent variable, independent variable**, and **multivariate relationship**.

case(s) The individual country or countries that feature in a comparison.

case-oriented Type of comparison that emphasizes the holistic qualities of the individual cases (or countries) that are being compared. This method of analysis is opposed to **variable-oriented** analysis.

coding The process by which either numerical or categorical values are assigned to observed political phenomena, such as 'violent' or 'non-violent' political protest, 'left' vs. 'right' ideological position, or the 'degree of democracy' in a political system. See also **measurement**.

configurative Holistic aspects of observed political phenomena, such as the necessary and sufficient conditions for revolution. Emphasis is not the additive independent effects, but the combination of favourable conditions. See also **case-oriented**.

control The practice of isolating the effects of some variables while examining the effects of others. Control can be introduced through statistical methods in many-country studies, or through the intentional selection of countries in few-country studies.

co-efficient Measure of association between two variables that results from regression analysis. The unstandardized version of a co-efficient will reflect the unit of measurement of the variables. See **regression**.

correlation Any significant association between two or more variables, such as age and income, or education and income. Mathematically, a correlation of 0 means no relationship, while a correlation of 1 means a perfect relationship. Correlation does not mean causation. See also **bivariate relationship** and **multivariate relationship**.

counterfactual Hypothetical situations that examine what may have happened given a different set of conditions. For example, what would have happened in the 1997 General Election in the United Kingdom if the electoral system were based on proportional representation? Since history cannot be repeated, comparativists compare similar countries with different electoral systems to examine their effects on party systems. In this way, comparison is a substitute for the counterfactual.

culturalist approaches Theoretical perspectives that concentrate on the shared meanings, understandings, identities, and overall 'world-view' within identifiable communities of people. For example, the 'moral economy' is a concept that captures the ethos of reciprocity and the shared sense of economic vulnerability among individuals in peasant communities (Scott 1976). See also **rationalist approaches** and **structuralist approaches**.

data Any information collected and organized systematically by a comparative scholar. The word 'data' is plural (as opposed to 'datum'), and may be quantitative or qualitative in nature.

data set The organized collection of data. In quantitative comparative studies, data are organized into a matrix of columns and rows, while in qualitative analysis, data may be organized into files, transcripts, recordings, archives, scanned text, etc.

deduction The logical process where conclusions are derived from starting assumptions. For example, one version of game theory assumes the presence of two players with two options from which four possible outcomes can be deduced. Such logical deduction identifies all possible outcomes, which are then reflected in real-world events. See also **induction**.

degrees of freedom The number of pieces of information that can vary independently from one another. In comparative politics, it is important for a research design to have a sufficient number of countries to allow the variables in the analysis to have full variation. Few-country comparativists argue that careful selection of countries alleviates this problem.

dependent variable The political outcome, event, or situation that is to be explained by the comparative analysis. This variable is identified by the research question and specified in the theory and research design of the comparison. For example, in the study of institutional design and democratic performance, democratic performance is presumed to be dependent on institutional design. The dependent variable is alternatively referred to as an outcome variable, an endogenous variable, or the explanandum. See also **independent variable**.

deviant cases (or countries) Those countries that appear to be the exception, or 'outlier' to an empirical generalization. Such countries are normally identified through the quantitative analysis of many countries. For example, in the many-country quantitative study of economic development and democracy, both Saudi Arabia and Costa Rica appear as deviant countries since the former is a rich non-democratic country while the latter is a poor democratic country.

diachronic Comparison over time. See also **synchronic**.

dialectic relationship Two-way relationship between two antagonistic forces or agents that ultimately becomes resolved by a new set of conditions. For example, Karl Marx posited a dialectic relationship under capitalism between the bourgeoisie and the proletariat, which through social revolution would bring about the establishment of communism.

dichotomous Any concept, idea, or category that has two values. For example, countries may be democratic or non-democratic, experience social revolution or not experience social revolution, have a democratic breakdown or not have a democratic breakdown.

dummy variable Any variable with two values or two categories that helps introduce control into systematic analysis. For example, in a comparison of all Latin American countries, the analysis may include a dummy variable for Central America and the Southern Cone to control for presumed sub-regional variation. Thus, in the sample of countries, each dummy variable is coded '1' for the countries that fit the criteria (Central America or Southern Cone) and '0' for those that do not.

ecological fallacy Drawing false conclusions about individuals through the analysis of aggregates. For example, Gurr (1968) compares 114 countries across a range of indicators to make inferences about individual violent political behaviour. See also **individualist fallacy**.

empirical generalization Making inferences about empirical relationships and event regularities without specifying a direct cause for the outcomes that are observed. For example, the following statements are empirical generalizations: 'Countries with proportional representation tend to have multiple political parties'; 'Rich countries tend to be democratic'; 'Democracies tend not to fight one another.'

equivalence The same underlying meaning associated with different actions, terms, structures, or categories. Survey instruments develop different questions that have the same meaning across different countries, and comparativists identify different structures that perform similar functions in different contexts. For example, the World Values Survey uses a battery of questions to construct measures of post-materialism across 43 societies, and some comparativists look for the key structures in society that perform the functions of interest articulation and interest aggregation. In both examples, the underlying equivalence of measures or functions allows for comparison.

external validity The extent to which the inferences of a study can be extended beyond the scope of countries in the original analysis. See also **internal validity**.

functional form The actual shape of a relationship between two or more variables. For example, the relationship between the level of income inequality and political violence can be in the shape of a U, an inverted U, a straight line, or some other form. Each form suggests a different type of relationship. The linear form is still the most common form of relationship that is posited in comparative politics. See also **monotonic relationship** and **regression**.

human rights A set of individual and collective rights that have been formally promoted and protected through international and domestic law since the UN Declaration of Human Rights in 1948. Arguments, theories, and protections of such rights have been in existence for a much longer period, but since the UN Declaration, the evolution of their express legal protection has grown rapidly.

hypothesis A statement about a possible relationship between two or more variables derived from a more general theory and tested using systematic comparative analysis. Hypotheses generally take the form: if A, then B. For example, a typical hypothesis would be stated as follows: 'A reduction in government repression will lead to an increase in social movement activity.'

independent variable The variable or variables included in the comparative analysis that are presumed to account for some or all of the variation in the **dependent variable**. The independent variable is alternatively labelled a causal variable, an explanatory variable, an exogenous variable, or the explicandum.

indeterminate research design A comparative analysis that is designed in such a way that the research question cannot truly be answered. For example, a comparative study may identify four independent variables for an outcome that is to be explained, but have only two countries in the comparison. There are not enough countries for the variables to assume their different values and logical combinations. This is a problem of insufficient **degrees of freedom** or 'too many variables, not enough countries'.

individualist fallacy Drawing false conclusions about aggregates through the analysis of individuals. For example, Inglehart (1997) compares surveys with approximately 2,000 respondents from 43 countries to identify cultural clusterings, but it is not clear that a country can be considered 'traditional' even if all of the respondents in the survey express such attitudes. See also **ecological fallacy**.

induction The process by which conclusions are drawn from direct observation of empirical evidence. See also **deduction**.

inference The process by which comparative researchers use facts they do know about the world to make statements about things they do not know.

internal validity The extent to which the inferences drawn from a study are due precisely to the factors that have been analysed and not to some other factors. See also **external validity**.

intervening variable An explanatory variable presumed to provide the causal link between two other variables. For example, the positive association between income and health is explained by the presence of expenditure on healthcare, the intervening variable.

level of analysis The degree to which political units are aggregated for comparative analysis. For example, a single-country study can examine individuals, cities, regions (counties), and sub-regions (states, federal districts). Few- and many-country comparisons use the nation state as the basic unit of analysis. The higher the level of analysis, the less specificity a study can have and vice versa.

macro-causal A specification of causal relationships among macro-level variables, such as class, class alliances, the state, and processes of socio-economic modernization.

majoritarian Refers to an electoral system that produces and gives power to majority political parties in the legislative assembly.

measurement Assigning values to objects of comparative inquiry for further quantitative analysis. See also **coding**.

method of agreement Part of J.S. Mill's logic that identifies similar features across different units. Forms the basis of the **most different systems design**.

method of difference Part of J.S. Mill's logic that identifies different features across similar units. Forms the basis of the **most similar systems design**.

methodology The study of different methods of research, including the identification of research questions, the formulation of theories to explain certain events and political outcomes, and the development of research design.

model A simplified representation of relationships between variables usually depicted graphically. The different relationships that form the structure of the model can then be tested empirically.

monotonic relationship Any **bivariate relationship** where an increase in one variable necessarily is associated with an increase in the other variable.

most different systems design A research design that compares instances of similar variation across different countries.

most similar systems design A research design that compares instances of different variation across similar countries.

multivariate relationship A significant relationship with at least two **independent variables** that account for the **dependent variable**.

observable implications All possible instances in which expected political outcomes ought to occur, or where significant relationships ought to be upheld.

observations The values that variables take on specific units. For example, a code of 1 for 'democracy' at time t in country A is an observation.

operationalize The process by which theoretical concepts become transformed into variables for quantitative or qualitative comparative analysis. See also **coding** and **measurement**.

parsimonious explanation The type of explanation that uses the least amount of evidence to explain the most amount of variation. This is also referred to as maximizing the analytical leverage of a comparative study.

post-behaviouralism A period (after 1970)/methodology of political science that accepts that observation and analysis of the political world are not free from certain theoretical and value biases, yet strives to make strong inferences through empirical analysis.

qualitative analysis   Any method that examines the inherent traits, characteristics, and qualities of the political objects of inquiry. Examples of qualitative analysis include comparative history, participant observation, in-depth interviews, and ethnographic field research. Studies in this vein tend to be more holistic and interpretative, as well as conducted for a small selection of countries.

quantitative analysis   Any method that uses numerical indicators of political phenomena and seeks to establish the existence of relationships between them across a selection of countries, time periods or both.

r-square   Measure of the 'goodness of fit' for a statistical model that fits a line to **data**. It is the ratio of explained variation in a particular **dependent variable** to its total variation and ranges from 0 (i.e. the model explains no variation in the dependent variable) to 1 (i.e. the model explains all of the variation in the dependent variable).

rationalist approaches   Theoretical perspectives that place the actions and choices of individuals at the centre of the analysis. These individuals are assumed to have sets of preferences, the utility of which is maximized through rational 'cost-benefit' analysis.

regression   An analytical technique that estimates relationships between two or more **variables** by fitting a line to data points that minimizes the distance between actual observations and those predicted by the analytical model. Standard regression fits a straight line to these data points (called linear regression), while more advanced versions of the technique fit curves of various shapes to the data points. See also **functional form**.

research design   The framework of analysis that is derived both from the research question and the theoretical attempt to provide a plausible answer to the research question. Research design includes the choice of countries, the ways in which the **dependent** and **independent variables** are **operationalized**, and the collection and analysis of the evidence. A good research design should answer the three questions: (1) What does the analysis seek to find out? (2) How does it propose to find it out? (3) How will the researcher know if the answer is wrong?

sample   A group of countries selected from a larger group of countries, which when analysed will reveal something about the larger group (known as the population). Even comparisons of many countries represent a sample, since their analysis is limited to a particular time-frame, and their **inferences** are meant to extend to all time. The general rule in comparative politics is that the larger the sample, the stronger the inferences that can be drawn about the population.

selection bias   The problem of choosing countries based on criteria that are somehow related to the **dependent variable**. For example, selection bias is present in studies that analyse exclusively countries in which only the outcome to be explained is present, such as military coups, revolutions, or democratic transitions.

solidarity rights   Rights to public goods such as development and the environment. This collection of rights seeks to guarantee that all individuals and groups have the right to share in the benefits of the earth's natural resources, as well as those goods and products that are made through processes of economic growth, expansion, and innovation. See also **human rights**.

spuriousness The false establishment of an empirical relationship between two or more variables that is actually due to a third variable not included in the analysis. For example, the seemingly positive relationship between authoritarian governments and superior economic performance is spurious, since authoritarian governments tend to collapse in periods of poor economic performance, while democracies extend over periods of good and bad economic performance.

structuralist approaches Theoretical perspectives that concentrate on the sets of relations, networks, and interconnectedness between and among individuals, and how these 'structures' constrain or facilitate human agency.

synchronic A comparison of countries at one point in time. See also **diachronic**.

theory A definitive and logical statement (or groups of statements) about how the world (or some key aspect of the world) 'works'. Known collectively as empirical theory (as opposed to normative theory), these statements make claims about relationships between variables that can be tested using systematic comparative analysis.

theory confirming Crucial single-country studies which are either 'least likely' or 'most likely' can confirm the expectations of a theory. For example, the presence of social revolution in Mexico and continued mobilization from subordinate rural groups confirms a number of theories about peasant rebellion.

theory infirming Crucial single-country studies which are either 'least likely' or 'most likely' can infirm the expectations of a theory. For example, the absence of social revolution in Brazil despite the presence of key socio-economic conditions infirms certain theories of revolution.

time-series Data that are collected over time and arranged in chronological order. These data have special attributes that need to be addressed when using advanced quantitative methods.

unit of analysis The objects of comparative political inquiry upon which data are collected, such as individuals, elections, or countries. See also **case(s)**.

value bias The introduction of contamination in measurement due to the cultural or theoretical predispositions of the researcher.

variable Any object in comparative analysis whose values vary across units, such as income across individuals, or the degree of democracy across countries.

variable-oriented Type of comparative analysis that emphasizes the empirical relationships between variables across a selection of countries. See also **case-oriented**.

References

Abouharb, M.R. and Cingranelli, D.L. (2004) 'Human Rights and Structural Adjustment: The Importance of Selection', in S.C. Carey and S.C. Poe (eds) *Understanding Human Rights Violations: New Systematic Studies*, Aldershot: Ashgate, 127–141.

Abouharb, M.R. and Cingranelli, D.L. (2007) *Human Rights and Structural Adjustment*, Cambridge: Cambridge University Press.

Achen, C.H. and Snidal, D. (1989) 'Rational Deterrence Theory and Comparative Case Studies', *World Politics*, 41(2): 143–169.

Adcock, R. and Collier, D. (2001) 'Measurement Validty: A Shared Standard for Qualitative and Quantitative Research', *American Political Science Review*, 95(3): 529–546.

Almond, G. (1990) *A Discipline Divided: Schools and Sects in Political Science*, Newbury Park, CA: Sage.

—— (1996) 'Political Science: The History of the Discipline', in R.E. Goodin and H. Klingemann (eds) *The New Handbook of Political Science*, Oxford: Oxford University Press.

Almond, G. and Bingham Powell, G. (1966) *Comparative Politics: A Developmental Approach*, Boston, MA: Little, Brown.

Almond, G. and Genco, S.J. (1977) 'Clouds, Clocks, and the Study of Politics', *World Politics*, 29(4): 489–522.

Almond, G. and Verba, S. (1963) *The Civic Culture: Political Attitudes and Democracy in Five Nations*, Princeton, NJ: Princeton University Press.

Alston, P. and Crawford, J. (eds) (2000) *The Future of UN Human Rights Treaty Monitoring*, Cambridge: Cambridge University Press.

Anderson, L. (1994) *The Political Ecology of the Peasant: Calculation and Community*, Baltimore, MD: Johns Hopkins University Press.

Andrain, C.F. (1994) *Comparative Political Systems*, Armonk, NY: M.E. Sharpe.

Apter, D.E. (1958) 'A Comparative Method for the Study of Politics', *American Journal of Sociology*, 64 (November): 221–237.

—— (1996) 'Comparative Politics, Old and New', in R.E. Goodin and H. Klingemann (eds) *The New Handbook of Political Science*, Oxford: Oxford University Press, 372–397.

Aristotle (1958) *The Politics*, trans. E.Barker, Oxford: Clarendon Press.

Arrighi, G. (1994) *The Long Twentieth Century*, London: Verso.

REFERENCES

Axelrod, R. (1984) *The Evolution of Cooperation*, New York: Basic Books.

Babst, D.Y. (1964) 'Elective Governments – A Force for Peace', *The Wisconsin Sociologist*, 3:9–14.

—— (1972) 'A Force for Peace', *Industrial Research* (April): 55–58.

Ball, P., Asher, J., Sulmont, D., and Manrique, D. (2003) 'How Many Peruvians Have Died?' Washington DC: American Association for the Advancement of Science (AAAS), http://shr.aaas.org/hrdag/peru/aaas_peru_5.pdf

Ball, P.B., Spirer, H. F., and Spirer, L. (eds) (2000) *Making the Case: Investigating Large Scale Human Rights Violations Using Information Systems and Data Analysis*, Washington DC: American Association for the Advancement of Science.

Banks, A.S. (1994) *Cross-Polity Time-Series Data Archive*, Binghamton, NY: State University of New York at Binghamton.

Barbalet, J.M. (1988) *Citizenship: Rights, Struggle and Class Inequality*, Milton Keynes: Open University Press.

Barratt, B. (2004) 'Aiding or Abetting: British Foreign Aid Decisions and Recipient Country Human Rights', in S.C. Carey and S.C. Poe (eds), *Understanding Human Rights Violations: New Systematic Studies*, Aldershot: Ashgate, 43–62.

Barsh, R.L. (1993) 'Measuring Human Rights: Problems of Methodology and Purpose', *Human Rights Quarterly*, 15: 87–121.

Bashevkin, S. (1998) *Women on the Defensive: Living through Conservative Times*, Chicago: University of Chicago Press.

Bates, G. (1989) *Beyond the Market: The Political Economy of Agrarian Development in Kenya*, Cambridge: Cambridge University Press.

Bayefsky, A.F. (2001) *The UN Human Rights Treaty System: Universality at the Crossroads*, York University Human Rights Project (www.yorku.ca/hrights).

Beck, N. and Katz, J.N. (1995) 'What to Do (and Not to Do) with Time-Series Cross-Section Data', *American Political Science Review*, 89(3):634–647.

Beer, C. and Mitchell, N.J. (2006) 'Comparing Nations and States: Human Rights and Democracy in India', *Comparative Political Studies*, 39(8): 996–1018.

Beer, F. and Balleck, B. (1994) 'Realist/Idealist Texts: Psychometry and Semantics', *Peace Psychology Review*, 1: 38–44.

Bennett, S.E. (2002) '"Perestroika" Lost: Why the Latest "Reform" Movement in Political Science Should Fail', *PS: Political Science and Politics*, 35(2): 177–179.

Berman, S. (2007a) 'How Democracies Emerge, II: Lessons from Europe, *Journal of Democracy*, 18 (1): 12–27.

—— (2007b) 'Exchange, III: The Vain Hope for Correct Timing', *Journal of Democracy*, 18 (3): 14–17.

Bill, J. and Hardgrave, R.L., Jr. (1973) *Comparative Politics: The Quest for Theory*, Columbus, OH: Charles Merrill Co.

Birch, S. (2000) *Elections and Democratization in Ukraine*, New York: St Martin's Press.

Black, D. (1999) 'The Long and Winding Road: International Norms and Domestic Political Change in South Africa', in T. Risse, S.C. Ropp, K. Sikkink (eds) *The Power of Human Rights: International Norms and Domestic Change*, Cambridge: Cambridge University Press, 78–108.

Blalock, H.M., Jr. (1961) *Causal Inferences in Nonexperimental Research*, Chapel Hill, NC: University of North Carolina Press.

Bob, C. (2005) *The Marketing of Rebellion: Insurgents, Media, and International Activism*, Cambridge: Cambridge University Press.

Boix, C. (2003) *Democracy and Redistribution*, Cambridge: Cambridge University Press.

Boix, C. and Stokes, S. (2003) 'Endogenous Democratization', *World Politics*, 55 (July): 517–49.

Bollen, K. (1979) 'Political Democracy and the Timing of Development', *American Sociological Review*, 44 (August): 572–587.

—— (1992) 'Political Rights and Political Liberties in Nations: An Evaluation of Rights Measures, 1950 to 1984', in T.B. Jabine and R.P. Claude (eds) *Human Rights and Statistics: Getting the Record Straight*, Philadelphia, PA: University of Pennsylvania Press, 188–215.

Boyle, K. (1995) 'Stock-taking on Human Rights: The World Conference on Human Rights, Vienna 1993', *Political Studies*, 43: 79–95.

Boyle, K. and Sheen, J. (1997) *The Freedom of Religion and Thought: A World Report*, London: Routledge.

Brady, H. and Collier, D. (eds) (2004) *Rethinking Social Inquiry: Diverse Tools, Shared Standards*, Lanham, MD: Rowman and Littlefield.

Brady, H.E., Collier, D., and Seawright, J. (2006) 'Toward a Pluralistic Vision of Methodology', *Political Analysis*, 14: 353–368.

Bratton, M. and van de Walle, N. (1997) *Democratic Experiments in Africa: Regime Transitions in Comparative Perspective*, Cambridge: Cambridge University Press.

Bremer, Stuart A. (1992) 'Dangerous Dyads: Conditions Affecting the Likelihood of Interstate War, 1816–1965', *Journal of Conflict Resolution*, 36(2): 309–341

Bremer, Stuart A. (1993) 'Democracy and Militarized Interstate Conflict,' *International Interactions*, 18: 231–249

Brockett, C. (2005) *Political Movements and Violence in Central America*, Cambridge: Cambridge University Press.

Brohman, J. (1996) *Popular Development*, Oxford: Blackwell.

Browne, E.C., Frendreis, J.P., and Gleiber, D.W. (1986) 'The Process of Cabinet Dissolution: An Exponential Model of Duration and Stability in Western Democracies', *American Journal of Political Science*, 30: 628–650.

Brysk, A. (1994a) *The Politics of Human Rights in Argentina: Protest, Change, and Democratization*, Stanford, CA: Stanford University Press.

—— (1994b) 'The Politics of Measurement: The Contested Count of the Disappeared in Argentina', *Human Rights Quarterly*, 16: 676–92.

Brysk, A. and Shafir, G. (eds) (2007) *National Insecurity and Human Rights: Democracies Debate Counterterrorism*, Berkeley, CA: University of California Press.

Budge, I., Klingemann, H., Volkens, A., Bara, J., and Tanenbaum, E. (2001) *Mapping Policy Preferences: Estimates for Parties, Electors, and Governments 1945–1998*, Oxford: Oxford University Press.

Budge, I., Robertson, D., and Hearl, D. (1987) *Ideology, Strategy, and Party Change: Spatial Analysis of Post-war Election Programmes in 19 Democracies*, Cambridge: Cambridge University Press.

Burkhart, R.E. and Lewis-Beck, M. (1994) 'Comparative Democracy, the Economic Development Thesis', *American Political Science Review*, 88(4): 903–910.

Burton, M., Gunther, R., and Higley, J. (1992) 'Introduction: Elite Transformation and Democratic Regimes', in John Higley and Richard Gunther (eds), *Elites and Democratic Consolidation in Latin America and Southern Europe*, Cambridge: Cambridge University Press, 1–37.

Cammack, P. (1997) *Capitalism and Democracy in the Third World: The Doctrine for Political Development*, London and Washington: Leicester University Press.

Campbell, C. and Connolly, I. (2006) 'Making War on Terror? Global Lessons from Northern Ireland', *Modern Law Review*, 69(6): 935–955.

Campbell, D.T. (1975) '"Degrees of Freedom" and the Case Study', *Comparative Political Studies*, 8(2): 178–193.

Campbell, D.T. and Stanley, J.C. (1963) *Experimental and Quasi-experimental Designs for Research*, Chicago: Rand McNally.

Caporaso, J.A. (1995) 'Research, Falsification, and the Qualitative-Quantitative Divide', *American Political Science Review*, 89 (June): 457–460.

Carey, S. (2007) 'Human Rights Versus Bureaucratic Inertia', *Journal of Peace Research*, 44 (4): 447–464.

Carey, S. and Poe, S. (2004) *Understanding Human Rights Violations: New Systematic Studies*, Aldershot: Ashgate.

Carothers, T. (2007a) 'How Democracies Emerge, I: The "Sequencing" Fallacy', *Journal of Democracy*, 18(1): 12–27.

—— (2007b) 'Exchange, III: The Vain Hope for Correct Timing', *Journal of Democracy*, 18(3): 18–22.

Carlsnaes, W., Risse, T., and Simmons, B. (2002) *Handbook of International Relations*, London: Sage.

Carr, R. and Fusi, J.P. (1979) *Spain: Dictatorship to Democracy*, 2nd edn, London: Allen & Unwin.

Castells, M. (1997) *The Information Age: Economy, Society, and Culture, Volume II: The Power of Identity*, Oxford: Blackwell.

Caterino, B. and Schram, S. F. (2006) *Making Political Science Matter: Debating Knowledge, Research and Method*, New York: New York University Press.

Cavarozzi, M. (1986) 'Political Cycles in Argentina since 1955', in G. O'Donnell, P. Schmitter, and L. Whitehead (eds) *Transitions from Authoritarian Rule: Latin America*, Baltimore, MD: Johns Hopkins University Press, 19–48.

Chan, S. (1984) *International Relations in Perspective: the Pursuit of Security, Welfare and Justice*, New York: Macmillan.

Chilcote, R.H. (1994) *Theories of Comparative Politics: The Search for a Paradigm Reconsidered*, 2nd edn, Boulder, CO: Westview Press.

Cingranelli, D.L. and Richards, D.L. (1999) 'Measuring the Level, Pattern, and Sequence of Government Respect for Physical Integrity Rights', *International Studies Quarterly*, 43: 409–10.

Cioffi-Revilla, C. (1981) 'Fuzzy Sets and Models of International Relations', *American Journal of Political Science*, 25: 129–159.

—— (1984) 'The Political Reliability of Italian Governments: An Exponential Survival Model', *American Political Science Review*, 78: 318–337.

—— (1998) *Politics and Uncertainty: Theory, Models and Applications*, Cambridge: Cambridge University Press.

Cioffi-Revilla, C. and Landman, T. (1999) 'The Rise and Fall of Maya City States in the Ancient Meso-American System', *International Studies Quarterly*, 43: 559–598.

Clarke, S.E. and Gaile, G. (1998) *The Work of Cities*, Minneapolis, MN and London: University of Minnesota Press.

Claude, R.P. (1976) 'The Classical Model of Human Rights Development', in R.P. Claude (ed.) *Comparative Human Rights*, Baltimore, MD and London: Johns Hopkins University Press, 6–50.

Claude, R.P. and Jabine, T.B. (1992) 'Exploring Human Rights Issues with Statistics', in T.B. Jabine and R.P. Claude (eds) *Human Rights and Statistics: Getting the Record Straight*, Philadelphia, PA: University of Pennsylvania Press, 5–34.

Cohen, J. and Arato, A. (1992) *Civil Society and Political Theory*, Cambridge, MA: MIT Press.

Cohen, Y. (1987) 'Democracy from Above: The Origins of Military Dictatorship in Brazil', *World Politics*, 30–54.

—— (1994) *Radicals, Reformers, and Reactionaries: The Prisoner's Dilemma and the Collapse of Democracy in Latin America*, Chicago: University of Chicago Press.

Collier, D. (ed.) (1979) *The New Authoritarianism in Latin America*, Princeton, NJ: Princeton University Press.

—— (1991) 'New Perspectives on the Comparative Method', in D.A. Rustow and K.P. Erickson (eds) *Comparative Political Dynamics: Global Research Perspectives*, New York: Harper Collins, 7–31.

—— (1993) 'The Comparative Method', in A. Finifter (ed.) *Political Science: The State of the Discipline*, Washington, DC: The American Political Science Association.

—— (1995) 'Translating Quantitative Methods for Qualitative Researchers: The Case of Selection Bias', *American Political Science Review*, 89 (June): 461–466.

Collier, D. and Collier, R.B. (1991) *Shaping the Political Arena: Critical Junctures, the Labor Movement, and Regime Dynamics*, Princeton, NJ: Princeton University Press.

Collier, D. and Mahoney, J. (1996) 'Insights and Pitfalls: Selection Bias and Qualitative Research', *World Politics*, 49: 56–91.

Collier, R.B. (1999) *Paths Toward Democracy: The Working Class and Elites in Western Europe and South America*, Cambridge: Cambridge University Press.

Colomer, J.M. (1991) 'Transitions by Agreement: Modelling the Spanish Way', *American Political Science Review*, 85(4): 1283–1302.

Colomer, J.M. and Pascual, M. (1994) 'The Polish Games of Transition', *Communist and Post-communist Studies*, 27(3): 275–294.

Comisión Nacional de Verdad y Reconciliación (1991) *Informe de la Comisión Nacional de Verdad y Reconciliacion*, Santiago: La Nación.

CONDADEP (1986) *Nunca más: (Never Again): a report by Argentina's National Commission on Disappeared People*, Buenos Aires.

Constable, P. and Valenzuela, A. (1993) *A Nation of Enemies: Chile Under Pinochet*, New York: W. W. Norton.

Costain, A.N. (1992) *Inviting Women's Rebellion: A Political Process Interpretation of the Women's Movement*, Baltimore, MD: Johns Hopkins University Press.

Costain, A.N. and Majstorovic, S. (1994) 'Congress, Social Movements and Public Opinion: Multiple Origins of Women's Rights Legislation', *Political Research Quarterly*, 47(1): 111–135.

Cotler, J. (1986) 'Military Interventions and "Transfer of Power to Civilians" in Peru', in G. O'Donnell, P. Schmitter, and L. Whitehad (eds) *Transitions from Authoritarian Rule: Latin America*, Baltimore, MD: Johns Hopkins University Press, 148–172.

Couvalis, G. (1997) *The Philosophy of Science: Science and Objectivity*, London: Sage.

Crighton, E. H. (2003) Review of Gurr, T.R. (2000) *People Versus States: Minorities at Risk in the New Century*, Washington DC: United States Institute of Peace, Perspectives on Politics, 1(1): 232–233.

Cutright, P. (1963) 'National Political Development: Its Measurement and Social Correlates', in N. Polsby, R.A. Denther, and P.A. Smith (eds) *Political and Social Life*, Boston, MA: Houghton Mifflin, 569–582.

Cutright, P. and Wiley, J.A. (1969) 'Modernization and Political Representation: 1927–1966', *Studies in Comparative International Development*, 5(2): 23–44.

Czempiel, E.O. (1992) 'Governance and Democratization', in J. Rosenau (ed.) *Governance without Government: Order and Change in World Politics*, Cambridge: Cambridge University Press.

Dahl, R. (1961) *Who Governs: Democracy and Power in an American City*, New Haven, CT: Yale University Press.

Dahl, R.A. (1971) *Polyarchy: Participation and Opposition*, New Haven, CT: Yale University Press.

—— (1998) *On Democracy*, New Haven, CT: Yale University Press.

REFERENCES

Dalton, R. (1988) *Citizen Politics in Western Democracies*, Chatham, NJ: Chatham House Publishers.

—— (1994) *Green Rainbow: Environmental Groups in Western Europe*, New Haven, CT: Yale University Press.

Dassin, J. (ed.) (1986) *Torture in Brazil, A Report by the Archdiocese of São Paulo*, New York: Vintage Books.

Davidson, S. (1993) *Human Rights*, Buckingham: Open University Press.

De Brito, A.B. (1997) *Human Rights and Democratization in Latin America: Uruguay and Chile*, Oxford: Oxford University Press.

De Mesquita, B., Morrow, J.D., and Zorick, E.R. (1997) 'Capabilities, Perception, and Escalation', *American Political Science Review*, 91 (March): 15–27.

De Meur, G. and Berg-Schlosser, D. (1994) 'Comparing Political Systems: Establishing Similarities and Dissimilarities', *European Journal of Political Research*, 26: 193–219.

De Schweinitz, K. (1964) *Industrialization and Democracy: Economic Necessities and Political Possibilities*, New York: Free Press.

De Tocqueville, A. (2007) *Democracy in America*, ed. J.P. Mayer, trans. George Lawrence, abridged by Scott A. Sandage, New York: Harper.

De Vaus, D.A. (1991) *Surveys in Social Research*, 2nd edn, London: Unwin Hyman.

Della Porta, D. (1996) 'Social Movements and the State: Thoughts on the Policing of Protest', in D. McAdam, J. McCarthy, and M.N. Zald (eds) *Comparative Perspectives on Social Movements*, Cambridge: Cambridge University Press, 62–92.

Della Porta, D. and Reiter, H. (1998) *Policing Protest: The Control of Mass Demonstrations in Western Democracies*, Minnesota, MN: University of Minnesota Press.

Devine, F. (1995) 'Qualitative Analysis', in D. Marsh and G. Stoker (eds) *Theories and Methods in Political Science*, London: Macmillan, 137–153.

Diamandouros, P.N. (1986) 'Regime Change and the Prospects for Democracy in Greece: 1974–1983', in G. O'Donnell, P. Schmitter, and L. Whitehead (eds) *Transitions from Authoritarian Rule: Southern Europe*, Baltimore, MD: Johns Hopkins University Press, 138–164.

Diamond, L. (1999) *Developing Democracy: Toward Consolidation*, Baltimore, MD: Johns Hopkins University Press.

Dion, Douglas (1998) 'Evidence and Inference in the Comparative Case Study', *Comparative Politics*, 30(2): 127–145.

Dixon, William J. (1994) 'Democracy and the Peaceful Settlement of International Conflict', *American Political Science Review*, 88(1): 14–32

Dogan, M. and Kazancigil, A. (1994) *Comparing Nations: Concepts, Strategies, Substance*, Oxford: Blackwell.

Dogan, M. and Pelassy, D. (1990) *How to Compare Nations: Strategies in Comparative Politics*, 2nd edn, Chatham, NJ: Chatham House.

Donnelly, J. (1989) *Human Rights in Theory and Practice*, Ithaca, NY and London: Cornell University Press.

—— (1998) *International Human Rights*, 2nd edn, Boulder, CO: Westview Press.

—— (1999) 'Democracy, Development, and Human Rights', *Human Rights Quarterly*, 21(3): 608–632.

—— (2000) *Realism and International Relations*, Cambridge: Cambridge University Press.

Doorenspleet, R. (2000) 'Reassessing the Three Waves of Democratization', *World Politics*, 52(3): 384–406.

—— (2001) 'The Fourth Wave of Democratization: Identification and Explanation', PhD Thesis Manuscript, University of Leiden.

—— (2005) *Democratic Transitions: Exploring the Structural Sources of the Fourth Wave*, Boulder, CO: Lynne Rienner.

Doyle, Michael W. (1983) 'Kant, Liberal Legacies, and Foreign Affairs', reprinted in Michael E. Brown, Sean M. Lynn-Jones, and Steven E. Miller (eds) (1996) *Debating the Democratic Peace*, Cambridge, MA: MIT Press.

—— (1995) 'Reflections on the Democratic Peace', reprinted in Michael E. Brown, Sean M. Lynn-Jones, and Steven E. Miller (eds) (1996) *Debating the Democratic Peace*, Cambridge, MA: MIT Press.

—— (1996) 'Michael Doyle on the Democratic Peace – Again', reprinted in Michael E. Brown, Sean M. Lynn-Jones, and Steven E. Miller (eds) (1996) *Debating the Democratic Peace*, Cambridge, MA: MIT Press.

—— (1999) 'Liberalism and World Politics', in Paul R. Viotti and Mark V. Kauppi, *International Relations Theory*, 4th edn, Boston, MA: Allyn and Bacon.

Drass, K.A. and Ragin, C.C. (1991) *Qualitative Comparative Analysis 3.0*, Evanston, IL: Center for Urban Affairs and Policy Research, Northwestern University.

Drazen, A. (2000) *Political Economy in Macroeconomics*, Princeton, NJ: Princeton University Press.

Dryzek, J.S. and Holmes, L. (2002) *Post-Communist Democratization: Political Discourses across Thirteen Countries*, Cambridge: Cambridge University Press.

Duverger, M. (1951) *Political Parties, their Organization and Activity in the Modern State*, London: Methuen.

—— (1954) *Political Parties*, trans. B. and R. North, London: Methuen.

Eckstein, H. (1964) *Internal War*, New York: Free Press.

—— (1975) 'Case-study and Theory in Political Science', in F.I. Greenstein and N.S. Polsby (eds) *Handbook of Political Science*, Vol. 7: Strategies of Inquiry, Reading, MA: Addison-Wesley, 79–137.

Enders, W. and Sandler, T. (2006) *The Political Economy of Terrorism*, Cambridge: Cambridge University Press.

Erickson, K.P. and Rustow, D.A. (1991) 'Global Research Perspectives: Paradigms, Concepts and Data in a Changing World', in D.A. Rustow and K.P. Erickson (eds) *Comparative Political Dynamics: Global Research Perspectives*, New York: HarperCollins, 441–459.

Ersson, S. and Lane, J.E. (1996) 'Democracy and Development: A Statistical Exploration', in A. Leftwich (ed.) *Democracy and Development*, Cambridge: Polity, 45–73.

Escobar, A. and Alvarez, S.E. (eds) (1992) *The Making of Social Movements in Latin America: Identity, Strategy, and Democracy*, Boulder, CO: Westview.

Eulau, H. (1996) *Micro-Macro Dilemmas in Political Science: Personal Pathways through Complexity*, Norman, OK: University of Oklahoma Press.

Falk, R. (2000) *Human Rights Horizons: The Pursuit of Justice in a Globalizing World*, London: Routledge.

Farber, Henry S., and Gowa, Joanne (1995) 'Polities and Peace', reprinted in Michael E. Brown, Sean M. Lynn-Jones, and Steven E. Miller (eds) (1996) *Debating the Democratic Peace*, Cambridge, MA: MIT Press

Faure, A.M. (1994) 'Some Methodological Problems in Comparative Politics', *Journal of Theoretical Politics*, 6(3): 307–322.

Fay, B. (1975) *Social Theory and Political Practice*, London: Allen & Unwin.

Ferguson, N. (ed.) (1997a) *Virtual History: Alternatives and Counterfactuals*, London: Picador.

—— (1997b) 'Virtual History: Towards a Chaotic Theory of the Past', in N. Ferguson (ed.) *Virtual History: Alternatives and Counterfactuals*, London: Picador, 1–90.

Feyerabend, P. (1993) *Against Method*, London: Verso Press.

Finer, S.E. (1997) *The History of Government*, Vol. I: Ancient Monarchies and Empires, Oxford: Oxford University Press.

Fiorina, M.P. (1996) *Divided Goverment*, 2nd edn, Needham Heights, MA: Simon & Schuster.

REFERENCES

Firebaugh, G. (1980) 'Cross-national Versus Historical Regression Models: Conditions of Equivalence in Comparative Analysis', *Comparative Social Research*, 3: 333–344.

Fischer, M.E. (ed.) (1996) *Establishing Democracies*, Boulder, CO: Westview Press.

Fitzgibbon, R.H. (1967) 'Measuring Democratic Change in Latin America', *Journal of Politics*, 29: 129–166.

Flyvbjerg, B. (2001) *Making Social Science Matter*, Cambridge: Cambridge University Press.

—— (2006) 'A Perestroikan Straw Man Answers Back: David Laitin and Phronetic Social Science', in Sanford F. Schram and Brian Caterino (eds) *Making Political Science Matter: Debating Knowledge, Research, and Methods*, New York: New York University Press, 56–85.

Forsythe, D. (2006) *Human Rights in International Relations*, Cambridge: Cambridge University Press.

Foweraker, J. (1989) *Making Democracy in Spain: Grassroots Struggle in the South, 1955–1975*, Cambridge: Cambridge University Press.

—— (1995) *Theorizing Social Movements*, London: Pluto.

—— (1998) 'Institutional Design, Party Systems and Governability: Differentiating the Presidential Regimes of Latin America', *British Journal of Political Science*, 28: 651–676.

Foweraker, J. and Landman, T. (1997) *Citizenship Rights and Social Movements: A Comparative and Statistical Analysis*, Oxford: Oxford University Press.

—— (1999) 'Individual Rights and Social Movements: A Comparative and Statistical Inquiry', *British Journal of Political Science*, 29 (April): 291–322.

—— (2002) 'Constitutional Design and Democratic Performance', *Democratization*, 9 (2):43–66.

—— (2004) 'Economic development and Democracy Revisited: Why Dependency Theory is Not Yet Dead', *Democratization*, 11(1): 1–21.

Foweraker, J., Landman, T., and Harvey, N. (2003) *Governing Latin America*, Cambridge: Polity Press.

Fox, J. (1997) *Applied Regression Analysis, Linear Models, and Related Methods*, Thousand Oaks and London: Sage Publications.

Franzosi, R. (2004) *From Words to Numbers: Narrative, Data, and Social Science*, Cambridge: Cambridge University Press.

Freedom House (1995) *Freedom in the World: Political and Civil Liberties, 1994–1995*, New York: Freedom House.

—— (1999) *Freedom in the World: Political and Civil Liberties, 1998–1999*, New York: Freedom House.

Freeman, M. (2001) 'Is a Political Science of Human Rights Possible?', *Netherlands Quarterly of Human Rights*, 19(2): 121–137.

Fuentes, M. and Frank, G.A. (1989) 'Ten Theses on Social Movements', *World Development*, 17(2):179–191.

Fukuyama, F. (1992) *The End of History and the Last Man*, New York: Avon Books.

—— (2007) 'Exchange, II: Liberalism versus State Building', *Journal of Democracy*, 18 (3): 10–13.

Gallie, W.B.(1956), 'Essentially Contested Concepts', *Proceedings of the Aristotelian Society*, 56: 167–198.

Gamson, W.A. (1975) *The Strategy of Social Protest*, Homewood, IL: Dorsey Press.

Garreton, M.A. (1986) 'The Political Evolution of the Chilean Military Regime and Problems in the Transition to Democracy', in G. O'Donnell, P. Schmitter, and L. Whitehead (eds) *Transitions from Authoritarian Rule: Latin America*, Baltimore, MD: Johns Hopkins University Press, 95–122.

Gastil, R.D. (1980) *Freedom in the World: Political Rights and Civil Liberties*, Westport, CT: Greenwood Press.

Gautier, D. (1986) *Morals by Agreement*, Oxford: Clarendon Press.

Geddes, B. (1990) 'How the Cases You Choose Affect the Answers You Get: Selection Bias in Comparative Politics', *Political Analysis*, 2: 131–150.

—— (1991) 'A Game Theoretic Model of Reform in Latin American Democracies', *American Political Science Review*, 85 (June): 371–392.

—— (1994) *Politician's Dilemma: Building State Capacity in Latin America*, Berkeley and Los Angeles: University of California Press.

Geertz, C. (1973) 'Thick Description: Toward an Interpretative Theory of Culture', in C. Geertz *The Interpretation of Cultures*, New York: Basic Books, 3–30.

Gelpi, C. and Griesdorf, M. (2001) 'Winners or Losers? Democracies in International Crisis, 1918–94', *American Political Science Review*, 95(3): 633–647.

George, A. L. (1979) 'The Causal Nexus between Cognitive Beliefs and Decision-making Behaviour: The "Operational Code" Belief System', in L. S. Falkowski (ed.) *Psychological Models in International Politics*, Boulder, CO: Westview Press.

George, A.L. and Bennett, A. (2005) *Case Studies and Theory Development in the Social Sciences*, Cambridge: Cambridge University Press.

Gerring, J. (2004) 'What is a case study and what is it good for?' *American Political Science Review*, 98: 341–354.

—— (2006) *Case Study Research: Principles and Practice*, Cambridge: Cambridge University Press.

Gerschenkron, A. (1962) *Economic Backwardness in Historical Perspective*, Cambridge, MA: Belknap Press of Harvard University Press.

Gibney, M. and Dalton, M. (1996) 'The Political Terror Scale', in D.L. Cingranelli (ed.) *Human Rights and Developing Countries*, Greenwich, CT: JAI Press, 73–84.

Gillespie, C.G. (1986) 'Uruguay's Transition from Collegial Military-Technocratic Rule', in G. O'Donnell, P. Schmitter, and L. Whitehead (eds) *Transitions from Authoritarian Rule: Latin America*, Baltimore, MD: Johns Hopkins University Press, 173–196.

Glaser, D. (1995) 'Normative Theory', in D. Marsh and G. Stoker (eds) *Theories and Methods in Political Science*, London: Macmillan, 21–41.

Gleditsch, K.S. (2002) *All International Politics is Local: The Diffusion of Conflict, Integration, and Democratization*, Ann Arbor, MI: University of Michigan Press.

Gleditsch, K. and Ward, M. (1997) 'Double Take: A Re-examination of Democracy and Autocracy in Modern Polities', *Journal of Conflict Resolution*, 41(3): 361–383.

Glynos, J. and Howarth, D. (2007) *Logics of Critical Explanation in Social and Political Theory*, Oxford and London: Routledge.

Golembewski, R.T., Welsh, W.A., and Crotty, W.J. (eds) (1969) *A Methodological Primer for Political Scientists*, Chicago: Rand McNally.

Goodin, R.E. and Klingemann, H. (1996a) 'Political Science: The Discipline', in R.E. Goodin and H. Klingemann (eds) *The New Handbook of Political Science*, Oxford: Oxford University Press, 3–49.

—— (eds) (1996b) *The New Handbook of Political Science*, Oxford: Oxford University Press.

Goodwin, J. and Skocpol, T. (1989) 'Explaining Revolutions in the Contemporary Third World', *Politics and Society*, 17(4): 489–509.

Gordon, S. (1991) *The History and Philosophy of Social Science*, London: Routledge.

Gränzer, S. (1999) 'Changing Discourse: Transnational Advocacy Networks in Tunisia and Morocco', in T. Risse, S.C. Ropp, and K. Sikkink (eds) *The Power of Human Rights: International Norms and Domestic Change*, Cambridge: Cambridge University Press, 109–133.

Gray, J. (1999) *False Dawn: The Delusions of Global Capitalism*, London: Granta Books.

Grofman, B. (2001) *Political Science as Puzzle Solving*, Ann Arbor, MI: Michigan University Press.

Gross, P.R. and Levitt, N. (1994) *Higher Superstition: The Academic Left and Its Quarrels with Science*, Baltimore, MD: Johns Hopkins University Press.

Guest, I. (1990) *Behind the Disappearances: Argentina's Dirty War Against Human Rights and the United Nations*, Philadelphia: The University of Pennsylvania Press.

Gujarati, D.N. (1988) *Basic Econometrics*, 2nd edn, London: McGraw-Hill.

Gurr, T.R. (1968) 'A Causal Model of Civil Strife', *American Political Science Review*, 62: 1104–1124.

—— (1970) *Why Men Rebel*, Princeton, NJ: Princeton University Press.

—— (1993) 'Why Minorities Rebel: A Global Analysis of Communal Mobilization and Conflict since 1945', *International Political Science Review*, 14(2): 161–201.

—— (2000) *People Versus States: Minorities at Risk in the New Century*, Washington DC: United States Institute of Peace.

Haas, M. (1962) 'Comparative Analysis', *The Western Political Quarterly*, 15 (June): 292–304.

Haas, M. and Stack, S. (1983) 'Economic Development and Strikes: A Comparative Analysis', *The Sociological Quarterly*, 24 (Winter): 43–58.

Hafner-Burton, E.M. and Tsutsui, K. (2005) 'Human Rights in a Globalizing World: The Paradox of Empty Promises', *American Journal of Sociology*, 110(5): 1373–1411.

Hafner-Burton, E.M. and Tsutsui, K. (2007) 'Justice Lost! The Failure of International Human Rights Law to Matter Where Needed Most', *Journal of Peace Research*, 44(4): 407–425.

Hagopian, F. (1996) *Traditional Politics and Regime Change in Brazil*, Cambridge: Cambridge University Press.

Hague, R., Harrop, M., and Breslin, S. (1992) *Political Science: A Comparative Introduction*, New York: St Martin's Press.

Harris, D. (1998) 'Regional Protection of Human Rights: The Inter-American Achievement', in D. Harris and S. Livingstone (eds) *The Inter-American System of Human Rights*, Oxford: Oxford University Press, 1–29.

Hartlyn, J. and Valenzuela, A. (1994) 'Democracy in Latin America since 1930', in L. Bethell (ed.) *Cambridge History of Latin America, Volume VI: Part 2*, Cambridge: Cambridge University Press.

Hartz, L. (1955) *The Liberal Tradition in America; An Interpretation of American Political Thought since the Revolution*, New York: Harcourt Brace.

Harvey, N. (1998) *The Chiapas Rebellion: The Struggle for Land and Democracy*, Raleigh, NC: Duke University Press.

Hathaway, O. (2002) 'Do Treaties Make a Difference? Human Rights Treaties and the Problem of Compliance', *Yale Law Journal*, 111: 1932–2042.

Hawkins, D. (2001) 'Democratization Theory and Non-Transitions: Insights from Cuba', *Comparative Politics*, 33(4): 441–461.

—— (2002) *International Human Rights and Authoritarian Rule in Chile*, Lincoln, NB: University of Nebraska Press.

—— (forthcoming) 'Single Case Studies', in T. Landman and N. Robinson (eds) *The Sage Handbook of Comparative Politics*, London: Sage.

Hay, C. (1995) 'Structure and Agency', in D. Marsh and G. Stoker (eds) *Theories and Methods in Political Science*, London: Macmillan, 189–206.

—— (2002) *Political Analysis*, London: Palgrave.

Hayner, P.B. (1994) 'Fifteen Truth Commissions – 1974–1994: A Comparative Study', *Human Rights Quarterly*, 16: 597–655.

—— (2002) *Unspeakable Truths: Facing the Challenge of Truth Commissions*, London: Routledge.

Held, D., McGrew, A., Goldblatt, D., and Perraton, J. (1999) *Global Transformations: Politics, Economics, and Culture*, Cambridge: Polity Press.

Helliwell, J.F. (1994) 'Empirical Linkages between Democracy and Economic Growth', *British Journal of Political Science*, 24: 225–248.

Henderson, C. (1993) 'Population Pressures and Political Repression', *Social Science Quarterly*, 74: 322–33.

Hertel, S. Minkler, L., and Wilson, R.A. (2007) *Economic Rights: Conceptual, Measurement, and Policy Issues*, Cambridge: Cambridge University Press.

Hibbs, D. (1973) *Mass Political Violence: A Cross-national Causal Analysis*, New York: Wiley.

Hirschman, A.O. (1971) 'The Search for Paradigms as a Hindrance to Understanding', *World Politics*, 22: 329–343.

Hobbes, T. [1651] (1985) *The Leviathan*, Harmondsworth: Penguin Classics.

Holm, J.D. (1996) 'Development, Democracy, and Civil Society in Botswana', in A. Leftwich (ed.) *Democracy and Development*, Cambridge: Polity Press, 97–113.

Holt, R.T. and Turner, J.E. (eds) (1970) *The Methodology of Comparative Research*, New York: The Free Press.

Howarth, D. (1995) 'Discourse Theory', in D. Marsh and G. Stoker (eds) *Theories and Methods in Political Science*, London: Macmillan, 115–136.

—— (1998a) 'Discourse Theory and Political Analysis', in E. Scarbrough and E. Tanenbaum (eds) *Research Strategies in the Social Sciences: A Guide to New Approaches*, Oxford: Oxford University Press, 268–293.

—— (1998b) 'Paradigms Gained? A Critique of Theories and Explanations of Democratic Transition in South Africa', in D. Howarth and A. Norval (eds) *South Africa in Transition: New Theoretical Perspectives*, London: Macmillan, 182–214.

—— (2000) *Discourse*, Buckingham: Open University Press.

Howarth, D., Norval, A., and Stavrakakis, Y. (eds) (2000) *Discourse Theory and Political Analysis: Identities, Hegemonies and Social Change*, Manchester: Manchester University Press.

Hume, D. [1748] (1962) *On Human Nature and the Understanding*, ed. Antony Flew, New York: Collier Books.

Huntington, S.P. (1968) *Political Order in Changing Societies*, New Haven, CT: Yale University Press.

—— (1991) *The Third Wave: Democratization in the Late Twentieth Century*, Norman, OK: University of Oklahoma Press.

—— (1996) *The Clash of Civilizations and the Remaking of the New World Order*, New York: Simon & Schuster.

Hutchings, K. (1999) *International Political Theory*, London: Sage Publications.

Imig, D. and Tarrow, S. (eds) (2001) *Contentious Europeans: Protest and Politics in an Emerging Polity*, Lanham, MD: Rowan and Littlefield.

Inglehart, R. (1977) *The Silent Revolution: Changing Values and Political Styles among Western Publics*, Princeton, NJ: Princeton University Press.

—— (1990) *Culture Shift in Advanced Industrial Societies*, Princeton, NJ: Princeton University Press.

—— (1997) *Modernization and Postmodernization*, Princeton, NJ: Princeton University Press.

—— (1998) 'Political Values', in Jan W. van Deth (ed.) *Comparative Politics: The Problem of Equivalence*, London: Routledge.

Inglehart, R. and Welzel, C. (2005) *Modernization, Cultural Change, and Democracy: The Human Development Sequence*, Cambridge: Cambridge University Press.

Innes, J.E. (1992) 'Human Rights Reporting as a Policy Tool: An Examination of the State Department Country Reports', in T.B. Jabine and R.P. Claude (eds) *Human Rights and Statistics: Getting the Record Straight*, Philadelphia: University of Pennsylvania Press , 235–257.

International Council on Human Rights Policy (2002) *Beyond Voluntarism: Human Rights and the Developing Legal Obligations of Companies*, Geneva: ICHRP.

Jackman, R.W. (1973) 'On the Relation of Economic Development to Democratic Performance', *American Journal of Political Science*, 17(3): 611–621.

—— (1975) *Politics and Social Equality*, New York: Wiley.

—— (1985) 'Cross-national Statistical Research and the Study of Comparative Politics', *American Journal of Political Science*, 29(1): 161–182.

Jackson, J.E. (1996) 'Political Methodology: An Overview', in R.E. Goodin and H. Klingemann (eds) *The New Handbook of Political Science*, Oxford: Oxford University Press, 717–748.

Jaggers, K. and Gurr, T.R. (1995) 'Tracking Democracy's Third Wave with the Polity III Data', *Journal of Peace Research*, 32(4): 469–482.

Janos, A.C. (1997) 'Paradigms Revisited: Productionism, Globality, and Postmodernity in Comparative Politics', *World Politics*, 50:118–149.

Jetschke, A. (1999) 'Linking the Unlinkable? International Norms and Nationalism in Indonesia and the Philippines', in T. Risse, S.C. Ropp, and K. Sikkink (eds) *The Power of Human Rights: International Norms and Domestic Change*, Cambridge: Cambridge University Press, 134–171.

Jones, M.P. (1995) *Electoral Laws and the Survival of Presidential Democracies*, Notre Dame, IN: University of Notre Dame Press.

Jones, P. (1994) *Rights*, London: Macmillan.

Kalleberg, A. (1966) 'The Logic of Comparison: A Methodological Note for the Comparative Study of Political Systems', *World Politics*, 19 (January): 69–82.

Kant, I. (1795) *Perpetual Peace and Other Essays on Politics, History and Morals*, Indianapolis, IN: Hackett.

—— (1977) *Prolegomena to any Future Metaphysics*, trans. J.W.Ellington, Indianapolis: Hackett Publishing.

—— [1785] (1990) *Foundations of the Metaphysics of Morals*, 2nd edn, trans. L.White Beck, London: Macmillan.

Karl, T.L. (1986) 'Petroleum and Political Pacts: The Transition to Democracy in Venezuela', in G. O'Donnell, P. Schmitter, and L. Whitehead (eds) *Transitions from Authoritarian Rule: Latin America*, Baltimore, MD: Johns Hopkins University Press, 196–220.

—— (1990) 'Dilemmas of Democratization in Latin America', *Comparative Politics*, 23: 1–21.

Katznelson, I. (1997) 'Structure and Configuration in Comparative Politics', in M. Lichbach and A. Zuckerman (eds) *Comparative Politics: Rationality, Culture, and Structure*, Cambridge: Cambridge University Press, 81–112.

Kaviraj, S. (1996) 'Dilemmas of Democratic Development in India', in A. Leftwich (ed.) *Democracy and Development*, Cambridge: Polity Press, 114–138.

Keck, M. and Sikkink, K. (1998a) 'Transnational Advocacy Networks in the Movement Society', in D.S. Meyer and S. Tarrow (eds) *The Social Movement Society: Contentious Politics for a New Century*, Lanham, MD: Rowman & Littlefield, 217–238.

—— (1998b) *Activists beyond Borders: Advocacy Networks in International Politics*, Ithaca, NY: Cornell University Press.

Keith, L.C. (1999) 'The United Nations International Covenant on Civil and Political Rights: Does it Make a Difference in Human Rights Behavior?' *Journal of Peace Research*, 36(1): 95–118.

Kelley, S.Q. (1993) 'Divided We Govern: A Reassessment', Polity 25: 475–484.

Keman, H. (1993) *Comparative Politics*, Amsterdam: Free University Press.

Keohane, R. (1984) *After Hegemony: Cooperation and Discord in World Political Economy*, Princeton, NJ: Princeton University Press.

—— (2001) 'Governance in a Partially Globalized World', *American Political Science Review*, 95(1): 1–13.

—— (2002) *Governance in a Partially Globalized World*, London: Routledge.

King, G. (1989) *Unifying Political Methodology: The Likelihood Theory of Statistical Inference*, Cambridge: Cambridge University Press.

—— (1997) *A Solution to the Ecological Inference Problem: Reconstructing Individual Behaviour from Aggregate Data*, Princeton, NJ: Princeton University Press.

King, G., Keohane, R.O., and Verba, S. (1994) *Designing Social Inquiry: Scientific Inference in Qualitative Research*, Princeton, NJ: Princeton University Press.

Kirkpatrick, J. (1979) 'Dictatorships and Double Standards', *Commentary*, November: 34–45.

Kitschelt, H. (1986) 'Political Opportunity Structures and Political Protest: Anti-nuclear Movements in Four Democracies', *British Journal of Political Science*, 16 (January): 57–85.

Klein, N. (2001) *No Logo*, London: Flamingo Press.

Klingemann, H.D., Hofferbert, R.I., and Budge, I. (1994) *Parties, Policies, and Democracy*, Boulder, CO: Westview Press.

Knack, S. (2003) *Democracy, Governance, and Growth*, Ann Arbor, MI: University of Michigan Press.

Knapp, T.R. (1996) *Learning Statistics through Playing Cards*, Thousand Oaks, CA: Sage.

Kohli, A., Evans, P., Katzenstein, P.J., Przeworski, A., Rudolph, S.H., Scott, J.C., and Skocpol, T. (1995) 'The Role of Theory in Comparative Politics: A Symposium', *World Politics*, 48: 1–49.

Kopstein, J. (2006) 'The Transatlantic Divide Over Democracy Promotion', *Washington Quarterly*, 29(2): 85–98.

Kornbluh, P. (2003) *The Pinochet File: A Declassified Dossier on Atrocity and Accountability*, New York: New Press.

Krasner, S. (1993) 'Sovereignty, Regimes and Human Rights', in V. Rittberger and P. Mayer (eds) *Regime Theory and International Relations*, Oxford: Oxford University Press, 139–167.

Kriesi, H. (1996) 'The Organizational Structure of New Social Movements in a Political Context', in D. McAdam, J.D. McCarthy, and M.N. Zald (eds) *Comparative Perspectives on Social Movements*, Cambridge: Cambridge University Press, 152–184.

Kriesi, H., Koopmans, R., Duyvendak, J.W., and Giugni, M.G. (1995) *New Social Movements in Western Europe*, London: UCL Press.

Kuhn, T. (1970) *The Structure of Scientific Revolutions*, Chicago: University of Chicago Press.

La Polombara, J. (1968) 'Macro-theories and Micro-applications in Comparative Politics: A Widening Chasm', *Comparative Politics*, 1 (October): 52–78.

—— (1974) *Politics within Nations*, Englewood Cliffs, NJ: Prentice-Hall.

Laakso, M. and Taagepera, R. (1979) '"Effective" Number of Parties: A Measure with Application to Western Europe', *Comparative Political Studies*, 12(1): 3–27.

Laitin, D. (1995) 'Disciplining Political Science', *American Political Science Review*, 89 (June): 454–456.

Laitin, D. and Warner, C.M. (1992) 'Structure and Irony in Social Revolutions', *Political Theory*, 20(1): 147–151.

Lakatos, I. (1970) 'Falsification and the Methodology of Scientific Research Programs', in I. Lakatos and A. Musgrave (eds) *Criticism and Growth of Knowledge*, Cambridge: Cambridge University Press, 91–196.

Landman, T. (1995) '"El Chiripero" wins: The Venezuelan Elections of 1993', *Electoral Studies*, 14(1): 100–109.

—— (1999) 'Economic Development and Democracy: The View from Latin America', *Political Studies*, 47(4): 607–626.

REFERENCES

—— (2001) 'The Economic Requirements of Democracy', in J. Foweraker and P.B. Clarke (eds) *Encyclopaedia of Democratic Thought*, London: Routledge, 235–239.

—— (2002) 'Comparative Politics and Human Rights', *Human Rights Quarterly*, 43(4): 890–923.

—— (2004) 'Measuring Human Rights: Principle, Practice, and Policy', *Human Rights Quarterly*, 26 (November): 906–931.

—— (2005a) 'Review Article: the Political Science of Human Rights', *British Journal of Political Science*, 35(3): 549–572.

—— (2005b) *Protecting Human Rights: A Global Comparative Study*, Washington DC: Georgetown University Press.

—— (2005c) *Protecting Human Rights: A Cross-national Time-Series Dataset*, Colchester: University of Essex.

—— (2005d) 'Democracy Analysis' in *International IDEA 10th Anniversary Handbook*, Stockholm: International IDEA, 19–27.

—— (2006a) 'Development, Democracy, and Human Rights in Latin America' in Janet Dine and Andrew Fagan (eds) *Capitalism and Human Rights*, Cheltenham: Edward Elgar Publishers, 330–357.

—— (2006b) *Studying Human Rights*, Oxford and New York: Routledge.

—— (2008) 'Imminence and Proportionality: The US and UK Response to Terrorism', *California Western International Law Journal* (forthcoming).

Lane, R. (1996) 'Positivism, Scientific Realism, and Political Science: Recent Developments in the Philosophy of Science', *Journal of Theoretical Politics*, 8(3): 361–382.

Lawson, T. (1997) *Economics and Reality*, London: Routledge.

Lees, C. (2006) 'We Are All Comparativists Now: Why and How Single-Country Scholarship Must Adapt and Incorporate the Comparative Politics Approach', *Comparative Political Studies*, 39(9): 1084–1108.

Leftwich, A. (ed.) (1996) *Democracy and Development*, Cambridge: Polity Press.

Legro, J. and Moravcsik, A. (1999) 'Is Anybody Still a Realist?' *International Security*, 24 (2): 5–55.

Lerner, D. (1958) *The Passing of Traditional Society: Modernizing the Middle East*, Glencoe, IL: The Free Press of Glencoe.

Levi, M. (1997) 'A Model, a Method, and a Map: Rational Choice in Comparative and Historical Analysis', in M. Lichbach and A. Zuckerman (eds) *Comparative Politics: Rationality, Culture, and Structure*, Cambridge: Cambridge University Press, 19–41.

Levine, D. (1989) 'Paradigm Lost: Dependency to Democracy', *World Politics*, 40(3): 377–394.

Levy, J.S. (1989) 'Domestic Politics and War', in R.I. Rothberg and T.K. Rabb (eds) *The Origin and Prevention of Major Wars*, Cambridge: Cambridge University Press.

—— (2002) 'War and Peace', in W. Carlsnaes, T. Risse, and B. Simmons, *Handbook of International Relations*, London: Sage, 350–368.

Lewis, D. (1973) *Counterfactuals*, Cambridge, MA: Harvard University Press.

Lewis-Beck, M. (1980) *Applied Regression: An Introduction*, London: Sage.

Li, Q. (2005) 'Does Democracy Promote Transnational Terrorism?' *Journal of Conflict Resolution*, 49(2): 278–297.

Li, Q. and Reuveny, R. (2003) 'Economic Globalization and Democracy: An Empirical Analysis', *British Journal of Political Science*, 33: 29–54.

Lichbach, M. (1989) 'An Evaluation of "Does Economic Inequality Breed Political Conflict" Studies', *World Politics*, 41: 431–470.

—— (1994) 'What Makes Rational Peasants Revolutionary? Dilemma, Paradox, and Irony in Peasant Collective Action', *World Politics*, 46 (April): 382–417.

—— (1995) *The Rebel's Dilemma*, Ann Arbor, MI: University of Michigan Press.

—— (1997) 'Social Theory and Comparative Politics', in M. Lichbach and A. Zuckerman (eds) *Comparative Politics: Rationality, Culture, and Structure*, Cambridge: Cambridge University Press, 239–276.

Lichbach, M. and Kopstein, J. (2000) *Comparative Politics: Interests, Identities, and Institutions in a Changing Global Order*, Cambridge: Cambridge University Press.

Lichbach, M. and Zuckerman, A. (eds) (1997) *Comparative Politics: Rationality, Culture, and Structure*, Cambridge: Cambridge University Press.

Lieberson, S. (1987) *Making It Count: The Improvement of Social Research and Theory*, Berkeley: University of California Press.

—— (1991) 'Small N's and Big Conclusions: An Examination of the Reasoning in Comparative Studies Based on a Small Number of Cases', *Social Forces*, (December): 307–320.

—— (1994) 'More on the Uneasy Case for Using Mill-Type Methods in Small-N Comparative Studies', *Social Forces*, 72 (June): 1225–1237.

Lieberson, S. and Hansen, L.K. (1974) 'National Development, Mother Tongue Diversity, and the Comparative Study of Nations', *American Sociological Review*, 39: 523–541.

Lijphart, A. (1968) *The Politics of Accommodation: Pluralism and Democracy in the Netherlands*, Berkeley: University of California Press.

—— (1971) 'Comparative Politics and Comparative Method', *The American Political Science Review*, 65(3): 682–693.

—— (1975) 'The Comparable Cases Strategy in Comparative Research', *Comparative Political Studies*, 8(2):158–177.

—— (1994a) *Electoral Systems and Party Systems: A Study of Twenty-seven Democracies, 1945–1990*, Oxford: Oxford University Press.

—— (1994b) 'Democracies: Forms, Performance, and Constitutional Engineering', *European Journal of Political Research*, 25:1–17.

—— (1999) *Patterns of Democracy: Government Forms and Performance in Thirty-Six Countries*, New Haven, CT: Yale University Press.

Lindberg, S. (2006) *Democracy and Elections in Africa*, Baltimore, MD: Johns Hopkins University Press.

Linz, J.J. (1964) 'An Authoritarian Regime: Spain', in E. Allardt and S. Rokkan (eds) *Mass Politics*, New York: Free Press.

—— (1990) 'The Perils of Presidentialism', *Journal of Democracy*, 1: 51–69.

Linz, J.J. and Stepan, A. (1978) *The Breakdown of Democratic Regimes*, Baltimore, MD: Johns Hopkins University Press.

—— (1996) *Problems of Democratic Transition and Consolidation: South America, Southern Europe, and Post-Communist Europe*, Baltimore, MD: Johns Hopkins University Press.

Lipset, S.M. (1959) 'Some Social Requisites for Democracy: Economic Development and Political Legitimacy', *The American Political Science Review*, 53: 69–105.

—— (1960) *Political Man*, London: Heinemann.

—— (1994) 'The Social Requisites of Democracy Revisited', *American Sociological Review*, 59 (February): 1–22.

Lipset, S.M. and Marks, G. (2000) *It Didn't Happen Here: Why Socialism Failed in the United States*, New York: W.W.Norton.

Lipset, S.M. and Rokkan, S. (1967) *Party Systems and Voter Alignments: Cross-national Perspectives*, New York: Free Press.

Luebbert, G. (1991) *Liberalism, Fascism, or Social Democracy: Social Classes and the Political Origins of Regimes in Inter-war Europe*, New York: Oxford University Press.

Lustick, I. (1996) 'History, Historiography, and Political Science: Multiple Historical Records and the Problem of Selection Bias', *American Political Science Review*, 90(3): 605–618.

—— (2006) *Trapped in the War on Terror*, Philadelphia: University of Pennsylvania Press.

McAdam, D., McCarthy, J.D., and Zald, M.N. (1996) *Comparative Perspectives on Social Movements*, Cambridge: Cambridge University Press.

McCarthy, J.D., and Zald, M.N. (1977) 'Resource Mobilization and Social Movements: A Partial Theory', *American Journal of Sociology*, 82: 1212–1241.

Macauley, N. (1967) *The Sandino Affair*, Chicago: Quadrangle Books.

McClelland, J.S. (1997) *A History of Western Political Thought*, London: Routledge.

McCormick J.M. and Mitchell, N.J. (1997) 'Human Rights Violations, Umbrella Concepts, and Empirical Analysis', *World Politics*, 49:510–525.

Macintyre, A. (1967) *After Virtue*, London: Duckworth.

—— (1971) 'Is a Science of Comparative Politics Possible?', *Against the Self-images of the Age*, London: Duckworth, 260–279.

McKay, D. (1994) 'Review Article: Divided and Governed? Recent Research on Divided Government in the United States', *British Journal of Political Science*, 24: 517–534.

Machiavelli [153] (1952) *The Prince*, New York and Toronto: New American Library.

Mackie, T. and Marsh, D. (1995) 'The Comparative Method', in D. Marsh and G. Stoker (eds) *Theory and Methods in Political Science*, London: Macmillan, 173–188.

Macridis, R.C. and Brown, B.E. (eds) (1986) *Comparative Politics*, 6th edn, Chicago: Dorsey Press.

Mahoney, J. and Goertz, G. (2004) 'The Possibility Principle: Choosing Negative Cases in Comparative Research', *American Political Science Review*, 98(4): 653–669.

Mahoney, J and Rueschemeyer, D. (2003) *Comparative Historical Analysis in the Social Sciences*, Cambridge: Cambridge University Press.

Mainwaring, S. (1993) 'Presidentialism, Multipartism, and Democracy: The Difficult Combination', *Comparative Political Studies*, 26(2): 198–228.

Mainwaring, S. and Perez-Liñan (2003) 'Level of Development and Democracy: Latin-American Exceptionalism, 1945–1966', *Comparative Political Studies* 36(9): 1031–1067.

Mainwaring, S. and Scully, T.R. (1995) 'Introduction: Party Systems in Latin America', in S. Mainwaring and T.R. Scully (eds) *Building Democratic Institutions: Party Systems in Latin America*, Stanford, CA: Stanford University Press, 1–34.

Mair, P. (1996) 'Comparative Politics: An Overview', in R.E. Goodin and H. Klingemann (eds) (1996) *The New Handbook of Political Science*, Oxford: Oxford University Press, 309–335.

Mansfield, E. D. and Snyder, J. (2005) *Electing to Fight: Why Emerging Democracies Go to War*, Cambridge, MA: MIT Press.

—— (2007) 'Exchange, I: The Sequencing "Fallacy"', *Journal of Democracy*, 18(3): 5–9.

Manzetti, L. (1993) *Institutions, Parties, and Coalitions in Argentine Politics*, Pittsburgh, PA: University of Pittsburgh Press.

Maravall, J.M. and Santamaría, J. (1986) 'Political Change in Spain and the Prospects for Democracy', in G. O'Donnell, P. Schmitter, and L.Whitehead (eds) *Transitions from Authoritarian Rule: Southern Europe*, Baltimore, MD: Johns Hopkins University Press, 71–108.

March, J.G. and Olsen, J.P. (1984) 'New Institutionalism: Organizational Factors in Political Life', *American Political Science Review*, 78: 734–749.

Marsh, D. and Stoker, G. (eds) (1995) *Theories and Methods in Political Science*, London: Macmillan.

Marshall, T.H. (1963) 'Citizenship and Social Class', in *Sociology at the Crossroads and Other Essays*, London: Heinemann.

Martin, L.L. and Sikkink, K. (1993) 'US Policy and Human Rights in Argentina and Guatemala, 1973–1980', in P.B. Evans, H.K. Jacobson, and R.D. Putnam (eds) *Double-edged Diplomacy: International Bargaining and Domestic Politics*, Los Angeles: University of California Press, 330–362.

Martins, L. (1986) 'The "Liberalization" of Authoritarian Rule in Brazil', in G. O'Donnell, P. Schmitter, and L. Whitehead (eds) *Transitions from Authoritarian Rule: Latin America*, Baltimore, MD: Johns Hopkins University Press, 72–94.

Maxwell, K. (1986) 'Regime Overview and the Prospects for Democratic Transition in Portugal', in G. O'Donnell, P. Schmitter, and L.Whitehead (eds) *Transitions from Authoritarian Rule: Southern Europe*, Baltimore, MD: Johns Hopkins University Press, 109–137.

—— (1995) *The Making of Portuguese Democracy*, Cambridge: Cambridge University Press.

Mayer, P., Rittberger, V. and Zürn, M. (1997) 'Regime Theory: State of the Art and Perspectives', in V. Rittberger, *Regime Theory and International Relations*, Oxford: Clarendon, 391–430.

Mayer, L.C. (1983) 'Practicing What We Preach: Comparative Politics in the 1980s', *Comparative Political Studies*, 16(2): 173–194.

—— (1989) *Redefining Comparative Politics: Promise versus Performance*, Newbury Park, CA: Sage.

Mayhew, D. (1993) *Divided We Govern: Party Control, Lawmaking, and Investigations, 1946–1990*, New Haven, CT: Yale University Press.

Mearsheimer, J.J. (1994–1995) 'The False Promise of International Institutions', *International Security*, 19(3): 5–49.

Mearsheimer, J.J. (2001) *The Tragedy of Great Power Politics*, New York: W. W. Norton.

Mendus, S. (1995) 'Human Rights in Political Theory', *Political Studies*, Special Issue 43: 10–24.

Merkl, P.H. (1970) *Modern Comparative Politics*, New York: Holt, Rinehart, & Winston.

Merritt, R.L. (1970) *Systematic Approaches to Comparative Politics*, Chicago: Rand McNally.

Meyer, W. H. (1996) 'Human Rights and MNCs: Theory vs. Quantitative Evidence', *Human Rights Quarterly*, 18(2): 368–397.

—— (1998) *Human Rights and International Political Economy in Third World Nations: Multinational Corporations, Foreign Aid, and Repression*, Westport, CT: Praeger.

—— (1999a) 'Confirming, Infirming, and Falsifying Theories of Human Rights: Reflections on Smith, Bolyard, and Ippolito Through the Lens of Lakatos', *Human Rights Quarterly*, 21(1): 220–228.

—— (1999b) 'Human Rights and International Political Economy in Third World Nations: Multinational Corporations, Foreign Aid, and Repression', *Human Rights Quarterly*, 21(3): 824–830.

Middlebrook, K. (1986) 'Political Liberalization in an Authoritarian Regime: The Case of Mexico', in G. O'Donnell, P. Schmitter, and L.Whitehead (eds) *Transitions from Authoritarian Rule: Latin America*, Baltimore, MD: Johns Hopkins University Press, 123–147.

Midlarsky, M.I. (1999) *The Evolution of Inequality: War, State Survival and Democracy in Comparative Perspective*, Stanford, CA: Stanford University Press.

Midlarsky, M. and Roberts, K. (1985) 'Class, State, and Revolution in Central America: Nicaragua and El Salvador Compared', *Journal of Conflict Resolution*, 29(2): 163–193.

Mill, J.S. (1843) *A System of Logic*, London: Longman.

Miller, W.L. (1995) 'Quantitative Analysis', *Theories and Methods in Political Science*, London: Macmillan, 154–172.

Mitchell, N. and Beer, C. (2004) 'Democracy and Human Rights in the Mexican States: Elections or Social Capital', *International Studies Quarterly*, 48(2): 293–312.

Mitchell, N., Bohara, A., and Nepal, M. (2006) 'Opportunity, Democracy and Political Violence: A Sub-national Analysis of Conflict in Nepal', *Journal of Conflict Resolution*, 50(1): 108–128.

Mitchell, N.J. and McCormick, J.M. (1988) 'Economic and Political Explanations of Human Rights Violations', *World Politics*, 40: 476–498.

Moon, C. and Kim, Y. (1996) 'A Circle of Paradox: Development, Politics and Democracy in South Korea', in A. Leftwich (ed.) *Democracy and Development*, Cambridge: Polity Press, 139–167.

Moore, B. (1966) *The Social Origins of Dictatorship and Democracy: Lord and Peasant in the Making of the Modern World*, Boston, MA: Beacon Press.

—— (1978) *Injustice: The Social Bases of Obedience and Revolt*, London: Macmillan.

Moravcsik, A. (1997) 'Taking Preferences Seriously: A Liberal Theory of International Politics', *International Organization*, 51(4): 513–553.

—— (2000) 'The Origins of Human Rights Regimes: Democratic Delegation in Postwar Europe', *International Organization*, 54 (Spring): 217–52.

Morgenthau, H. (1960) *Politics among Nations: The Struggle for Power and Peace*, 3rd edn, New York: Alfred A.Knopf.

—— (1961) *Politics among Nations: The Struggle for Power and Peace*, 3rd edition, New York: Alfred A Knopf.

Muller, E.N. and Seligson, M.A. (1987) 'Inequality and Insurgency', *American Political Science Review*, 81(2): 425–451.

Neubauer, D.E. (1967) 'Some Conditions of Democracy', *American Political Science Review* 61: 1002–1009.

Neumayer, E. (2005) 'Do International Human Rights Treaties Improve Respect for Human Rights?' *Journal of Conflict Resolution*, 49(6): 925–953.

Neumayer, E. and Plümper, T., 'International Terrorism and the Clash of Civilizations: Was Huntington Right After All?' A SSRN Working Paper (December 17, 2006). Available at SSRN: http://ssrn.com/abstract=952208

Nichols, E. (1986) 'Skocpol and Revolution: Comparative Analysis vs. Historical Conjuncture', *Comparative Social Research*, 9: 163–186.

Nugent, D. (1993) *Spent Cartridges of Revolution: An Anthropological History of Namiquipa, Chihuahua*, Chicago: University of Chicago Press.

Nye, J.E. (2004) *Soft Power: The Means to Success in World Politics*, New York: Public Affairs.

O'Donnell, G. (1973) *Modernization and Bureaucratic Authoritarianism: Studies in South American Politics*, Berkeley, CA: Institute of International Studies.

O'Donnell, G. and Schmitter, P.C. (1986) *Transitions from Authoritarian Rule: Tentative Conclusions about Uncertain Democracies*, Baltimore and London: Johns Hopkins University Press.

O'Donnell, G., Schmitter, P.C., and Whitehead, L. (eds) (1986a) *Transitions from Authoritarian Rule: Southern Europe*, Baltimore and London: Johns Hopkins University Press.

—— (1986b) *Transitions from Authoritarian Rule: Latin America*, Baltimore and London: Johns Hopkins University Press.

—— (1986c) *Transitions from Authoritarian Rule: Comparative Perspectives*, Baltimore and London: Johns Hopkins University Press.

Ogburn, W.F. and Goltra, I. (1919) 'How Women Vote: A Study of an Election in Portland, Oregon', *Political Science Quarterly*, 34: 413–433.

O'Laughlin, J., Ward, M.D., Lofdahl, C.L., Cohen, J.S., Brown, D.S., Reilly, D., Gleditsch, K.S., and Shin, M. (1998) 'The Diffusion of Democracy, 1946–1994', *Annals of the Association of American Geographers*, 88(4): 545–574.

Olson, M. (1965) *The Logic of Collective Action*, Cambridge, MA: Harvard University Press.

Opp, K.D., Finkel, S.E., Muller, E.N., Wolsfield, G., Dietz, H.A., and Green, J.D. (1995) 'Left-Right Ideology and Collective Political Action: A Comparative Analysis of Germany,

Israel, and Peru', in J.C. Jenkins and B. Klandermans (eds), *The Politics of Social Protest: Comparative Perspectives on States and Social Movements*, London: UCL Press, 63–95.

Owen, John M. (1994) 'How Liberalism Produces Democratic Peace', reprinted in Michael E. Brown, Sean M. Lynn-Jones, and Steven E. Miller (eds) (1996) *Debating the Democratic Peace*, Cambridge, MA: MIT Press.

Page, E. (1990) 'British Comparative Politics and Political Science', *Political Studies*, 38: 275–305.

Paige, J. (1975) *Agrarian Revolution: Social Movements and Export Agriculture in the Underdeveloped World*, New York: Free Press.

Parsa, M. (2000) *States, Ideologies, and Social Revolutions: A Comparative Analysis of Iran, Nicaragua, and the Philippines*, Cambridge: Cambridge University Press.

Pasquino, G. (1986) 'The Demise of the First Fascist Regime and Italy's Transition to Democracy: 1943–1948', in G. O'Donnell, P. Schmitter, and L. Whitehead (eds) *Transitions from Authoritarian Rule: Southern Europe*, Baltimore, MD: Johns Hopkins University Press, 45–70.

Payne, L. (2000) *Uncivil Movements: The Armed Right Wing and Democracy in Latin America*, Baltimore, MD: Johns Hopkins University Press.

Peeler, J.A. (1992) 'Elite Settlements and Democratic Consolidation: Colombia, Costa Rica, and Venezuela', in J. Higley and R. Gunther (eds) *Elites and Democratic Consolidation in Latin America and Southern Europe*, Cambridge: Cambridge University Press, 81–112.

Pennings, P., Keman, H., and Kleinnijenhuis, J. (1999) *Doing Research in Political Science: An Introduction to Comparative Methods and Statistics*, London: Sage.

Peters, Guy (1998) *Comparative Politics: Theory and Methods*, New York: New York University Press.

Peterson, P. and Greene, J.P. (1993) 'Why Executive-Legislative Conflict in the United States Is Dwindling', *British Journal of Political Science*, 24: 33–55.

Plümper, T. and Troeger, V. (2007) 'Efficient Estimation of Time Invariant and Rarely Changing Variables in Panel Data Analysis with Unit Effects', *Political Analysis*, Spring 2007(15): 124–139.

Poe, S. (1990) 'Human Rights and Foreign Aid: A Review of Quantitative Studies and Suggestions for Future Research', *Human Rights Quarterly* 12: 499–509.

—— (1992) 'Human Rights and Economic Aid Allocation', *American Journal of Political Science*, 36: 147–167.

Poe, S.C. and Tate, C.N. (1994) 'Repression of Human Rights to Personal Integrity in the 1980s: A Global Analysis', *American Political Science Review*, 88(4): 853–872.

Poe, S., Pilatovcky, S., Miller, B., and Ogundele, A. (1994) 'Human Rights and US Foreign Aid Revisited: The Latin American Region', *Human Rights Quarterly*, 16: 539–558.

Poe, S.C., Tate, C.N. and Keith, L.C. (1999) 'Repression of the Human Right to Personal Integrity Revisited: A Global Cross-national Study Covering the Years 1976–1993', *International Studies Quarterly*, 43: 291–313.

Poe, S.C., Wendel-Blunt, D., and Ho, K. (1997) 'Global Patterns in the Achievement of Women's Human Rights to Equality', *Human Rights Quarterly*, 19: 813–835.

Popkin, S. (1979) *The Rational Peasant: the Political Economy of Rural Society in Vietnam*, Berkeley: University of California Press.

Popper, K. (1959) *The Logic of Scientific Discovery*, London: Hutchinson.

—— (1997) *The Lesson of This Century*, London: Routledge.

Porter, M. E. (1990) *The Competitive Advantage of Nations*, New York: Free Press.

Poulantzas, N. (1976) *The Crisis of the Dictatorships: Portugal, Spain, Greece*, New York: Schocken Books.

Powell, G. Bingham (1982) *Contemporary Democracies: Participation, Stability, and Violence*, Cambridge, MA: Harvard University Press.

Przeworski, A. (1985) 'Marxism and Rational Choice', *Politics and Society* 14(4): 379–409.

—— (1991) *Democracy and the Market*, Cambridge: Cambridge University Press.

Przeworski, A. and Limongi, F. (1993) 'Political Regimes and Economic Growth', *Journal of Economic Perspectives*, 7(3): 51–69.

—— (1997) 'Modernization: Theories and Facts', *World Politics*, 49 (January): 155–183.

Przeworski, A. and Teune, H. (1970) *The Logic of Comparative Social Inquiry*, New York: Wiley.

Przeworski, A., Alvarez, M.E., Cheibub, J.A., and Limongi, F. (2000) *Democracy and Development: Political Institutions and Well-being in the World, 1950–1990*, Cambridge: Cambridge University Press.

Putnam, R. (1988) 'Diplomacy and Domestic Politics: The Logic of Two-Level Games', *International Organization*, 42 (3): 427–460.

Putnam, R. (1993a) *Making Democracy Work: Civic Traditions in Modern Italy*, Princeton, NJ: Princeton University Press.

Putnam, R. (1993b) 'Diplomacy and Domestic Politics: the Logic of Two-Level Games', in P.B. Evans, H.K. Jacobson, and R.D. Putnam (eds) *Double-Edged Diplomacy: International Bargaining and Domestic Politics*, Los Angeles: University of California Press, 431–468.

Rae, D. (1967) *The Political Consequences of Electoral Laws*, New Haven, CT: Yale University Press.

Ragin, C. (1987) *The Comparative Method: Moving beyond Qualitative and Quantitative Strategies*, Berkeley: University of California Press.

—— (1994) 'Introduction to Qualitative Comparative Analysis', in T. Janoski and A. Hicks (eds) *The Comparative Political Economy of the Welfare State*, Cambridge: Cambridge University Press, 299–320.

—— (2000) *Fuzzy Set Social Science*, Chicago: University of Chicago Press.

Ragin, C., Berg-Schlosser, D., and de Meur, G. (1996) 'Political Methodology: Qualitative Methods', in R.E. Goodin and H. Klingemann (eds) *The New Handbook of Political Science*, Oxford: Oxford University Press, 749–768.

Raustiala, K. and Slaughter, A. (2002) 'International Law, International Relations and Compliance', in W. Carlsnaes, T. Risse, and B. Simmons (eds) *Handbook of International Relations*, London: Sage, 538–558.

Rawls, J. (1971) *A Theory of justice*, Cambridge, MA: Harvard University Press.

Renteln, A.D. (1988) 'Relativism and the Search for Human Rights', *American Anthropologist*, 90: 64

Risse, T. and Sikkink, K. (1999) 'The Socialization of International Human Rights Norms into Domestic Practices: Introduction', in T. Risse, S.C. Ropp, and K. Sikkink (eds) *The Power of Human Rights: International Norms and Domestic Change*, Cambridge: Cambridge University Press, 1–38.

Risse, T., Ropp, S.C. and Sikkink, K. (eds) (1999) *The Power of Human Rights: International Norms and Domestic Change*, Cambridge: Cambridge University Press.

Robertson, A.H. and Merrills, J.G. (1996) *Human Rights in the World: An Introduction to the Study of the International Protection of Human Rights*, 4th edn, Manchester: University of Manchester Press.

Robinson, W.S. (1950) 'Ecological Correlations and the Behaviour of Individuals', *American Sociological Review*, 15: 351–357.

Ropp, S.C. and Sikkink, K. (1999) 'International Norms and Domestic Politics in Chile and Guatemala', in T. Risse, S.C. Ropp, and K. Sikkink (eds) *The Power of Human Rights: International Norms and Domestic Change*, Cambridge: Cambridge University Press, 171–204.

Rosato, Sebastian (2003) 'The Flawed Logic of Democratic Peace Theory', *American Political Science Review*, 97(4): 585–602.

Rosenau, P.M. (1992) *Post-Modernism and the Social Sciences: Insights, Inroads, and Intrusions*, Princeton, NJ: Princeton University Press.

Ross, M.H. (1997) 'Culture and Identity in Comparative Political Analysis', in M. Lichbach and A. Zuckerman (eds) *Comparative Politics: Rationality, Culture, and Structure*, Cambridge: Cambridge University Press, 42–80.

Ross, M. and Homer, E. (1976) 'Galton's Problem in Cross-National Research', *World Politics*, 29(1): 1–28.

Rostow, W.W. (1961) *The Stages of Economic Growth: A Non-communist Manifesto*, Cambridge: Cambridge University Press.

Rubin, B.R. and Newberg, P.R. (1980) 'Statistical Analysis for Implementing Human Rights Policy', in P.R. Newberg (ed.) *The Politics of Human Rights*, New York: New York Press.

Rueschemeyer, D., Stephens, E.H., and Stephens, J. (1992) *Capitalist Development and Democracy*, Cambridge: Polity Press.

Russett, Bruce (1993a) *Grasping the Democratic Peace: Principles for a Post-Cold War Peace*, Princeton, NJ: Princeton University Press.

Russett, Bruce (1993b) 'The Fact of Democratic Peace', reprinted in Michael E. Brown, Sean M. Lynn-Jones, and Steven E. Miller (eds) (1996) *Debating the Democratic Peace*, Cambridge, MA: MIT Press.

Russett, Bruce (1993c) 'Why Democratic Peace?' reprinted in Michael E. Brown, Sean M. Lynn-Jones, and Steven E. Miller (eds) (1996) *Debating the Democratic Peace*, Cambridge, MA: MIT Press.

Russett, Bruce (1995) 'The Democratic Peace – And Yet It Moves' reprinted in Michael E. Brown, Sean M. Lynn-Jones, and Steven E. Miller (eds) (1996) *Debating the Democratic Peace*, Cambridge, MA: MIT Press.

Russett, Bruce, Oneal, John R., and Davis, David R. (1998) 'The Third Leg of the Kantian Tripod for Peace: International Organizations and Militarized Disputes, 1950–85', *International Organization*, 5(3): 441–467

Russett, Bruce M., O'Neal, John R., and Cox, Michaelene (2000) 'Clash of Civilizations, or Realism and Liberalism Déjà Vu? Some Evidence', *Journal of Peace Research*, 37(5): 583–608.

Russett, B. and O'Neal, J. (2001) *Triangulating Peace: Democracy, Interdependence and International Organizations*, New York: W. W. Norton

Rustow, D.A. (1970) 'Transitions to Democracy: Toward a Dynamic Model', *Comparative Politics*, 2: 337–363.

Rustow, D.A. and Erickson, K.P. (1991) 'Introduction', in D.A. Rustow and K.P. Erickson (eds) *Comparative Political Dynamics: Global Research Perspectives*, New York: HarperCollins, 1–4.

Sanders, D. (1981) *Patterns of Political Instability*, London: Macmillan.

—— (1994) 'Methodological Considerations in Comparative Cross-national Research', *International Social Science Journal*, 46: 43–49.

—— (1995) 'Behavioural Analysis', in D. Marsh and G. Stoker (eds) *Theories and Methods in Political Science*, London: Macmillan, 58–75.

Sands, P. (2005) *Lawless World: America and the Making and Breaking of Global Rules*, London: Allen Lane.

Sartori, G. (1970) 'Concept Misinformation in Comparative Politics', *American Political Science Review*, 64: 1033–1053.

—— (ed.) (1984) *Social Science Concepts: A Systematic Analysis*, Beverly Hills, CA: Sage.

—— (1994) 'Compare Why and How: Comparing, Miscomparing and the Comparative Method', in M. Dogan and A. Kazancigil (eds) *Comparing Nations: Concepts, Strategies, Substance*, London: Basil Blackwell, 14–34.

Savolainen, J. (1994) 'The Rationality of Drawing Conclusions Based on Small Samples: In Defense of Mill's Methods', *Social Forces*, 72 (June): 1217–1224.

Scarrow, H.A. (1969) *Comparative Political Analysis: An Introduction*, New York: Harper & Row.

Scheuch, E.K. (1966) 'Cross-national Comparisons Using Aggregate Data: Some Substantive and Methodological Problems', in R.L. Merritt and S. Rokkan (eds) *Comparing Nations: The Use of Quantitative Data in Cross-national Research*, New Haven, CT: Yale University Press, 131–167.

—— (1969) 'Social Context and Individual Behaviour', in M. Dogan and S. Rokkan (eds) *Quantitative Ecological Analysis in the Social Sciences*, Cambridge, MA: MIT Press, 133–155.

Schmidt, B.C. (2002) 'On the History and Historiography of International Relations', in W. Carlsnaes, T. Risse, and B. Simmons (eds) *Handbook of International Relations*, London: Sage, 3–22.

Schmitz, H.P. (1999) 'Transnational Activism and Political Change in Kenya and Uganda', in T. Risse, S.C. Ropp, and K. Sikkink, (eds) *The Power of Human Rights: International Norms and Domestic Change*, Cambridge: Cambridge University Press, 39–77.

Scott, J. (1976) *The Moral Economy of the Peasant: Rebellion and Subsistence in Southeast Asia*, New Haven and London: Yale University Press.

—— (1985) *Weapons of the Weak: Everyday Forms of Peasant Resistance*, New Haven, CT: Yale University Press.

Schram, S. and Caterino, B. (eds) (2006) *Making Political Science Matter: Debating Knowledge, Research, and Method*, New York: New York University Press.

Seligson, M. (1987) 'Development, Democratization, and Decay: Central America at the Crossroads', in J. Malloy and M. Seligson (eds) *Authoritarians and Democrats: Regime Transition in Latin America*, Pittsburgh, PA: University of Pittsburgh Press.

Serra, J. (1979) 'Three Mistaken Theses Regarding the Connections between Industrialization and Authoritarian Regimes', in D. Collier (ed.) *The New Authoritarianism in Latin America*, Princeton, NJ: Princeton University Press, 99–164.

Shugart, M. and Carey, J.M. (1992) *Presidents and Assemblies: Constitutional Design and Electoral Dynamics*, Cambridge: Cambridge University Press.

Shugart, M. and Carey, J.M. (eds) (1998) *Executive Decree Authority*, New York: Cambridge University Press.

Sigelman, L. and Gadbois, G. (1983) 'Contemporary Comparative Politics: An Inventory and Assessment', *Comparative Political Studies*, 16(3): 275–307.

Sigelman, L. and Simpson, M. (1977) 'A Cross-national Test of the Linkage between Economic Inequality and Political Violence', *Journal of Conflict Resolution*, 21(1): 105–128.

Singer, M. (1997) 'What is Happening in History?', *PS: Political Science and Politics*, 30(1): 27–33.

Skocpol, T. (1979) *States and Social Revolutions: A Comparative Analysis of France, Russia, and China*, Cambridge: Cambridge University Press.

—— (1994) *Social Revolutions in the Modern World*, Cambridge: Cambridge University Press.

Skocpol, T. and Somers, M. (1980) 'The Uses of Comparative History in Macrosocial Inquiry', *Comparative Studies in Society and History*, 22: 174–197.

Small, M. and Singer, D. (1970) 'Patterns in International Warfare, 1816–1965', *Annals of the American Academy of Political and Social Science*, 391: 15–155.

Smelser, N. (1976) *Comparative Methods in the Social Sciences*, Englewood Cliffs, NJ: Prentice-Hall.

Smith, R. (2002) 'Putting the Substance Back in Political Science', *Chronicle of Higher Education*, 5 April, B10–11.

Smith, J., Bolyard, M. and Ippolito, A. (1999) 'Human Rights and the Global Economy: A Response to Meyer', *Human Rights Quarterly*, 21: 207–219.

Spirer, H. (1990) 'Violations of Human Rights – How Many? *American Journal of Economics and Sociology*, 49: 199–204.

Starr, H. (1991) 'Democratic Dominoes: Diffusion Approaches to the Spread of Democracy in the International System', *Journal of Conflict Resolution*, 35(2): 356–381.

Steiner, H.J. and Alston, P. (1996) *International Human Rights in Context: Law, Politics, Morals*, Oxford: Oxford University Press.

Steinmo, S., Thelen, K., and Longstreth, F. (eds) (1992) *Structuring Politics: Historical Institutionalism in Comparative Analysis*, Cambridge: Cambridge University Press.

Stepan, A. (1978) 'Political Leadership and Regime Breakdown: Brazil', in J.J. Linz and A. Stepan (eds) *The Breakdown of Democratic Regimes: Latin America*, Baltimore, MD: Johns Hopkins University Press, 110–137.

Stepan, A. and Skach, C. (1993) 'Constitutional Frameworks and Democratic Consolidation: Parliamentarism and Presidentialism', *World Politics* 46 (October): 1–22.

—— (1994) 'Presidentialism and Parliamentarism in Comparative Perspective', in J.Linz and A.Valenzuela (eds) *The Failure of Presidential Democracy*, Baltimore, MD: Johns Hopkins University Press, 119–136.

Stiglitz, J.E. (2002) *Globalization and Its Discontents*, New York: Allen Lane/The Penguin Press.

Stimson, J. (1985) 'Regression in Space and Time: A Statistical Essay', *American Political Science Review*, 29: 914–947.

Stoker, G. (1995) 'Introduction', in D. Marsh and G. Stoker (eds) *Theory and Methods in Political Science*, London: Macmillan.

Strouse, J.C. and Claude, R.P. (1976) 'Empirical Comparative Rights Research: Some Preliminary Tests of Development Hypotheses', in R.P. Claude (ed.) *Comparative Human Rights*, Baltimore and London: Johns Hopkins University Press, 51–67.

Suleiman, E. (1994) 'Presidentialism and Political Stability in France', in J. Linz and A. Valenzuela (eds) *The Failure of Presidential Democracy*, Baltimore, MD: Johns Hopkins University Press, 137–162.

Sunar, I. and Sayari, S. (1986) 'Democracy in Turkey: Problems and Prospects', in G. O'Donnell, P. Schmitter, and L. Whitehead (eds) *Transitions from Authoritarian Rule: Southern Europe*, Baltimore, MD: Johns Hopkins University Press, 165–186.

Sundquist, J.L. (1988) 'Needed: A Political Theory for the New Era of Coalition Government in the United States', *Political Science Quarterly*, 103: 613–635.

Tarrow, S. (1989) *Democracy and Disorder: Protest and Politics in Italy, 1965–1975*, Oxford: Clarendon Press.

—— (1994) *Power in Movement: Social Movements, Collective Action, and Politics*, Cambridge: Cambridge University Press.

—— (1995) 'Bridging the Quantitative-Qualitative Divide in Political Science', *American Political Science Review*, 89(2): 471–474.

—— (2005) *The New Transnational Activism*, Cambridge: Cambridge University Press.

Taylor, C. and Hudson, M. (1972) *World Handbook of Political and Social Indicators*, 2nd edn, New Haven, CT: Yale University Press.

Taylor, C. and Jodice, D.A. (1983) *World Handbook of Political and Social Indicators*, 3rd edn, New Haven, CT: Yale University Press.

Tetlock, P.E. and Lebow, R.N. (2001) 'Poking Counterfactual Holes in Covering Laws: Cognitive Styles and Historical Reasoning', *American Political Science Review*, 95(4): 829–843.

Teune, H. (1975) 'Comparative Research, Experimental Design, and Comparative Method', *Comparative Political Studies*, 8(2): 195–199.

Therborn, G. (1977) 'The Rule of Capital and the Rise of Democracy', *New Left Review*, 103: 3–42.

Thomas, D.C. (1999) 'The Helsinki Accords and Political Change in Eastern Europe', in T. Risse, S.C. Ropp, and K. Sikkink (eds) *The Power of Human Rights: International Norms and Domestic Change*, Cambridge: Cambridge University Press, 204–233.

Thucydides (1982) *The Peloponnesian War*, Harmondsworth: Penguin Classics.

Tilly, C. (1978) *From Mobilization to Revolution*, Englewood Cliffs, NJ: Prentice-Hall.

—— (1984) *Big Structures, Large Processes, Huge Comparisons*, New York: Russell Sage.

—— (1986) *The Contentious French*, Cambridge, MA: Belknap Press.

—— (1997) 'Means and Ends of Comparison in Macrosociology', *Comparative Social Research*, 16: 43–53.

Tilly, C., Tilly, L., and Tilly, R. (1975) *The Rebellious Century 1830–1930*, Cambridge, MA: Harvard University Press.

Todaro, M.P. (1994) *Economic Development*, 5th edn, London: Longman.

—— (1997) *Economic Development*, 6th edn, London: Longman.

Tsebelis, G. (1990) *Nested Games: Rational Choice in Comparative Politics*, Berkeley: University of California Press.

UNDP (1999) *Human Development Report*, New York: Oxford University Press.

—— (2002) *Human Development Report*, New York: Oxford University Press.

Valenzuela, A. (1988) 'Political Science and the Study of Latin America', in C.Mitchell (ed.) *Changing Perspectives in Latin American Studies: Insights from Six Disciplines*, Stanford, CA: Stanford University Press, 63–86.

Valenzuela, J.S. and Valenzuela, A. (1978) 'Modernization and Dependency: Alternative Perspectives in the Study of Latin American Underdevelopment', *Comparative Politics*, 10, 535–557.

Van Evera, S. (1997) *Guide to Methods for Students of Political Science*, Ithaca, NY: Cornell University Press.

Vanhanen, T. (1984) *The Emergence of Democracy: A Comparative Study of 119 States, 1850–1979*, Helsinki: The Finnish Society of Science and Letters.

—— (1990) *The Process of Democratization: A Comparative Study of 147 States, 1980–1988*, New York: Crane Russak.

—— (1997) *The Prospects of Democracy*, London: Routledge.

—— (2003) *Democratization: A Comparative Analysis of 170 Countries*, London: Routledge.

Varshney, A. (2002) *Ethnic Conflict and Civic Life: Hindus and Muslims in India*, New Haven, CT: Yale University Press.

Verba, S. (1967) 'Some Dilemmas in Comparative Research', *World Politics*, 20 (October): 111–127.

Vincent, R.J. (1986) *Human Rights and International Relations*, Cambridge: Cambridge University Press.

Viotti, P.R. and Kauppi, M.V. (1999) *International Relations Theory: Realism, Pluralism, and Beyond*, Boston, MA: Allyn and Bacon.

Vogt, W.P. (1999) *Dictionary of Statistics and Methodology: A Non-Technical Guide for the Social Sciences*, 2nd edn, London: Sage.

Von Wright, G.H. (1971) *Explanation and Understanding*, London: Routledge & Kegan Paul.

Wade, R. (1992) 'East Asia's economic success: Conflicting Perspectives, Partial Insights, Shaky Evidence', *World Politics*, 44: 270–320.

Waisman, C.H. (1989) 'Argentina: Autarkic Industrialization and Illegitimacy', in L. Diamond, J.J. Linz, and S.M. Lipset (eds) *Democracy in Developing Countries*, Vol. 4: Latin America, London: Adamantine Press, 59–109.

Waltz, K. (1979) *Theory of International Politics*, New York: Random House.

Wang, T.Y. (1993) 'Inequality and Political Violence Revisited', *American Political Science Review* , 87(4): 979–993.

Ward, H. (1995) 'Rational Choice Theory', in D. Marsh and G. Stoker (eds) *Theories and Methods in Political Science*, London: Macmillan, 76–93.

Ward, M. and Gleditsch, K. (1998) 'Democratizing for Peace', *American Political Science Review*, 92(1): 51–61.

Weber, M. (1949) *On Methodology of the Social Sciences*, ed. E. Shils, New York: Free Press.

Weissbrodt, D. and Bartolomei, M.L. (1991) 'The Effectiveness of International Human Rights Pressures: The Case of Argentina, 1976–1983', *Minnesota Law Review*, 75: 1009–1035.

Wendt, A. (1999) *Social Theory of International Politics*, Cambridge: Cambridge University Press.

Whitehead, L. (1996a) 'Comparative Politics: Democratization Studies', in R.E. Goodin and H. Klingemann (eds) *The New Handbook of Political Science*, Oxford: Oxford University Press.

—— (1996b) *The International Dimensions of Democratization*, Oxford: Oxford University Press.

—— (2002) *Democratization: Theory and Experience*, Oxford: Oxford University Press.

Whiteley, P. (1999) 'The Origins of Social Capital', in Jan Van Deth, Marco Maraffi, Ken Newton and Paul Whiteley, *Social Capital and European Democracy*, London: Routledge, 25–44.

—— (2000) 'Economic Growth and Social Capital', *Political Studies*, 48: 443–466.

Wickham-Crowley, T. (1993) *Guerrillas and Revolution in Latin America*, Princeton, NJ: Princeton University Press.

Wilensky, H. (2003) *Rich Democracies: Political Economy, Public Policy, and Performance*, Berkeley: University of California Press.

Wolf, E. (1969) *Peasant Wars of the Twentieth Century*, New York: Harper Torchbooks.

Womack, J. (1969) *Zapata and the Mexican Revolution*, New York: Knopf.

Wood, E.J. (2003) *Insurgent Collective Action and War in El Salvador*, Cambridge: Cambridge University Press.

World Bank (1992) *Development and Good Governance*, Washington DC: World Bank.

Young, O.R. (1980) 'International Regimes: Problems of Concept Formation', *World Politics*, 32: 331–356.

—— (1999) *Governance in World Affairs*, Ithaca, NY: Cornell University Press.

Zacher, M.W. (1992) 'The Decaying Pillars of the Westphalian Temple: Implications for International Order and Governance', in J.D. Rosenau and E. Czempiel (eds) *Governance without Government: Order and Change in World Politics*, Cambridge: Cambridge University Press.

Zakaria, F. (2003) *The Future of Freedom: Illiberal Democracy at Home and Abroad*, New York: W.W. Norton.

Zald, M.N. and Ash, R. (1966) 'Social Movement Organizations: Growth, Decay and Change', *Social Forces*, 44: 327–341.

Zanger, S.C. (2000) 'A Global Analysis of the Effect of Regime Changes on Life Integrity Violations, 1977–1993', *Journal of Peace Research*, 37(2): 217–233.

Zürn, M. (2002) 'From Inter-dependence to Globalization', in W. Carlsnaes, T. Risse, and B. Simmons (eds) *Handbook of International Relations*, London: Sage, 235–254.

Index

Afghanistan 309
Africa 75, 205, 211, 296, 307; and truth
    commissions 256, 288
agricultural sector, and collective violence
    72–3, 137–9, 145–7, 154–7, 286, 290,
    296
Alfonsín, Raúl 258
Algeria 144
Allende, Salvador 277
Alliance for Progress 309
Almond, G. 5, 13, 34
American Civil War 116, 119
Amnesty International 35, 244
analysis, levels of 19–20
Angola 20, 25, 93, 139, 145, 146
anti-nuclear movements 168–70
Apartheid 90, 251
Aquino, Corazon 150
Argentina 37, 38, 87, 122, 124, 230;
    democratic transition 244, 257, 259;
    'Dirty War' 244, 257, 291; domestic
    human rights movement 258, 259;
    human rights 257–9, 260, 291
Aristotle 6, 7, 308
Arrighi, G. 40
autocracy 189–90

Barratt, B. 246
Bartolomei, M.L. 257, 258, 259
Bashevkin, S. 168, 174–6, 181, 183
Beer, C. 26, 32

Berg-Schlosser, D. 75
binary comparison 147, 152
bivariate relationship 135, 177, 246, 286
Bob, C. 267–8, 272–3, 288, 289
Boix, C. 109, 192, 309
Bolivia 73, 75, 151
Bollen, K. 107, 126
Boolean algebra 79–80, 306
Botswana 122, 124–5, 289
Bratton, M. 71, 194, 204–5, 213, 259, 287,
    296, 307
Brazil 9, 20, 26, 32, 38, 79, 90, 168,
    172–4, 257
Britain, and democratization 113–14, 115,
    116
Brockett, C. 79, 144, 152–4, 289, 296
Brysk, A. 258, 259
Budge, I. 305
Burkhart, R.E. 12, 32, 62, 107, 108
Burma 147, 296
Burton, M. 103

Carey, J.M. 222–4, 225, 226, 230
Caribbean 79, 110, 118, 122, 191, 288
Caribbean Basin Initiative 309
Carter, Jimmy 258
case-oriented analysis 69, 306
cases (countries) 18–19; negative cases
    77–8;
selection 298, 310, *see also* comparing few
    countries, case selection; methodology,

347

eBooks - at www.eBookstore.tandf.co.uk

A library at your fingertips!

eBooks are electronic versions of print books. You can store them onto your PC/laptop or browse them online.

They have advantages for anyone needing rapid access to a wide variety of published, copyright information.

eBooks can help your research by enabling you to bookmark chapters, annotate and use instant searches to find specific words or phrases. Several eBook files would fit on even a small laptop or PDA.

NEW: Save money by eSubscribing: cheap, online acess to any eBook for as long as you need it.

Annual subscription packages

We now offer special low cost bulk subscriptions to packages of eBooks in certain subject areas. These are available to libraries or to individuals.

For more information please contact webmaster.ebooks@tandf.co.uk

We're continually developing the eBook concept, so keep up to date by visiting the website.

www.eBookstore.tandf.co.uk